Introduction ....

Chapter 1 Convenient Shortcuts 7
1-1 Device search "Ctrl + F" 9
1-2 Device usage list "Ctrl + D" 17
1-3 Comment, statement, note display "Ctrl + F5, F7, F8." 19
1-4 Statement list between lines "Ctrl + L" 34
1-5 Input/delete vertical/horizontal lines "Ctrl + arrow keys." 35
Exercise 1 (computer operation) 37
Practice Question 1 Answers 38

Chapter 2 Basic sequence control program 43
2-1 Creation of sequence control using a washing machine 44
2-2 Step 1 Creation of a washing machine automatic operation signal circuit 50
2-3 Step 2 Create a washing machine sequence control circuit. 57
2-4 Step 3 Washing machine interlock, creation of temporary stop circuit 67
2-5 Step 4 Create a circuit for the washing machine's optional course. 78
2-6 Step 5 Creation of touch panel screen for washing machine operation. 93
2-7 Step 6 Washing machine manual course circuit/screen creation 139
Exercise 2 (Bottle transfer sequence control: PLC program) 148
Practice Question 2 Answers 152
Exercise 3 (Bottle transfer sequence control: touch panel) 162
Exercise Question 3 Answers 163

Chapter 3 Specific examples of PLC/GOT improvement. ...175

3-1 Improvement example 1: Creation of energy-saving operation circuits for equipment/machinery............175

3-2 Improvement example 2: Creating a maintenance alarm circuit and screen based on the number of operations............198

3-3 Improvement example 3: Alarm circuit/screen creation due to reduced operating time............224

3-4 Improvement example 4: Creating a circuit and screen that acquires each operation time as a log............244

Chapter 4 3 Selections of Program Investigation Methods Useful in Trouble............265

4-1 Contact coil search "Ctrl + Alt + F7"............265

4-2 Investigation of defect cause using increment (INC) instruction 269

4-3 Investigation of defect occurrence step using increment (INC) instruction............275

At the end............279

Introduction

Thank you for picking up this book.

in this book

- **Shortcuts to improve the efficiency of PLC program creation.**
- **How to write a basic sequence control program.**
- **Specific PLC/GOT improvement cases: 4 cases.**
- **Three selections of program investigation methods that are useful when problems occur.**

I have explained as clearly as possible.

The tools used are GX Works2 and GT Designer3 GOT2000 series. The following book introduces the basic operation method, so if you are learning PLC or GOT for the first time, please learn from here.

- BASIC PLC PROGRAMMING FOR BEGINNERS
  (Mitsubishi Electric GX Works2)

- GOT Introduction to Industrial Panel Creation
  (Mitsubishi Electric GT Designer3 GOT2000 Series)

I think that many of the people reading this book are interested in PLCs and GOTs and need to use them in their work. It is a technology in a niche field that is not recognized at all by people other than those in specific departments.

But many factories equipment and robots are controlled using PLCs and GOTsdoing. andThere are more than 400,000 factories in JapanIt is said that. Furthermore, PLCs and GOTs are also used by Japanese companies overseas. Considering that, it is a niche and special technology, Technologies with high scarcity needs that will continue to be needed in the future I think you can say that.

Also, as I mentioned in my previous book, there is also the impact of labor shortages due to the recent declining birthrate and aging population. Innovation and improvement of the entire factory using DX, AI, IoT, etc. will be necessary in the future is becoming.

Where should you start when you want to innovate and improve?

It is a "**manufacturing site**".

because, Because the innovation and improvement of the "manufacturing site" is directly linked to sales and profits is.

The manufacturing industry is a company that makes things. Depending on the item to be manufactured, there is a lot of manual work, Considering the future declining birthrate and aging population, automation of manufacturing using machines and robots will be promoted. You can easily imagine that.

And the technology that supports the automation of various manufacturing industries issues various operation commands to machines and robots. Touch panel to enable the operation and monitoring of machines and robots. touch panel is essential.

That is why we can create PLC programs and touch panels. Skills that can improve the control of factory equipment and robots are as valuable to each company as human resources who can do DX and AI.

And the concept of this book is.

 · Sequence control program can be created
⇒Various control becomes possible by learning the basic writing style
 · Can improve PLC/GOT of specific equipment
⇒Learn improvement methods from 4 examples
 · Learning how to investigate problems
 ⇒ Leads to early resolution of problems

It is based on these three concepts.

This document first explains shortcuts that lead to more efficient PLC program creation.

Next, the sequence control program is explained. A sequence control program is a program that operates in order such as pouring water into the washing machine ⇒ washing ⇒ rinsing ⇒ dehydration I'm talking about By learning this control, it becomes possible to make machines and robots perform complex movements.

In the next chapter, four examples of facility improvement are introduced. Applied to the actual scene, if there are any points that could be improved, I would like you to change the PLC program and GOT touch panel.

In addition, since there are many problems with PLC programs at the site, we also introduce the investigation method in that case.

We believe that by mastering these skills, we will be able to control various aspects of factory equipment and troubleshoot problems.

We hope that this book will help you to become an excellent PLC programmer and touch panel production engineer who will be responsible for the factories and facilities of the future.

Chapter 1 Convenient Shortcuts

First, I will explain shortcuts that are useful to remember when operating GX Works2. Mastering the main shortcuts will lead to a reduction in program creation time and trouble investigation time.

This time, the following shortcuts are the same operations as Excel, so I will not describe the details, but I will describe them because they are frequently used shortcuts.

Copy "Ctrl + C"
Paste "Ctrl + V"
Cut "Ctrl + X."
Undo "Ctrl + Z"
Redo "Ctrl + Y"
Overwrite save "Ctrl + S."

In addition, the previous book
"BASIC PLC PROGRAMMING FOR BEGINNERS
 (Mitsubishi Electric GX Works2)" are also described.

Write mode "F2."
(Program can be edited)
Monitor mode "F3."
(Monitors write mode "Shift+F3")
Convert "F4"
(Conversion + Write during RUN "Shift+F4")
a contact "F5"
(a-contact OR is "Shift+F5")
b contact "F6"
(b contact OR is "Shift+F6")
Coil "F7"
Application command "F8"
Horizontal bar input "F9"
("Ctrl + F9" for horizontal bar deletion)
Vertical bar input "F10"
("Ctrl+F10" for vertical bar deletion)
Rising pulse "Shift+F7"
Falling pulse "Shift+F8"
Line insertion "Shift+Ins"
("Shift+Del" to delete a line)
Column insert "Ctrl+Ins."
("Ctrl+Del" to delete a column)

This time, I will introduce frequently used shortcuts other than the above and introduce their functions where necessary.

1-1 Device search "Ctrl + F"

device search **Used to find out where the device is being used**. You can search for devices by clicking the Search/Replace tab ⇒ Search for devices or by clicking the "Search/Replace window" button on the toolbar.

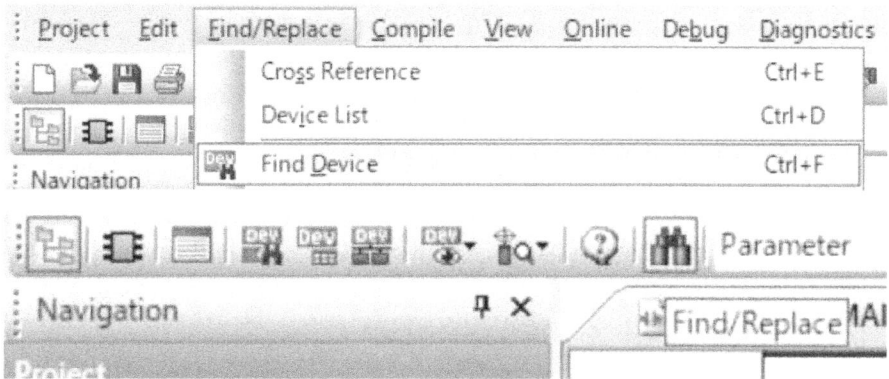

If the toolbar with the "Find/Replace Window" is not displayed, select the "View" tab at the top ⇒ Toolbar ⇒ Docking Window/Project Data Switcher. This is the circuit created in question 5 of the GX Works2 introductory edition.

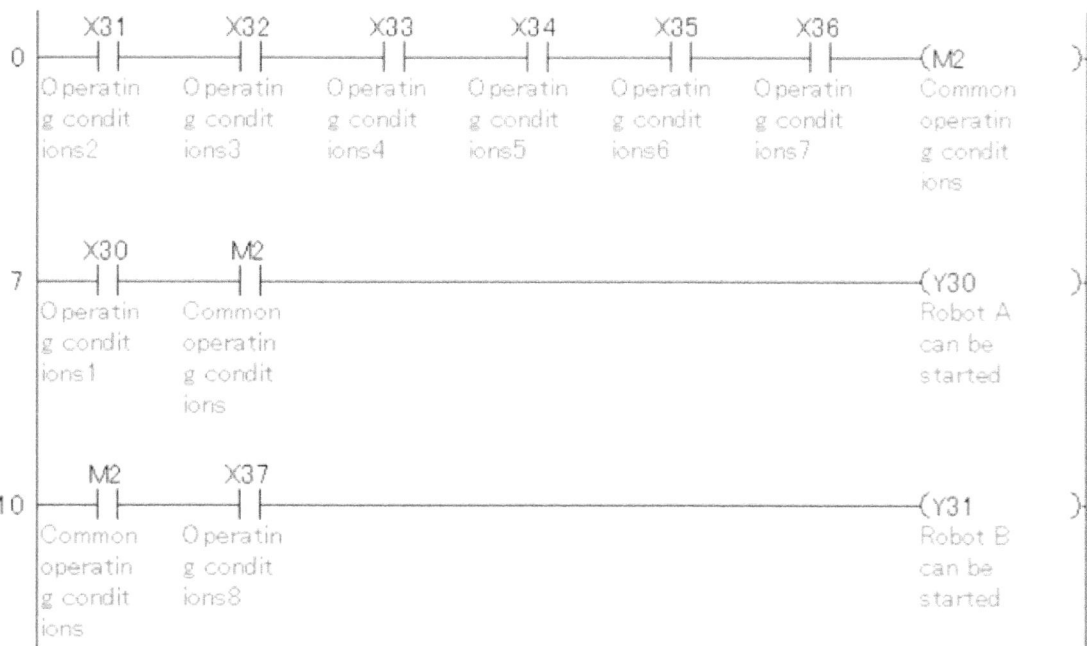

First, create the above program.

1. First, open GX Works2, click the "Project" tab at the top ⇒ New, change only the model to "Q02/Q02H", and then click OK.

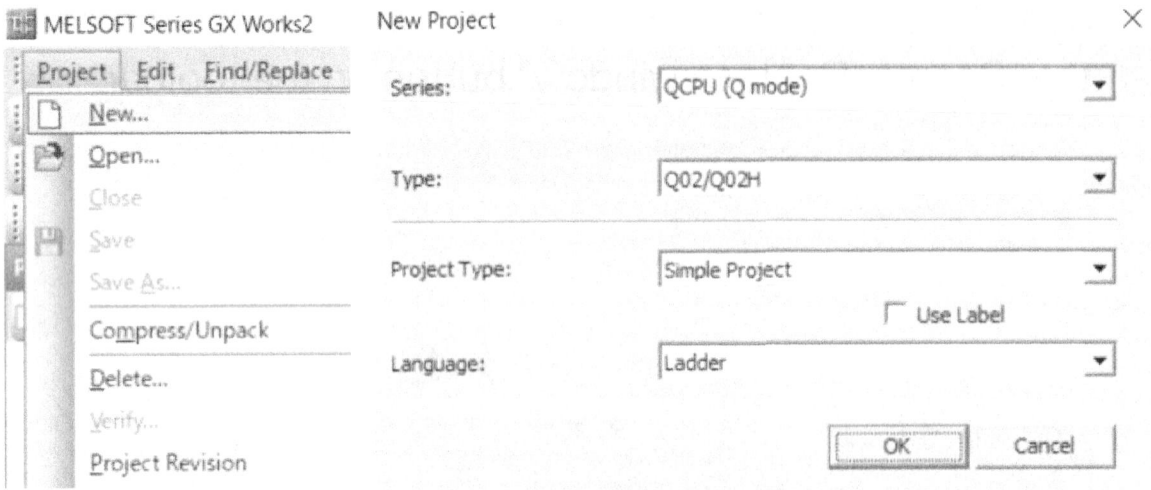

2. Then right-click on "MAIN" in the navigation ⇒ press change data name and change the data name to "Chapter 1".

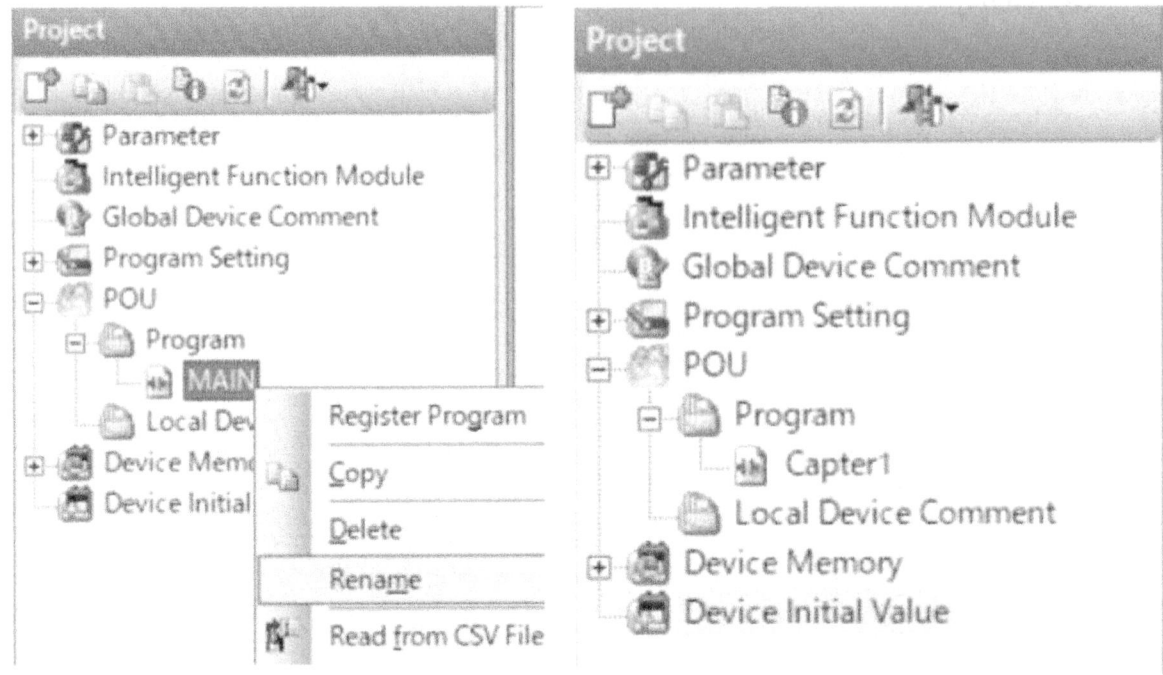

3. Click the "Tool" tab ⇒ Options at the top, click Program Editor ⇒ Ladder/SFC ⇒ Enter ladder, and check "Check duplicated coil" and "Enter label comment and device comment".

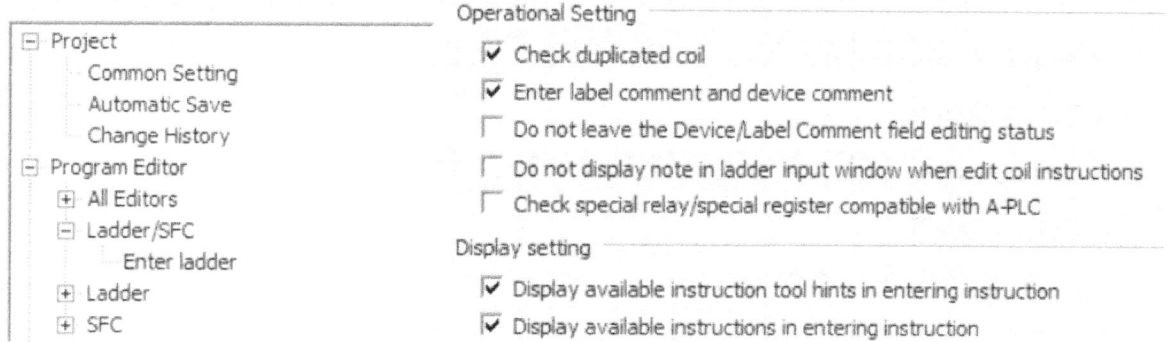

4. On the option screen, click Online Change, confirm that "Execute online change by Compile" is unchecked, and then click OK on the bottom right. (Uncheck if checked)

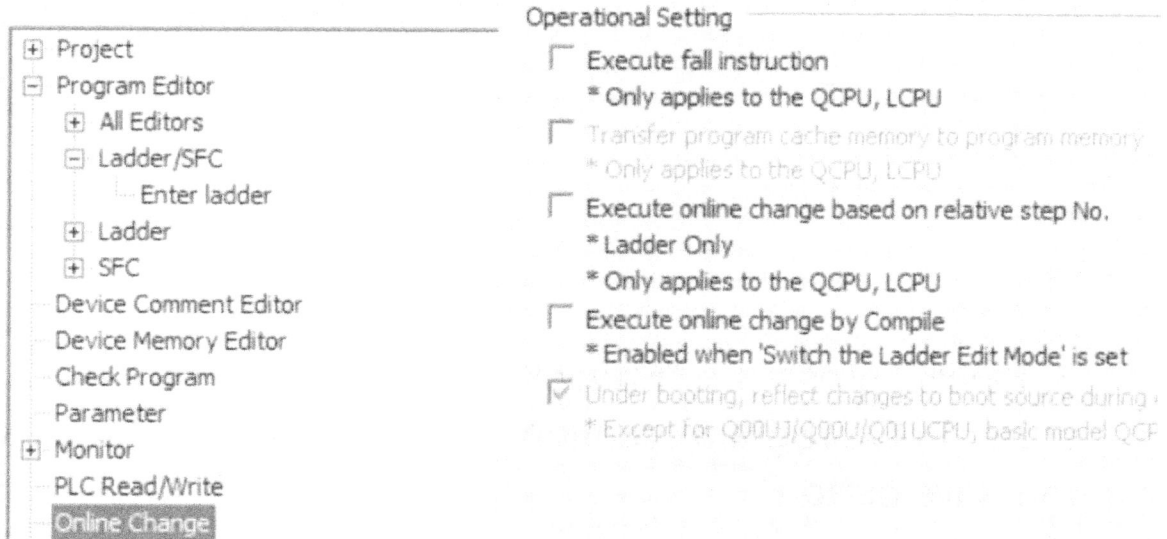

5. Using the shortcuts F5 (a contact) and F7 (coil), create the same circuit as the one created in question 5 of the GX Works2 introductory edition. If you type a comment and it doesn't appear, press Ctrl+F5. (Ctrl + F5 will be explained later)

X30 to X37, M2 NO contacts: Press F5 to enter device and comment.
Coils for M2, Y30, Y31: Press F7 to enter device and comment.
press F4 to convert.

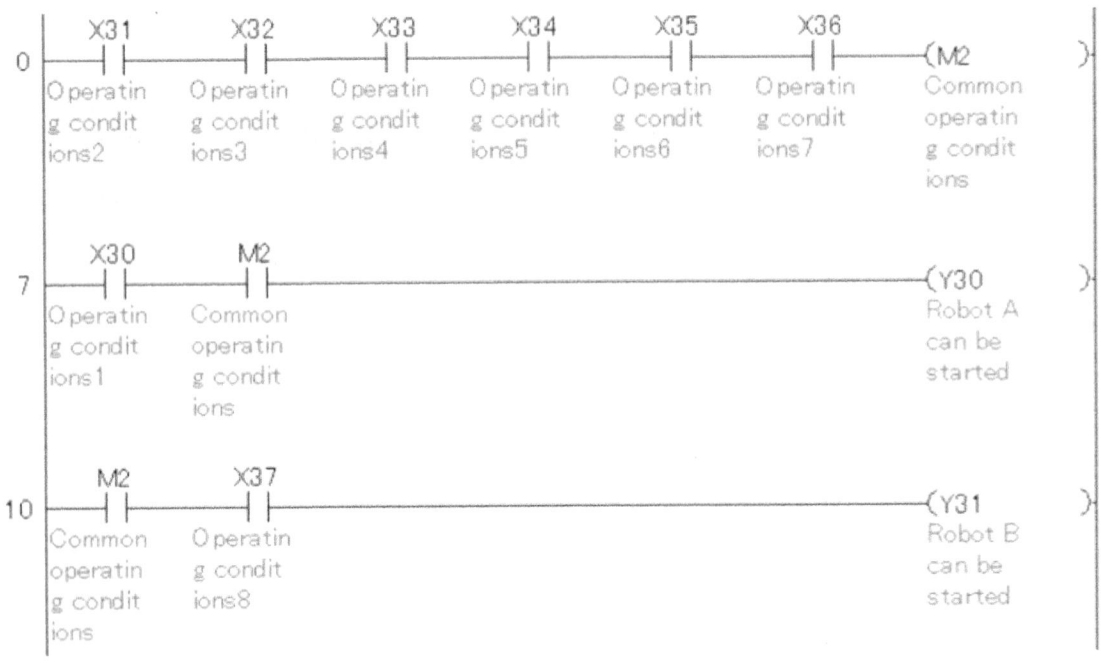

6. Finally, press the "Project" tab at the top ⇒ Save as, enter "PLC program creation" in the file name, and press the Save button.

Then, using this circuit, device search is performed with a shortcut.

Hover over the device you want to search for and press CTRL to bring up the Find/Replace window below. Also, it is OK to press Ctrl + F in a place other than the device and enter the device in the search device field.

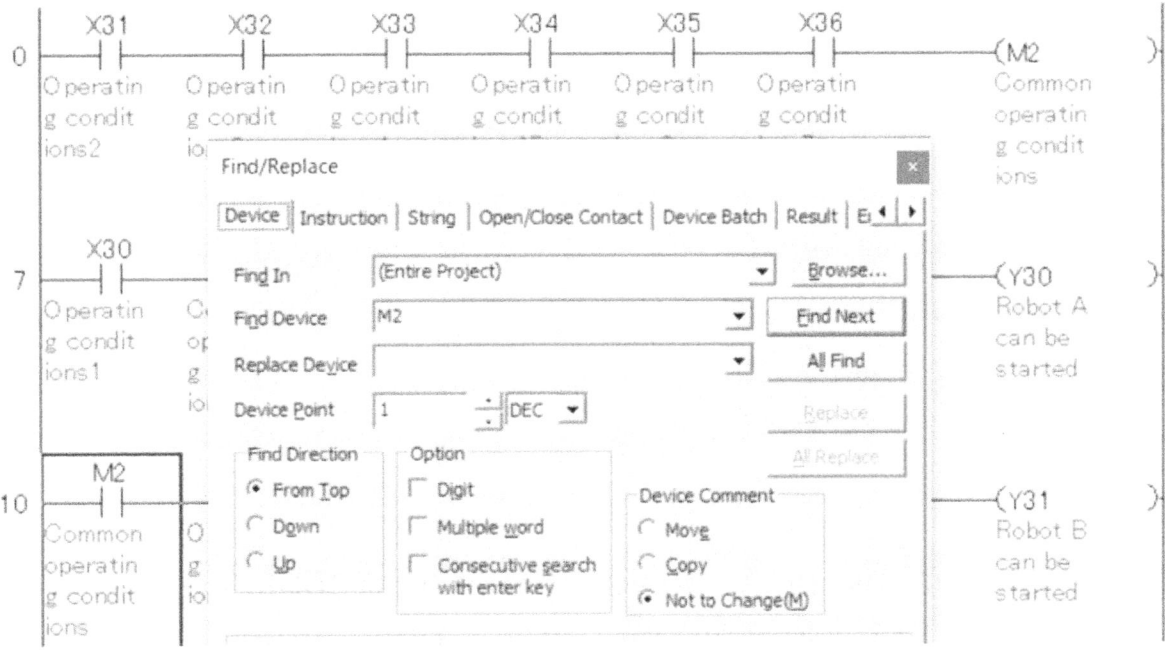

Press Enter in this state to search and move to the first M2.

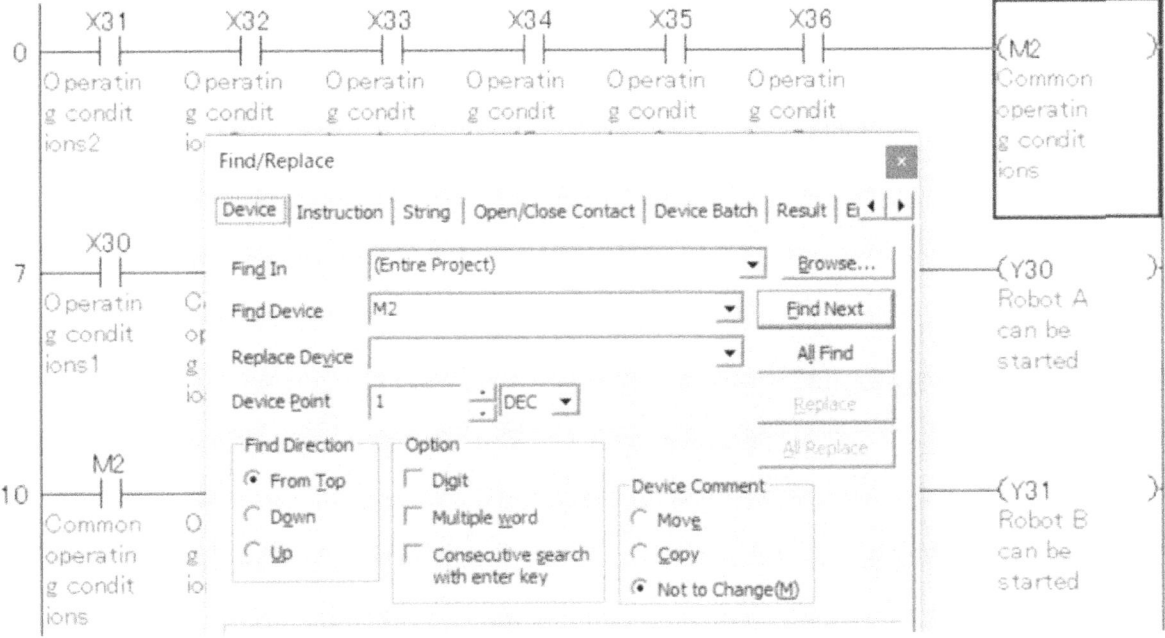

However, when I press Enter again, it becomes a circuit input, and I cannot search for the next M2.

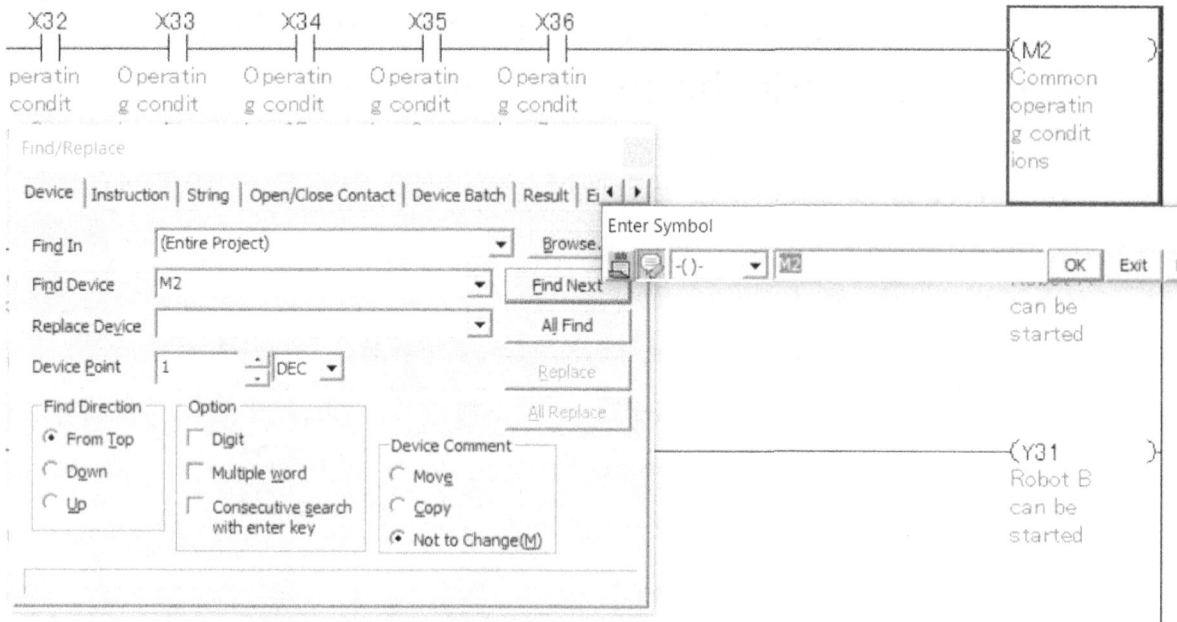

This is inconvenient, so you can enable continuous search with the Enter key by checking "Consecutive search with enter key" in the option frame of the Find/Replace window.

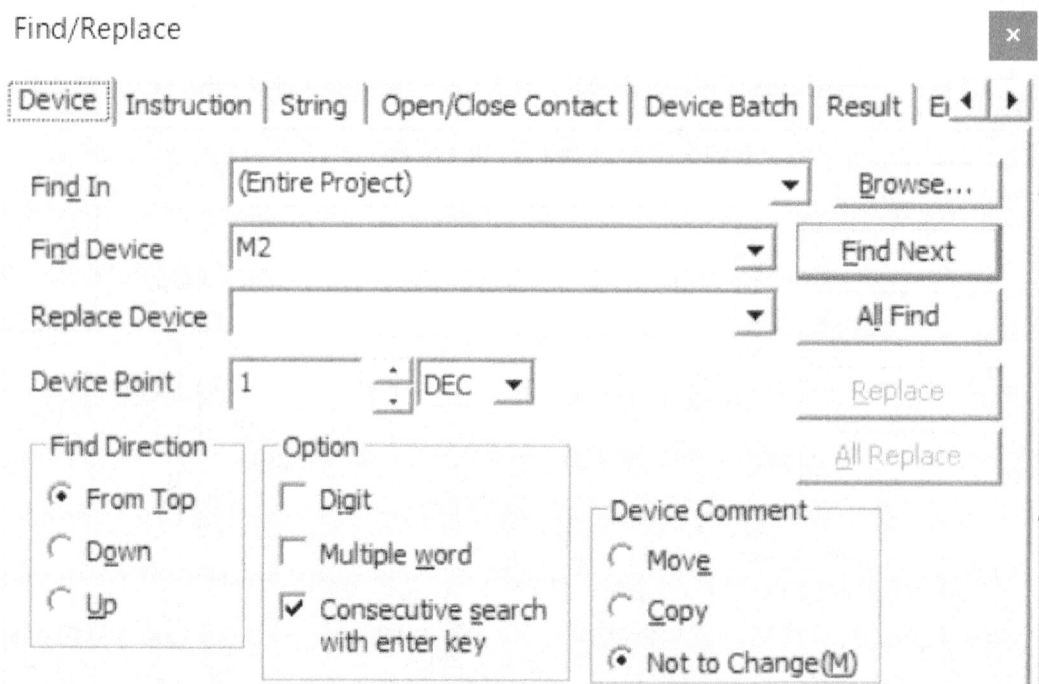

In addition to devices, you can switch between instruction search and character string search using the tabs above, but if you want to search continuously, you need to check "Consecutive search with Enter key" in the option frame of each tab.

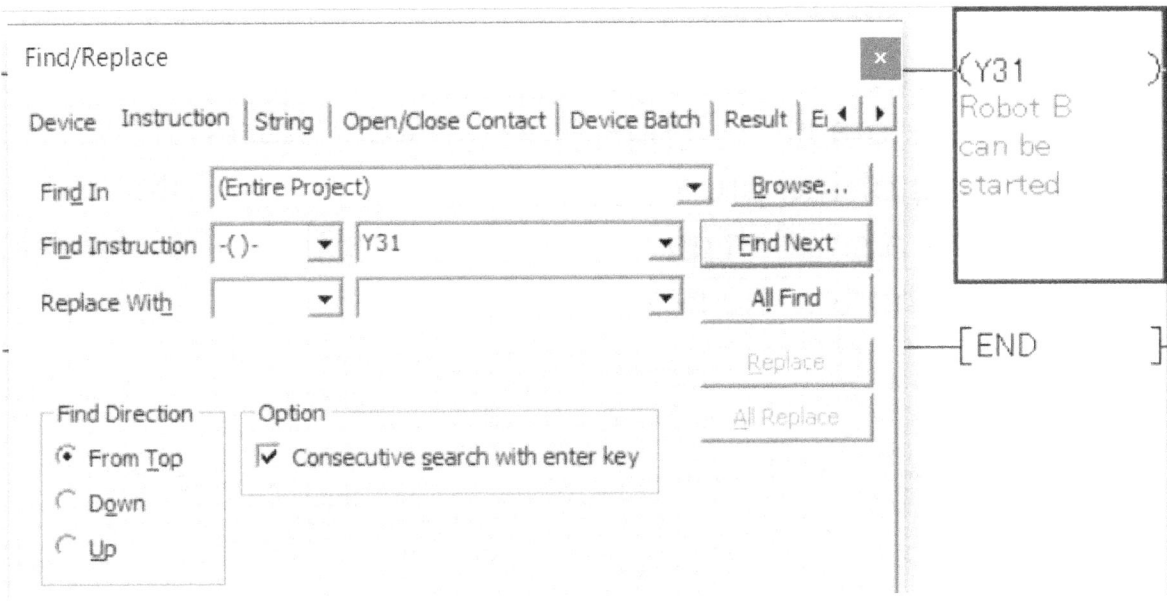

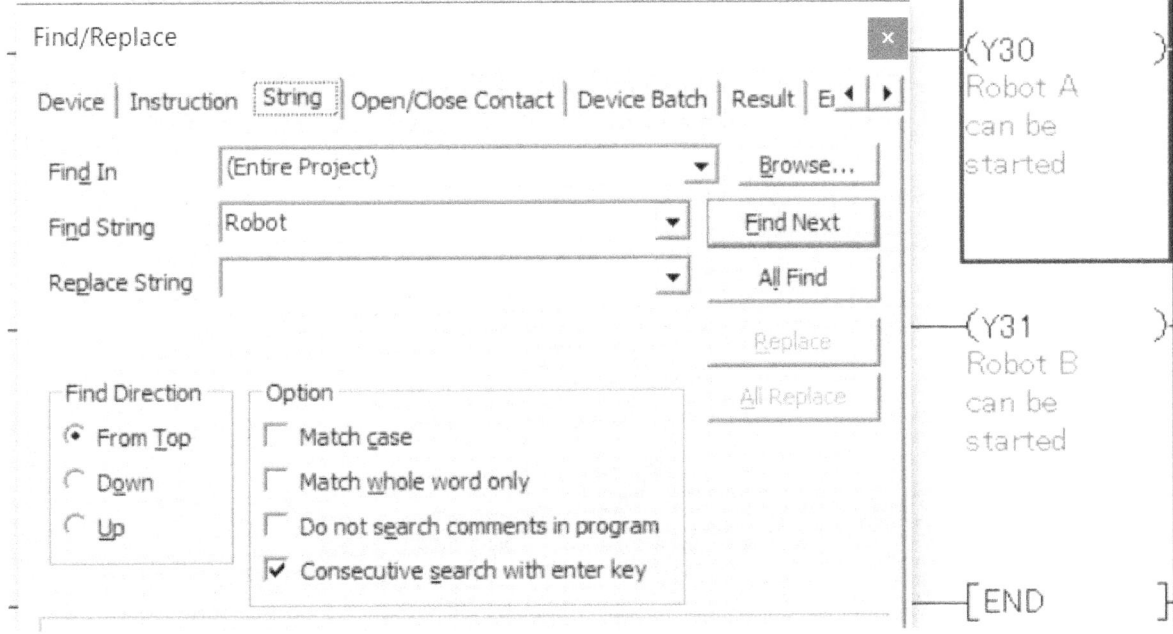

Also, if you search at the location where the cursor is currently positioned, the current search direction is "from the beginning", so the search will start from the beginning of the program. By checking it, you can search downward from the current device. (The first search searches itself)

I want to search from the current point onwards, but if I use the default settings, the search starts from the beginning of the program, and I must press Enter many times. It's a small thing, but by reducing this kind of work, you can shorten the search time.

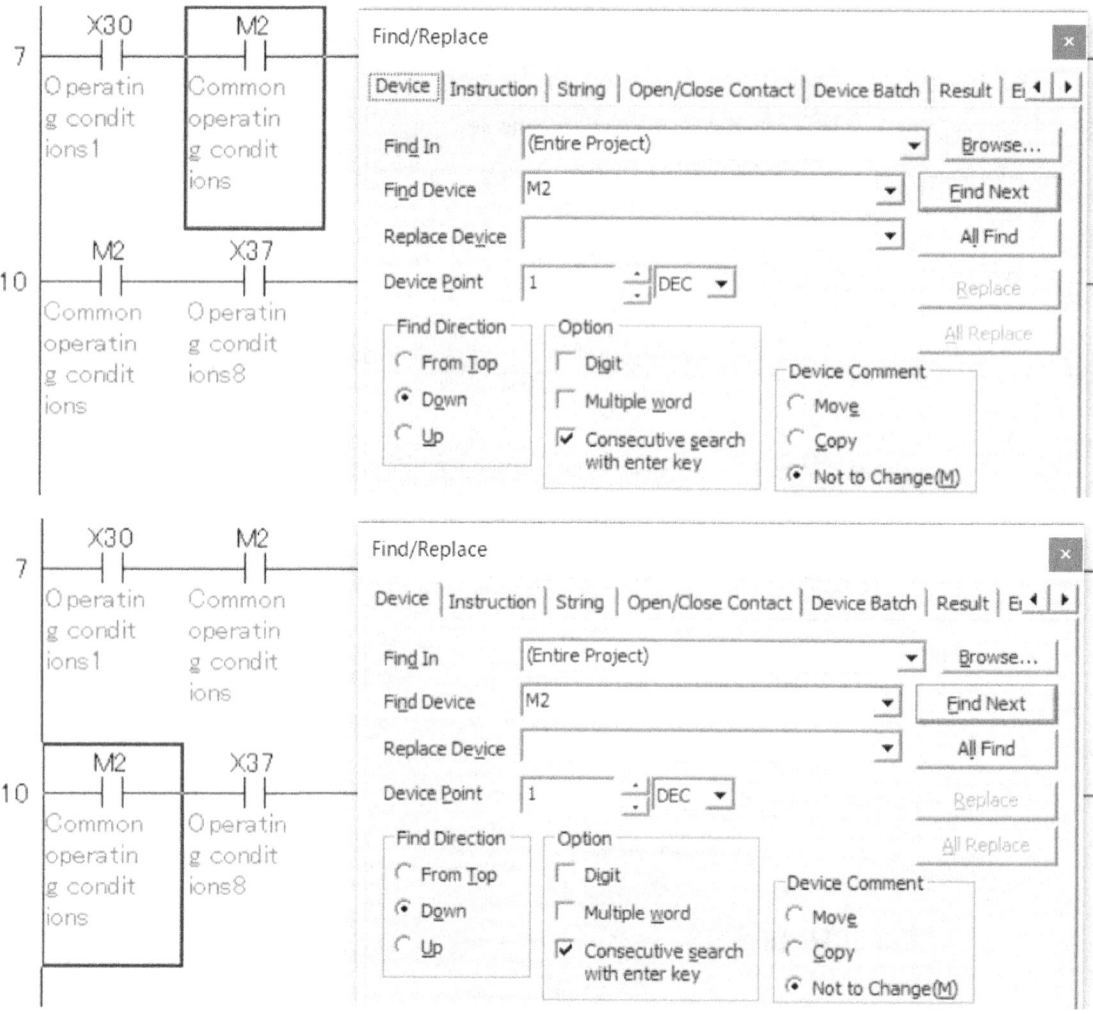

1-2 Device usage list "Ctrl + D"

As the name suggests, the device usage list is **You can check whether the device is used on the program**. It is often used to check which devices are unused when creating a new program. The device usage list can be displayed by clicking the "Find/Replace" tab ⇒ Device usage list, or by clicking the "Device usage list window" on the toolbar.

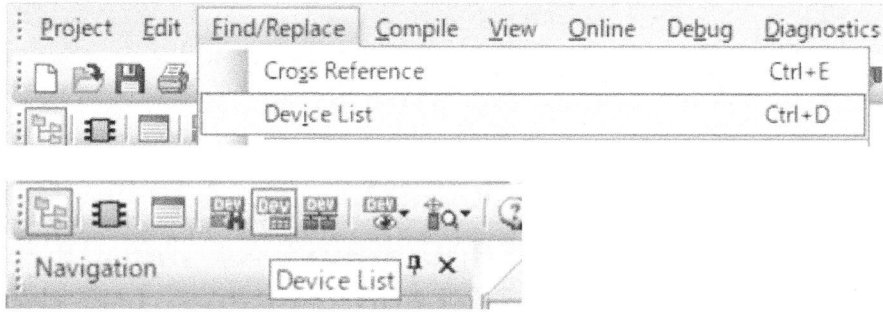

This will also be explained using the circuit created earlier. For example, if you place the cursor on M2 at step number 10 and press Ctrl + D, the device usage list will be displayed at the bottom of the screen. From this list, you can see that M2 is used for both contacts and coils, and M3 to M5 are not used for contacts and coils.

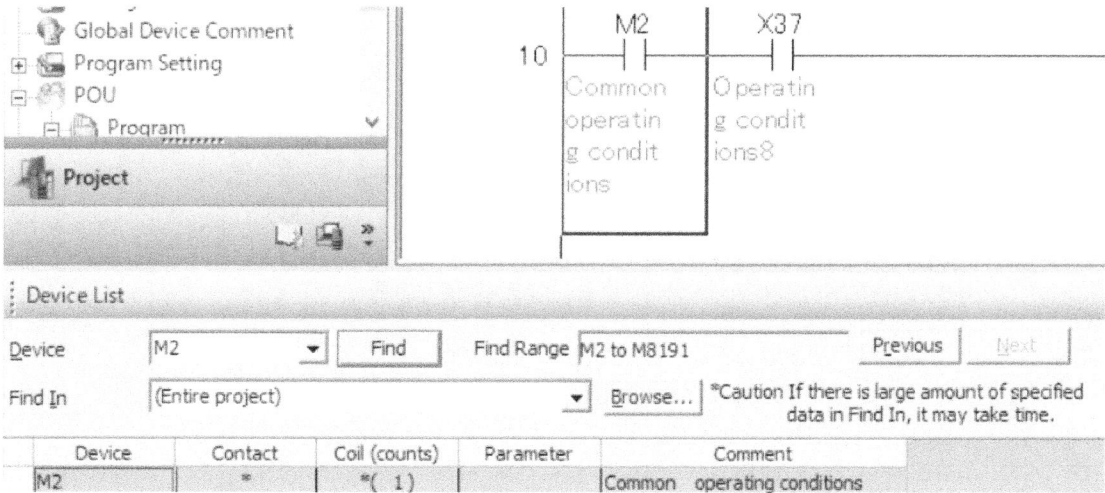

17

In addition, in the device use list, it is possible to display only the used devices and only unused devices, as well as the comment deletion function for devices with unused contacts and coils that have comments left.

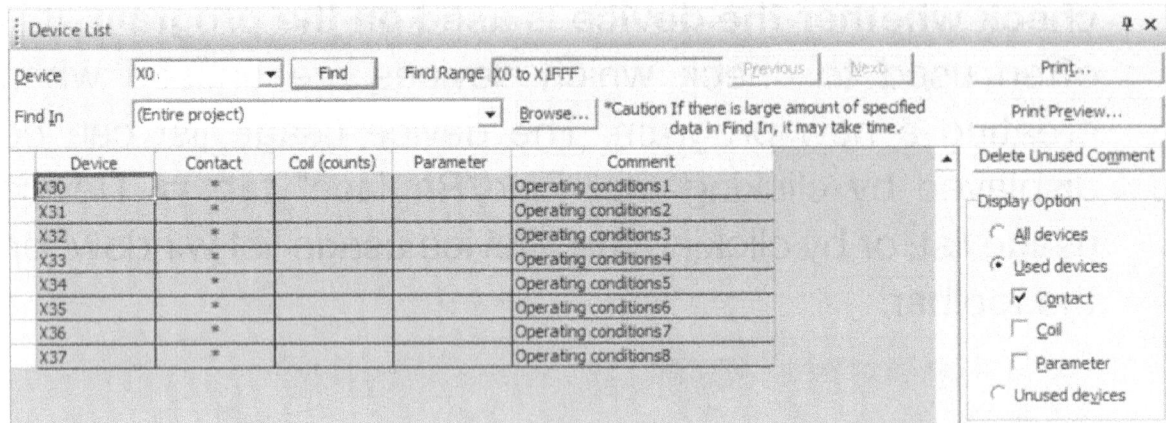

Also, by changing the search location, you can switch between viewing the device usage status for the entire project or viewing the device usage status for the currently opened screen.

If you want to see the device usage status of the screen that is currently open, select (Current window) in the search location and press Enter to switch.

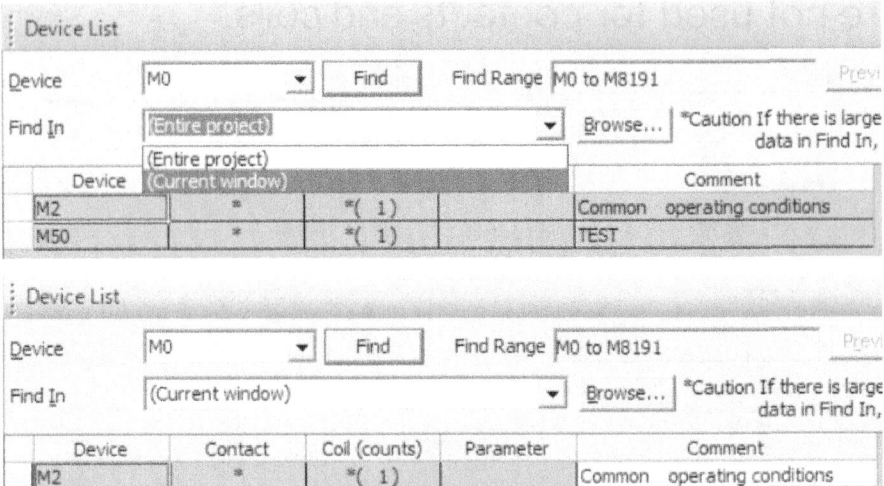

1-3 Comment, statement, note display "Ctrl + F5, F7, F8."

To make the contents of the program easier to understand, the comment, statement, and note writing functions are very important functions, so I will explain each function along with the introduction of shortcuts.

【comment】

Comments attached to each device It's about. The comment for M2 is "common operating conditions". If the comment is not displayed, you can display it with Ctrl + F5. You can also use Ctrl + F5 if you want to hide from the display state. *If no comment is entered, it will not be displayed even if it is displayed.

```
         M2        X37
10      ─┤ ├──────┤ ├──────────────────────────(Y31  )
```

```
         M2        X37
10      ─┤ ├──────┤ ├──────────────────────────(Y31  )
        Common    Operatin                      Robot B
        operatin  g condit                      can be
        g condit  ions8                         started
        ions
```

You can also switch in the same way from the "View" tab at the top ⇒ Comment view.

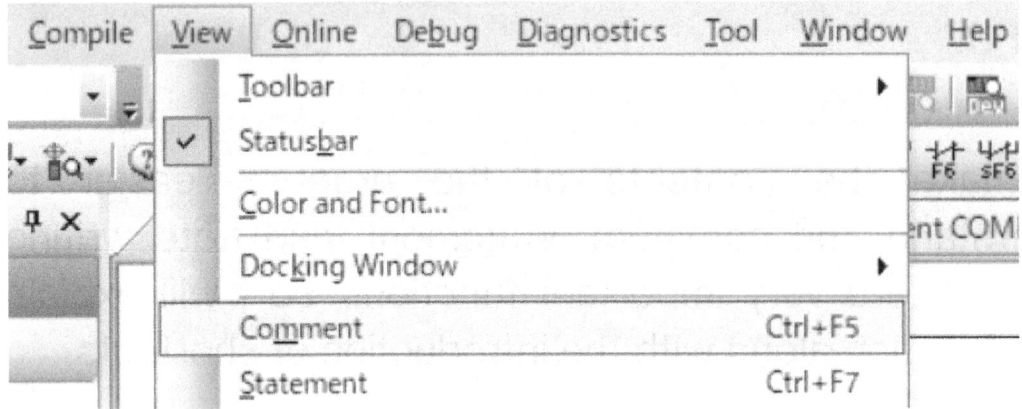

There are two ways to enter a comment: after entering the device, entering from the global device comment in the navigation, and entering only the comment by double-clicking the device. I will explain each.

＜**How to input after device input**＞
Open the "Tools" tab at the top ⇒ Options, click Program Editor ⇒ Ladder/SFC ⇒ Enter ladder in the tool on the left, and check "Enter label comment and device comment" in the operation settings. and press OK.

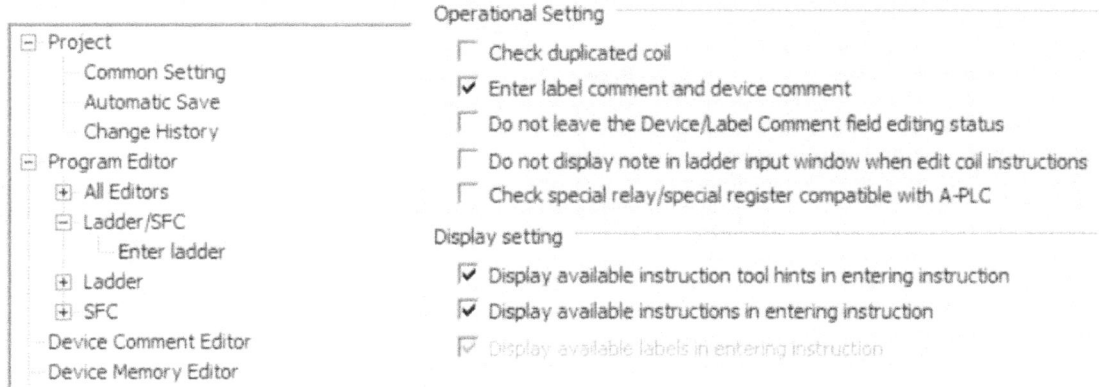

After that, when you double-click the device, the circuit input is displayed, so you can enter a comment by pressing OK.

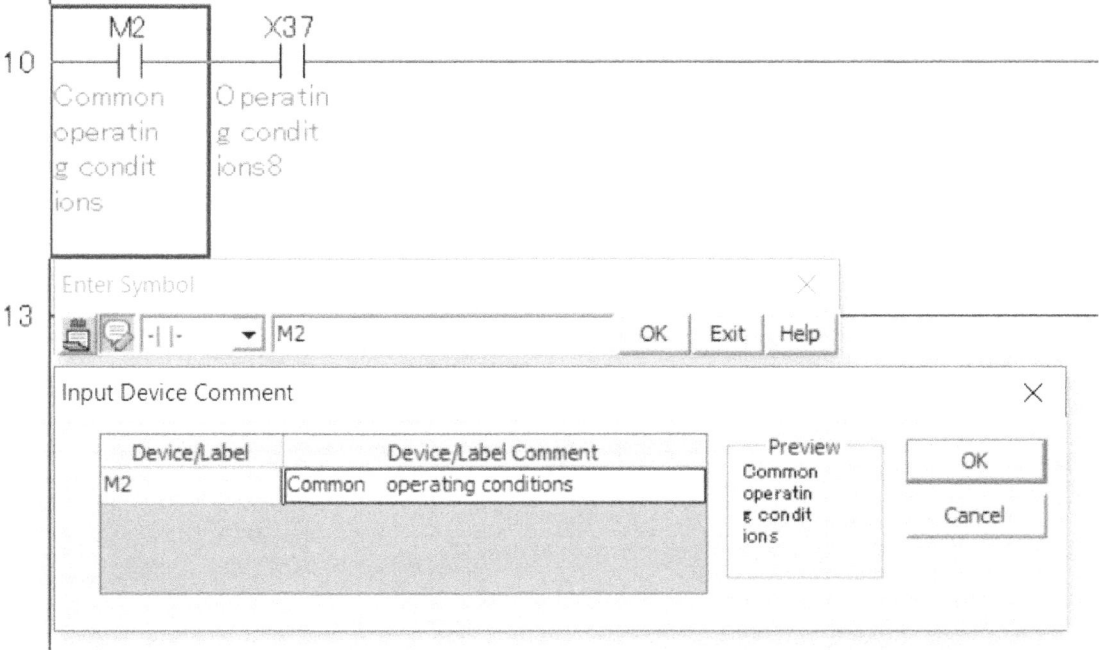

< **How to enter from global device comments in navigation**>

Double-click Global Device Comments in the left navigation. If the navigation is not displayed, you can display it with the "View" tab at the top ⇒ Docking window ⇒ Navigation.

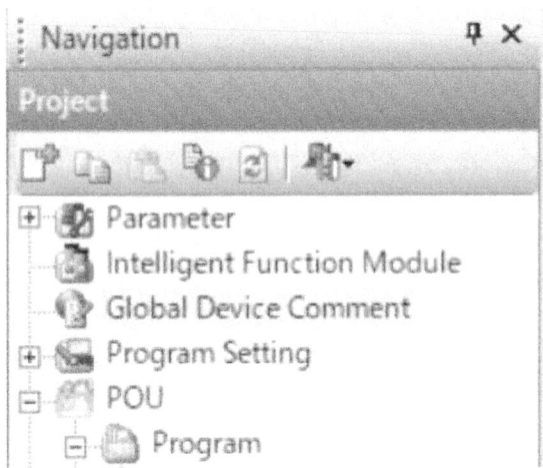

The following screen will be displayed. Add a comment to the required device. You can also search by entering a device in the device name field.

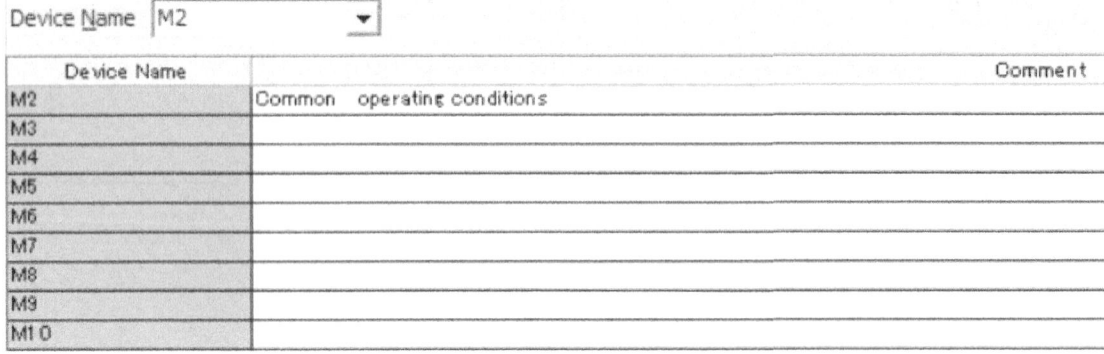

< **How to double-click a device and enter only comments** >

Click the "Edit" tab at the top ⇒ Documentation ⇒ Device comment, or press the "Edit device comment" button on the toolbar. If the toolbar with "Device Comment Edit" is not displayed, select "View" tab ⇒ Toolbar ⇒ Ladder at the top.

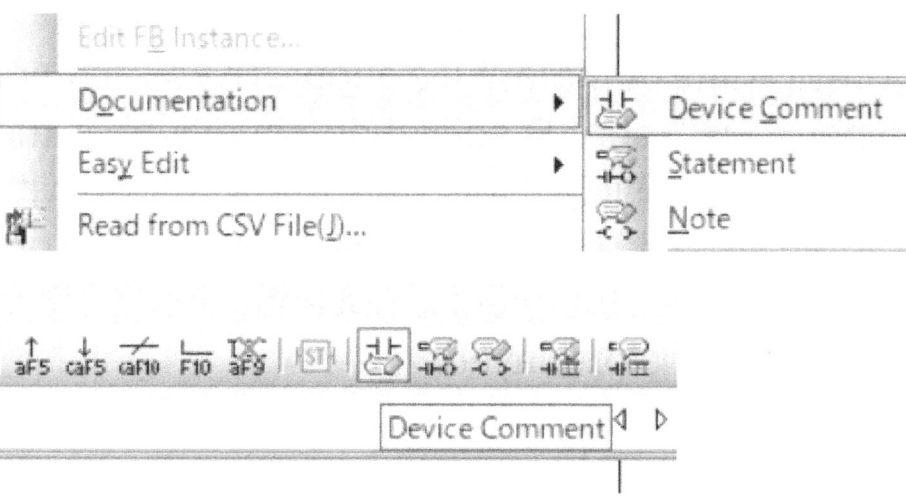

If you double-click the device in this state, you can enter a comment. To stop editing the device comment, press the Esc button on your computer.

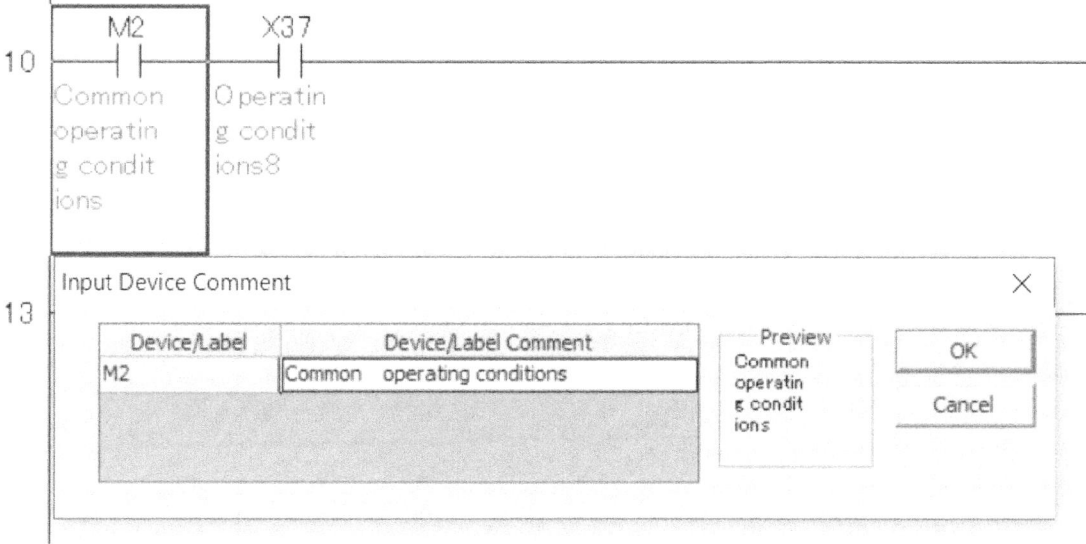

Comments are a very important part that expresses the contents of the program.is. Please try to write comments that other people can see and understand. Also, I think that any of the comment input methods described above are OK if they are suitable for you.

〔statement〕

this is not a device **line comment** It's about. The statement in step number 10 is "robot B activation condition". If the statements are not visible, you can show them with Ctrl+F7. You can also use Ctrl + F7 if you want to hide from the display state. *If the statement is not entered, it will not be displayed even if it is displayed.

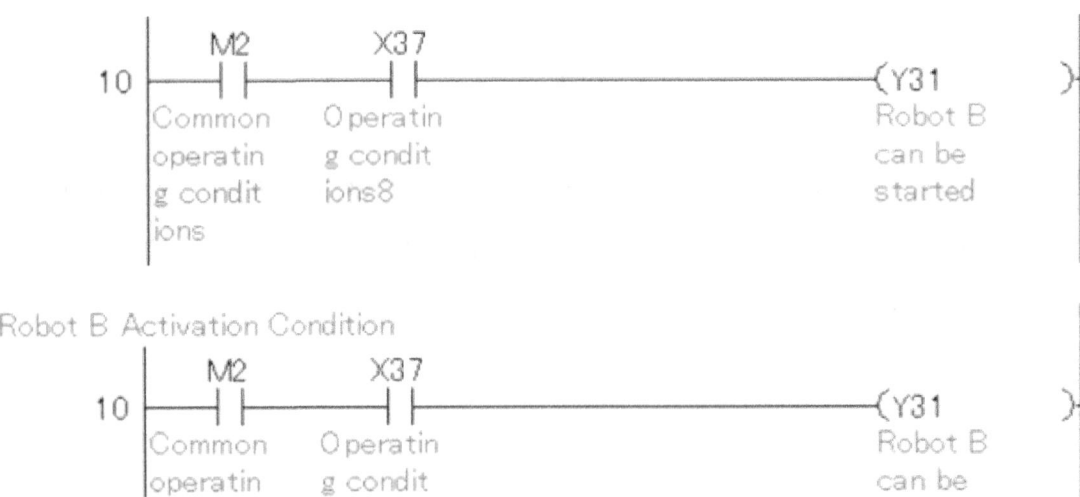

As for how to enter the statement, click the "Edit" tab at the top ⇒ Create document ⇒ Edit statement, or press the "Edit statement" button on the toolbar.

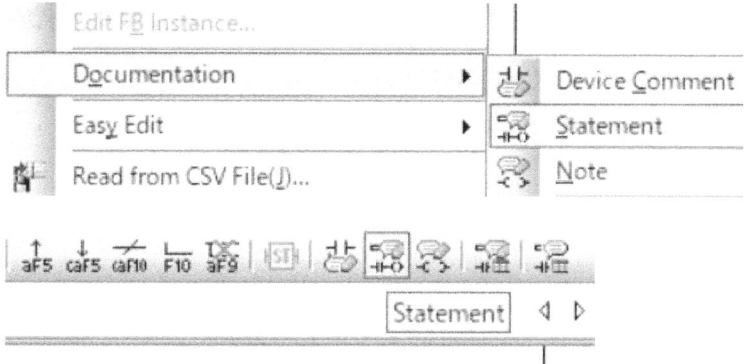

If you double-click on the line where you want to add a statement in this state, the statement input between lines will be displayed. After entering the statement, press OK to reflect the statement. (I will explain the whole thing and its surroundings later.) After inputting, double-click the statement if you want to modify it. If you want to delete it, click on the statement, and press the Del key.

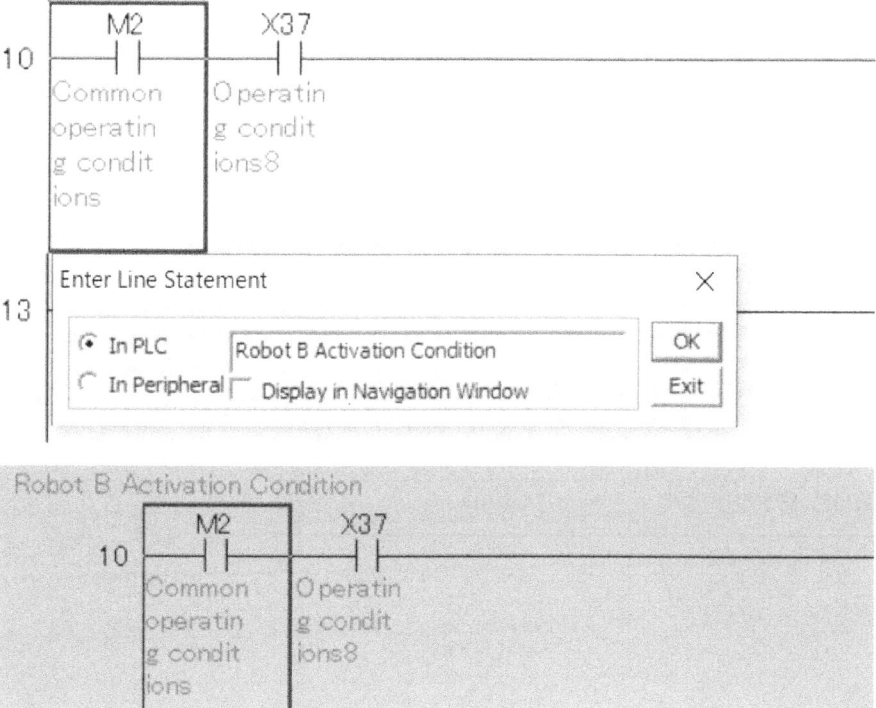

The gray status means that the conversion has not been completed yet, so press F4, or click the "Compile" tab ⇒ Build at the top, or press the "Build" button on the toolbar to convert. (If an error occurs currently, the corrective action is described on the next page.)

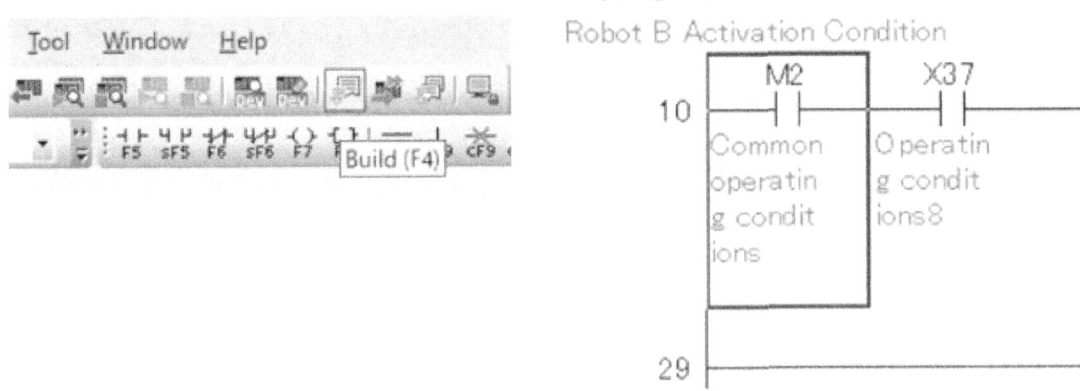

The following error may occur when executing the conversion.

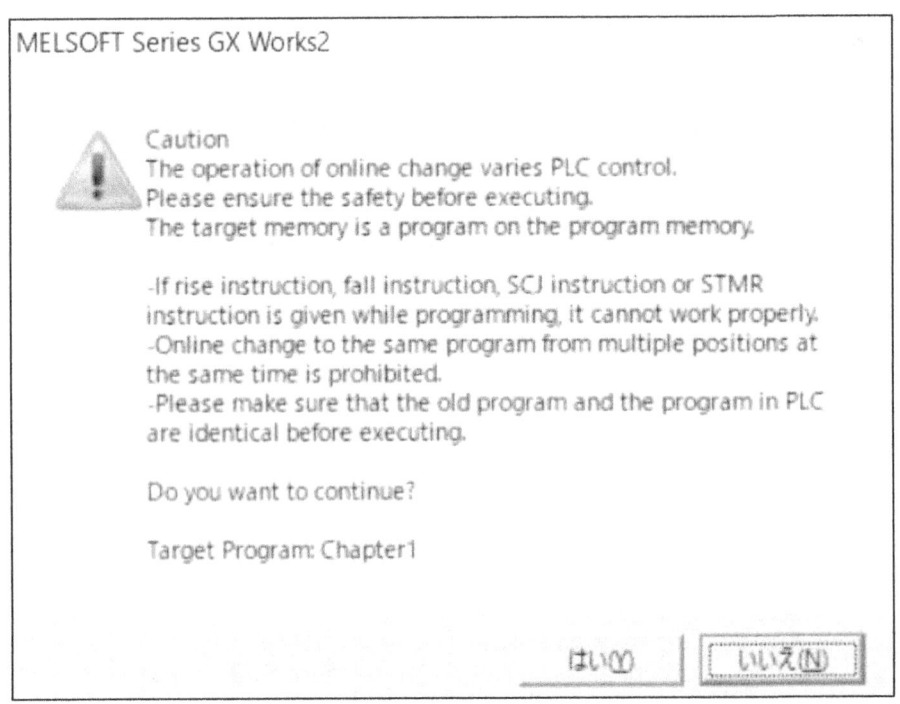

If this error occurs, click the "Tools" tab ⇒ Options at the top and uncheck "Execute online change by Compile". After that, you will be able to convert by performing the conversion.

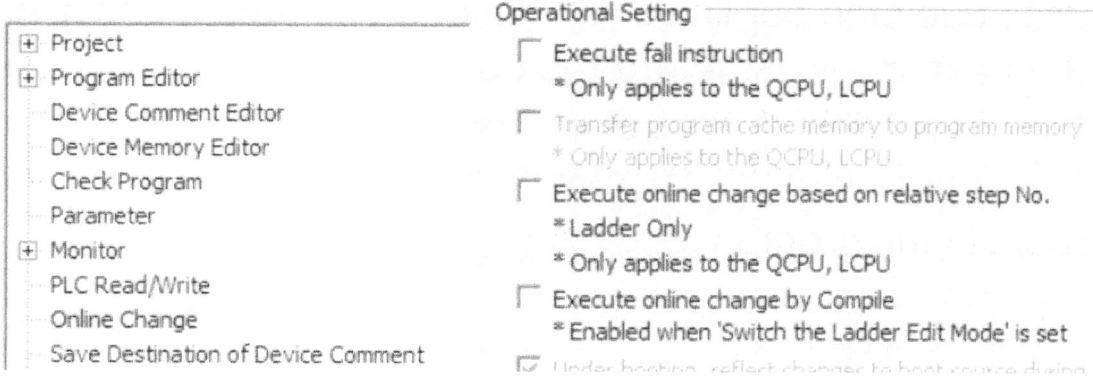

Interline statement input includes "In PLC", "In peripheral", and "Display in navigation window". I will also explain this.

· Interline Statement "In PLC"
The entered statement is saved in the PLC (equipment side) Therefore, when the program is read from the PLC, the statements are also read. However, it uses a lot of program capacity. The step number for the next line is 13 before the conversion, but it is 26 after the conversion. If there is room in the program capacity, I think that it is better to describe it.

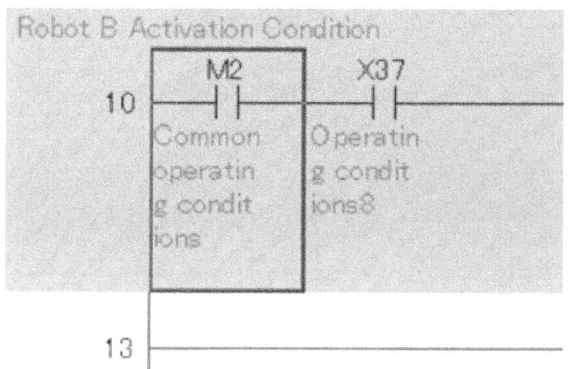
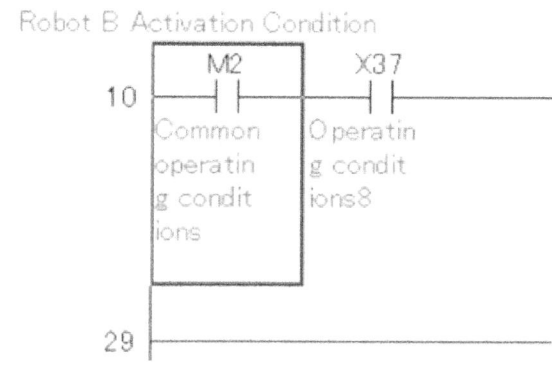

· **Interline Statement "In Peripheral"**
The entered statement is saved on the PC (software side) Therefore, even if you read the program from the PLC, the statement will not be read. The program capacity uses one step per line of statement. The step number for the next line is 13 before the conversion, but it is 14 after the conversion. If it is set to "Peripheral", * is attached to the beginning of the statement. It is used when there is no room in the program capacity.

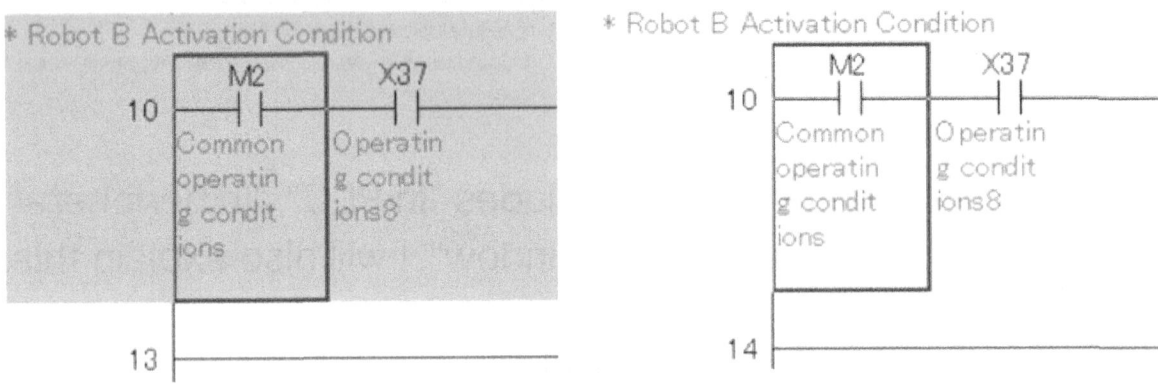

· **Display in the navigation window**
If you check "Show in navigation window", [Title] will be displayed at the top, so press OK and press F4 to convert.

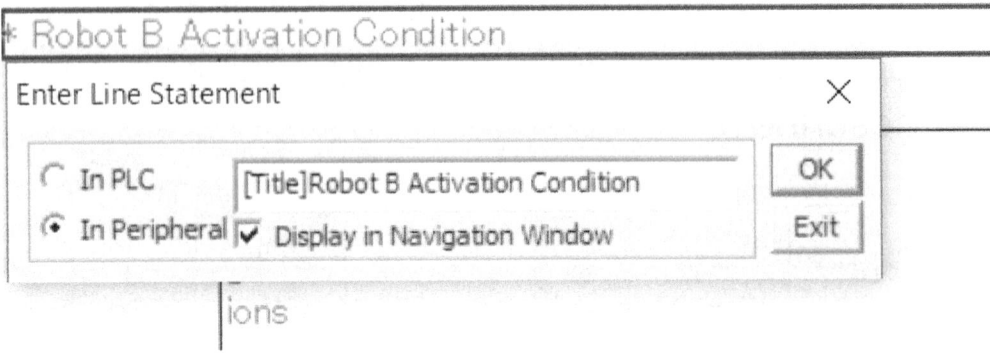

After conversion, a + mark will be displayed in the display program of the navigation. Click the + mark to display the statement name section.

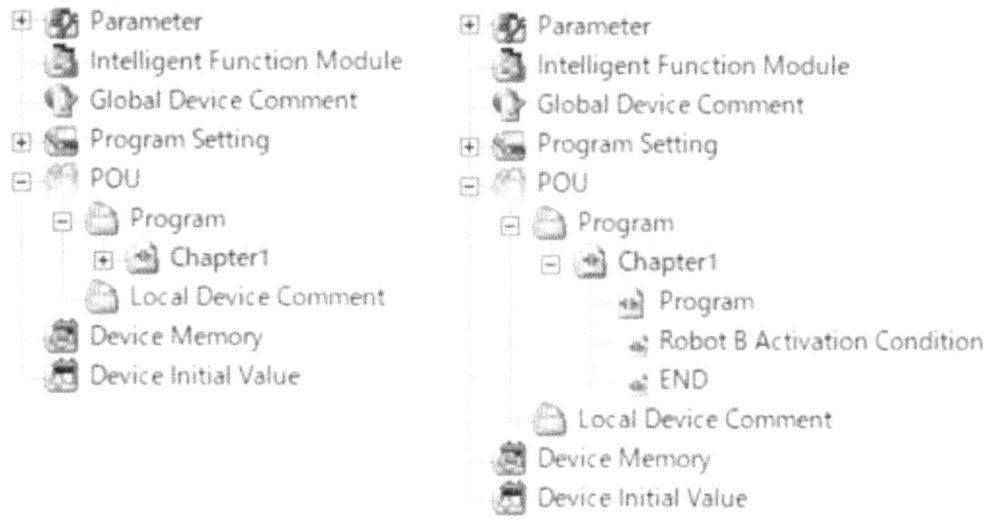

Double-clicking a statement name here will show you from the line where that statement is to where the next statement is.

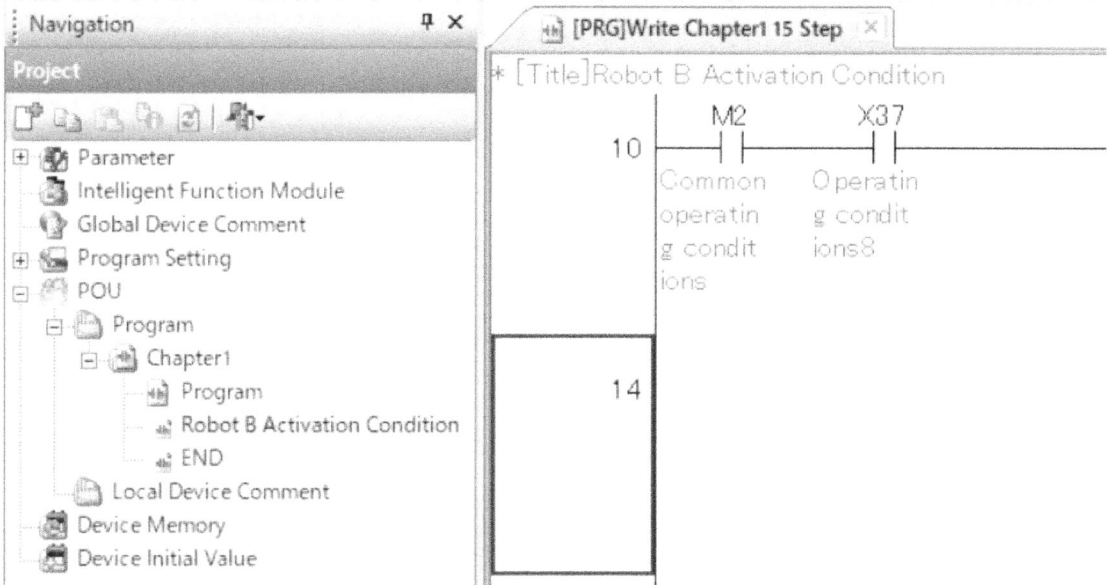

Press the Esc button when you want to finish entering the statement.

Device comments are also important when creating programs. **This statement is very important so that you can quickly move to the program you want to check when creating a program or troubleshooting later.**

In addition, you can improve the efficiency of various tasks by making good use of the "Show in navigation window" or the "List of statement between lines" shortcuts that will be introduced later.

【Note】

This is **Comments attached to outputs and instructions** It's about. The note for output Y31 is "Robot B: Workpiece transfer robot". If you don't see the notes, you can show them with Ctrl + F8. You can also use Ctrl + F8 if you want to hide from the display state. *If no note is entered, it will not be displayed even if it is displayed.

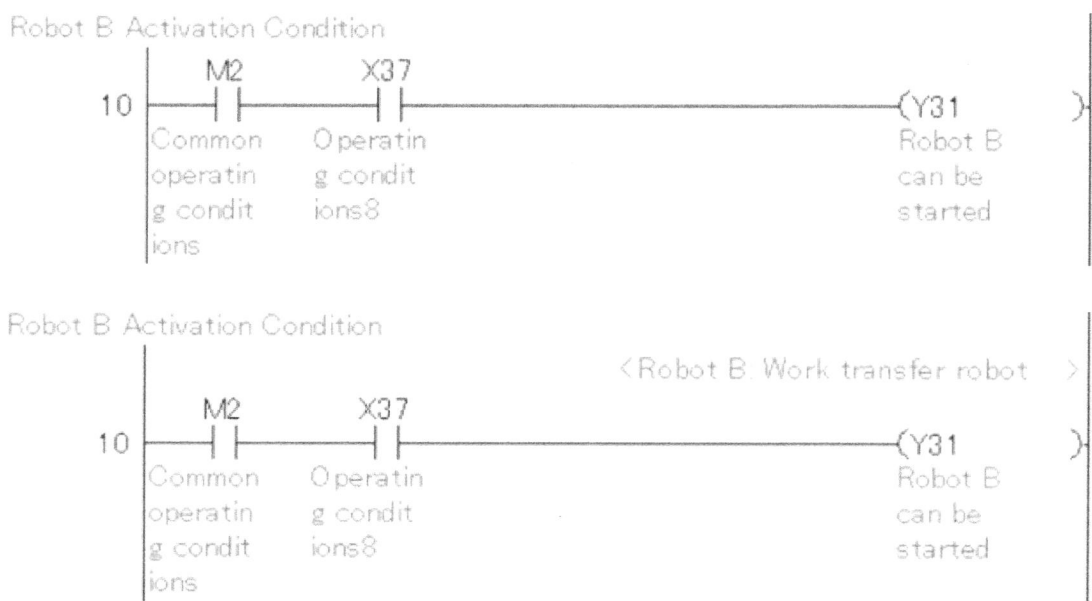

As for how to enter a note, click the "Edit" tab at the top ⇒ Document creation ⇒ Edit note, or press the "Edit note" button on the toolbar.

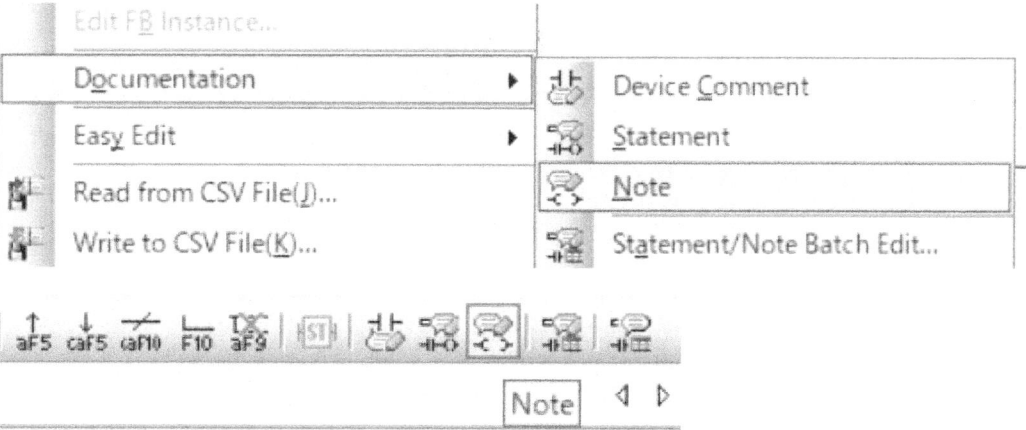

In this state, double-click on the output or instruction you want to add a note to display the note input, so after entering the note, press OK to reflect the note. (Integrated and peripheral have the same meaning as statements.) After entering, double-click the note if you want to modify it. If you want to delete it, click the note, and press the Del key.

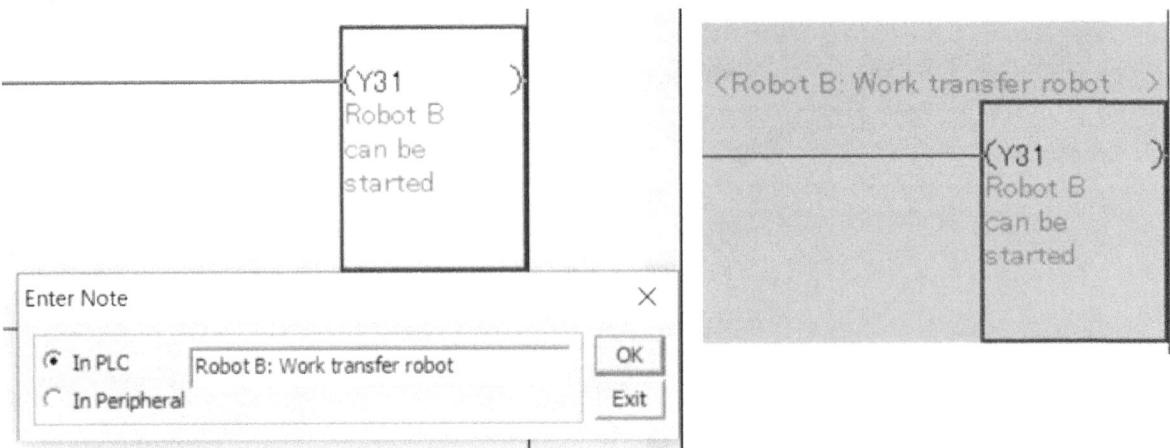

The gray status means that the conversion has not been completed yet, so press F4 or press the " Compile" tab ⇒ Build at the top to convert.

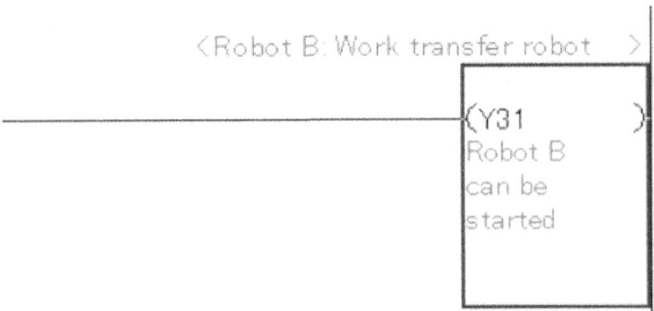

If you want to finish entering notes, press the Esc button. The maximum number of characters that can be displayed for a device comment is 32.**If you write the content that cannot be written in the device comment in a note as a supplement, it will be easier to understand when you look at the program later.**。

We've talked about comments, statements, and notes here, but **These features are very important for you and others to understand when they look at your program.** Therefore, we recommend that you include as much information as possible.

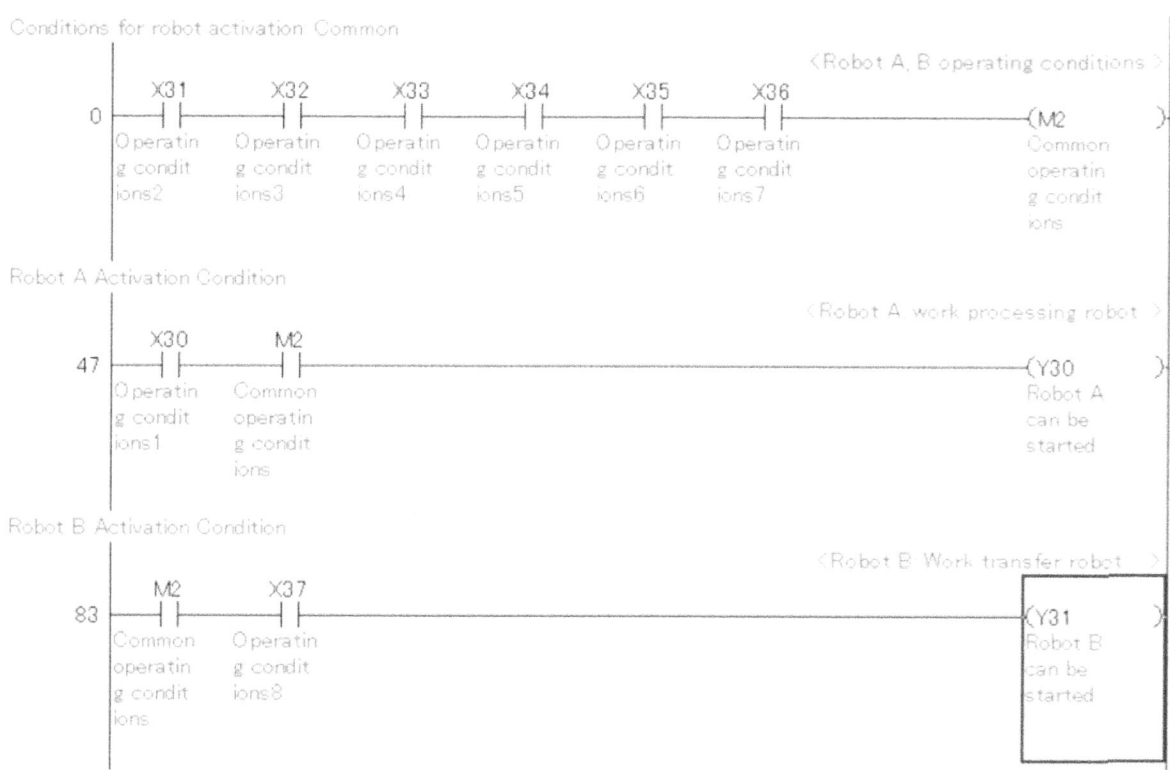

1-4 Statement list between lines "Ctrl + L"

Statements were explained in 1-3, but the list of statements between lines is **You can display a list of statements on the display program.** You can make it visible by pressing Ctrl + L. After displaying, you can move to the step where the statement is by double-clicking each step or name. You can also search by entering the name in the search field.

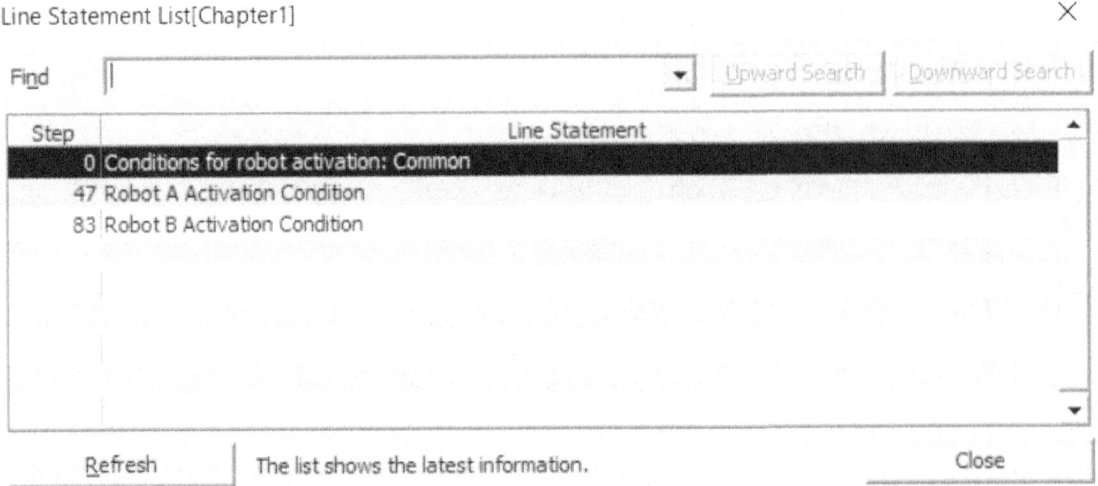

You can also display it by clicking the "Find/Replace" tab at the top ⇒ Line statement List, or by clicking the "Line statement List" button on the toolbar.

You can easily move to the step with the statement, so by attaching an easy-to-understand statement **It leads to shortening of search time when correcting programs or when trouble occurs.**

1-5 Input/delete vertical/horizontal lines "Ctrl + arrow keys."

For vertical/horizontal line input, enter horizontal bar "F9" (delete horizontal bar "Ctrl+F9"), vertical bar input "F10" (delete vertical bar "Ctrl+F10") It is possible, but **You can also enter using Ctrl + arrow keys.**

For example, if you place the cursor next to X37 (operating condition 8) and press Ctrl + ↓ key once and Ctrl + → key 4 times, you can draw vertical and horizontal lines as shown below. After that, you can delete the line by pressing Ctrl + ← key three times. Keeping this in mind will also save you time.

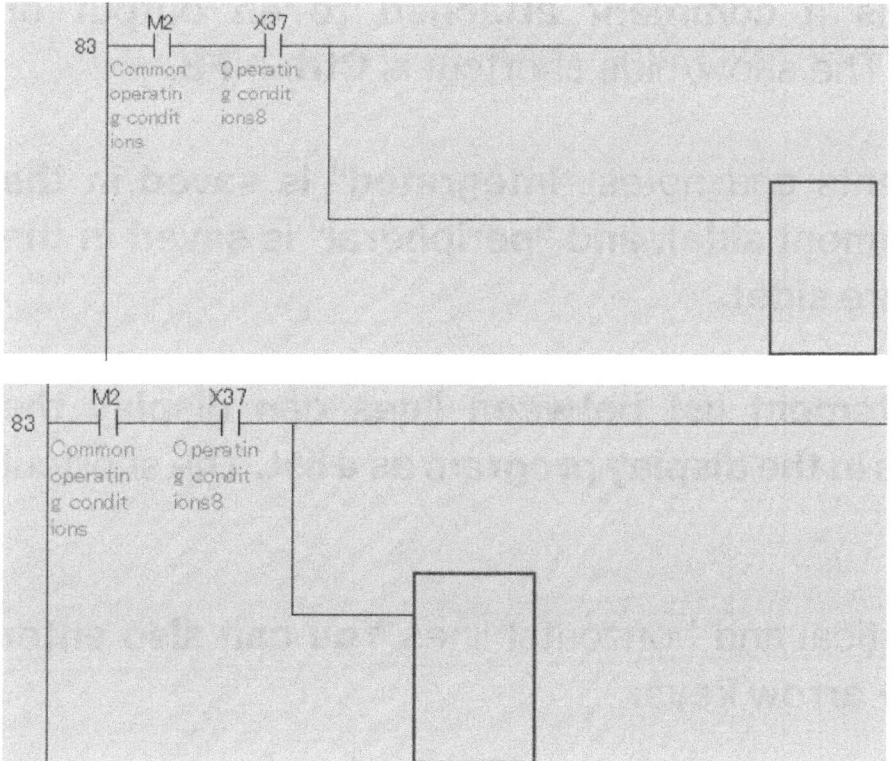

1-1 to 1-5 Summary

· **Device search is used to search where devices are used.** The shortcut is **Ctrl + F**.

· **The device usage list allows you to check whether the device is being used on the program.**. The shortcut is **Ctrl + D**.

· **Comment are comments attached to each device.** The show/hide shortcut is **Ctrl + F5**.

· **A statement is a comment attached to a line.** The show/hide shortcut is **Ctrl + F7**.

- **A note is a comment attached to an output or command.** The show/hide shortcut is **Ctrl + F8**.

· Statements and notes **"Integrated" is saved in the PLC (equipment side), and "peripheral" is saved in the PC (software side).**

· **The statement list between lines can display the statements in the display program as a list.** The shortcut is **Ctrl + L**.

· Enter vertical and horizontal lines **You can also enter using Ctrl + arrow keys.**

Exercise 1 (computer operation)

Press X300 (Ctrl key) and X310 (C key) to turn Y310 (Copy execution) ON, press X300 (Ctrl key) and X311 (V key) to turn Y311 (Paste execution) ON, Y311 note) is "invalid if copy is not executed", pressing X300 (Ctrl key) and X312 (X key) turns Y312 (Cut execution) ON, statement (integral) is "copy/paste/cut shortcut" Please create the following PLC program using shortcut keys as much as possible. (Open the "PLC program creation" file, create new program data "Task1", and then create it.)

```
Copy/Paste/Cut shortcut
       X300         X310
  0 ────┤├──────────┤├────────────────────────────(Y310)──┤
       Ctrl key    C key                           Copy
                                                   executio
                                                   n

                                          <Invalid if not running copy>
                    X311
                 ────┤├────────────────────────────(Y311)──┤
                    V key                          Paste
                                                   executio
                                                   n

                    X312
                 ────┤├────────────────────────────(Y312)──┤
                    X key                          Cut
                                                   executio
                                                   n
```

Practice Question 1 Answers

1. Open "PLC program creation" created in Chapter 1, right-click the program in the navigation ⇒ select Create new data, enter "Task1" in the data name, press OK at the bottom right to create program data "Task 1 " is newly created.

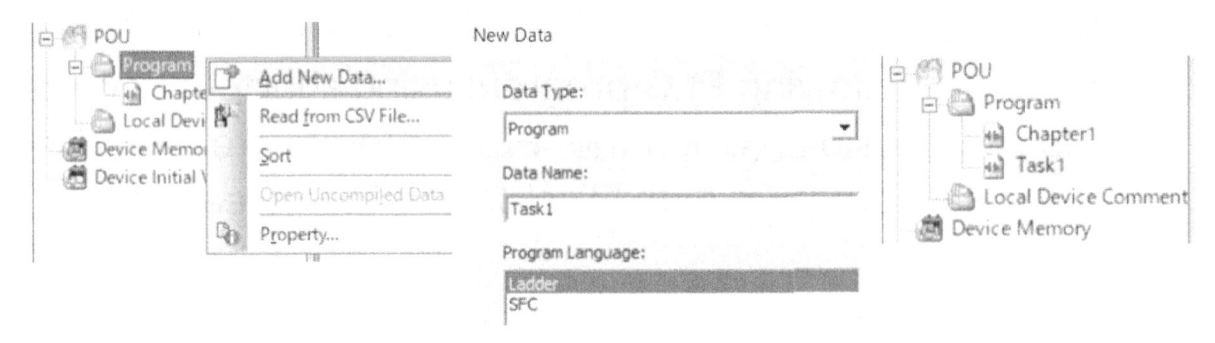

2. Next, use F5 and F7 to create the following program. Any of the three methods described in Chapter 1 can be used to enter comments. If you don't see comments, press Ctrl+F5.

3. With the cursor on X310, press Ctrl + Down arrow key to enter a vertical line, then use F5 and F7 to create the following program.

```
   X300        X310
   ─┤ ├─────────┤ ├──────────────────────(Y310  )─
   Ctrl key    C key                      Copy
                                          executio
                                          n
                           X311
                           ─┤ ├───────────(Y311  )─
                           V key          Paste
                                          executio
                                          n
```

4. In the same way, press Ctrl + Down arrow key to enter a vertical line, then use F5 and F7 to create the following program.

```
   X300        X310
   ─┤ ├─────────┤ ├──────────────────────(Y310  )─
   Ctrl key    C key                      Copy
                                          executio
                                          n
                           X311
                           ─┤ ├───────────(Y311  )─
                           V key          Paste
                                          executio
                                          n
                           X312
                           ─┤ ├───────────(Y312  )─
                           X key          Cut
                                          executio
                                          n
```

5. Click the "Edit" tab at the top ⇒ Documentation ⇒ statement, or click the statement button on the toolbar, double-click anywhere in the program, and select "Copy/Paste/Cut shortcut" in the interline statement input field. and press OK. If you don't see the statement, press Ctrl+F7.

```
Copy/Paste/Cut shortcut
       X300         X310
      ──┤├──────────┤├──────────────────────(Y310)─
       Ctrl key    C key                     Copy
                                             executio
                                             n

                    X311
                  ──┤├──────────────────────(Y311)─
                    V key                    Paste
                                             executio
                                             n

                    X312
                  ──┤├──────────────────────(Y312)─
                    X key                    Cut
                                             executio
                                             n
```

6. Click the "Edit" tab at the top ⇒ Documentation ⇒ note, or click the note button on the toolbar, double-click Y311, and enter "Disable if copy is not executed" in the note entry field, press OK. If you don't see the note, press Ctrl+F8.

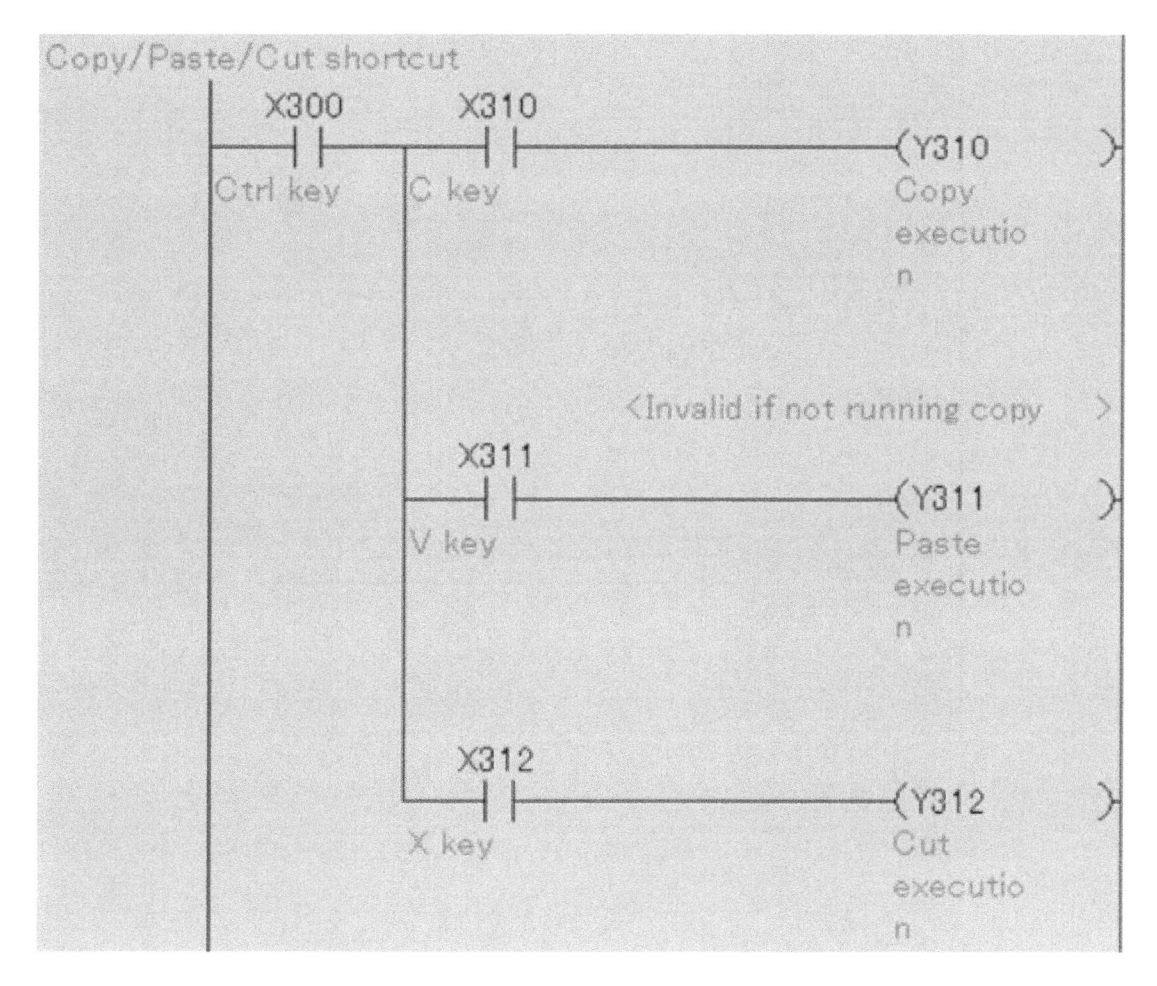

```
Copy/Paste/Cut shortcut
        X300      X310
        ─┤├──────┤├──────────────────(Y310  )
        Ctrl key  C key                Copy
                                       executio
                                       n

                           <Invalid if not running copy>
                  X311
                 ─┤├──────────────────(Y311  )
                  V key                Paste
                                       executio
                                       n

                  X312
                 ─┤├──────────────────(Y312  )
                  X key                Cut
                                       executio
                                       n
```

7. Press F4 or press "Compile" tab ⇒ Build at the top to convert. That's all. Press Ctrl + S to overwrite and save.

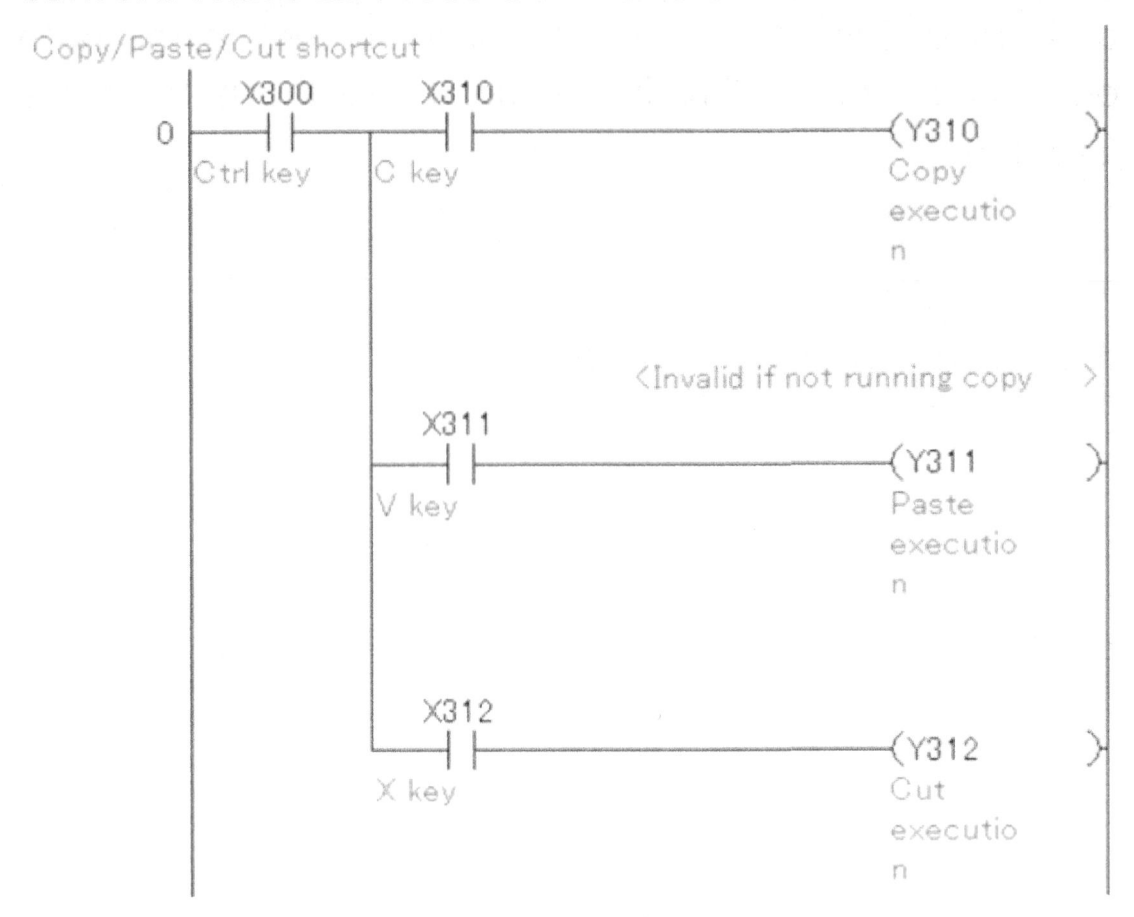

Copy/Paste/Cut shortcut

```
        X300      X310
0       ─┤├───────┤├──────────────────────(Y310)
        Ctrl key  C key                    Copy
                                           execution

                              <Invalid if not running copy>
                  X311
                  ─┤├──────────────────────(Y311)
                  V key                    Paste
                                           execution

                  X312
                  ─┤├──────────────────────(Y312)
                  X key                    Cut
                                           execution
```

Chapter 2 Basic sequence control program

In this chapter, I would like to introduce how to write a basic sequence control program. However, I think that each person has their own tastes and ways of writing programs, so please use this as a reference only. Sequence control is" **Control that advances each stage of control sequentially according to a predetermined order or procedure**".

For example, the control of a three-color traffic light repeats blue ⇒ yellow ⇒ red.

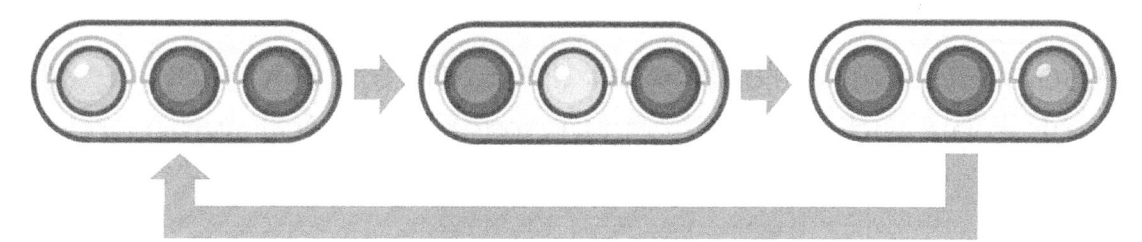

Pedestrian traffic light control repeats blue ⇒ flashing blue ⇒ red. This kind of operation is called sequence control.

2-1 Creation of sequence control using a washing machine

This time, we will learn about the basic creation method of sequence control while creating sequence control for a washing machine. The tools used this time are GX Works2 and GT Designer (GOT2000). If you search for "GX Works2 Trial Version" or "GT Designer3 Trial Version" on Google, you will find it, so you can download and install each trial version to use it for a trial period of 30 days. (* Can be used again by reinstalling)

Also, instead of creating all the controls at once, we will explain by adding functions in order in the following order.

[Step 1 Creation of a washing machine automatic operation signal circuit]

When the automatic operation start button of the washing machine is pressed while the washing machine power is on, the washing machine automatically operates signal is self-maintained and the operation lamp turns on. After creating a circuit that turns off the self-holding of the signal during automatic operation, check the operation with the simulation function.

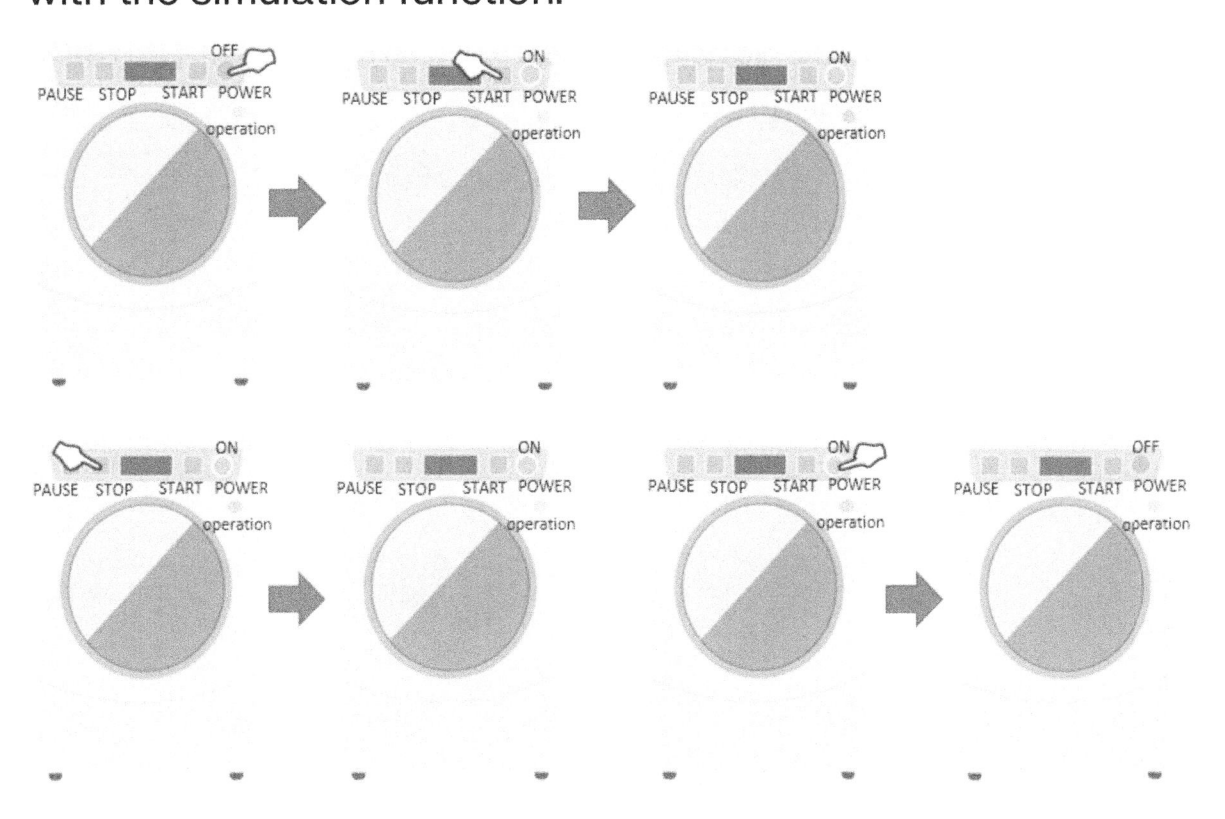

[Step 2 Creating a washing machine sequence control circuit]

While the washing machine automatic operation signal is ON, water supply starts ⇒ water supply complete ⇒ washing starts ⇒ washing complete ⇒ rinsing starts ⇒ rinsing complete ⇒ dehydration starts ⇒ dehydration complete ⇒ washing completion buzzer starts ⇒ washing completion buzzer complete ⇒ washing machine automatic operation complete After creating the circuit that performs the sequence control, check the operation with the simulation function.

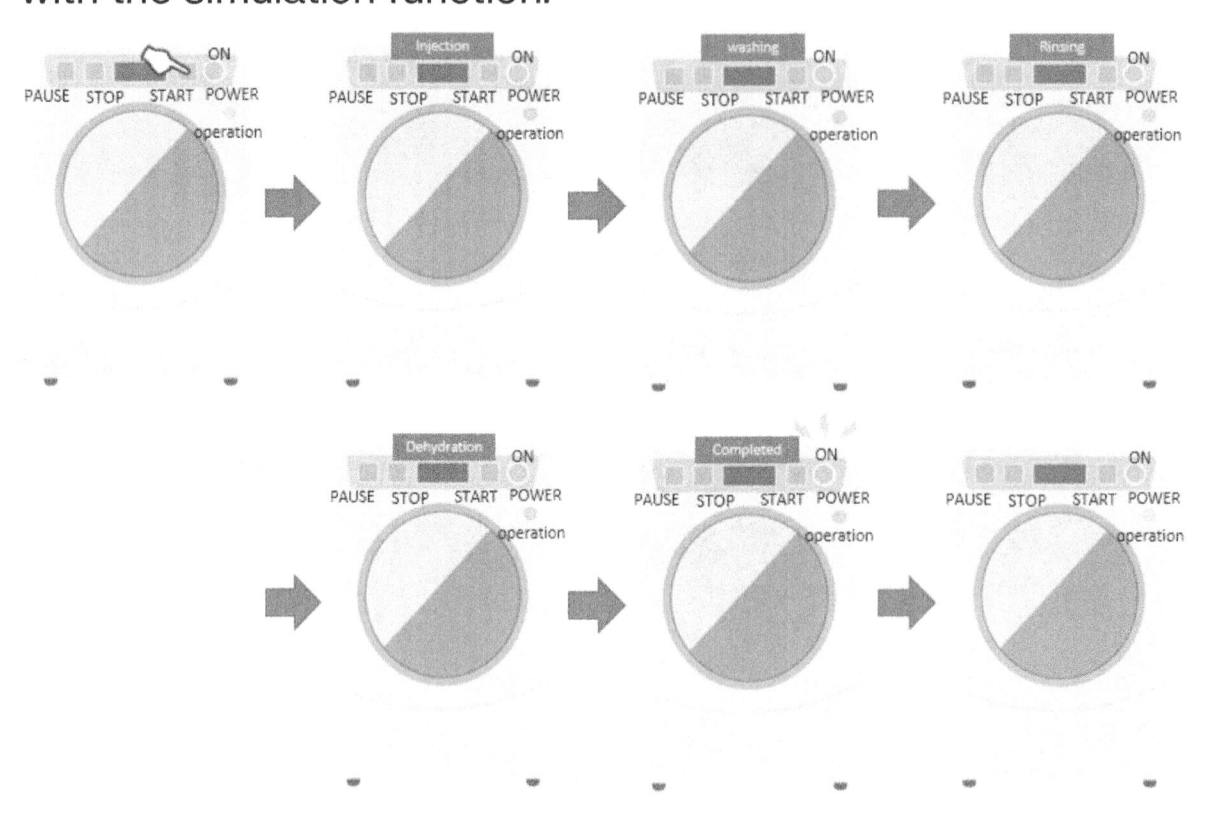

[Step 3 Creating a washing machine interlock and temporary stop circuit]

After adding an interlock signal that immediately stops the washing machine in the event of an abnormality, and creating a circuit that causes the running lamp to blink and automatic operation to pause when the pause button is pressed, check the operation with the simulation function. to hold.

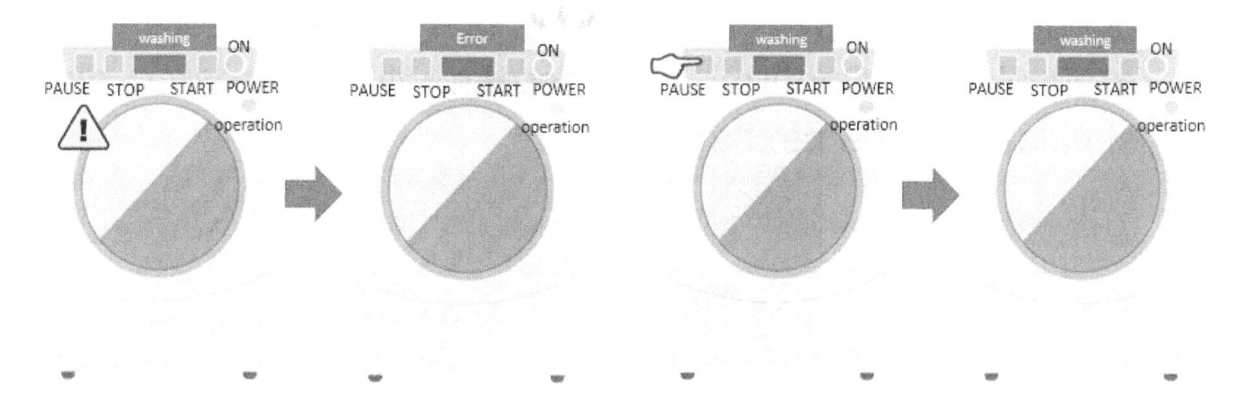

[Step 4 Creating a circuit for the washing machine's optional course]

After turning on the power to the washing machine, set the operation time for each process with the Omakase course button. After that, when the start button is pressed, water injection time 15 seconds ⇒ washing time 10 seconds ⇒ rinsing time 8 seconds ⇒ dehydration time 12 seconds ⇒ buzzer (intermittent sound) 3 seconds After creating a circuit that completes automatic operation, it operates in a simulation. Confirm. (The screen will be created and simulated in the next step 5)

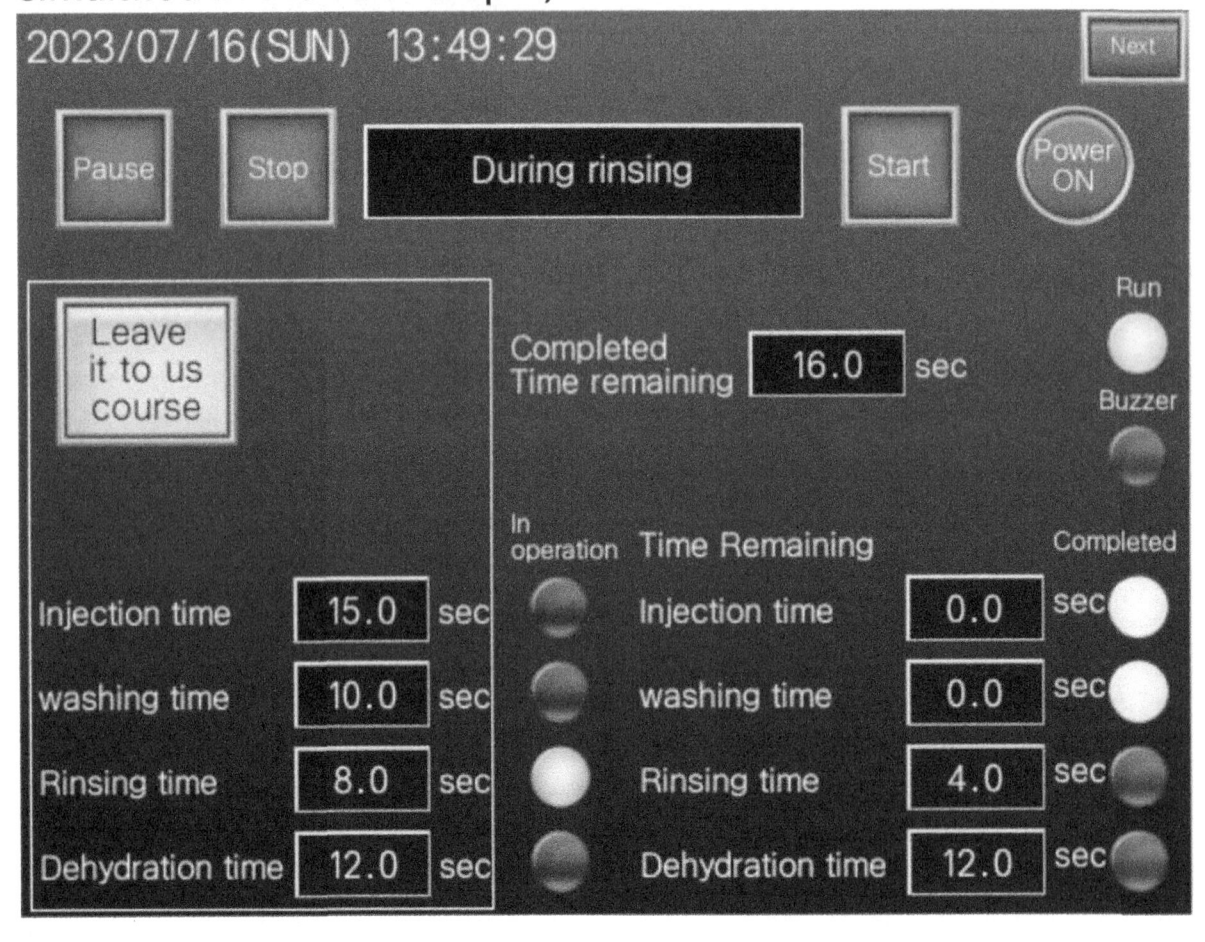

[Step 5 Creation of touch panel screen for washing machine operation]
After creating the touch panel screen from steps 1 to 4, check the operation using the simulation function.

[Step 6 Circuit and screen creation for manual washing machine course]
After adding a manual course where the time for each process can be set from the touch panel, we will check the operation with the simulation function.

Basic sequence control can be created by creating the above 6 steps and checking the operation by simulation. I would like to start from step 1.

2-2 Step 1 Creation of a washing machine automatic operation signal circuit

First, prepare for programming.

1. Open "PLC program creation", right-click the program in the navigation ⇒ select "Create new data", enter "washing machine" in the data name, press OK at the bottom right, and create a new program data "washing machine". increase.

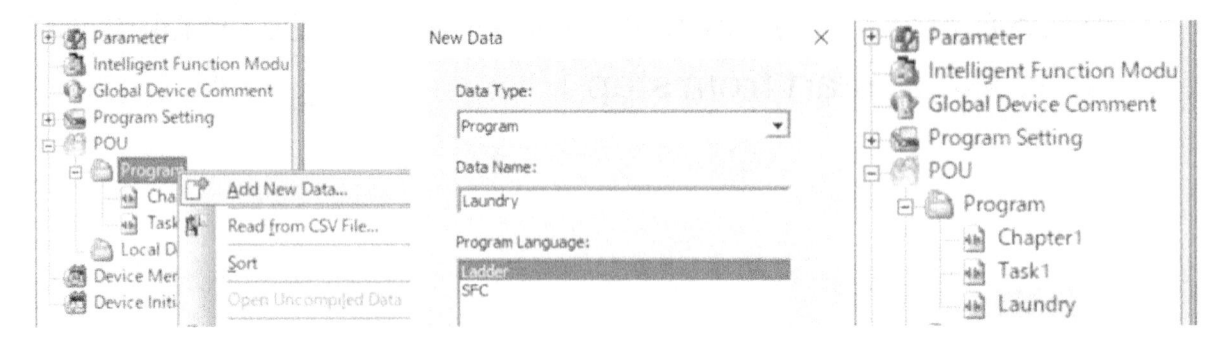

2. Double-click "Parameters" in the navigation, then double-click "PC Parameters" just below it. Then press the "Program Settings" tab, click "Washing Machine" in the program, press Insert, and press Exit Settings at the bottom right. (This setting is required during simulation)

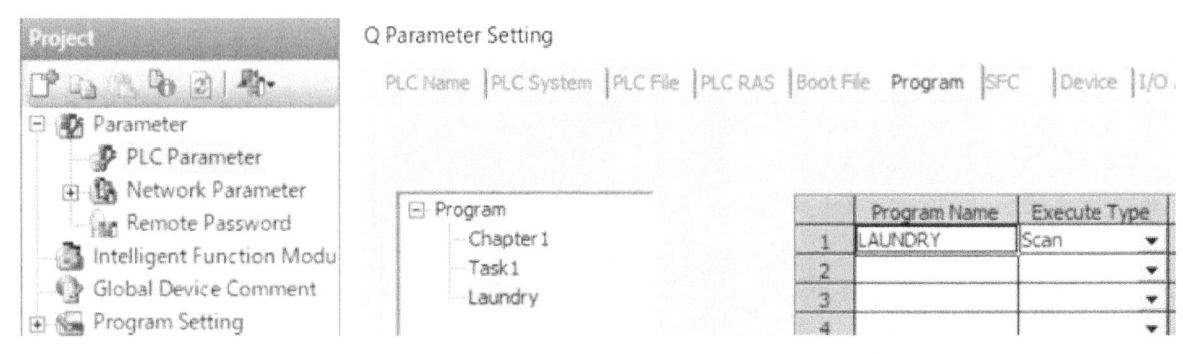

3. Press Ctrl+F5, Ctrl+F7, Ctrl+F8 to show comments, statements, and notes.

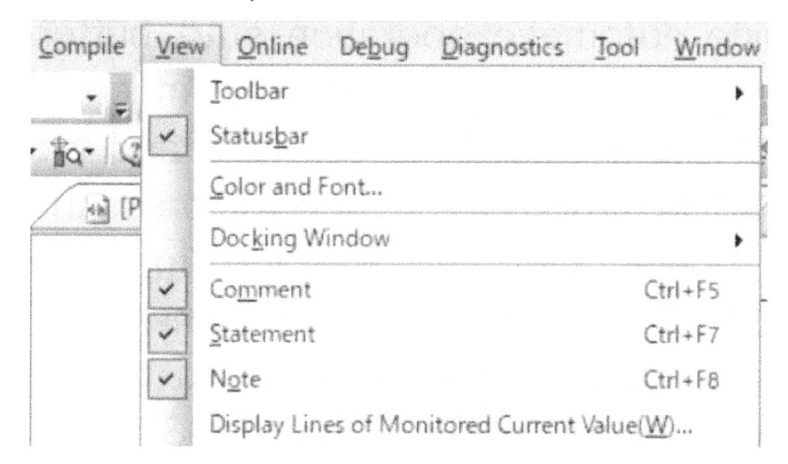

This completes the preparations before creating the program.

Let's create the program for step 1. When the washing machine power button (X320: Alternate) is turned ON and the washing machine automatic operation start button (X330: Momentary) is pressed, the washing machine automatic operation signal (M330) is self-held and the operation lamp (Y330) is turned ON. , When you press the washing machine power OFF or washing machine automatic operation stop button (X331: Momentary), create a circuit that turns off the self-holding of the washing machine automatic operation signal (M330).

Alternate: Holds the ON or OFF state when the button is pressed

Momentary: ON only while the button is pressed

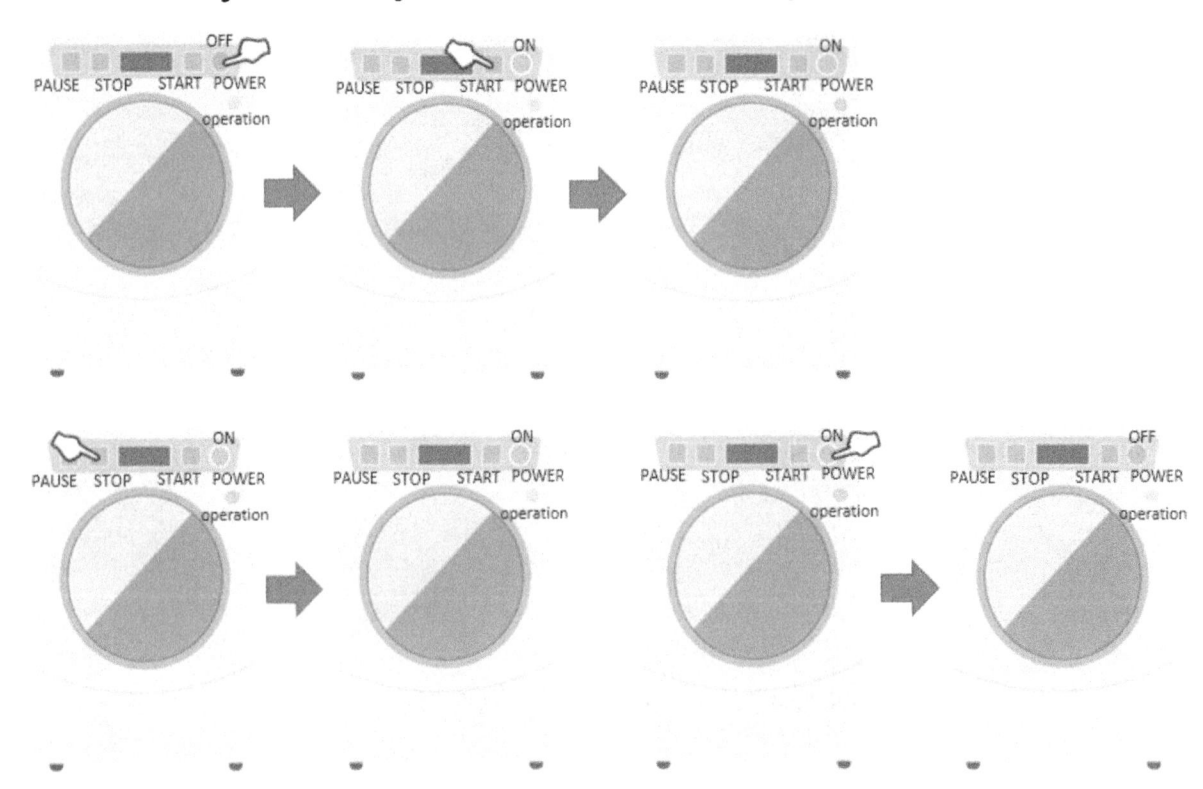

1. Since we learned about shortcuts in the previous chapter, we will create a program using shortcuts.

Rising pulse of X330: Press Shift + F7 and enter X330 and comment, X320 a-contact: Press F5 and enter X320 and comment, X331 b-contact: Press F6 and enter X331 and comment, M330 coil: Press F7 and M330 and comment, M330 for self-holding: Press F5 on the END line and enter M330, Horizontal and vertical lines: Press Ctrl and arrow button, Insert line: Press Shift + Ins to insert line,
M330 for lamp ON: Press F5 to enter M330, Y330 coil: Press F7 to enter Y330 and comment, finally press F4 to convert and create the following program.

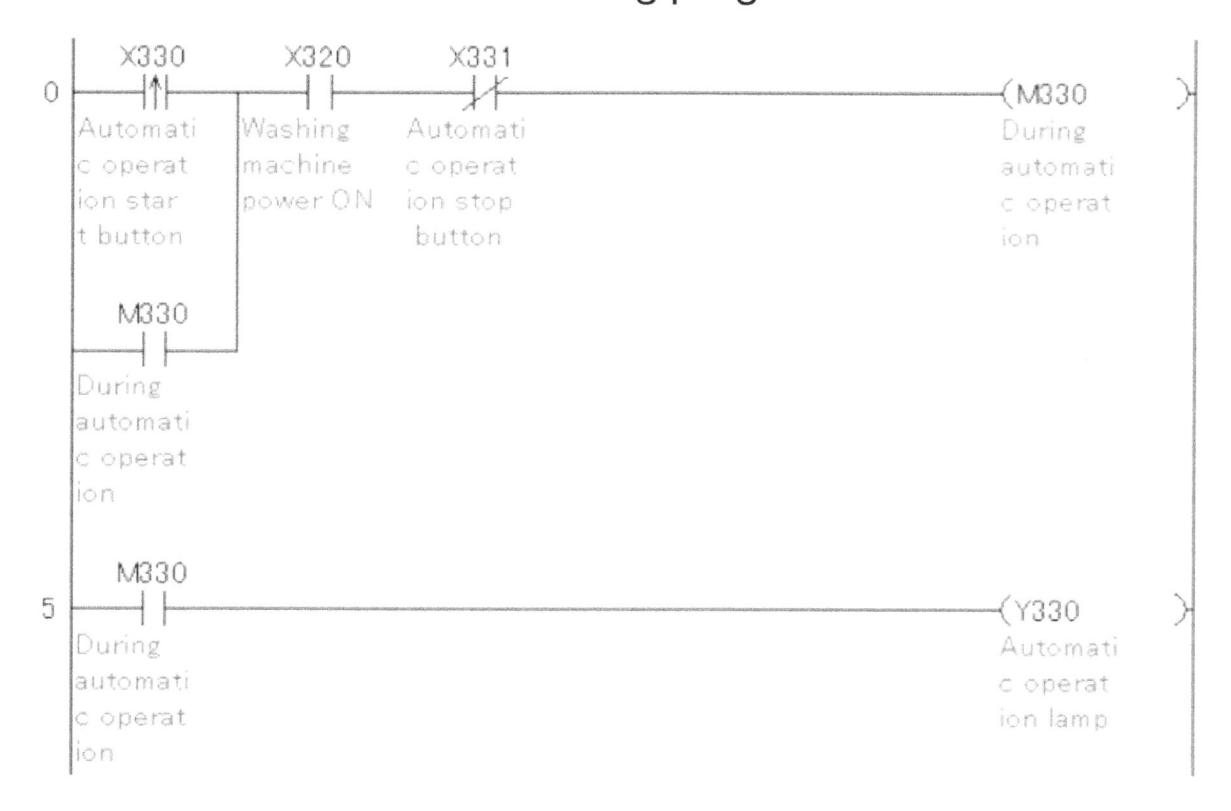

```
     X330           X320          X331
0 ────┤↑├───────────┤ ├───────────┤/├──────────────────────(M330)
     Automati      Washing       Automati                  During
     c operat      machine       c operat                  automati
     ion star      power ON      ion stop                  c operat
     t button                    button                    ion

     M330
     ┤ ├
     During
     automati
     c operat
     ion

     M330
5 ────┤ ├──────────────────────────────────────────────────(Y330)
     During                                                Automati
     automati                                              c operat
     c operat                                              ion lamp
     ion
```

2. Then add statements and notes.

・ Statement "Washing machine starts automatic operation"
After clicking the "Edit" tab at the top ⇒ Documentation ⇒ Statement, click somewhere in the circuit, enter the above comment all at once, and press OK.

・Note "Always ON during operation"
After clicking the "Edit" tab at the top ⇒ Documentation ⇒ Note, click the coil of M330, enter the above comment and press OK.

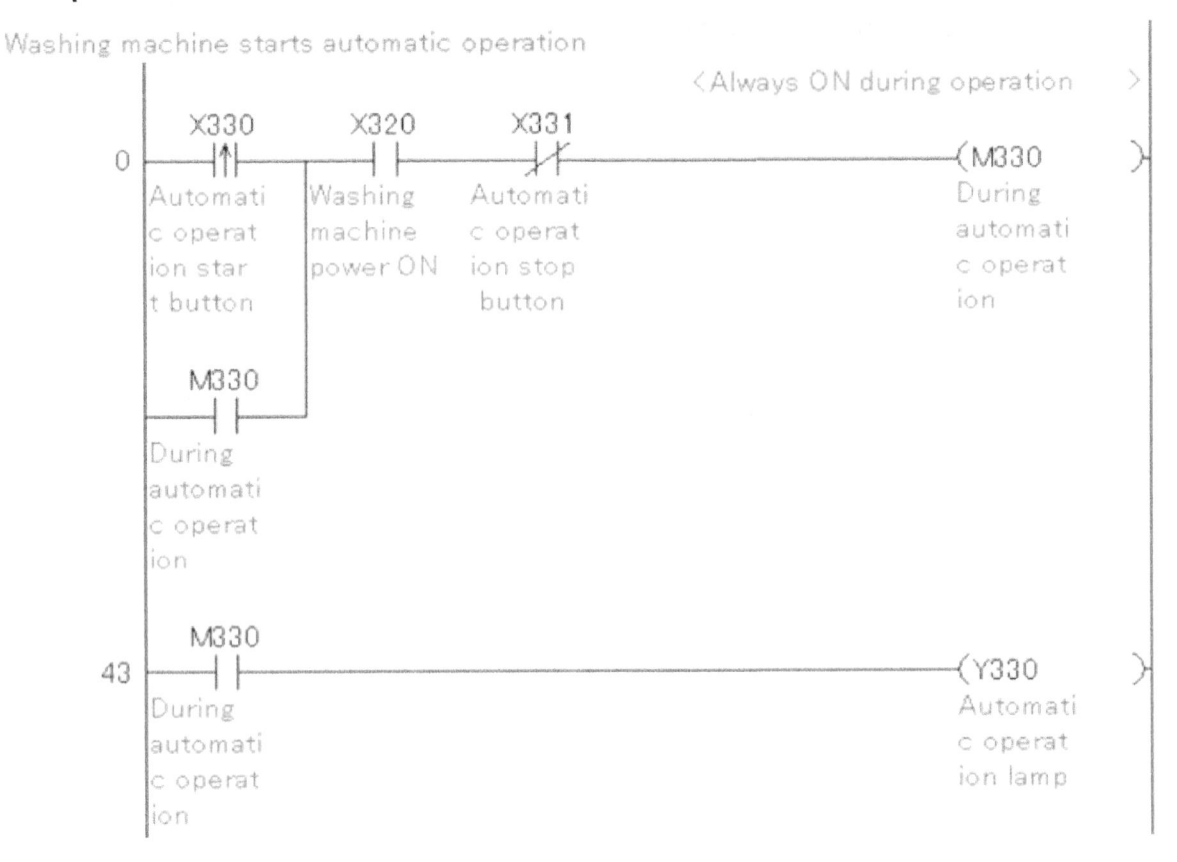

```
Washing machine starts automatic operation
                                                              <Always ON during operation>
       X330      X320      X331
  0 ────|↑|──┬───| |───────|/|──────────────────────────────(M330)
     Automati │ Washing   Automati                               During
     c operat │ machine   c operat                               automati
     ion star │ power ON  ion stop                               c operat
     t button │           button                                 ion
              │
       M330   │
      ───| |──┘
     During
     automati
     c operat
     ion

       M330
 43 ────| |──────────────────────────────────────────────────(Y330)
     During                                                      Automati
     automati                                                    c operat
     c operat                                                    ion lamp
     ion
```

54

3. Run the simulation to see if the program works correctly. When you press "Debug" ⇒ Start/Stop Simulation at the top, a pop-up for writing to PC will appear, so check "When processing ends, close this windows automatically" after writing on the debug is completed. and from now on the program will automatically close while it is open.

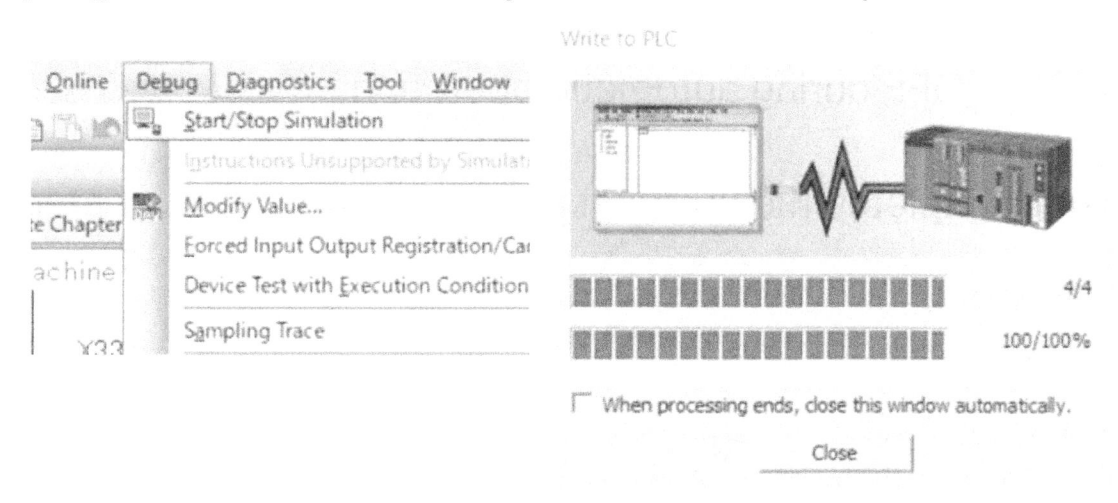

Each signal can be turned ON/OFF with Shift + Enter, so check the operation below.

・Start button ON when power is OFF ⇒ Must not be ON during automatic operation

・Start button ON when power is ON ⇒ self-hold + lamp ON when ON during automatic operation

・Power OFF or stop button during automatic operation ⇒ Turn OFF during automatic operation

This completes the creation and operation check of step 1.

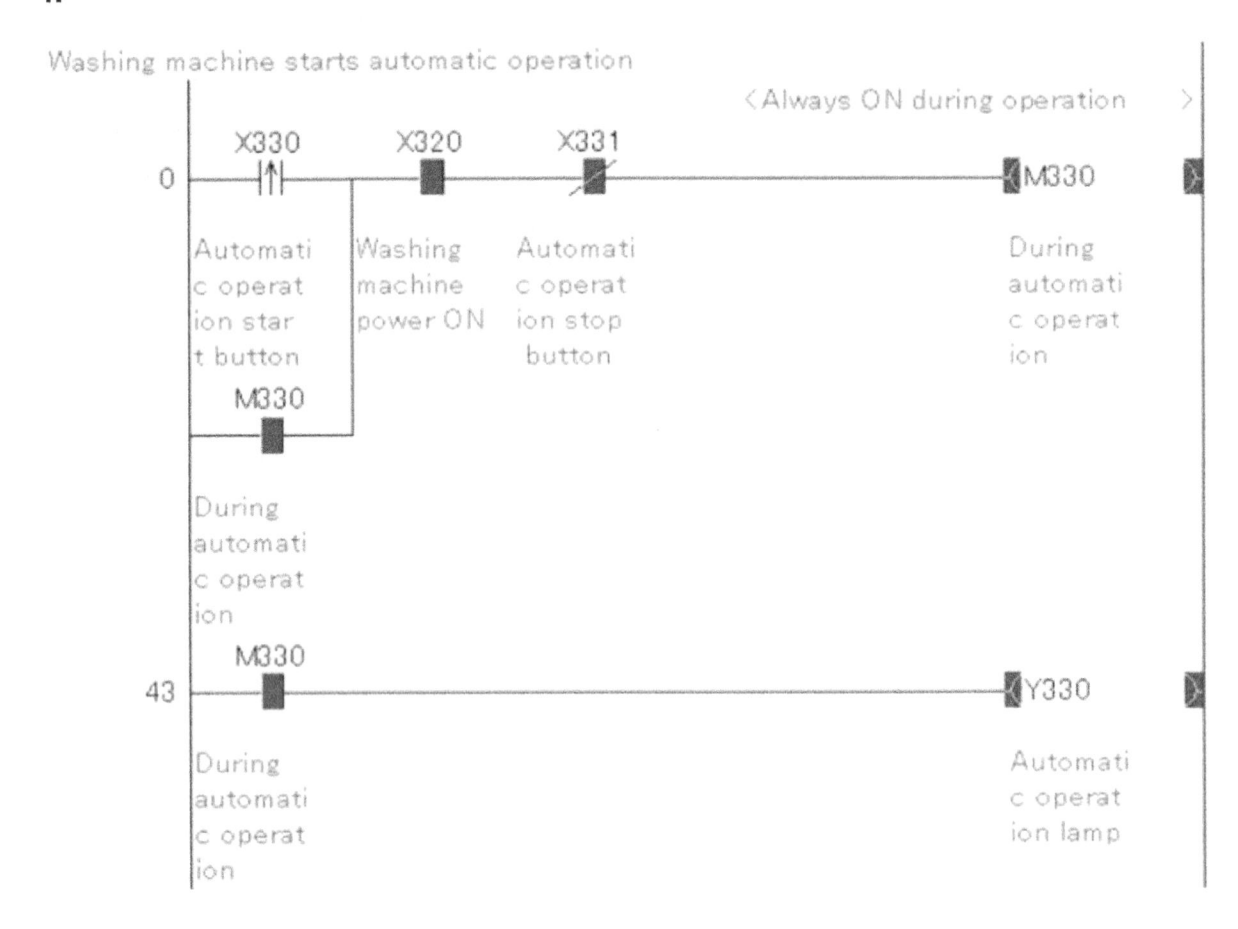

```
Washing machine starts automatic operation
                                                    <Always ON during operation>
        X330        X320        X331
    0 ───┤↑├────────┤ ├─────────┤/├──────────────────────────(M330)
        Automatic   Washing     Automatic                    During
        operation   machine     operation                    automatic
        start       power ON    stop                         operation
        button                  button
        M330
        ──┤ ├──
        During
        automatic
        operation

        M330
   43 ───┤ ├──────────────────────────────────────────────────(Y330)
        During                                               Automatic
        automatic                                            operation
        operation                                            lamp
```

2-3 Step 2 Create a washing machine sequence control circuit.

In step 2, create the sequence control circuit for the main washing machine.

While the washing machine automatic operation signal (M330) is ON, start pouring water (M331) ⇒ finish pouring water (M332) ⇒ start washing (M333) ⇒ finish washing (M334) ⇒ start rinsing (M335) ⇒ finish rinsing (M336) ⇒ Create a circuit that performs sequence control of dehydration start (M337) ⇒ dehydration completion (M338) ⇒ washing completion buzzer start (M339) ⇒ washing completion buzzer completion (M340) ⇒ washing machine automatic operation completion (M341). In addition, the output signal for each operation is water injection command (Y331), wash command (Y332), rinse command (Y333), dehydration command (Y334), washing completion buzzer command (Y335), and the completion signal of each operation is water injection completion signal (X335), washing completion signal (X336), rinsing completion signal (X337), dehydration completion signal (X338).

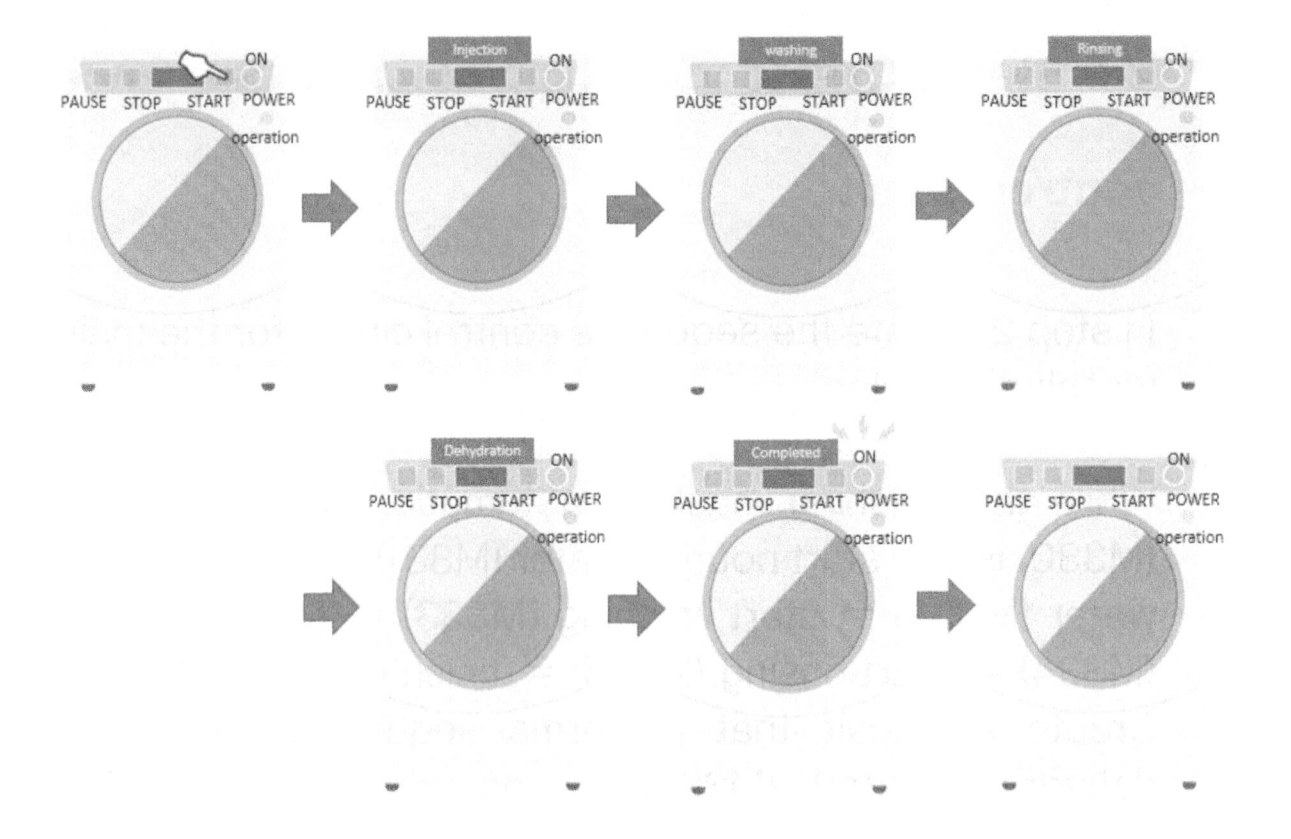

Then, we will create it step by step for each sequence control.

1. First, create a circuit that performs the water injection process after the automatic operation signal turns ON. Since only a contact, b contact, coil, and statement are required for program creation, they are omitted.

The flow of this circuit is automatic operation signal (M330) ON ⇒ water injection start (M331) ON ⇒ water injection command (Y331 ON) ⇒ water injection ⇒ water injection complete signal (X335) ON ⇒ water injection complete (M332) ON ⇒ Water injection command (Y331) OFF ⇒ Water injection stops. M332 is self-holding during automatic operation so that X335 can be turned off during automatic operation. (In the case of sensors, etc., they may turn ON/OFF during automatic operation.)

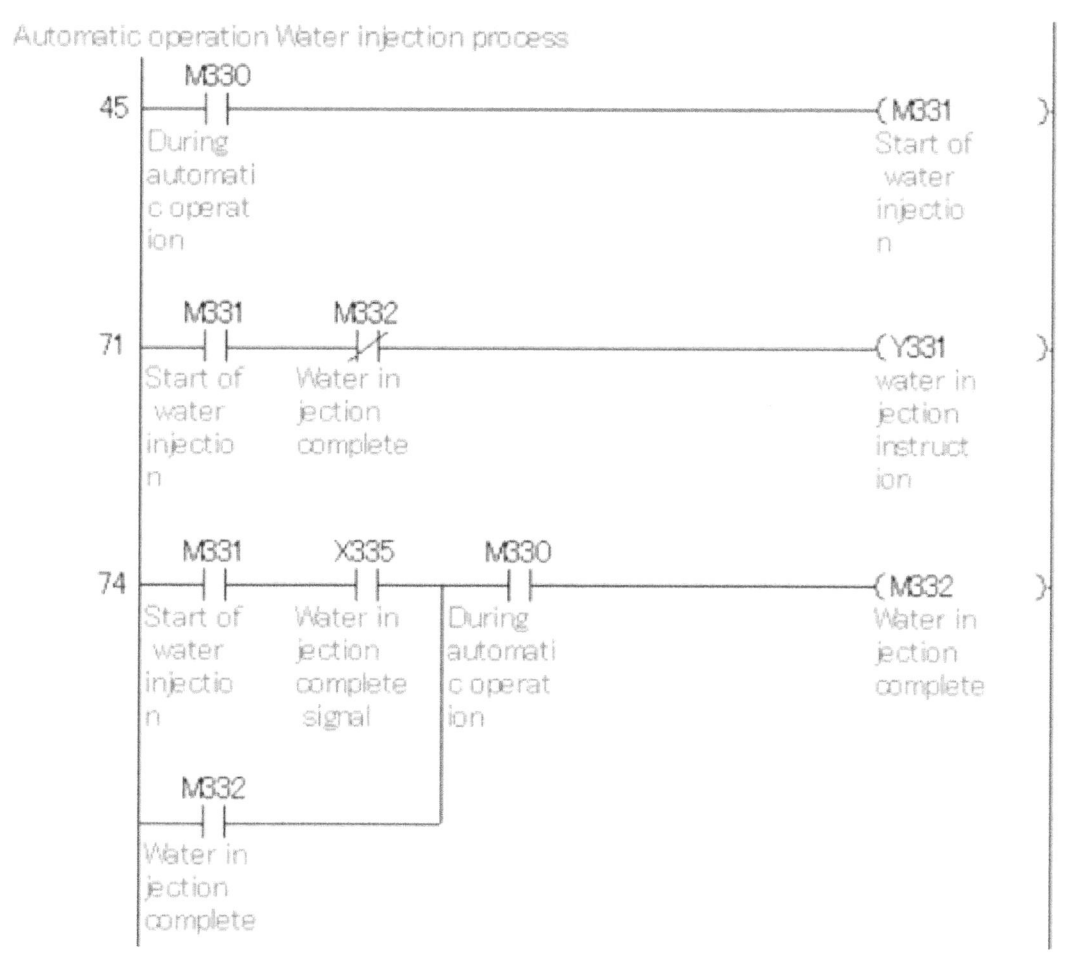

```
Automatic operation Water injection process
        M330
45 ─────┤ ├──────────────────────────────────────(M331)─
        During                                    Start of
        automati                                  water
        c operat                                  injectio
        ion                                       n

        M331      M332
71 ─────┤ ├──────┤/├──────────────────────────────(Y331)─
        Start of  Water in                        water in
        water     jection                         jection
        injectio  complete                        instruct
        n                                         ion

        M331      X335      M330
74 ─────┤ ├──────┤ ├──────┤ ├────────────────────(M332)─
        Start of  Water in  During                Water in
        water     jection   automati              jection
        injectio  complete  c operat              complete
        n         signal    ion

        M332
        ─┤ ├─
        Water in
        jection
        complete
```

Start flag ON ⇒ Start command ON ⇒ Running ⇒ Completion signal ON ⇒ Completion flag ON (retained) ⇒ Start command OFF ⇒ Operation stopped ⇒ To next step This circuit is the basic form of sequence control.

2. Create a circuit that performs washing, rinsing, and dehydration in the same procedure.

Washing process flow: Water injection complete (M332) ON ⇒ Washing start (M333) ON ⇒ Washing command (Y332 ON) ⇒ Washing ⇒ Washing complete signal (X336) ON ⇒ Washing complete (M334) ON ⇒ Washing command (Y332)OFF ⇒ Washing stops. M334 is self-holding during automatic operation so that X336 can be turned off during automatic operation. (In the case of sensors, etc., they may turn ON/OFF during automatic operation.)

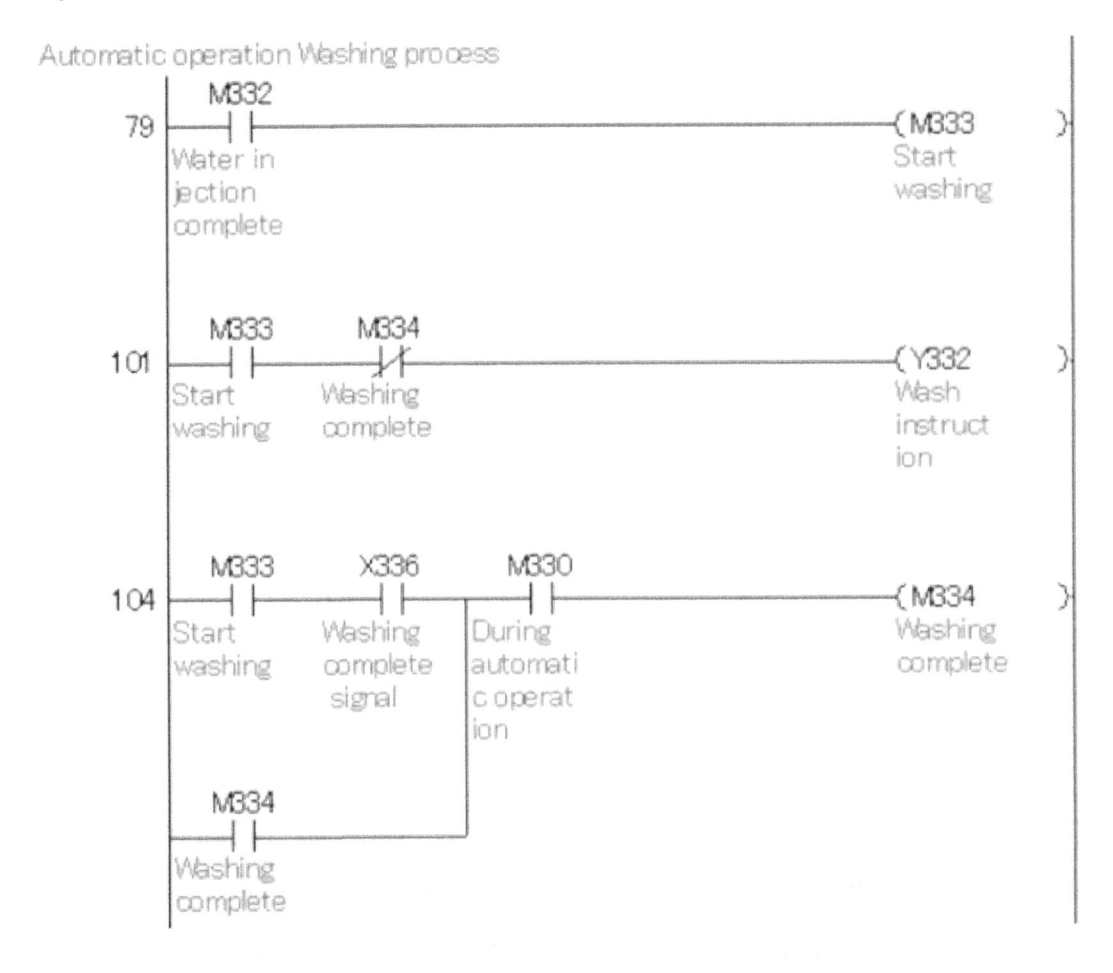

Automatic operation Washing process

```
         M332
79      ──┤ ├──────────────────────────────────( M333 )
        Water in                                Start
        jection                                 washing
        complete

         M333     M334
101     ──┤ ├─────┤/├────────────────────────────( Y332 )
        Start    Washing                         Wash
        washing  complete                        instruct
                                                 ion

         M333     X336     M330
104     ──┤ ├─────┤ ├──────┤ ├───────────────────( M334 )
        Start    Washing   During                Washing
        washing  complete  automati               complete
                 signal    c operat
                           ion
         M334
        ──┤ ├─────┘
        Washing
        complete
```

60

Rinsing process flow (flow): Washing complete (M334) ON ⇒ Rinsing start (M335) ON ⇒ Rinsing command (Y333 ON) ⇒ During rinsing ⇒ Rinsing complete signal (X337) ON ⇒ Rinsing complete (M336) ON ⇒ Rinsing command (Y333)OFF ⇒ Rinsing stops. M336 is self-holding during automatic operation so that X337 can be turned off during automatic operation. (In the case of sensors, etc., they may turn ON/OFF during automatic operation.)

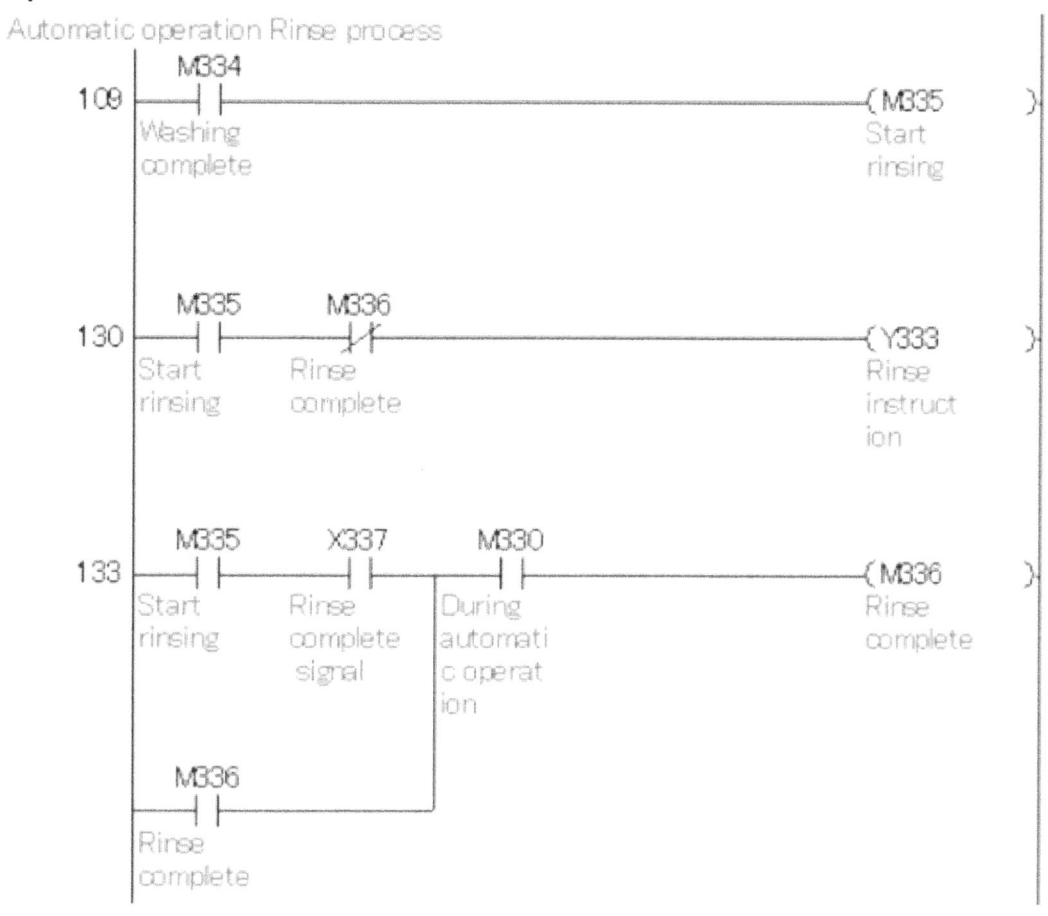

Automatic operation Rinse process

```
         M334
109    ──┤ ├──────────────────────────────────────( M335 )
         Washing                                    Start
         complete                                   rinsing

         M335    M336
130    ──┤ ├────┤/├────────────────────────────────( Y333 )
         Start   Rinse                              Rinse
         rinsing complete                           instruct
                                                    ion

         M335    X337    M330
133    ──┤ ├────┤ ├─────┤ ├────────────────────────( M336 )
         Start   Rinse   During                     Rinse
         rinsing complete automati                  complete
                 signal  c operat
                         ion
         M336
       ──┤ ├──┘
         Rinse
         complete
```

Dehydration process flow: Rinsing complete (M336) ON ⇒ Dehydration start (M337) ON ⇒ Dehydration command (Y334ON) ⇒ During dehydration ⇒ Dehydration completion signal (X338) ON ⇒ Dehydration complete (M338) ON ⇒ Dehydration command (Y334)OFF ⇒ Dehydration stops. M338 self-holds during automatic operation so that X338 can be turned off during automatic operation. (In the case of sensors, etc., they may turn ON/OFF during automatic operation.)

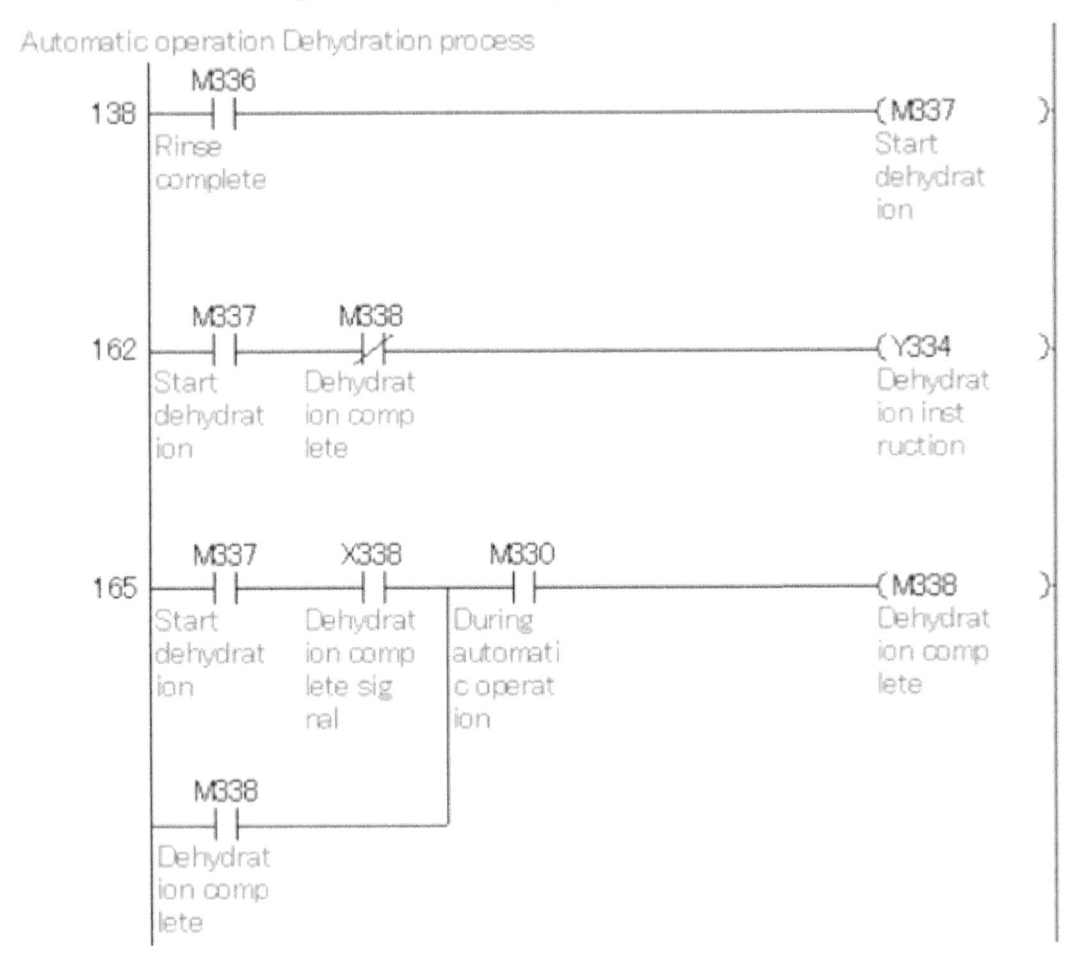

```
Automatic operation Dehydration process
          M336
138       ─┤ ├────────────────────────────────────( M337 )
          Rinse                                    Start
          complete                                 dehydrat
                                                   ion

          M337        M338
162       ─┤ ├────────┤/├──────────────────────────( Y334 )
          Start       Dehydrat                     Dehydrat
          dehydrat    ion comp                     ion inst
          ion         lete                         ruction

          M337        X338        M330
165       ─┤ ├────────┤ ├─────────┤ ├──────────────( M338 )
          Start       Dehydrat    During           Dehydrat
          dehydrat    ion comp    automati         ion comp
          ion         lete sig    c operat         lete
                      nal         ion

          M338
          ─┤ ├─
          Dehydrat
          ion comp
          lete
```

The above is the circuit that performs washing, rinsing, and spin-drying operations.

3. Create a circuit to turn on the washing completion buzzer after dehydration operation. For T335, press F7 and enter "T335 K30" as a comment. For SM412 (1-second clock: special relay), press F5 and enter SM412 as a comment.

Washing completion buzzer process flow: Dehydration completion (M338) ON ⇒ Washing completion buzzer start (M339) ON ⇒ Washing completion buzzer start command (Y335ON) ⇒ Buzzer ON for 3 seconds (intermittent sound) ⇒ Washing completion buzzer ON time (T335) ON ⇒ Buzzer OFF ⇒ End of washing completion buzzer (M340) ON.

```
Automatic operation Washing completion buzzer process
        M338
170 ────┤ ├──────────────────────────────────(M339)
        Dehydrat                              Laundry
        ion comp                              completi
        lete                                  on buzze
                                              r starts

        M339                                    K30
201 ────┤ ├──────────────────────────────────(T335)
        Laundry                               Buzzer
        completi                              ON time
        on buzze
        r starts

                      SM412    T335
                  ────┤ ├─────┤/├────────────(Y335)
                      1 second Buzzer         Buzzer
                      clock    ON time        start
                                              instruct
                                              ion

        T335
209 ────┤ ├──────────────────────────────────(M340)
        Buzzer                                Buzzer
        ON time                               end
```

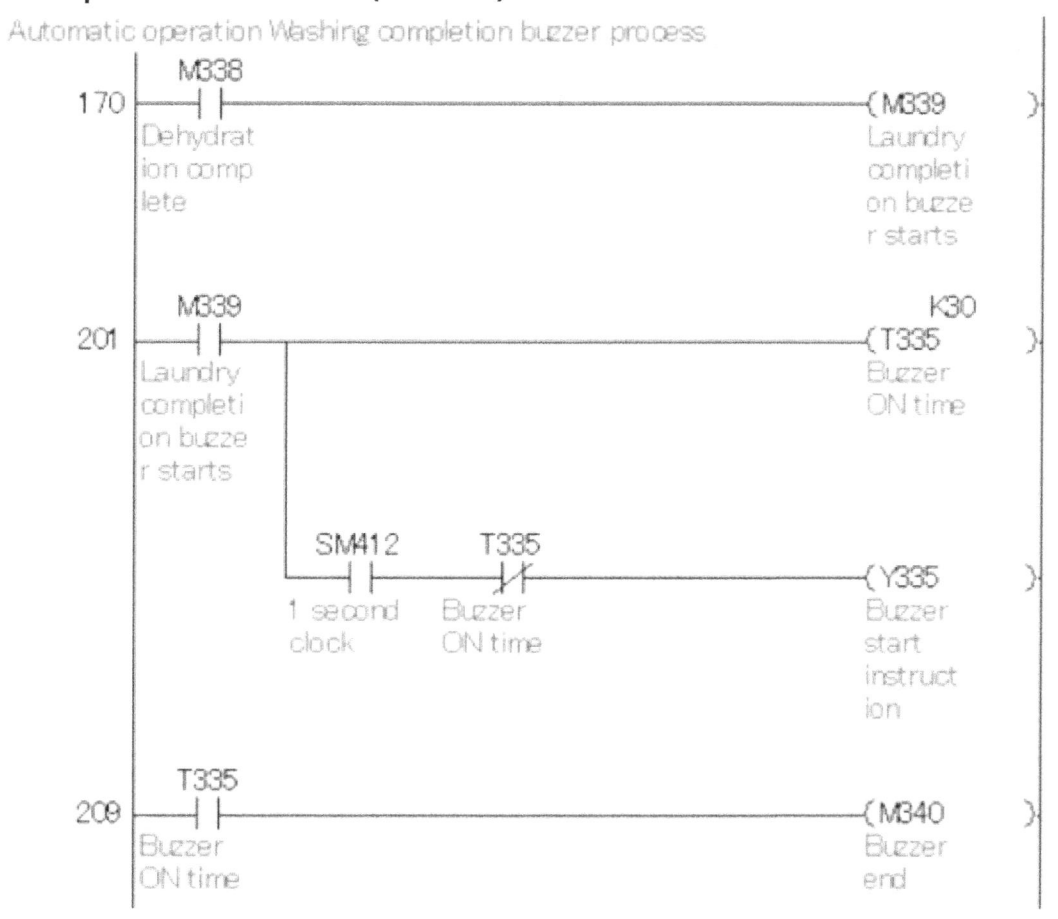

4. Now that all the steps have been completed, we will create the circuit after the automatic operation of the washing machine is complete. When the washing completion buzzer end (M340) turns ON, the washing machine automatic operation completion (M341) turns ON.

```
Automatic operation All processes completed
         M340
211 ─────┤ ├─────────────────────────────(M341)
         Buzzer                          Automati
         end                             c operat
                                         ion comp
                                         leted
```

When the washing machine automatic operation completion (M341) is ON, the washing machine automatic operation running (M330) is turned off. This completes the washing machine sequence control circuit.

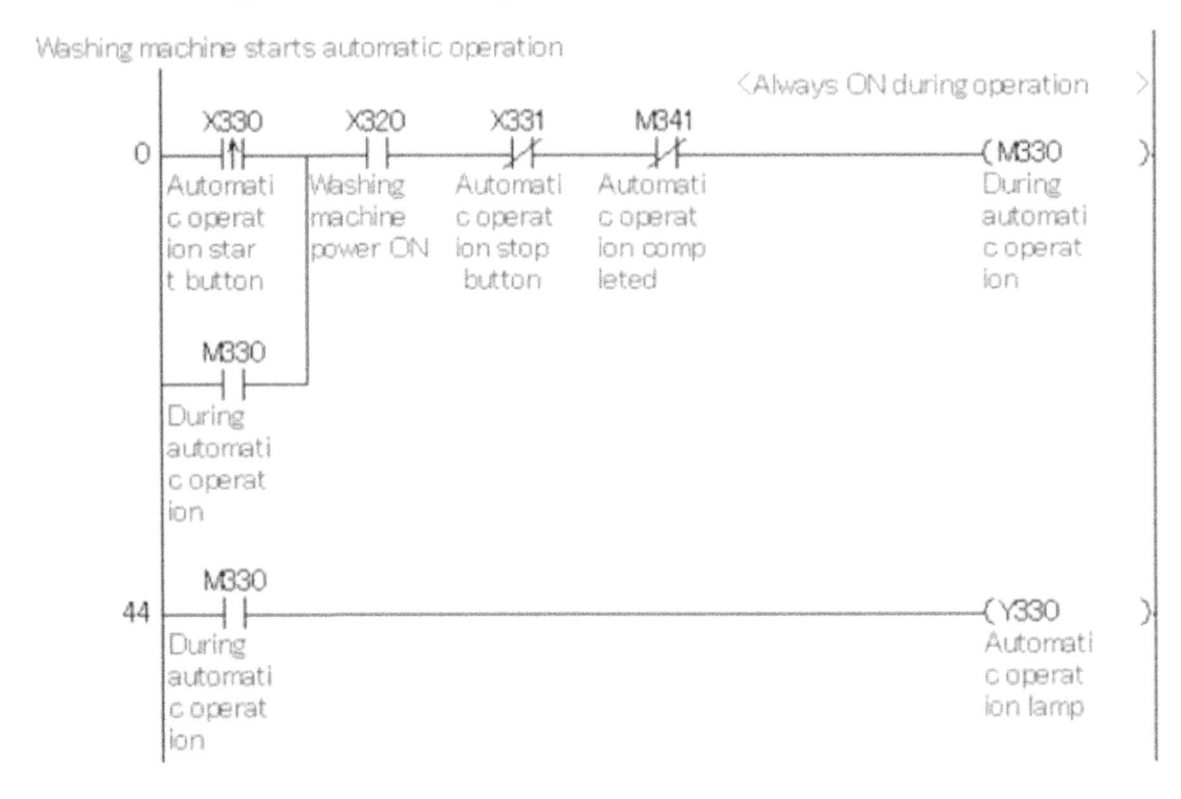

```
Washing machine starts automatic operation
                                                    <Always ON during operation>
     X330       X320      X331      M341
0 ───┤↑├───────┤ ├───────┤/├───────┤/├─────────────(M330)
     Automati  Washing   Automati  Automati        During
     c operat  machine   c operat  c operat        automati
     ion star  power ON  ion stop  ion comp        c operat
     t button            button    leted           ion

     M330
    ─┤ ├─
     During
     automati
     c operat
     ion

      M330
44 ───┤ ├──────────────────────────────────────────(Y330)
      During                                       Automati
      automati                                     c operat
      c operat                                     ion lamp
      ion
```

64

5. Run the simulation to see if the program works correctly. Start the simulation by pressing "Debug" at the top ⇒ Simulation start/stop. Each signal can be turned ON/OFF with Shift + Enter, so check the following operations.

1. During automatic operation (M330) ON
   Water injection command (Y331) is ON
2. Filling completed (X335) ON で
   Water injection command (Y331) is OFF
3. After filling the water,
   Wash command (Y332) is ON
4. Washing completed (X336) ON
   Wash command (Y332) is OFF
5. After washing,
   Rinsing command (Y333) is ON
6. Rinsing complete (X337) ON
   Rinsing command (Y333) is OFF
7. After rinsing,
   Dehydration command (Y334) is ON
8. Dehydration complete (X338) ON
   Dehydration command (Y334) is OFF
9. After dehydration,
   Washing completion buzzer start command (Y335) ON with SM412 (1 second clock)
10. After 3 seconds, the washing completion buzzer ends,
    Washing machine automatic operation completion (M341) is ON
11. Automatic operation (M330) OFF

This time, I explained how to write a basic sequence control circuit using a washing machine as an example. If you remember this way of writing, you can create sequence control that connects simple actions, so please remember it. The next step describes the interlock and pause circuits.

2-1 to 2-3 Summary

· What is sequence control? **Control that advances each stage of control sequentially according to a predetermined order or procedure"** says.

· **Start flag ON ⇒ Start command ON ⇒ Running ⇒ Completion signal ON ⇒ Completion flag ON (retained) ⇒ Start command OFF ⇒ Operation stopped ⇒ To next step** This circuit is the basic form of sequence control.

2-4 Step 3 Washing machine interlock, creation of temporary stop circuit

In step 3, an interlock signal is added to immediately stop the washing machine when something goes wrong with the washing machine, and a circuit is created that, when the pause button is pressed, causes the running lamp to blink, and pauses the machine in the middle of automatic operation. To do.

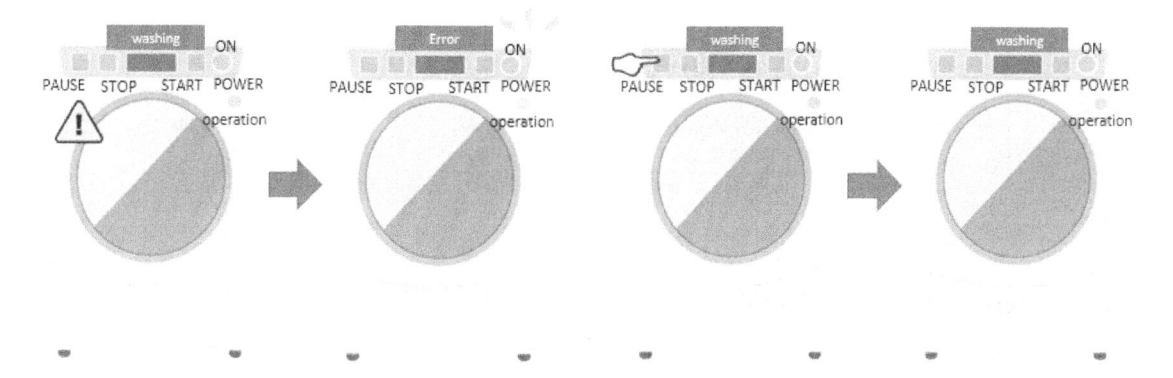

What is interlock **safety mechanism or safety circuit that disables or stops operation unless certain conditions are met,** I'm talking about Now let's create the interlock circuit.

1. As an interlock signal for the washing machine, it is possible to operate when the washing machine power supply (X320) is ON, the washing machine lid is open (X325) OFF, the washing machine filter clogging error (X326) is OFF, and the washing machine short circuit error (X327) is OFF. Create a washing machine interlock signal (M345) that does not start automatic operation if any of the conditions are not met and stops immediately if it is in automatic operation. Create a location just above Autorun (M330).

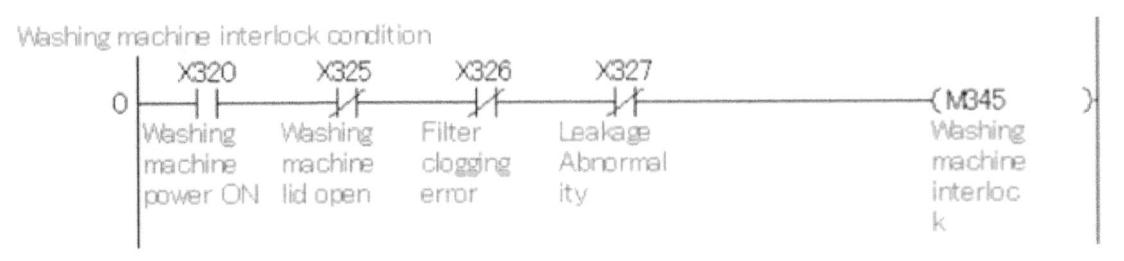

```
Washing machine interlock condition
      X320       X325      X326      X327
0 ─────┤├────────┤/├───────┤/├───────┤/├──────────────────( M345 )─
    Washing    Washing    Filter   Leakage              Washing
    machine    machine    clogging Abnormal             machine
    power ON   lid open   error    ity                  interlock
```

2. When the washing machine interlock signal (M345) turns OFF, a contact is added to turn off the maintenance during automatic operation (M330). Also, the washing machine power supply (X320) that was originally installed is included in the interlock signal, so delete it.

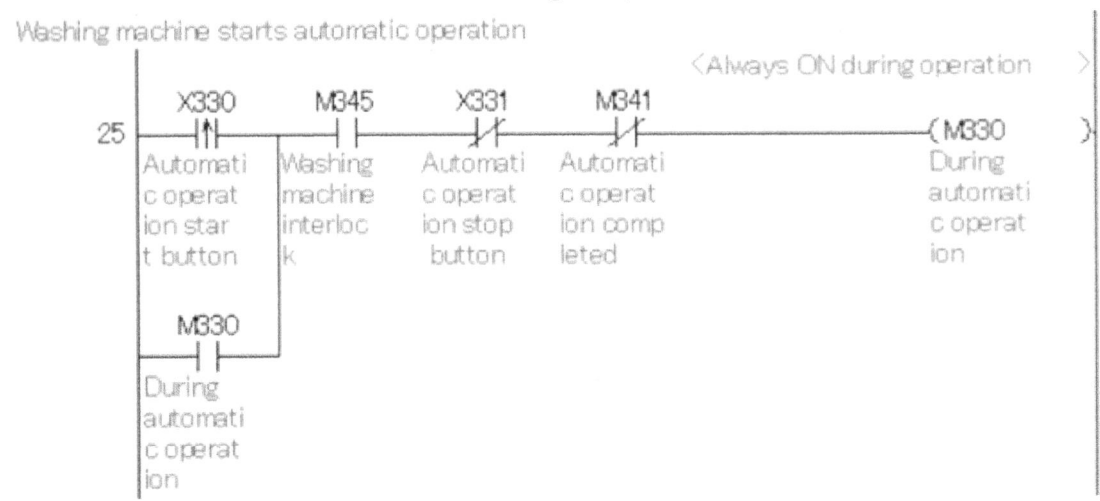

```
Washing machine starts automatic operation
                                                      <Always ON during operation>
       X330       M345      X331      M341
25 ─────┤↑├───┬───┤├────────┤/├───────┤/├──────────────────( M330 )─
     Automatic │ Washing   Automatic Automatic            During
     operation│ machine    operation operation            automatic
     start    │ interlock  stop      completed            operation
     button   │            button
              │
       M330   │
     ─────┤├──┘
     During
     automatic
     operation
```

68

With this, if the washing machine interlock signal (M345) is OFF, automatic operation cannot be started, and if it turns OFF during automatic operation, the washing machine will stop immediately, so it will be a safe operation.

For example, if the automatic operation continues with the lid of the washing machine open, it will be a serious problem. If the conditions are not met, it may lead to machine failure or dangerous operation. **The concept of interlock is very important in creating a PLC program** is. In the case of equipment that performs complex operations, an interlock is required for each sequence operation, so interlock lists may be collectively managed in Excel or the like.

Next, when you press the pause button (X322), after the automatic operation is paused, the running lamp blinks, and when you press the pause button (X322) again, the pause is canceled, and the circuit restarts automatic operation. I will create it. Create a place just below the coil of the washing machine automatic operation completion M341.

1. First, when the pause button (X322) is pressed, the automatic operation pause (M348) turns ON, and when the pause button (X322) is pressed while M348 is ON, M348 turns OFF.

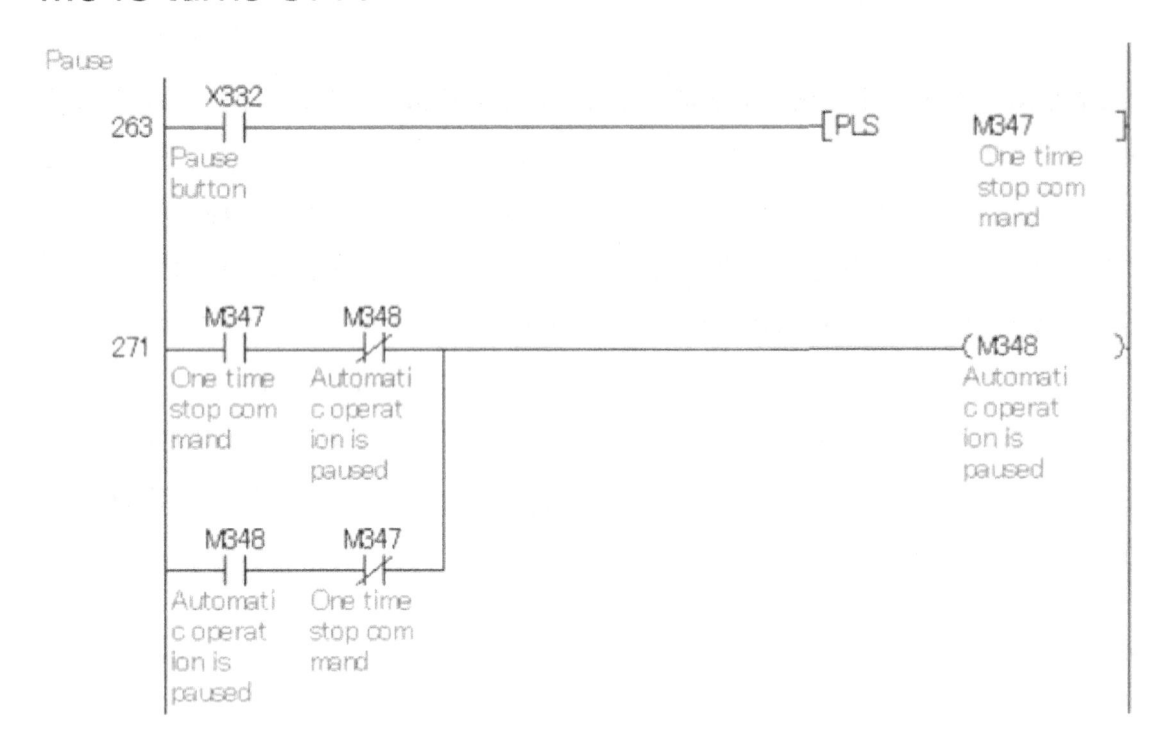

```
Pause
          X332
263       ─┤ ├──────────────────────────────[PLS   M347    ]
          Pause                                    One time
          button                                   stop com
                                                   mand


          M347      M348
271       ─┤ ├──────┤/├──────┬─────────────────────(M348    )
          One time  Automati │                     Automati
          stop com  c operat │                     c operat
          mand      ion is   │                     ion is
                    paused   │                     paused

          M348      M347     │
          ─┤ ├──────┤/├──────┘
          Automati  One time
          c operat  stop com
          ion is    mand
          paused
```

in this way **A circuit where the output (M348 this time) repeats ON and OFF with one input (X332 this time) of Flip-flop circuit (alternate circuit)** Is called. Since this method of writing circuits is often required when creating PLC programs, I will explain in detail how the mechanism works.

First, if you press the automatic operation pause button (X332) while the automatic operation pause (M348) is OFF, M347 will be ON and M348 will be ON for the first scan as shown in the figure below.

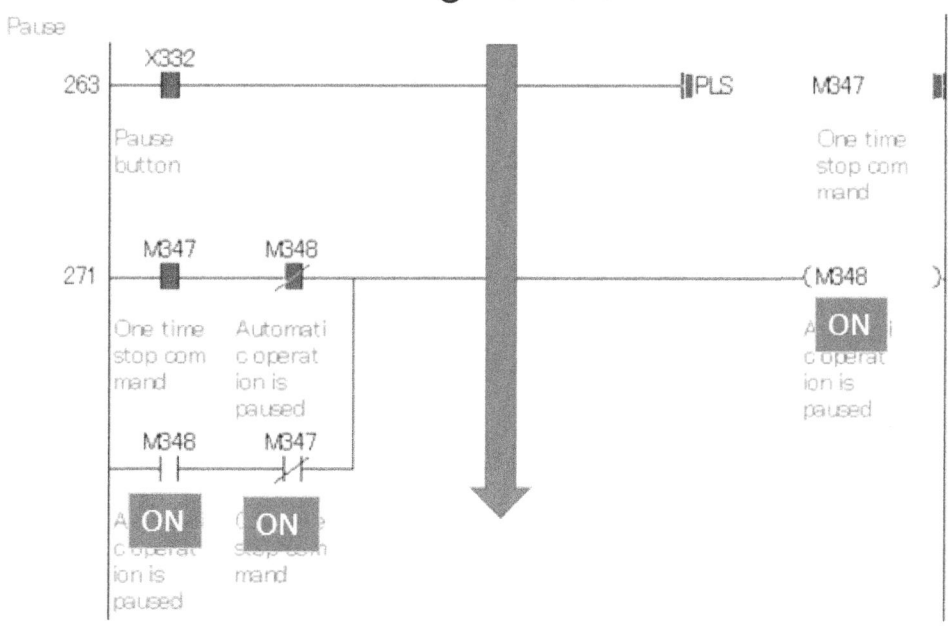

In the second scan, M347 is OFF and M348 is ON as shown in the figure below, so M348 is self-held and remains ON.

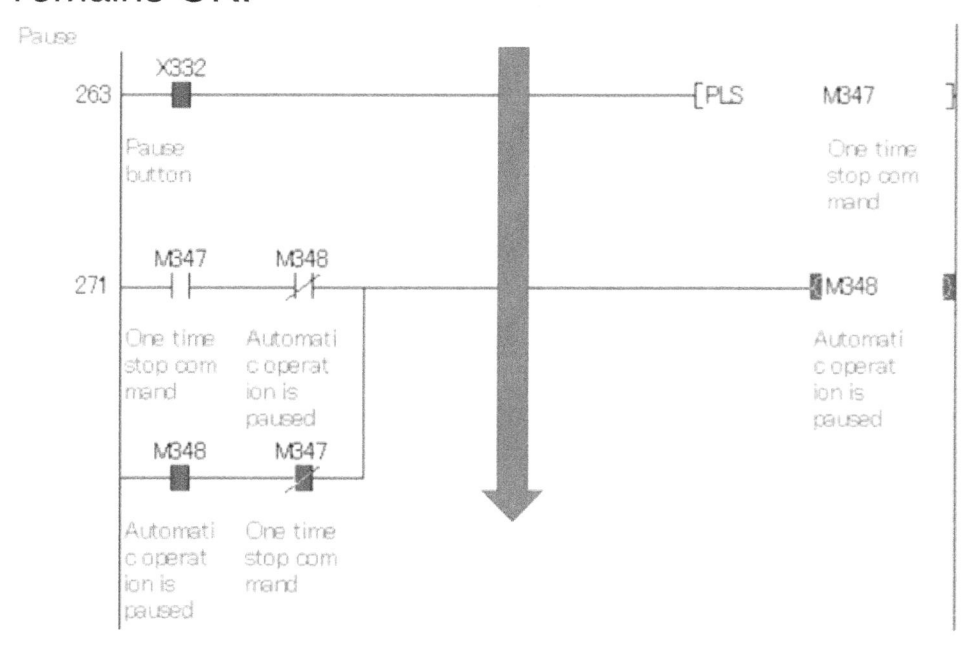

Next, after X332 is turned off, press the automatic operation pause button (X332) again. In the first scan, M347 is turned on as shown in the figure below, and the self-holding of M348 is cut off and M348 is turned off.

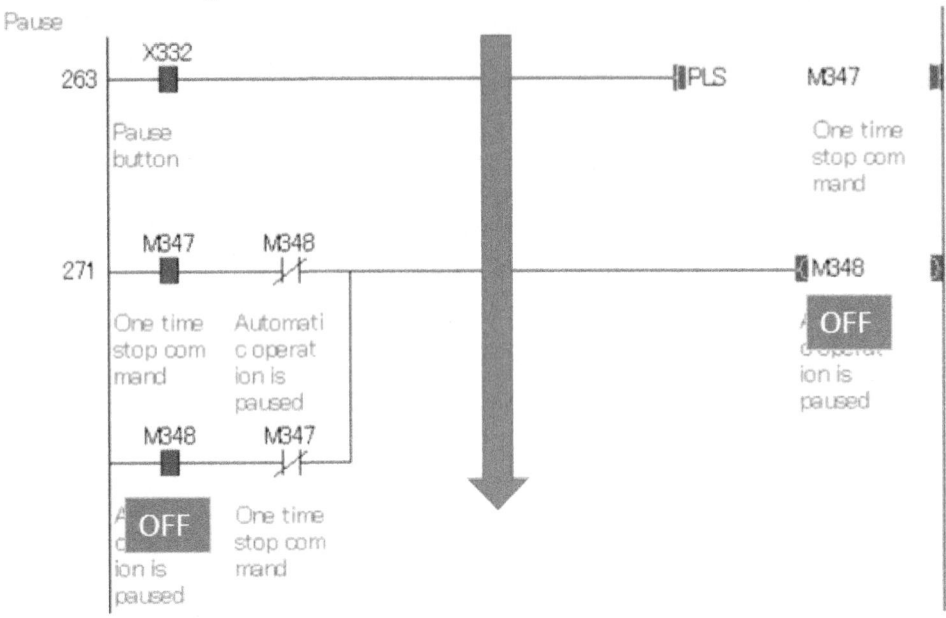

```
Pause
          X332
263       ─┤ ├──────────────────────────────[PLS    M347  ]
          Pause                                     One time
          button                                    stop com
                                                    mand

          M347    M348
271       ─┤ ├────┤/├──┬──────────────────────────( M348 )
          One time  Automati                        OFF
          stop com  c operat                        ion is
          mand      ion is                          paused
                    paused
          M348    M347
          ─┤ ├────┤/├──┘
          OFF      One time
          ion is   stop com
          paused   mand
```

In the second scan, M347 is OFF and M348 is OFF as shown in the figure below, so M348 does not turn ON and remains OFF. This is how a flip-flop circuit works.

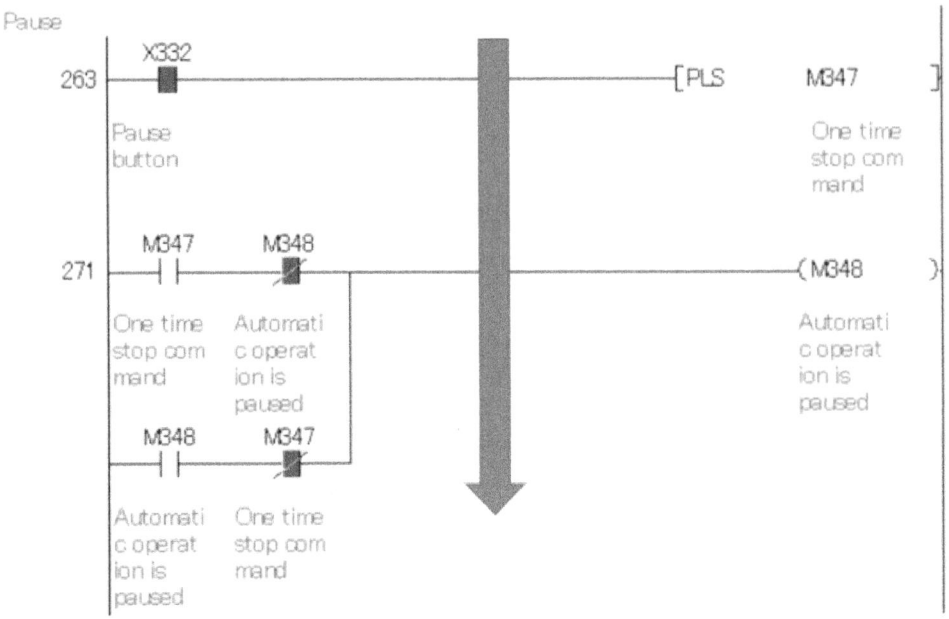

```
Pause
          X332
263       ─┤ ├──────────────────────────────[PLS    M347  ]
          Pause                                     One time
          button                                    stop com
                                                    mand

          M347    M348
271       ─┤ ├────┤/├──┬──────────────────────────( M348 )
          One time  Automati                        Automati
          stop com  c operat                        c operat
          mand      ion is                          ion is
                    paused                          paused
          M348    M347
          ─┤ ├────┤/├──┘
          Automati  One time
          c operat  stop com
          ion is    mand
          paused
```

And since there is no need to pause except during automatic operation, turn off self-holding of M348 during automatic operation (M330) OFF.

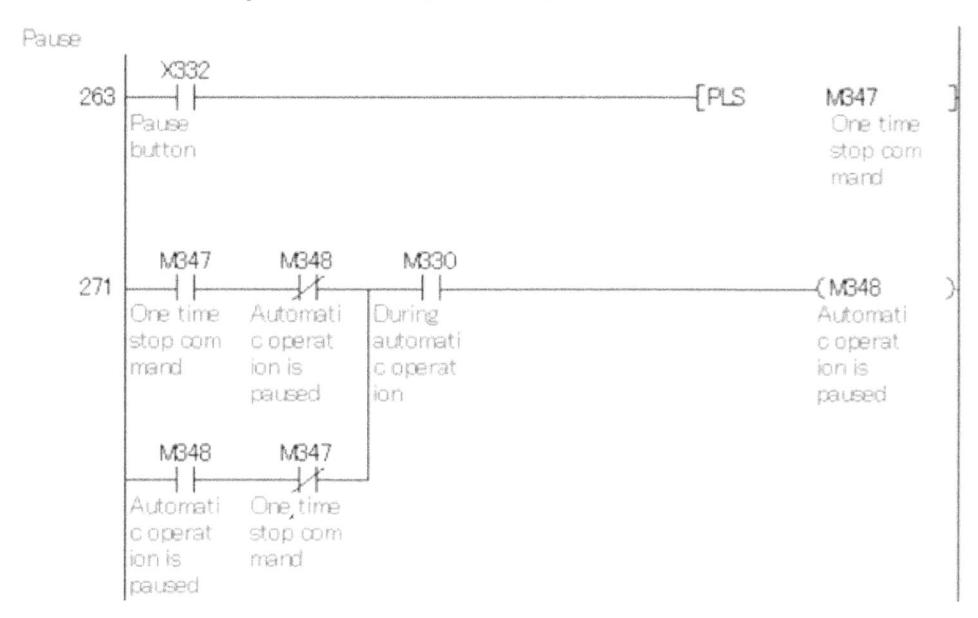

```
Pause
         X332
   263  ──┤ ├──────────────────────────────[PLS   M347    ]
         Pause                                    One time
         button                                   stop com
                                                  mand

         M347    M348    M330
   271  ──┤ ├────┤/├────┤ ├───────────────────────(M348   )
         One time Automati During                  Automati
         stop com c operat automati                c operat
         mand     ion is   c operat                ion is
                  paused   ion                     paused

         M348    M347
        ──┤ ├────┤/├──
         Automati One time
         c operat stop com
         ion is   mand
         paused
```

besides that, **Bit device output inversion instruction (FF)** can be used to create similar programs. (FF instructions are created by pressing F8 and entering "FF M348")

```
    X332
  ──┤ ├──────────────────────────────────────[FF    M348    ]
   Pause                                             Automati
   button                                            c operat
                                                     ion is
                                                     paused
```

This circuit can also operate in the same way as the above flip-flop circuit. However, some models such as the A series and FX series cannot be used. In that case, create a flip-flop circuit. In this creation, we will create and simulate with a flip-flop circuit that can be used universally for any model.

2. Next, put the automatic operation pause signal (M348) at the B contact before the output of each process. With this, operation output will not be output during temporary stop. Also, since the buzzer is only for notifying the completion of washing, it is unnecessary.

Water injection process

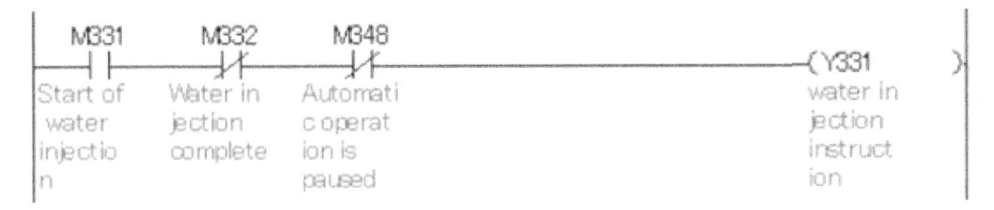

```
  M331          M332          M348
───┤ ├─────────┤/├──────────┤/├──────────────────────────(Y331)──
 Start of     Water in     Automati                      water in
  water       jection      c operat                      jection
 injectio     complete     ion is                        instruct
   n                       paused                         ion
```

washing process

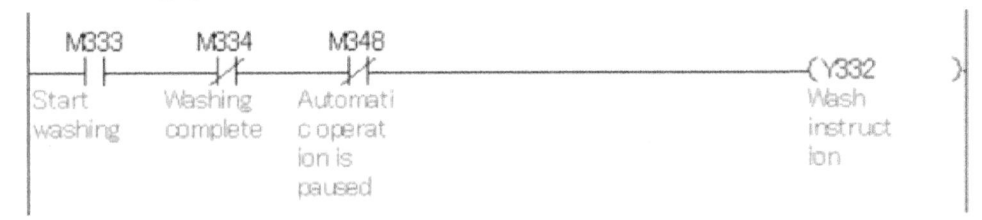

```
  M333          M334          M348
───┤ ├─────────┤/├──────────┤/├──────────────────────────(Y332)──
 Start        Washing       Automati                     Wash
 washing      complete      c operat                     instruct
                            ion is                        ion
                            paused
```

Rinsing process

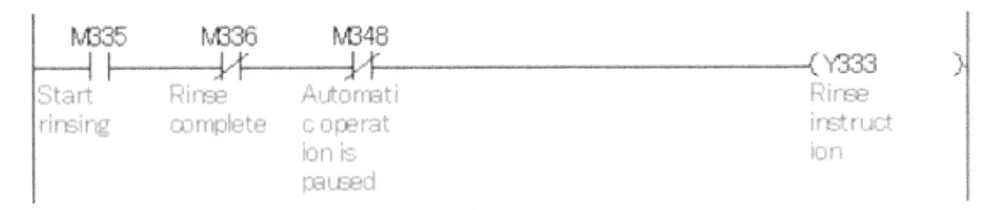

```
  M335          M336          M348
───┤ ├─────────┤/├──────────┤/├──────────────────────────(Y333)──
 Start        Rinse         Automati                     Rinse
 rinsing      complete      c operat                     instruct
                            ion is                        ion
                            paused
```

Dehydration process

```
  M337          M338          M348
───┤ ├─────────┤/├──────────┤/├──────────────────────────(Y334)──
 Start        Dehydrat      Automati                     Dehydrat
 dehydrat     ion comp      c operat                     ion inst
 ion          lete          ion is                       ruction
                            paused
```

3. Create a circuit in which the automatic operation lamp blinks during the pause. As shown below, when the automatic operation pause signal (M348) is ON, set SM412 (1 second clock) to enter the condition.

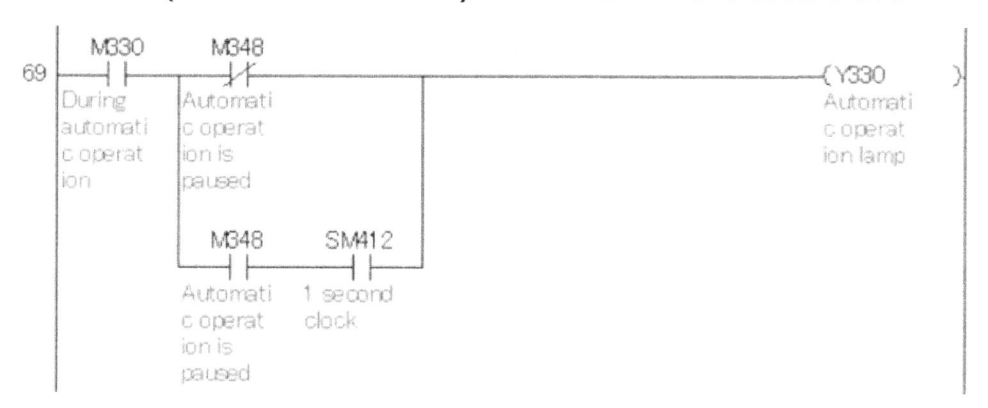

```
     M330      M348                                      (Y330)
69 ──┤ ├──────┤/├──────────────────────────────────────
     During   Automati                                   Automati
     automati c operat                                   c operat
     c operat ion is                                     ion lamp
     ion      paused

              M348      SM412
           ──┤ ├───────┤ ├──
              Automati  1 second
              c operat  clock
              ion is
              paused
```

4. Run the simulation to see if the program works correctly. Start the simulation by pressing "Debug" at the top ⇒ Simulation start/stop. Each signal can be turned ON/OFF with Shift + Enter, so check the operation below.

・ When the washing machine automatic operation (M330) is OFF and the washing machine interlock signal (M345) is OFF, pressing the washing machine automatic operation start button (X330) does not start automatic operation.

・ When the washing machine interlock signal (M345) is turned OFF while the washing machine is in automatic operation (M330), the washing machine is in automatic operation (M330) is turned OFF, the washing machine stops immediately, and the washing machine is automatically operated. Even if you press the start button (X330), it should not be in automatic operation.

· If you press the automatic operation pause button (X332) while the washing machine is automatically running (M330) is ON and the automatic operation pause signal (M348) is OFF, the automatic operation pause signal (M348) will turn ON. If you press the automatic operation pause button (X332) again in that state, the automatic operation pause signal (M348) will turn OFF.

· If the washing machine automatic operation (M330) is ON and the automatic operation pause signal (M348) is ON while each process command is ON, each process command will be turned OFF and the automatic operation pause signal (M348) will be generated. is turned OFF, the command for each process is turned ON, and operation continues from the continuation.

The explanation of the interlock circuit and the temporary stop circuit is over. If the concept of interlock is omitted, the machine will operate at a timing that should not operate and break down, or in a factory, it will lead to injury or disaster, so be sure to take this into consideration when creating programs for equipment and machines. Please do so.

2-4 Summary

・What is an interlock? **A safety mechanism or safety circuit that disables or stops operation unless certain conditions are met,** I'm talking about

・If the conditions are not met, it may lead to machine failure or dangerous operation. **The concept of interlock is very important in creating a PLC program** is.

・**A circuit in which the output repeats ON and OFF with one input** of **Flip-flop circuit (alternate circuit)**Is called.

・**Bit device output inversion instruction (FF)**can be used to create a program similar to a flip-flop circuit.

2-5 Step 4 Create a circuit for the washing machine's optional course.

In step 4, we will create a circuit for the washing machine Random course. This time, the time display **Integration timer (ST)**Use the. The integration timer (ST) will be explained later.

As a sequence, after selecting the Omakase course (X321) and starting automatic operation, water injection start (M331) ⇒ water injection 15 seconds (ST331, setting D350) ⇒ water injection complete (M332) ON ⇒ wash start (M333) ⇒ wash 10 seconds (ST332, setting D351) ⇒ washing complete (M334) ON ⇒ start rinsing (M335) ⇒ rinse 8 seconds (ST333, setting D352) ⇒ finish rinsing (M336) ON ⇒ dehydration start (M337) ⇒ dehydration 12 seconds (ST334, setting D353)) ⇒ Dehydration complete (M338) ON ⇒ Buzzer (Intermittent sound) After creating a circuit that completes the washing operation after 3 seconds, check the operation by simulation.

(The screen will be created and simulated in the next step 5)

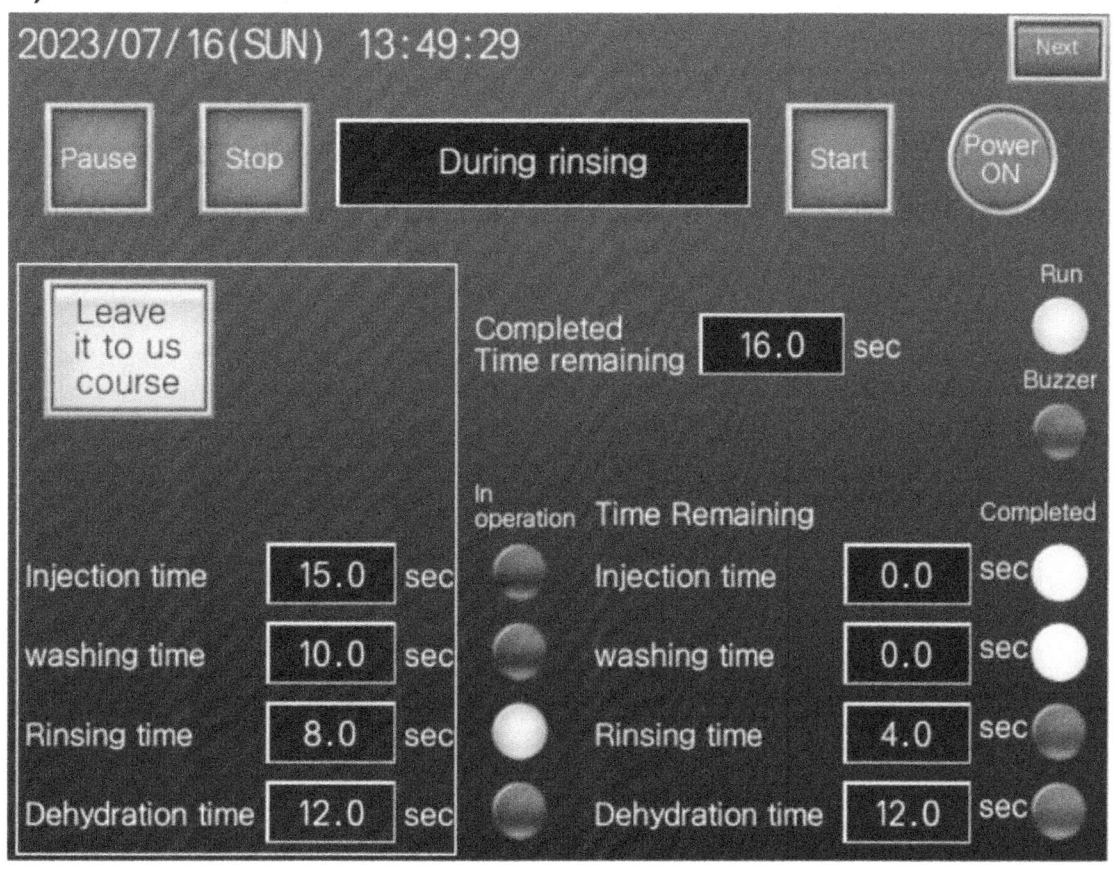

1. First, create a circuit that outputs and holds the washing machine's Random course (Y350) when you press the Random course button (X321). Also, it is valid only when the washing machine power supply (X320) is ON. Create a location above the washing machine interlock condition.

2. Next, create a circuit that sets the operation time for each process when Y350 is ON. For how to write MOV (transfer instruction), press F8, enter "MOV K○○○ D□□□" and press OK, then enter a comment and press OK. (15 seconds is set to K150 because it is used for timers in units of 100ms) Create the location just below the washing machine course setting above.

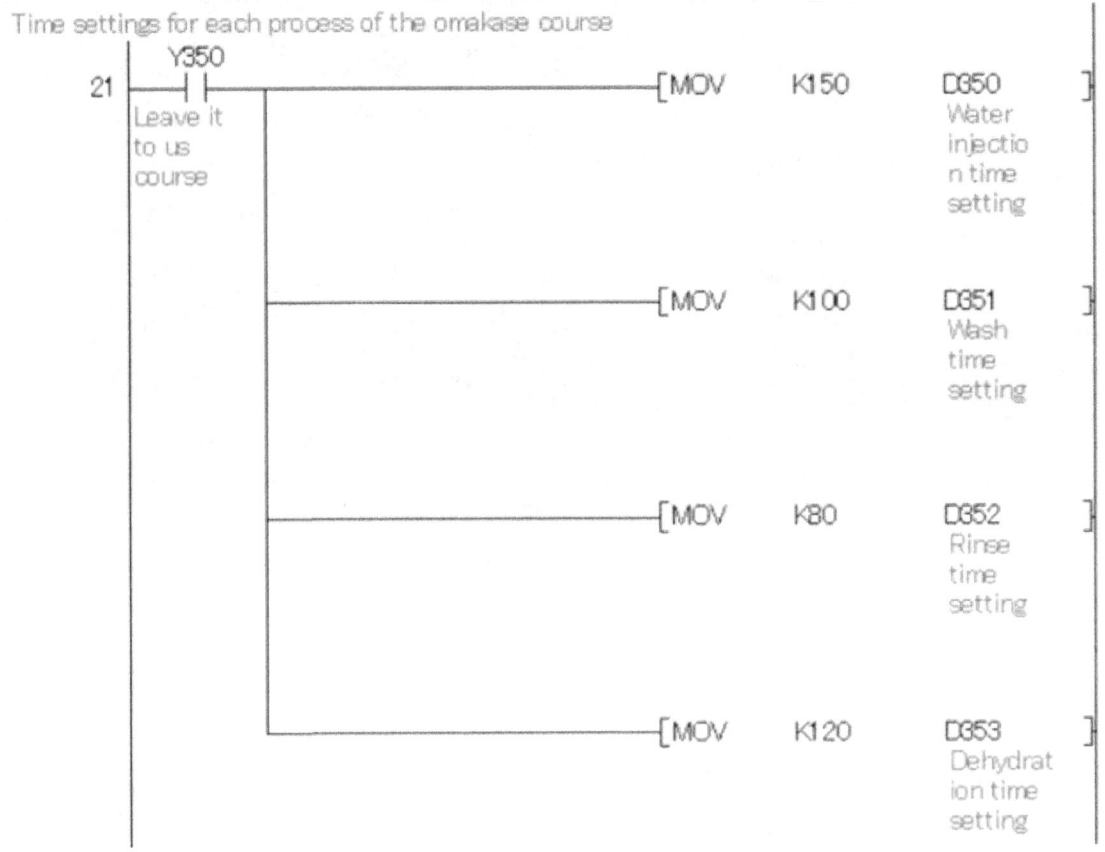

```
Time settings for each process of the omakase course
      Y350
 21   ─┤ ├─────────────────────────[MOV    K150    D350 ]
      Leave it                                     Water
      to us                                        injectio
      course                                       n time
                                                   setting

                       ─────────────[MOV    K100    D351 ]
                                                    Wash
                                                    time
                                                    setting

                       ─────────────[MOV    K80     D352 ]
                                                    Rinse
                                                    time
                                                    setting

                       ─────────────[MOV    K120    D353 ]
                                                    Dehydrat
                                                    ion time
                                                    setting
```

3. Create a circuit that resets the operation time setting for each process when the washing machine power supply (X320) is turned off. To write FMOV (batch transfer instruction), press F8, enter "FMOV K0 D350 K4", press OK, then enter a comment and press OK. Places should be created directly below each process time setting.

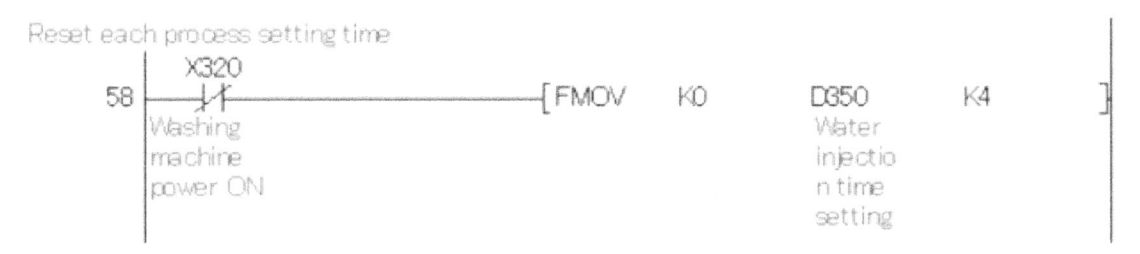

```
Reset each process setting time
         X320
  58 ─────┤/├─────────────────────[FMOV    K0      D350       K4 ]
         Washing                                  Water
         machine                                  injectio
         power ON                                 n time
                                                  setting
```

4. Create a washing machine automatic operation start able (M354). The conditions are that automatic operation can be started by turning on the Omakase course (Y350), turning on the washing machine interlock (M345), and turning off the automatic operation of the washing machine (M330). Create a location just below each process set time reset.

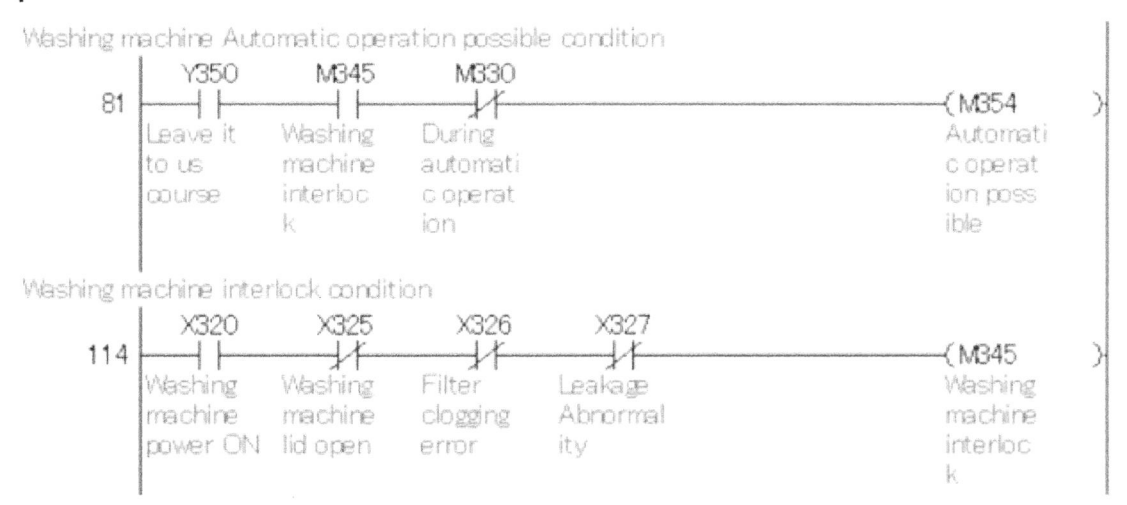

```
Washing machine Automatic operation possible condition
         Y350       M345       M330
  81 ────┤├─────────┤├─────────┤/├──────────────────────────(M354  )
         Leave it   Washing    During                       Automati
         to us      machine    automati                     c operat
         course     interloc   c operat                     ion poss
                    k          ion                          ible

Washing machine interlock condition
         X320       X325       X326       X327
 114 ────┤├─────────┤/├────────┤/├────────┤/├───────────────(M345  )
         Washing    Washing    Filter     Leakage           Washing
         machine    machine    clogging   Abnormal          machine
         power ON   lid open   error      ity               interloc
                                                            k
```

5. Add the washing machine automatic operation start possible (M354) created earlier to the condition of washing machine automatic operation (M330). M354 turns off during automatic operation, so add it next to the start button so as not to turn off self-holding.

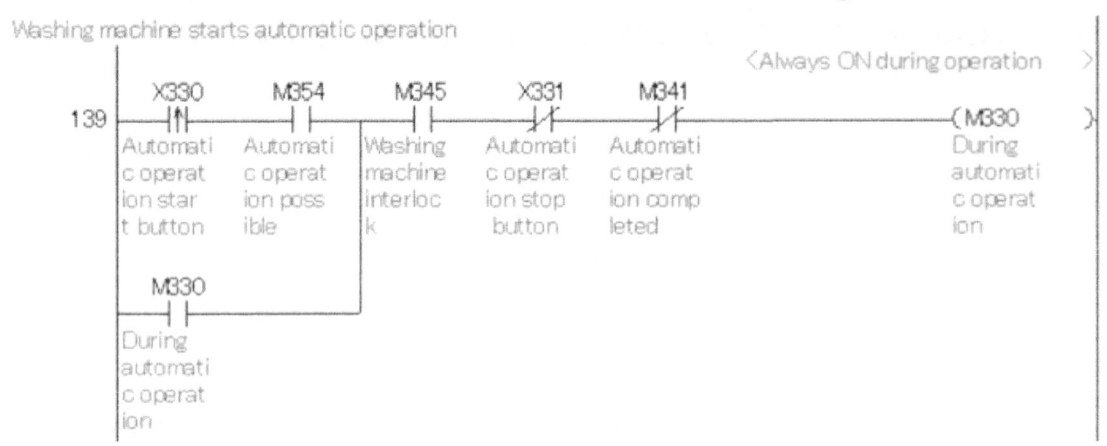

```
Washing machine starts automatic operation
                                                                    <Always ON during operation>
         X330      M354      M345      X331      M341
   139 ──┤↑├──────┤ ├───┬───┤ ├───────┤/├───────┤/├──────────────(M330)
         Automati  Automati │ Washing   Automati  Automati                During
         c operat  c operat │ machine   c operat  c operat                automati
         ion star  ion poss │ interloc  ion stop  ion comp                c operat
         t button  ible     │ k         button    leted                   ion
                            │
         M330               │
        ──┤ ├───────────────┘
         During
         automati
         c operat
         ion
```

6. From now on, we will create a program that will complete the water injection in 15 seconds from the start of the water injection process. After the stop is released, water injection will start again for 15 seconds.

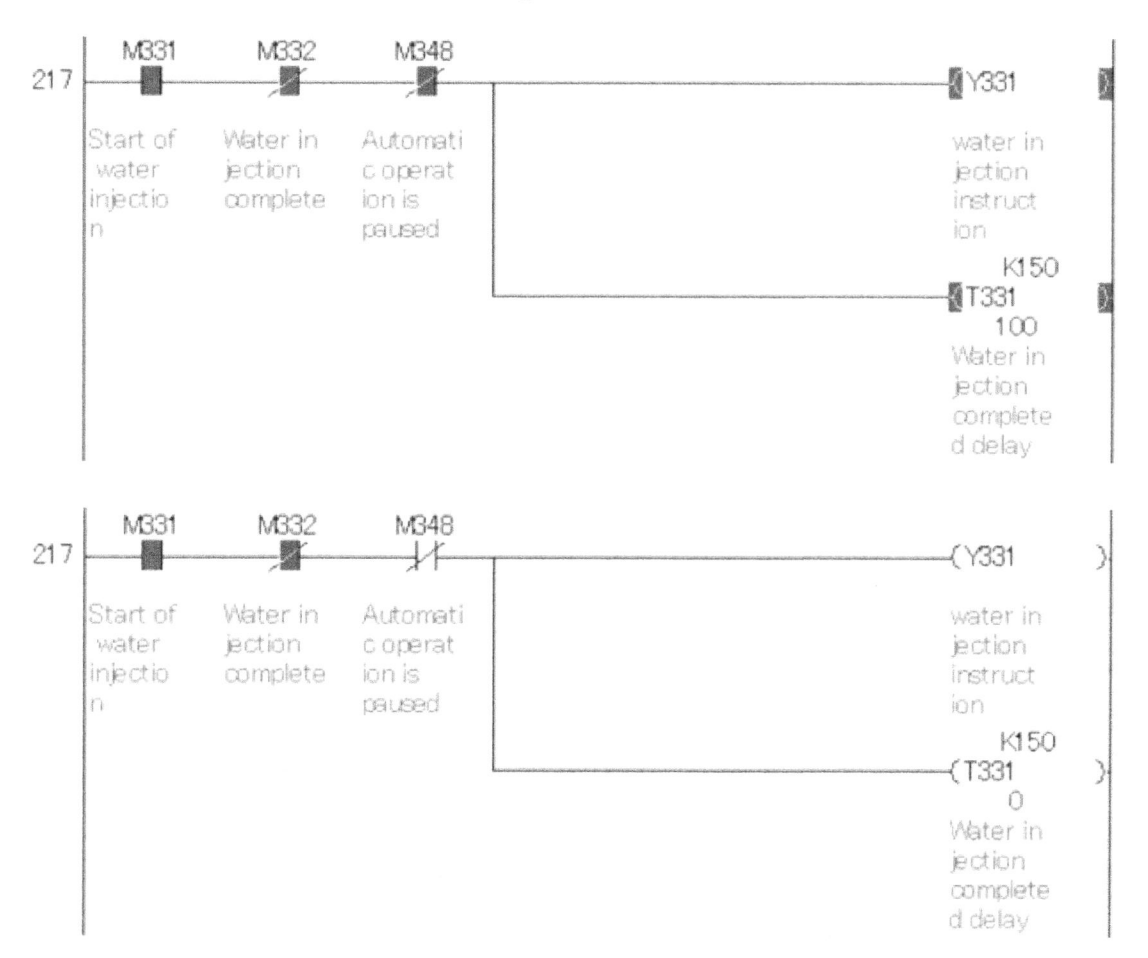

```
      M331     M332     M348
217 ───┤├──────┤/├──────┤/├──────────────────────────(Y331)
     Start of  Water in  Automati                    water in
     water     jection   c operat                    jection
     injectio  complete  ion is                      instruct
     n                   paused                      ion
                                                      K150
                                              ──────(T331)
                                                      100
                                                    Water in
                                                    jection
                                                    complete
                                                    d delay

      M331     M332     M348
217 ───┤├──────┤/├──────┤/├──────────────────────────(Y331)
     Start of  Water in  Automati                    water in
     water     jection   c operat                    jection
     injectio  complete  ion is                      instruct
     n                   paused                      ion
                                                      K150
                                              ──────(T331)
                                                       0
                                                    Water in
                                                    jection
                                                    complete
                                                    d delay
```

This does not work correctly, so this time **Integration timer (ST)**Use the. (There are other ways to do it, but this time we will create it with an integration timer.)

Using the integration timer (ST)**Even if the condition is turned off, the time until now remains**. Therefore, even if it is paused, the time until now remains, so it is possible to operate from the elapsed time so far.

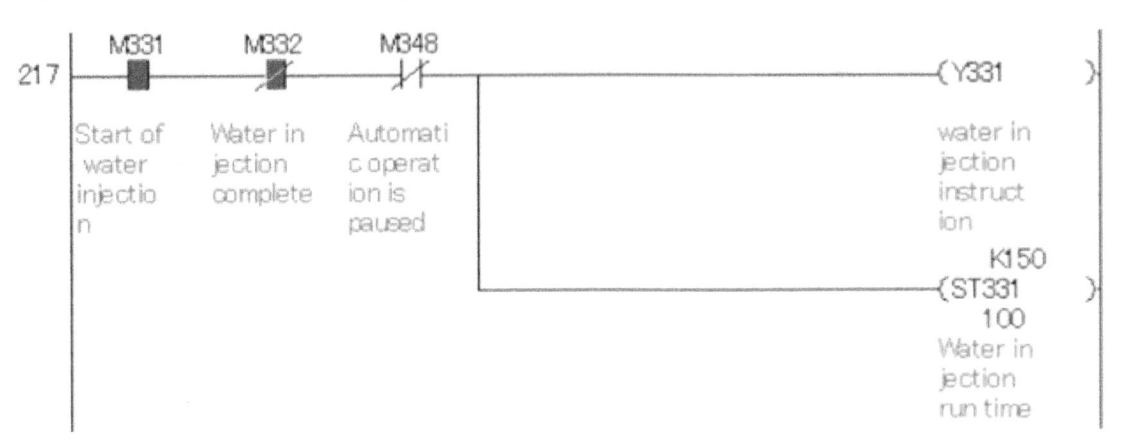

```
        M331      M332      M348
217 ────┤├────────┤/├───────┤/├──────────────────────────(Y331)
        Start of  Water in  Automati                     water in
        water     jection   c operat                     jection
        injectio  complete  ion is                       instruct
        n                   paused                       ion
                                                            K150
                                                      ──(ST331)
                                                           100
                                                         Water in
                                                         jection
                                                         run time
```

Now, let's create a water injection process using this integration timer. First, the integration timer cannot be used in the initial settings, so change the settings. After double-clicking Parameter ⇒ PLC Parameter in the navigation, click the "Device" tab. If the number of device points of the integration timer is OK, it cannot be used, so this time, change the number of device points of the timer to 1K and the number of device points of the Retentive timer to 1K, and then press "End" at the bottom right.

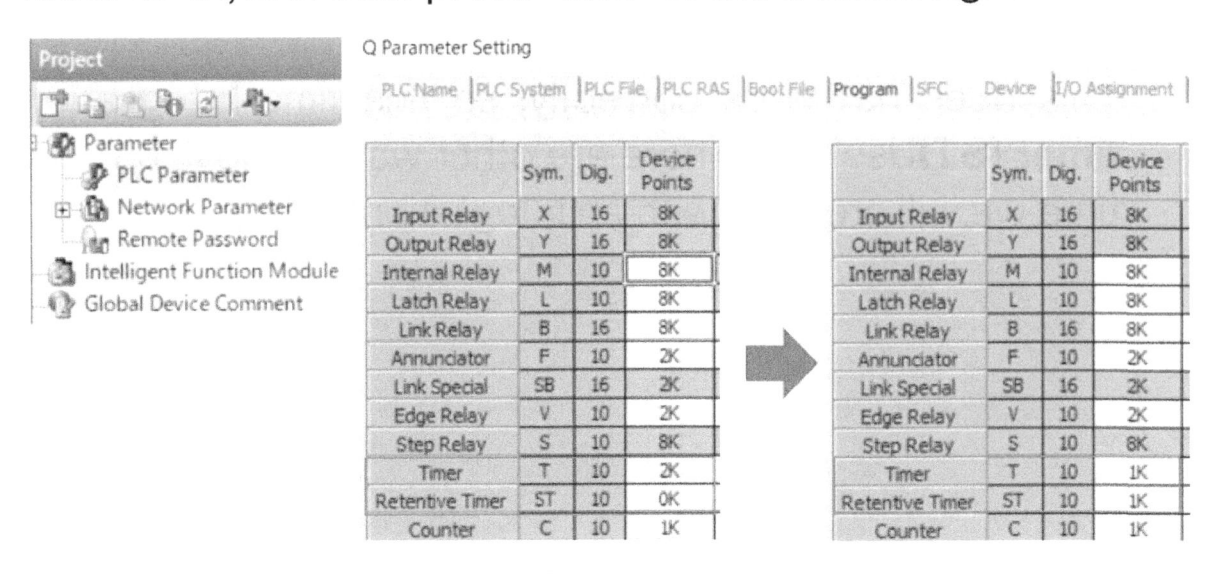

Q Parameter Setting

PLC Name | PLC System | PLC File | PLC RAS | Boot File | Program | SFC | Device | I/O Assignment

	Sym.	Dig.	Device Points
Input Relay	X	16	8K
Output Relay	Y	16	8K
Internal Relay	M	10	8K
Latch Relay	L	10	8K
Link Relay	B	16	8K
Annunciator	F	10	2K
Link Special	SB	16	2K
Edge Relay	V	10	2K
Step Relay	S	10	8K
Timer	T	10	2K
Retentive Timer	ST	10	0K
Counter	C	10	1K

➡

	Sym.	Dig.	Device Points
Input Relay	X	16	8K
Output Relay	Y	16	8K
Internal Relay	M	10	8K
Latch Relay	L	10	8K
Link Relay	B	16	8K
Annunciator	F	10	2K
Link Special	SB	16	2K
Edge Relay	V	10	2K
Step Relay	S	10	8K
Timer	T	10	1K
Retentive Timer	ST	10	1K
Counter	C	10	1K

Now that the integration timer can be used, create the following program. For the ST331 coil, press F7, enter "ST331 D350", press OK, then enter a comment and press OK. Since this D350 contains K150, ST331 turns ON after the ST331 coil counts 15 seconds in the integrated time. Also, after ST is turned ON, it is held until reset, so holding M332 is not necessary. (The reset method is explained in the next step.)

Program before change

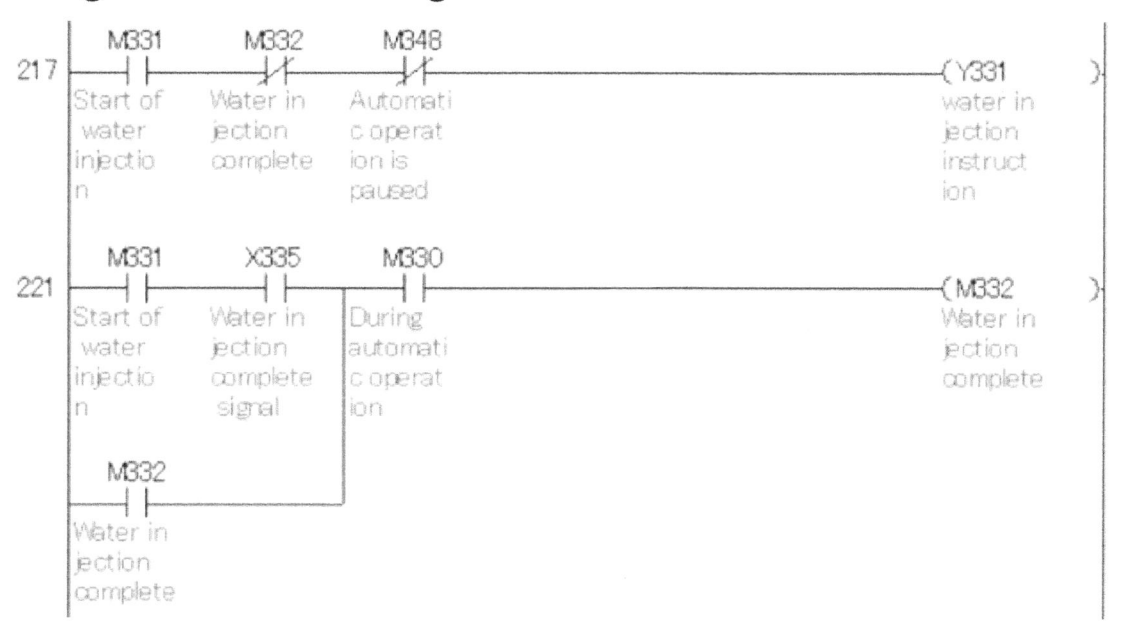

```
        M331         M332         M348
217 ─────┤ ├─────────┤/├─────────┤/├──────────────────────(Y331)─
        Start of    Water in    Automati                  water in
        water       jection     c operat                  jection
        injectio    complete    ion is                    instruct
        n                       paused                    ion

        M331         X335         M330
221 ─────┤ ├─────────┤ ├─────────┤ ├──────────────────────(M332)─
        Start of    Water in    During                    Water in
        water       jection     automati                  jection
        injectio    complete    c operat                  complete
        n           signal      ion

        M332
    ─────┤ ├
        Water in
        jection
        complete
```

Program after change

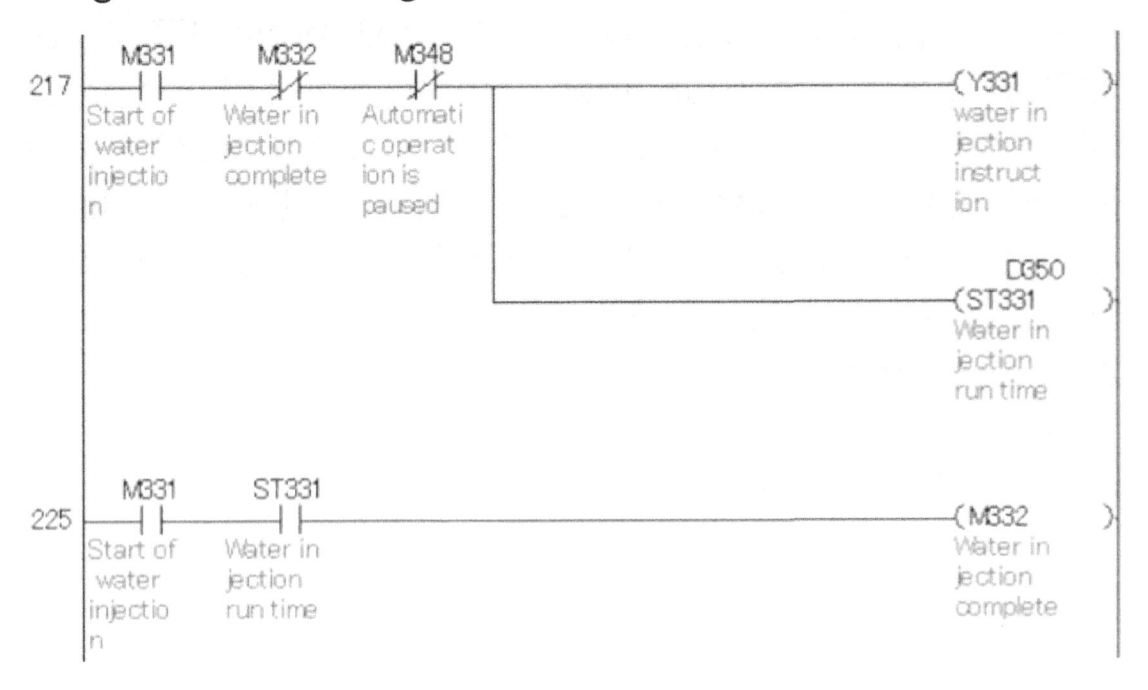

```
      M331      M332      M348
217 ──┤ ├──────┤/├──────┤/├─────────────────────────(Y331)
     Start of  Water in  Automati                   water in
     water     jection   c operat                   jection
     injectio  complete  ion is                     instruct
     n                   paused                     ion

                                                     D850
                                                   (ST331)
                                                   Water in
                                                   jection
                                                   run time

      M331      ST331
225 ──┤ ├──────┤ ├─────────────────────────────────(M332)
     Start of  Water in                             Water in
     water     jection                              jection
     injectio  run time                             complete
     n
```

After the integration timer turns ON, it remains ON. **Reset instruction (RST)** must be reset by the set and reset instructions are explained here.

Set command (SET)・・・Holds the set device in the ON state.

Reset command (RST): Holds the set device in the OFF state.

Turn M100 ON ⇒ Keep Y100 ON

```
   M100
───┤↑├──────────────────────────────────[SET    Y100  ]
  Lamp ON                                       Lamp ON
  button

   M101
───┤↑├──────────────────────────────────[RST    Y100  ]
  Lamp OFF                                      Lamp ON
  button
```

M101 ON ⇒ Y100 remains OFF

```
   M100
───┤↑├──────────────────────────────────[SET    Y100  ]
  Lamp ON                                       Lamp ON
  button

   M101
───┤↑├──────────────────────────────────[RST    Y100  ]
  Lamp OFF                                      Lamp ON
  button
```

This kind of operation is possible with the set instruction (SET) and reset instruction (RST). However, if you use this SET/RST command frequently, you will not be able to see the conditions that turn on the coil in one place, and the circuit may become difficult to see. again, **In the case of SET/RST instructions, even if the same coil is used multiple times, it will not become a double coil.** In this circuit, ST311 remains ON after it is turned ON due to the characteristics of the integration timer, so use the reset command (RST) at the necessary timing to turn it OFF. Please create a place just above the automatic water injection process of the washing machine.

The timing to reset this time is as follows.

· When automatic operation starts: Works correctly by resetting when automatic operation starts

· When automatic operation is completed: It is not necessary to display the execution time after completion

· When you press the automatic operation stop button: It is not necessary to display the execution time after stopping

· When the power is turned off: Because it is not necessary to display the execution time when the power is turned off.

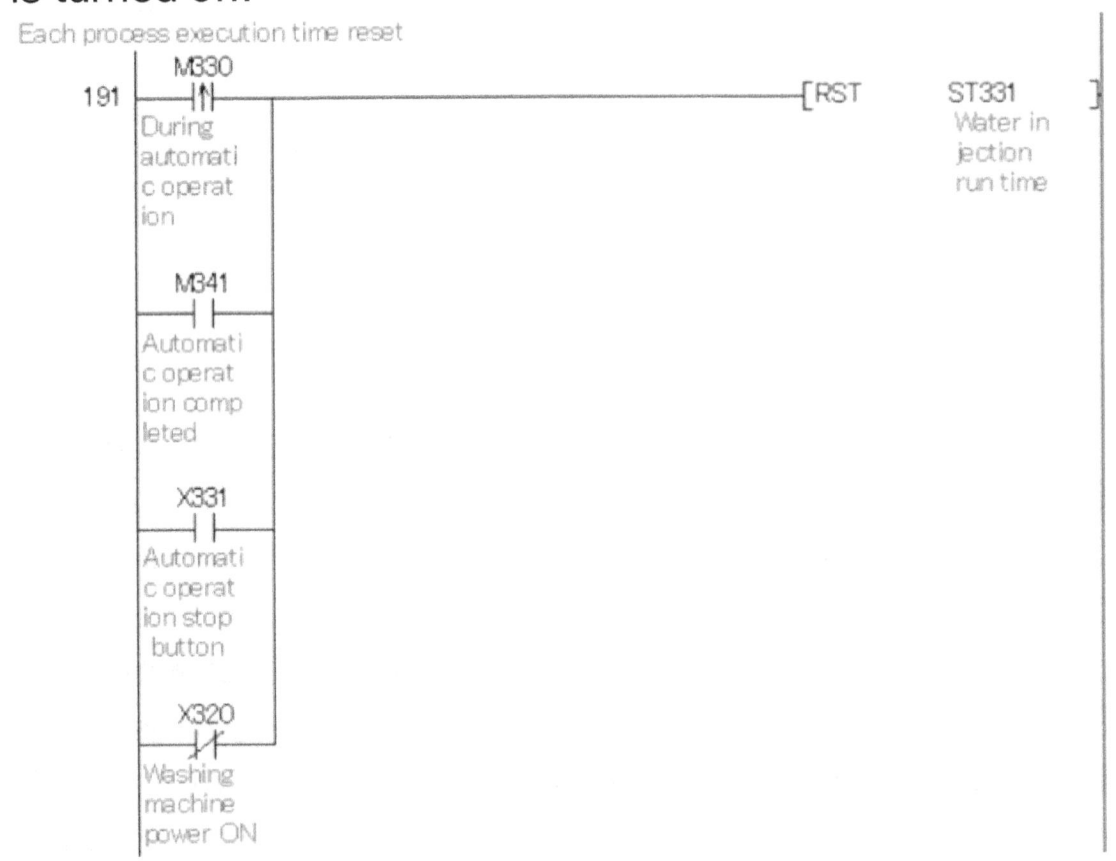

```
Each process execution time reset
            M330
191        ──┤↑├──────────────────────────[RST    ST331    ]
            During                                 Water in
            automati                               jection
            c operat                               run time
            ion

            M341
           ──┤ ├──
            Automati
            c operat
            ion comp
            leted

            X331
           ──┤ ├──
            Automati
            c operat
            ion stop
             button

            X320
           ──┤/├──
            Washing
            machine
            power ON
```

This completes the water injection process: water injection start (M331) ⇒ water injection 15 seconds (ST331, setting D350) ⇒ water injection complete (M332) ON sequence. If you are wondering what kind of operation it will be, please check the operation with the simulation function at this timing.

7. Create a program for the washing, rinsing, and dehydration processes in the same way as the water injection process.

Washing process After program change

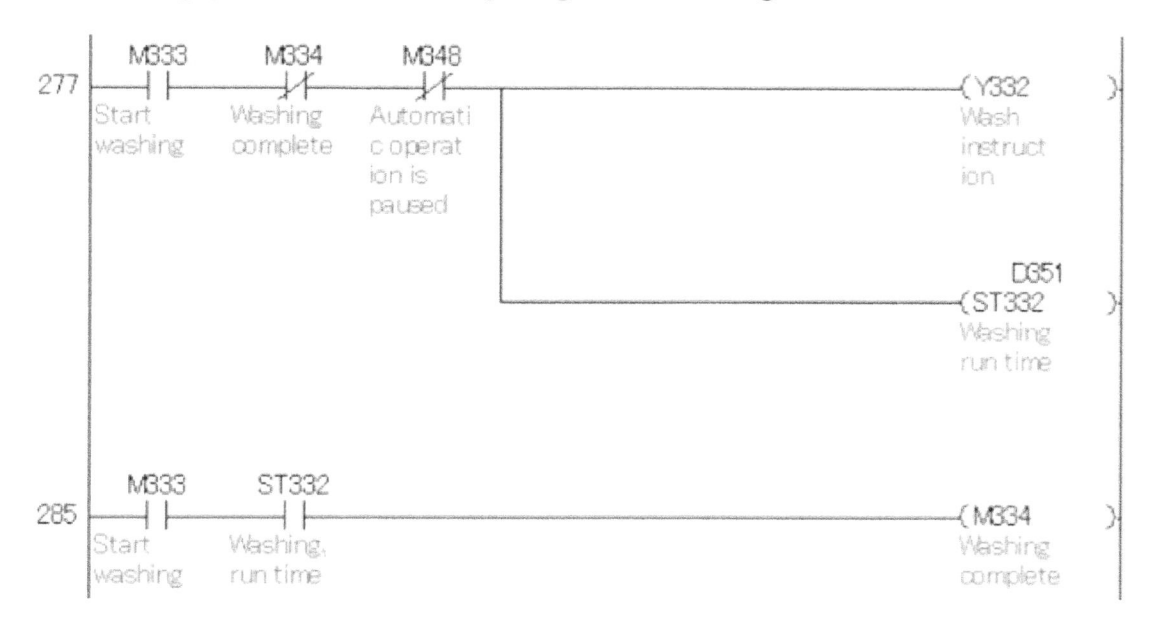

```
        M333      M334      M348
277 ─────┤├───────┤/├───────┤/├──────────────────────────(Y332)─
        Start    Washing   Automati                      Wash
        washing  complete  c operat                      instruct
                           ion is                        ion
                           paused

                                                          D651
                                              ───────────(ST332)─
                                                         Washing
                                                         run time

        M333      ST332
285 ─────┤├───────┤├─────────────────────────────────────(M334)─
        Start    Washing,                                Washing
        washing  run time                                complete
```

Rinsing process After program change

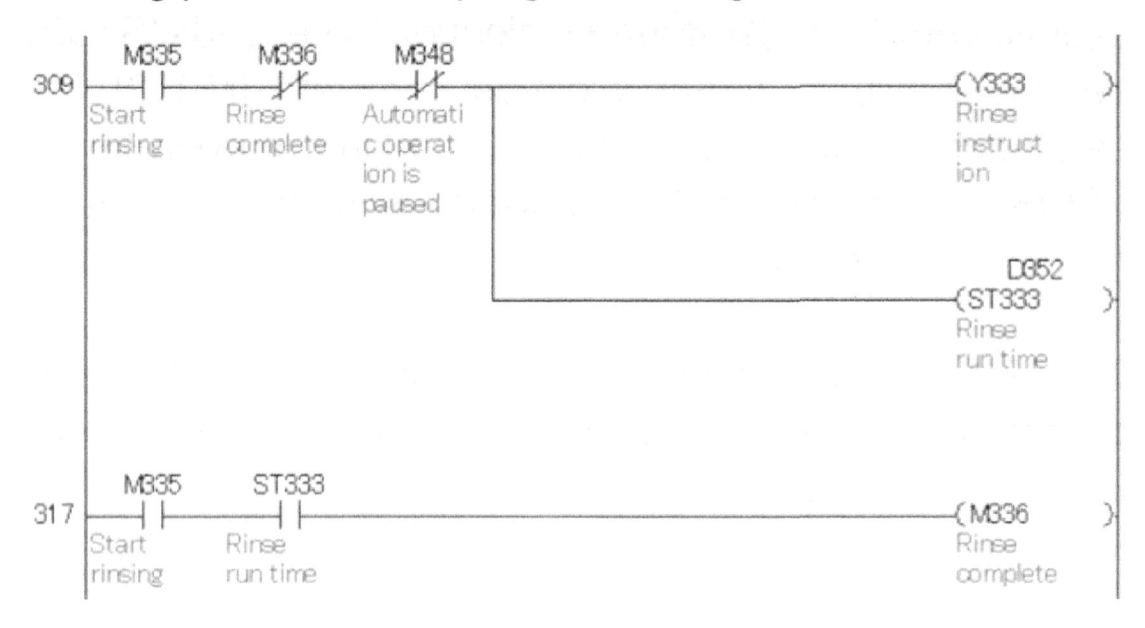

```
       M335      M336      M348                                              (Y333)
309 ----| |------|/|-------|/|---------------------------------------------
       Start    Rinse     Automati                                          Rinse
       rinsing  complete  c operat                                          instruct
                          ion is                                            ion
                          paused

                                                                      D652
                                                                     -(ST333)
                                                                      Rinse
                                                                      run time

       M335      ST333                                                      (M336)
317 ----| |------| |------------------------------------------------------
       Start    Rinse                                                       Rinse
       rinsing  run time                                                    complete
```

Dehydration process After program change

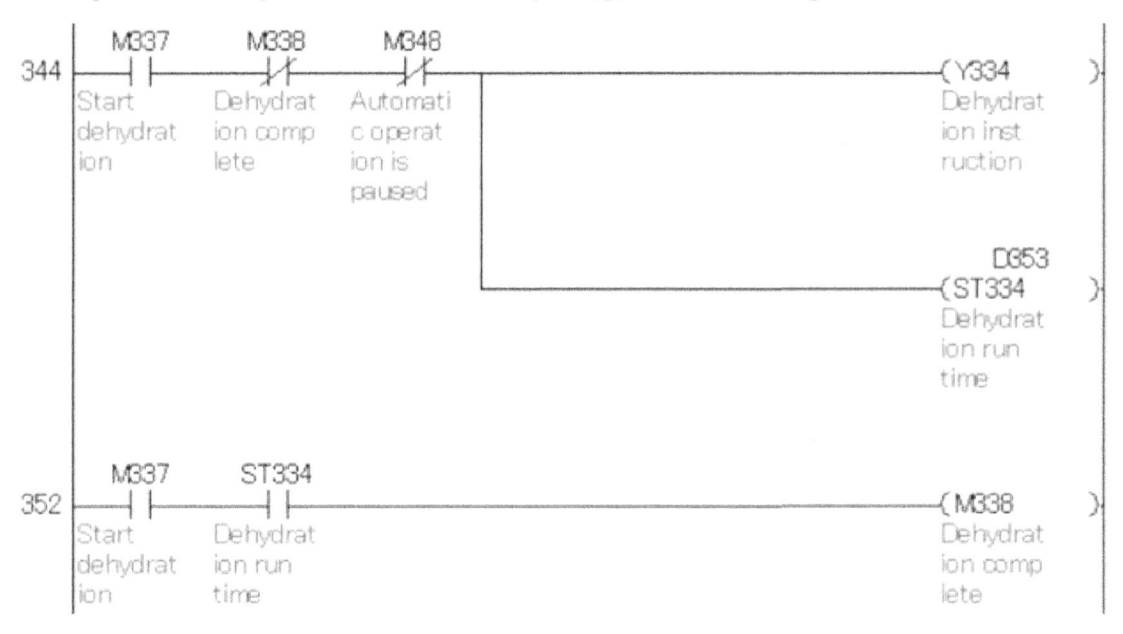

```
       M337      M338      M348                                              (Y334)
344 ----| |------|/|-------|/|---------------------------------------------
       Start    Dehydrat  Automati                                          Dehydrat
       dehydrat ion comp  c operat                                          ion inst
       ion      lete      ion is                                            ruction
                          paused

                                                                      D653
                                                                     -(ST334)
                                                                      Dehydrat
                                                                      ion run
                                                                      time

       M337      ST334                                                      (M338)
352 ----| |------| |------------------------------------------------------
       Start    Dehydrat                                                    Dehydrat
       dehydrat ion run                                                     ion comp
       ion      time                                                        lete
```

runtime reset circuit.

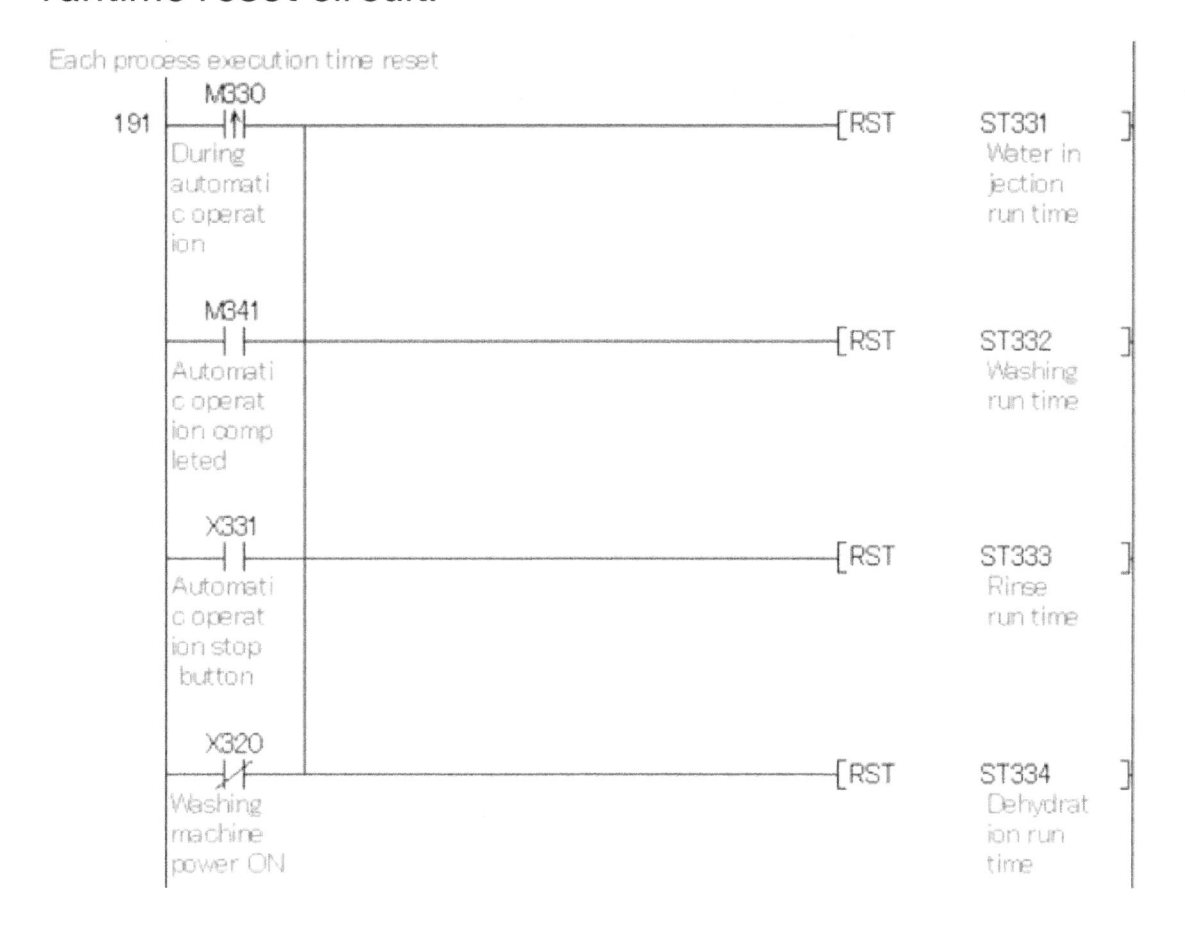

```
Each process execution time reset
        M330
191      ─┤↑├─                                    ─[RST    ST331   ]
        During                                            Water in
        automati                                          jection
        c operat                                          run time
        ion

        M341
         ─┤ ├─                                    ─[RST    ST332   ]
        Automati                                          Washing
        c operat                                          run time
        ion comp
        leted

        X331
         ─┤ ├─                                    ─[RST    ST333   ]
        Automati                                          Rinse
        c operat                                          run time
        ion stop
        button

        X320
         ─┤/├─                                    ─[RST    ST334   ]
        Washing                                           Dehydrat
        machine                                           ion run
        power ON                                          time
```

8. Run the simulation to see if the program works correctly. Start the simulation by pressing "Debug" at the top ⇒ Start/Stop Simulation.

・After turning on the washing machine, if you press the start button without pressing the auto course button, automatic operation will not start.

・When you press the auto course button after turning on the power of the washing machine, the operation time of each process is set to D350 to D353, and it is reset when the power is turned off.

· After turning on the power of the washing machine, set the operation time for each process with the automatic course button, and press the start button.) Complete automatic operation in 3 seconds

· If you press the pause button during each process (water injection, washing, rinsing, dehydration), the execution time will stop at the time you pressed it, and when you cancel the pause, it will start working from the continuation time.

· After automatic operation of the washing machine is completed, it should operate correctly even if automatic operation is performed again.

2-5 Summary

· Integration timer (ST)**Even if the condition is turned off, the time until now remains**. Therefore, even if it is paused, the time until now remains, so it is possible to operate from the elapsed time so far.

· Since the integration timer remains ON after it is turned ON, **Reset instruction (RST)** must be reset by.

· **In the case of SET/RST instructions, even if the same coil is used multiple times, it will not become a double coil.**

2-6 Step 5 Creation of touch panel screen for washing machine operation.

In step 5, after creating the touch panel screen from steps 1 to 4, check the operation using the simulation function. The contents of the screen to be created this time are as follows.

・Power ON/OFF button

・Automatic operation start/stop/pause button

・During operation/Buzzer/During operation of each process/Completion lamp of each process

・Omakase course button and set time display for each process

・Remaining time to complete washing and remaining time for each process

・Monitor display
(Filling water/washing/rinsing/dehydrating/washing complete/clogging/earth leakage)
・Current date and time display

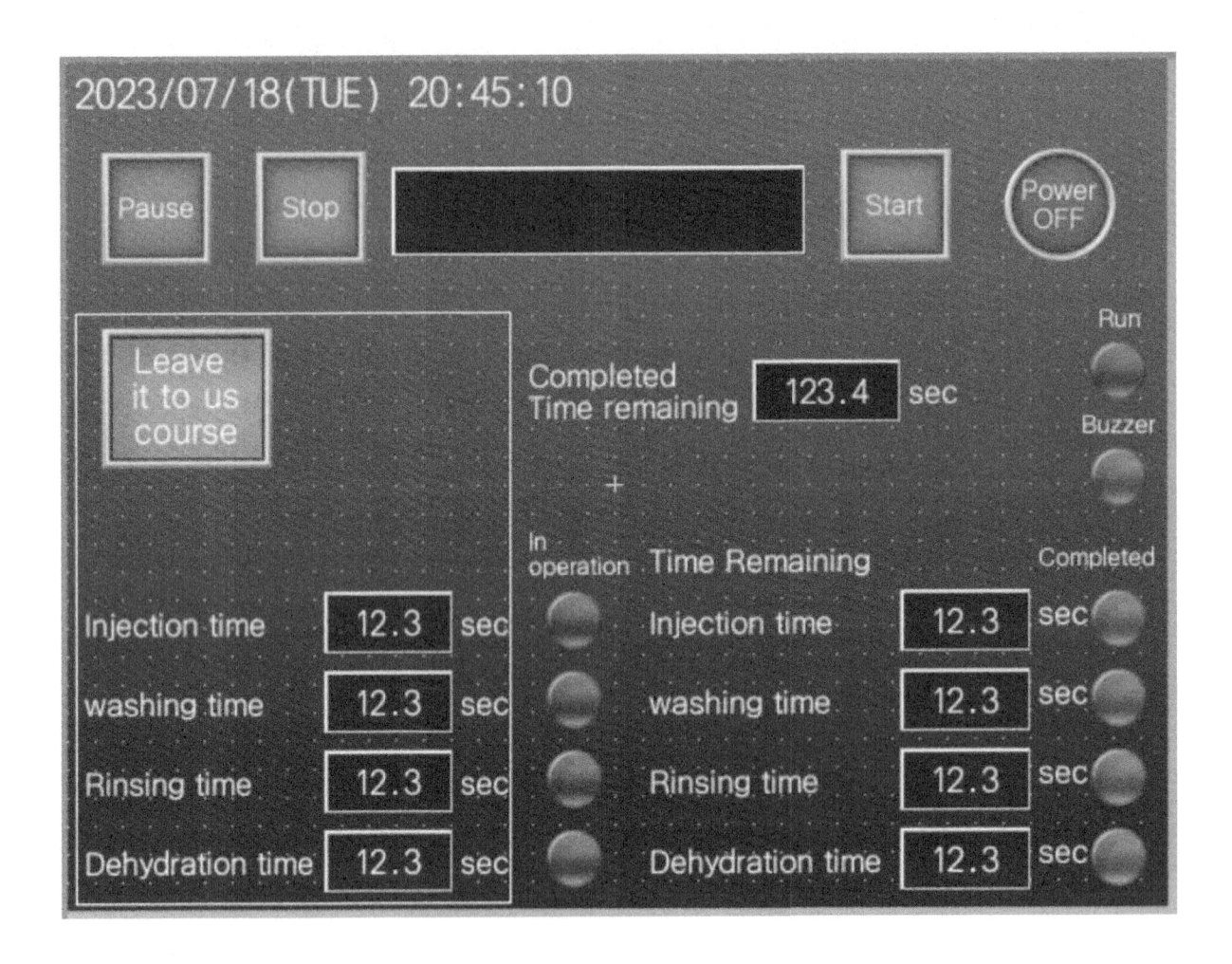

This time, it will be created with GT Designer (GOT2000).
Let's create one by one.

1. First, make the necessary preparations for screen creation. After starting GT Designer (GOT2000) and selecting "Create new", it is OK to leave the default settings other than the connected device settings, so press "Next" to proceed. /QS..." and "Next," then proceed with all default settings. (This is because the connected device is created with "Q02/Q02H" on the PLC side this time.)

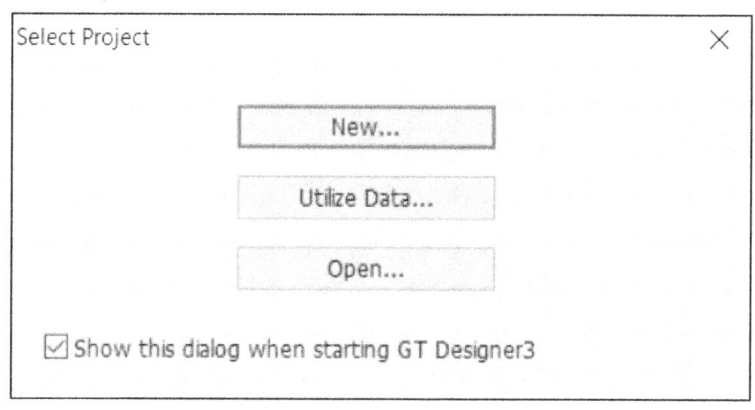

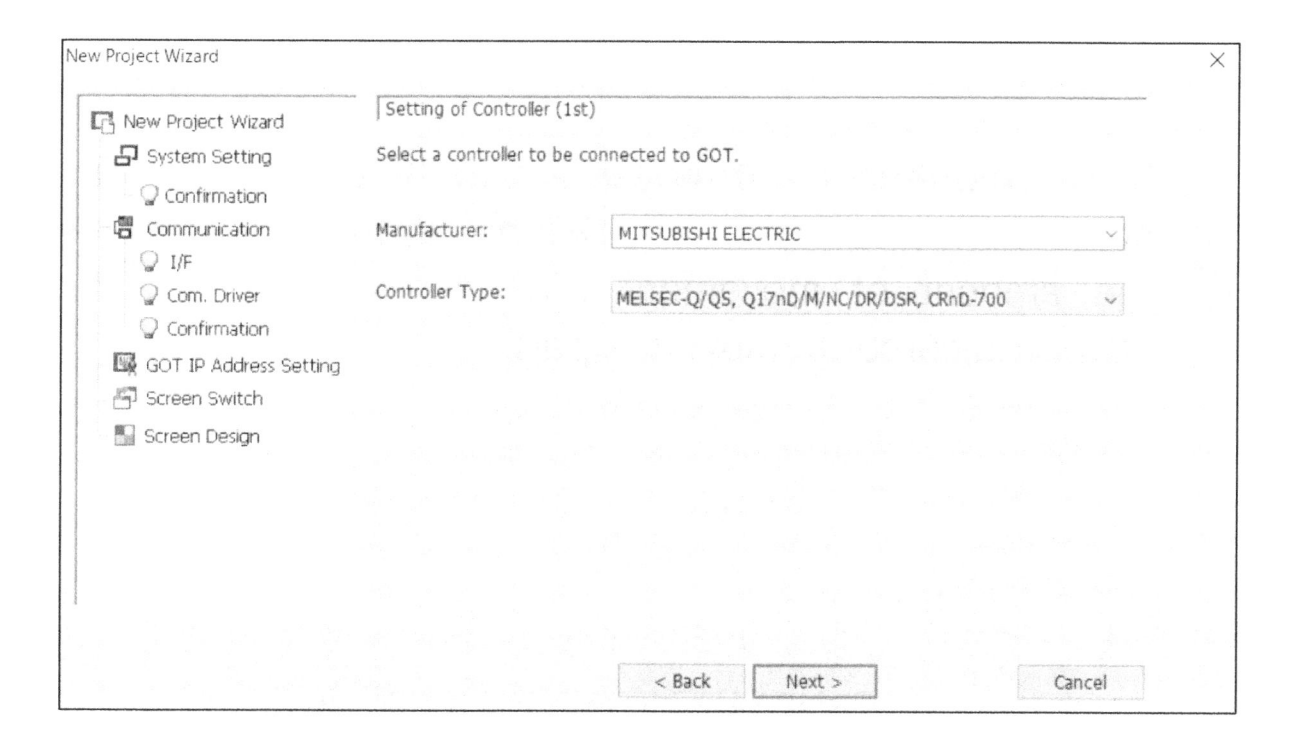

2. Next, change the name of the screen to "Washing machine operation screen". Right-click "1" on the left base screen ⇒ Open the screen properties, enter "washing machine operation screen" in the title and press OK at the bottom right. Alternatively, after clicking "1", you can also enter the properties displayed below.

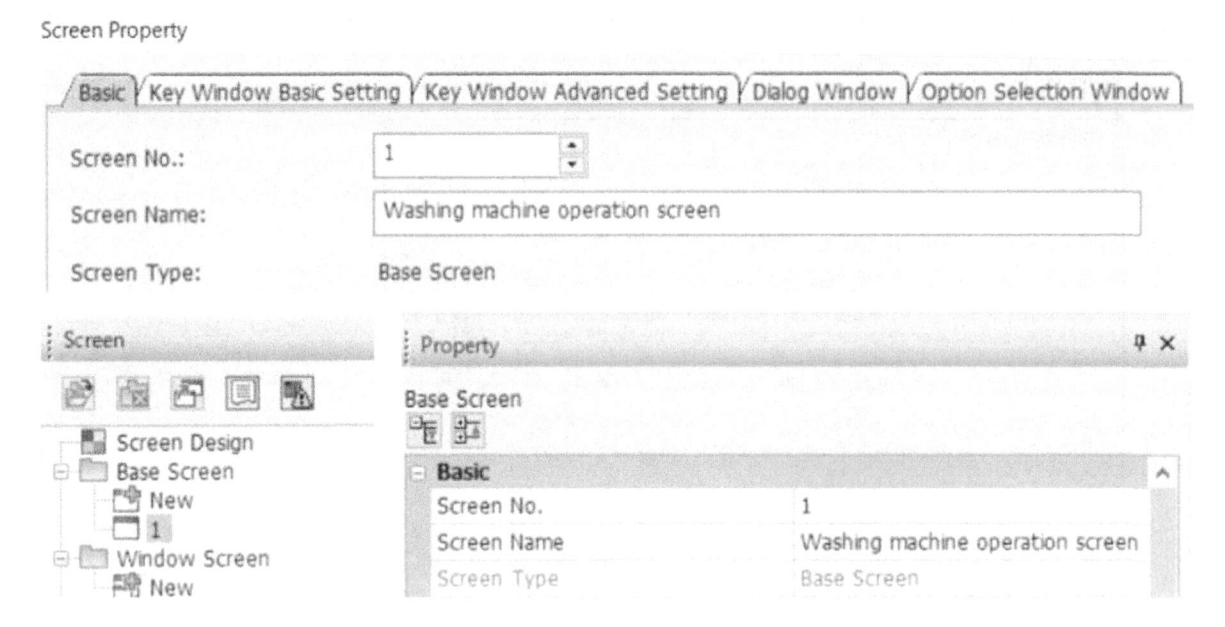

3. Set the amount of movement to "1" to facilitate fine adjustment of the position. This amount of movement is the amount of movement each time you press the keyboard cursor to move the part.

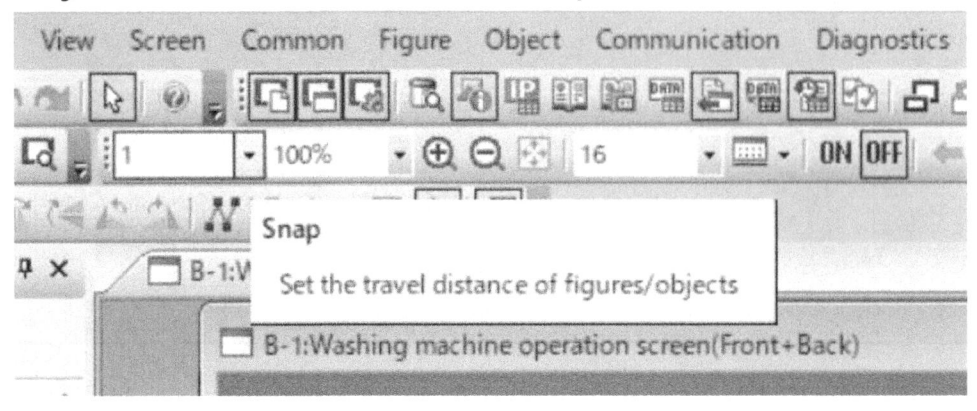

4. To make the screen easier to see, go to the "View" tab ⇒ Uncheck the display items except for objects and touch areas. If you want to check if the device is correct, display the device each time.

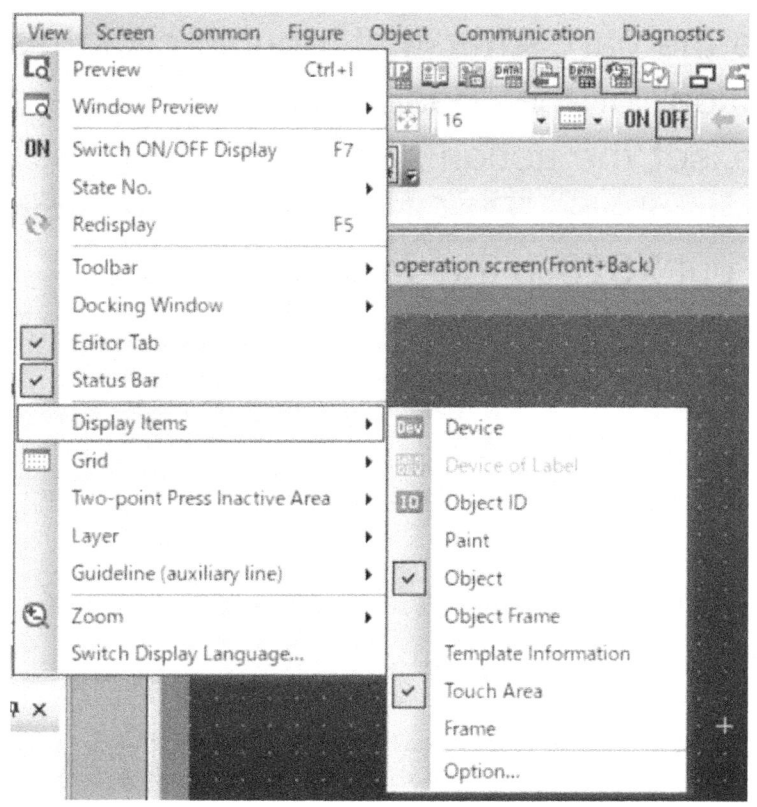

5. "Project" tab ⇒ Press "Save As" to save as "Screen creation". The file format will be saved in 1 file format this time, so if "Switch to 1 file format project" is displayed in the lower right, click it and save it as 1 file format.

This completes the preparations necessary for screen creation.

6. First, create a power ON/OFF button.

＜**Power ON/OFF button**＞

After clicking the "Object" tab ⇒ Switch ⇒ Switch, click the screen to place the part. After that, double-click this part, and click "Action" of the "Basic Settings" tab, set X320 as the device, set the action setting to "Alternate", and press OK. Then check "Bit-ON/OFF" in the lamp function below and put X320 in the device.

Next, select the "Style" tab and click "Shape..." to display a list of images, select "Red" for the color, select shape number 4. Then, after clicking the lamp ON in the display figure, select "Blue" for the color, select the shape No. 1 in "FA control switch figure A1" for the shape, and press OK on the lower right.

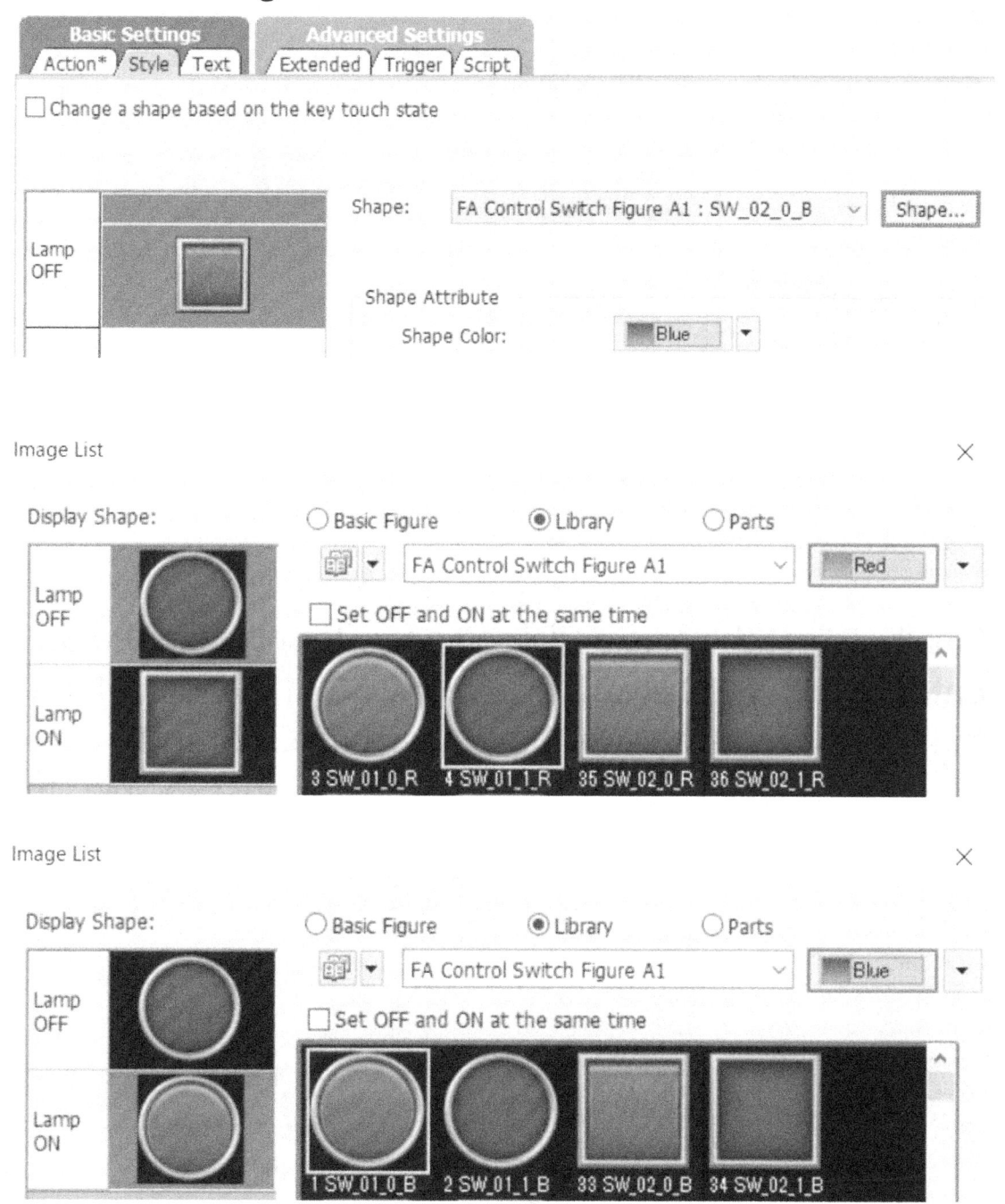

Next, select the "Text" tab, uncheck "OFF = ON" next to the nameplate type, click the lamp OFF on the left, and enter 16 for the character size and "Power OFF" for the character string. increase. Then, after clicking the lamp ON the left, enter 16 for the character size and "Power ON" for the character string, then press OK at the bottom right.

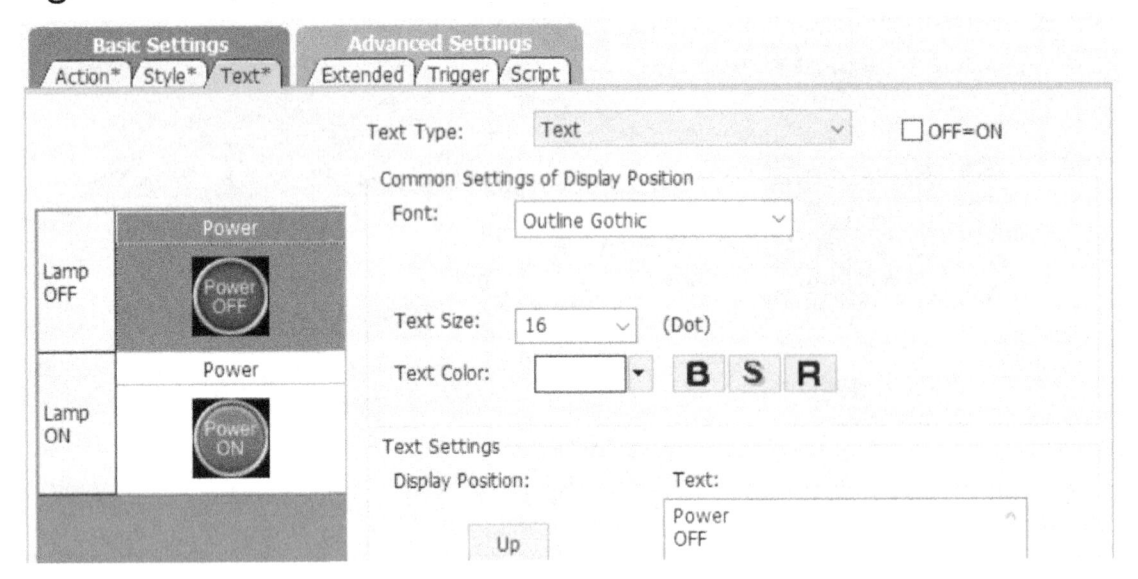

Finally adjust the size and position. After clicking the part, enter X: 545 Y: 50 Width 65 Height: 65 in the lower left of the screen to complete the power ON/OFF button. You can check the display with ON/OFF just below the "Communication" tab.

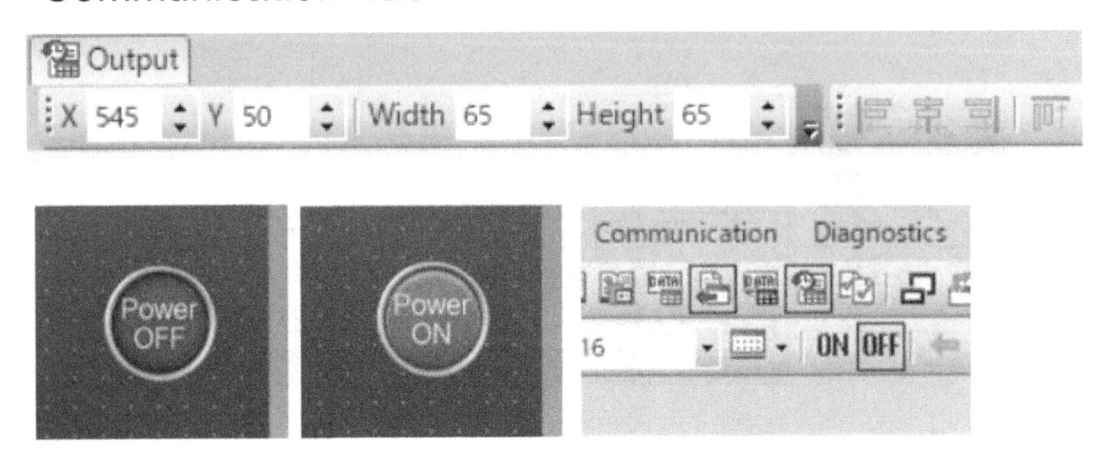

7. Next, create an automatic operation start/stop/pause button. We will copy and create the power ON / OFF button created earlier.

<Start button>

First, click the power ON/OFF button, then press Ctrl + C (copy), Ctrl + V (paste) and click the screen to place the same button.

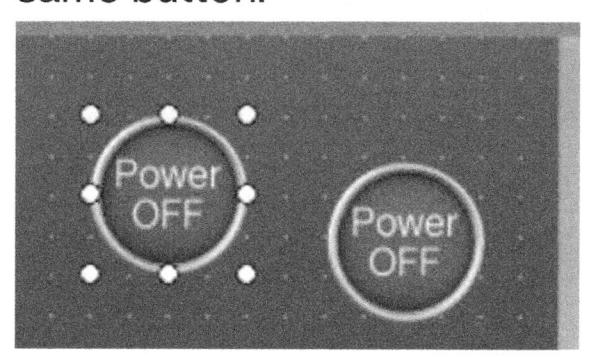

After double-clicking the newly created button, change the settings as follows using the same procedure as for the power ON/OFF button.

【Operation setting】
Action: Bit Momentary, Setting: X330, Device for Lamp Function: X330

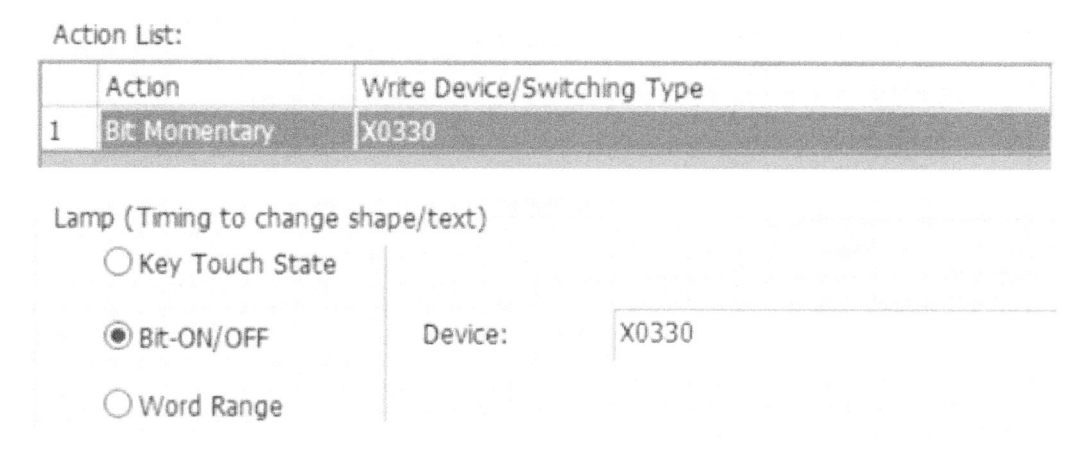

【style】

Lamp OFF: White, number 58 of "FA control switch figure A1"

Lamp ON: White, No. 57 of "FA control switch figure A1"

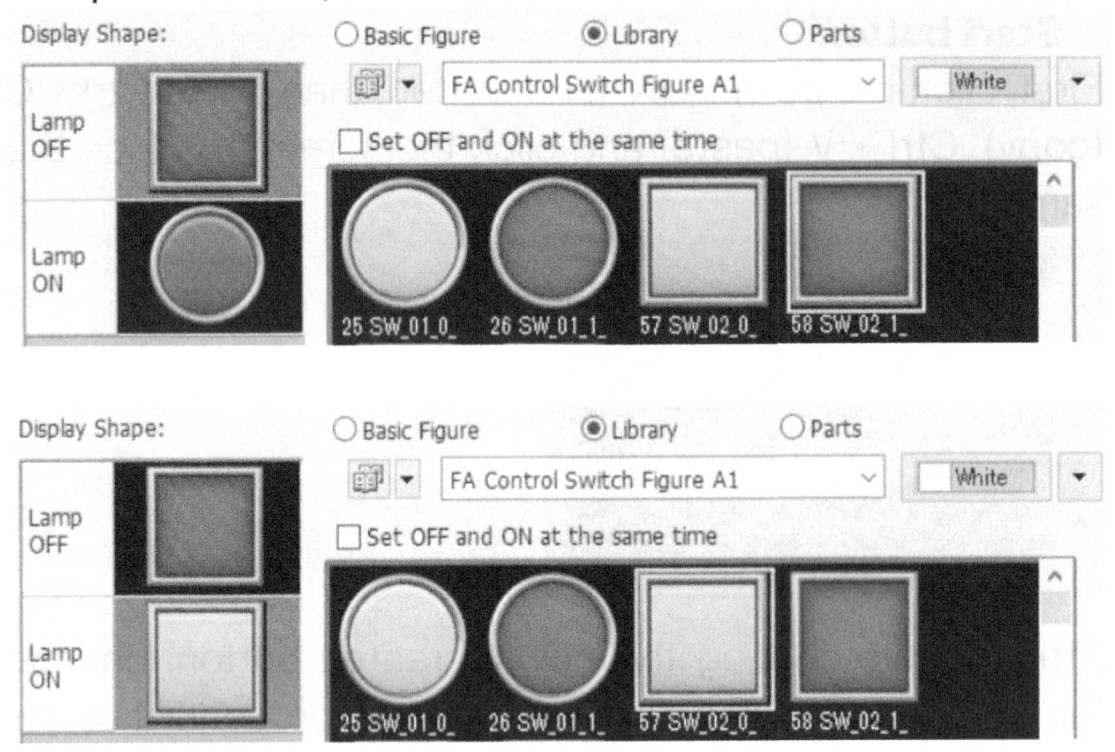

【letter】

Lamp OFF: Character color "white", character string "Start"

Lamp ON: Character color "black", character string "start"

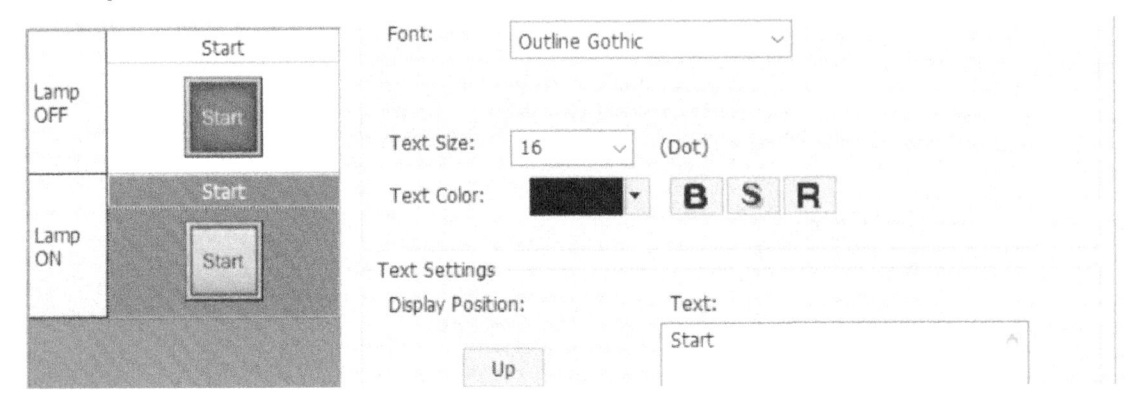

[Placement/size]
X: 450 Y: 50 Width: 65 Height: 65

Create a stop button and a pause button in the same way.

<**Stop button**>
Copy the start button ⇒ Paste ⇒ After clicking the screen, double-click the part to perform each setting
【Operation setting】
Action: Bit Momentary, Setting: X331
Device of lamp function: X331
【letter】
Lamp OFF: Character color "white", character string "Stop"
Lamp ON: Character color "black", character string "Stop"
[Placement/size]
X: 110 Y: 50 Width: 65 Height: 65

<**Pause button**>
Copy the pause button ⇒ Paste ⇒ After clicking the screen, double-click the part to perform each setting
【Operation setting】
Action: Bit Momentary, Setting: X332
Device of lamp function: M348

【letter】

Lamp OFF: Character color "white", character string "Pause"

Lamp ON: Character color "black", character string "On pause"

[Placement/size]

X: 20 Y: 50 Width: 65 Height: 65

8. Next, create a running lamp.

<Run lamp>

After clicking the "Object" tab ⇒ Lamp ⇒ Bit Lamp, click the screen to place the part. After that, double-click it and enter Y330 as the device in the "Device/Style" tab.

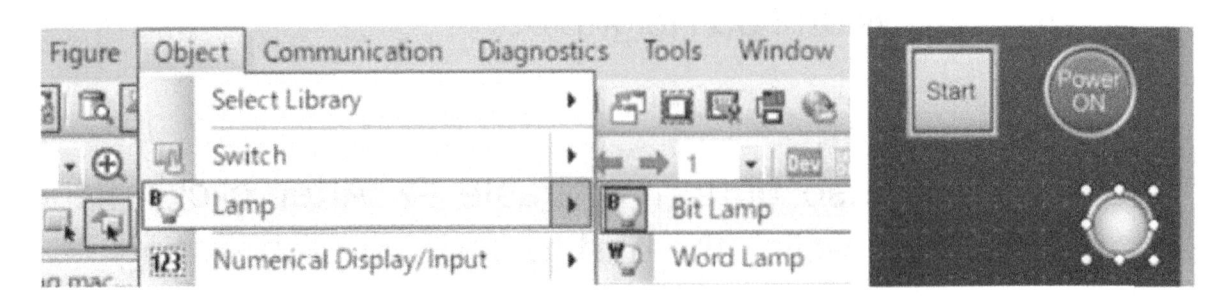

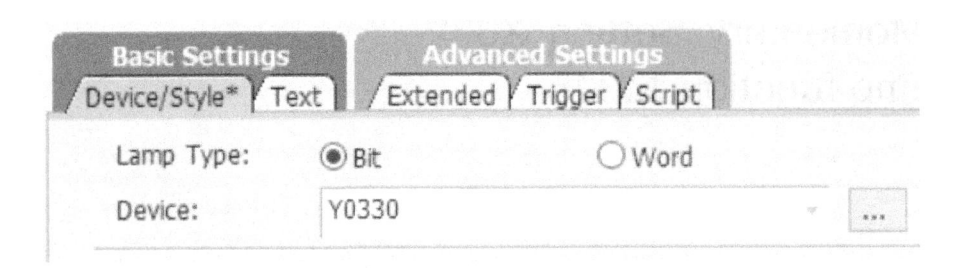

Then, when you click "Figure...", a list of images will be displayed. After clicking "Lamp OFF" in the display figure, set the color to "orange" and the shape to "FA control (no frame) lamp figure A1", number 9. Select the shape of Then, after clicking on the lamp ON of the display figure, select "Orange" for the color, select shape No. 10 in "FA control (no frame) lamp figure A1" for the shape, and press OK on the lower right.

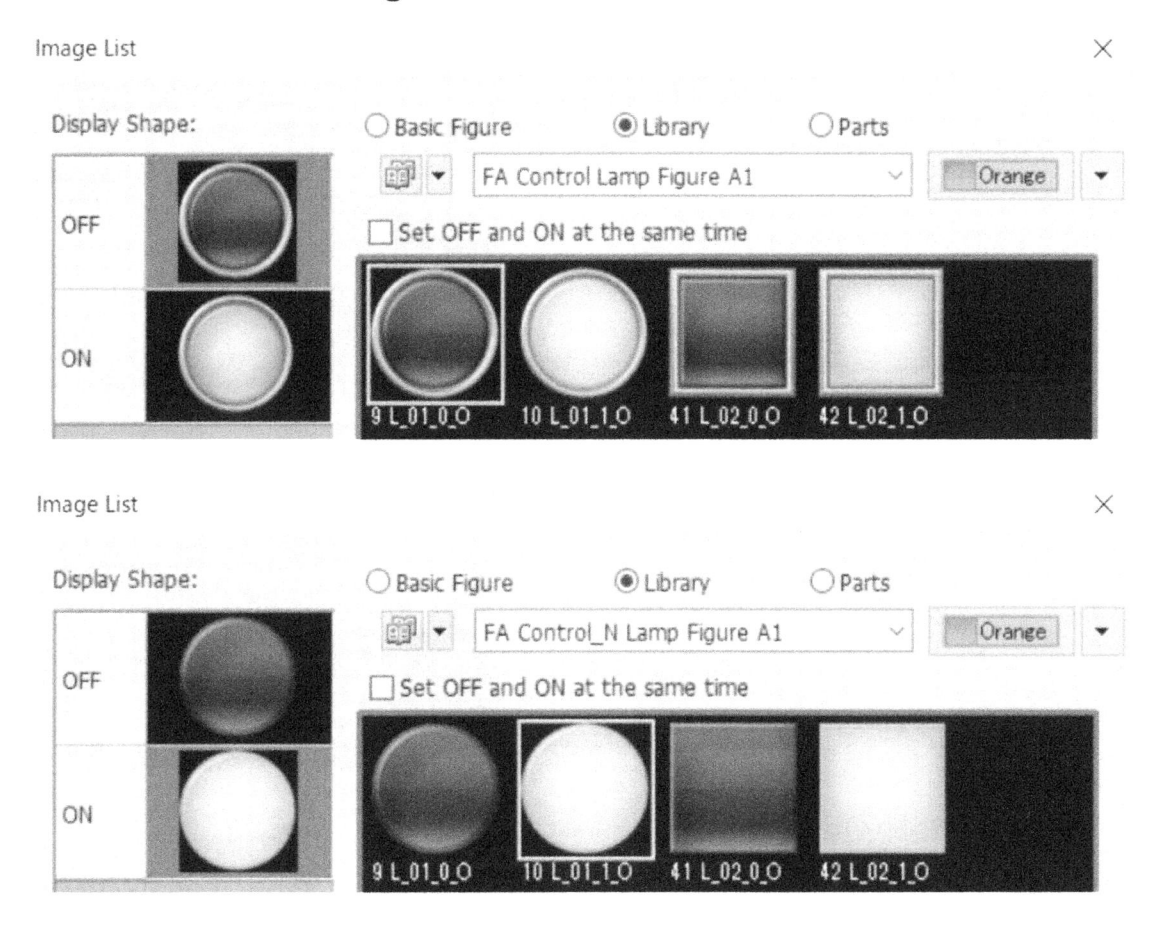

Set the size and position to X: 595 Y: 160 Width 33 Height: 33.

Then add the word "Run" above the lamp. "Figure" tab ⇒ Click the text, click the screen, set the text string to "Run", set the text size to 14, and press OK at the bottom right. And set the position to X: 600 Y: 145. This completes the creation of the running lamp.

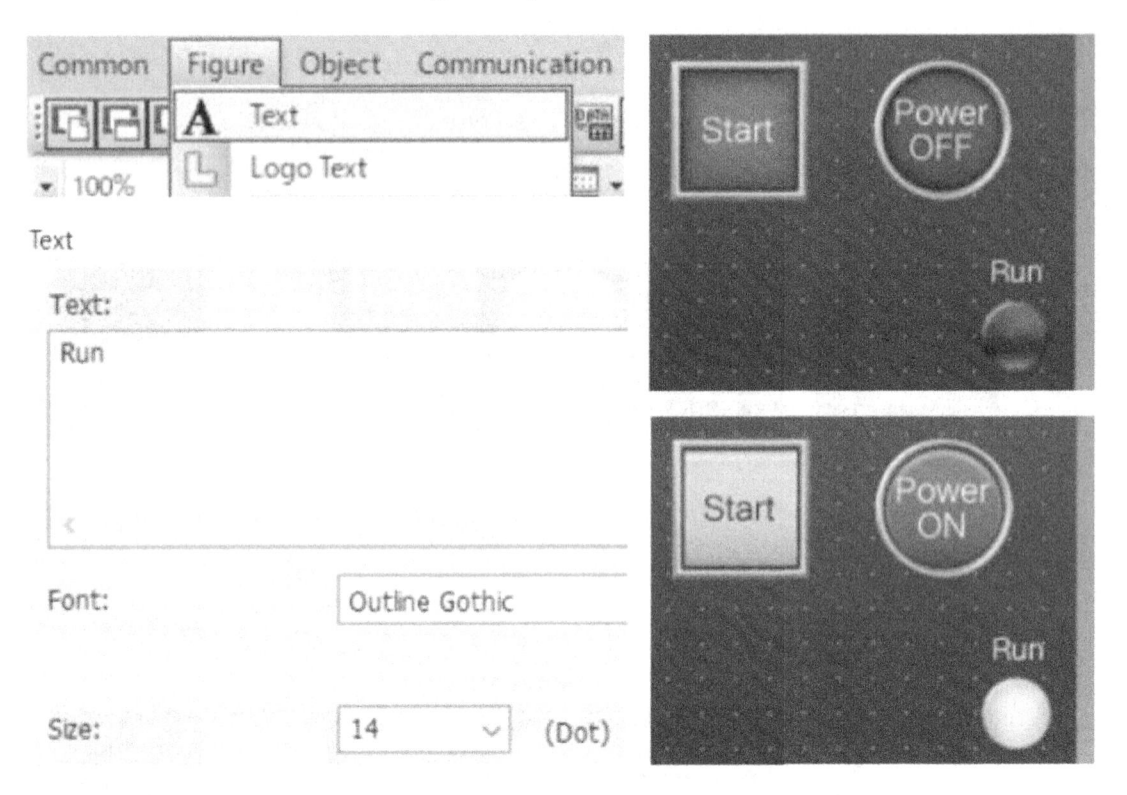

9. Next, create a buzzer/each process in progress/each process completed lamp. We will copy and create the driving lamp that we created earlier.

<buzzer lamp>

Copy the button during operation ⇒ Paste ⇒ After clicking the screen, double-click the part to perform each setting

[Device/Style]
Device: Y335
Figure color with lamp OFF: Yellow
Figure color when lamp is ON: Yellow
[Placement/size] X: 595 Y: 220 Width: 33 Height: 33

Copy the text "Run" ⇒ Paste ⇒ Click on the screen, then double-click on the part to perform each setting
[Character] String: Buzzer
[Placement/size] X: 580 Y: 200 Width: 54 (Height: 18)

<Operating lamp (filling water)>

Copy the button during operation ⇒ Paste ⇒ After clicking the screen, double-click the part to perform each setting

[Device/Style]
Device: Y331
Figure color with lamp OFF: blue
Figure color when lamp is ON: blue.
[Placement/Size] X: 280 Y: 300 Width: 33 Height: 33

Copy the text "Run" ⇒ Paste ⇒ Click on the screen, then double-click on the part to perform each setting
【letter】
Text column: In operation
[Placement/Size] X: 270 Y: 265 Width: 59 (Height: 28)

< **In-operation lamp (during washing, rinsing, dehydration)** >

After clicking the operating lamp (injection) created earlier, select the "Edit" tab ⇒ Consecutive Copy.

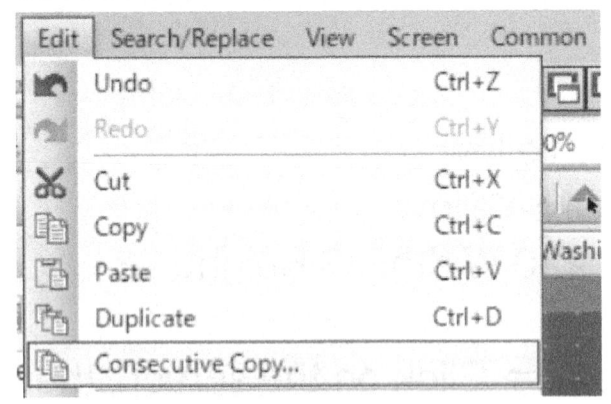

Edit	Search/Replace	View	Screen	Common
Undo			Ctrl+Z	
Redo			Ctrl+Y	
Cut			Ctrl+X	
Copy			Ctrl+C	
Paste			Ctrl+V	
Duplicate			Ctrl+D	
Consecutive Copy...				

On the continuous copy screen, Y direction: 4 * Enter the number including the operating lamp (filling). Spacing: Check Include figures/objects, Y direction: 46 * Enter the number for the spacing you want to open +1. Increment target: Check the device number, Increment setting: After entering 1 at once, press OK at the bottom right.

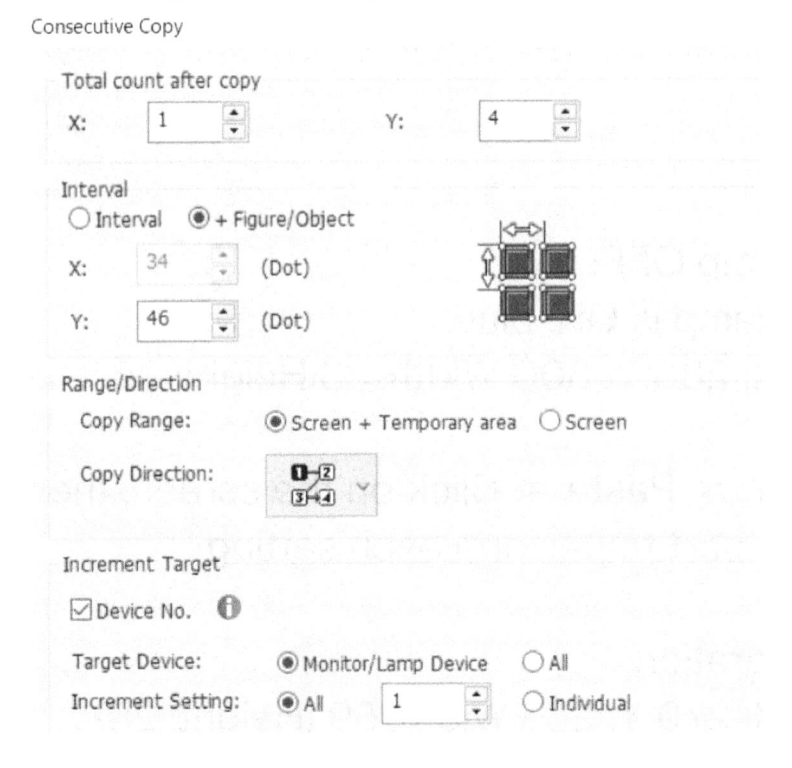

Consecutive Copy

Total count after copy
X: 1   Y: 4

Interval
○ Interval ● + Figure/Object
X: 34 (Dot)
Y: 46 (Dot)

Range/Direction
Copy Range: ● Screen + Temporary area   ○ Screen
Copy Direction: ①→②
                 ③→④

Increment Target
☑ Device No.
Target Device: ● Monitor/Lamp Device   ○ All
Increment Setting: ● All   1   ○ Individual

This completes the active lamps (washing, rinsing, spinning).

< **Completion lamp (filling completion, washing completion, rinsing completion, dehydration completion)** >

Enclose the 4 lamps other than the characters in operation while holding down the left click, copy ⇒ After pasting, click on the place where there was a line above the lamp in operation and to the left of the buzzer lamp, the position will be X: 595 will be If the position is misaligned, select 4 lamps, and set X: 595.

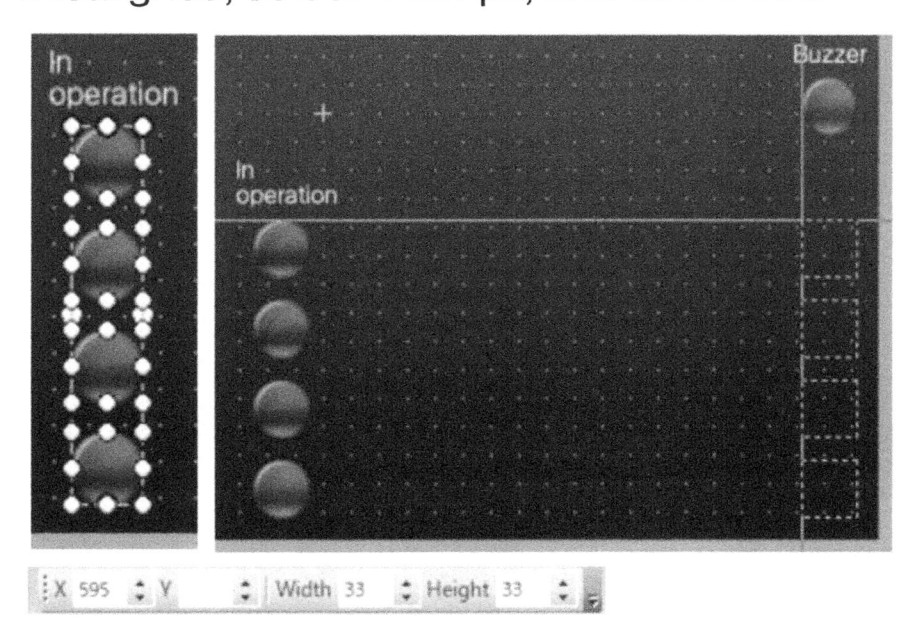

With the four lamps selected, press the condition OFF and condition ON + buttons in the properties at the bottom left to change the color of each figure to green. If the properties are not displayed, you can display them with Alt+1.

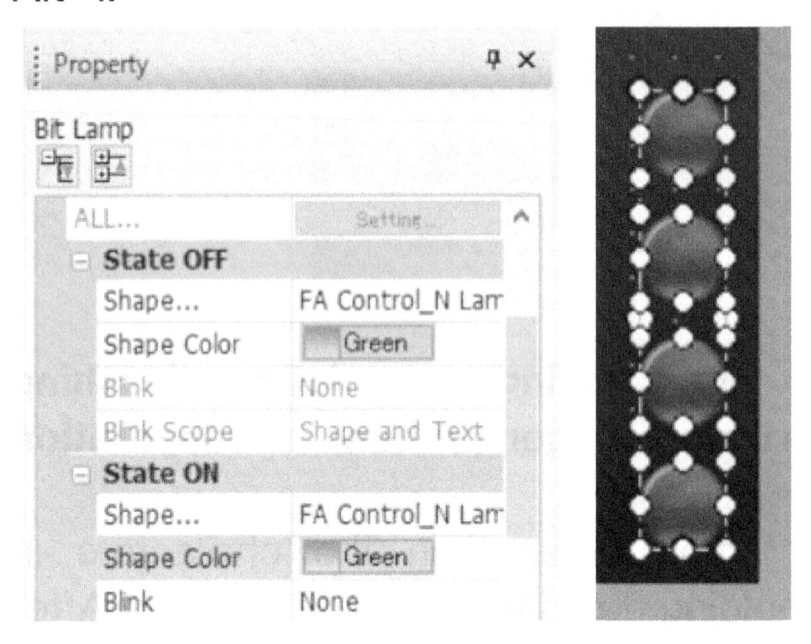

Batch change the device of the completion lamp. Press Ctrl + F3 with 4 lamps selected, or right click ⇒ Batch Edit ⇒ Select devices.

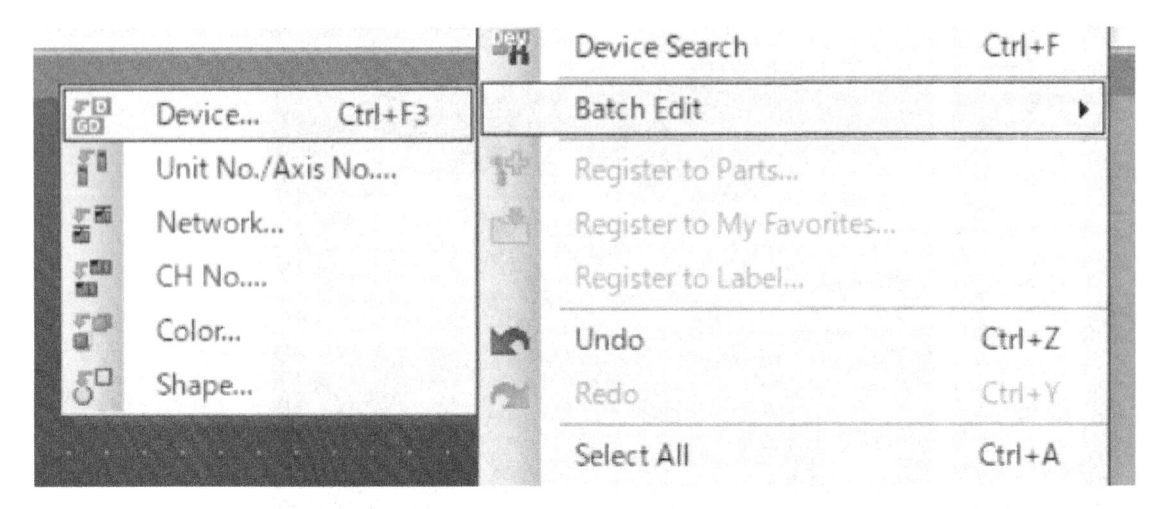

On the batch change screen, change the device after change as shown below, and then press Change.

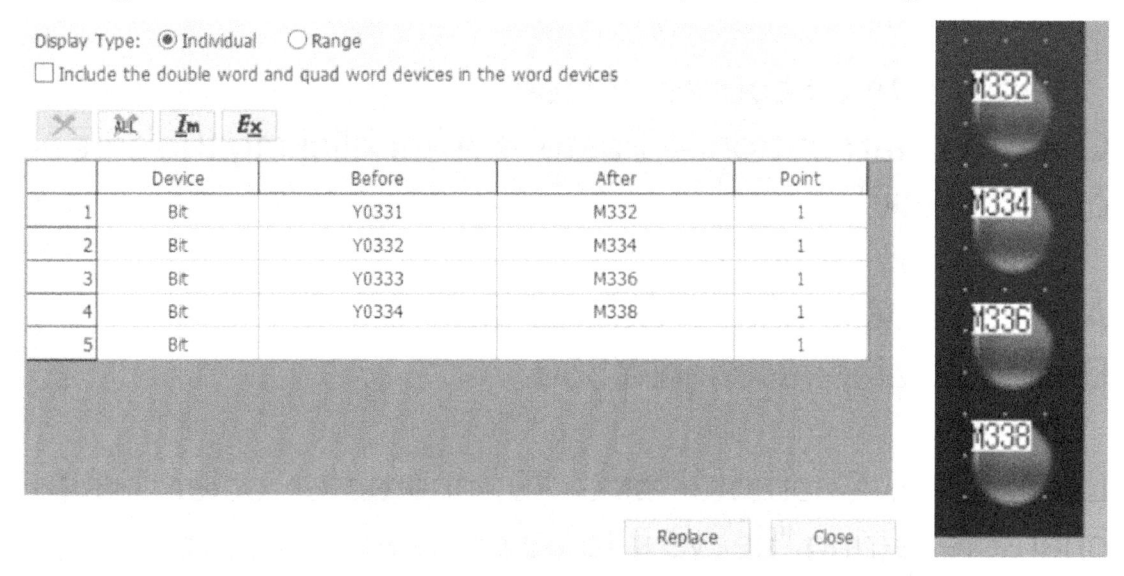

	Device	Before	After	Point
1	Bit	Y0331	M332	1
2	Bit	Y0332	M334	1
3	Bit	Y0333	M336	1
4	Bit	Y0334	M338	1
5	Bit			1

This completes the creation of each completed lamp.
Copy the text "In operation" ⇒ Paste ⇒ After clicking the screen, double-click the part to perform each setting
【letter】 String: Completed
[Placement/Size] X: 565 Y: 275 Width: 68 (Height: 14)

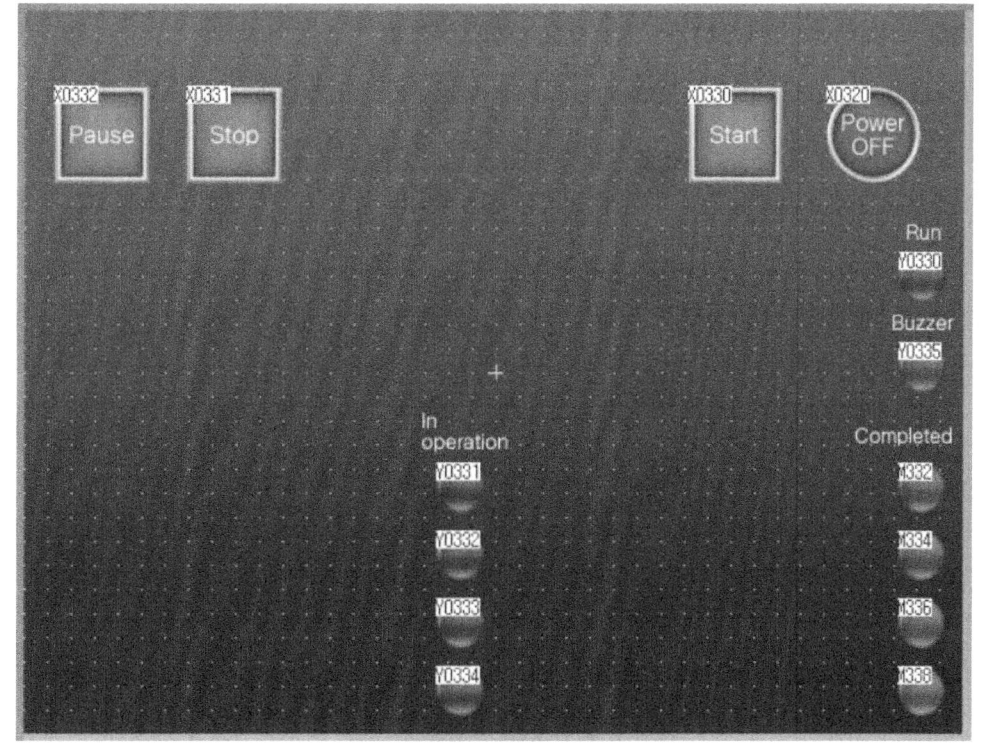

10. Next, create the Omakase course button and the setting time display for each process.

<Leave it to us course button>
Copy the start button ⇒ Paste ⇒ After clicking the screen, double-click the part to perform each setting
　【Operation setting】
Action: Bit Momentary, Setting: X321
Device of lamp function: Y350
　【letter】
Lamp OFF: Character size 20, character color "white", character string "Leave it to us course"
Lamp ON: Character size 20, character color "black", character string "Leave it to us course"
[Placement/size]
X: 20 Y: 150 Width: 100 Height: 80

<Injection work setting time display>
First, create the characters for "Injection time" and "Sec".

Copy the text of "Run" ⇒ Paste ⇒ Click on the screen
　【letter】
Character string: Injection time, character size: 18
[Placement/size] X: 10 Y: 310 Width: 106 (Height: 18)

Copy the text of " Injection time" ⇒ Paste ⇒ Click on the screen
　【letter】
Character string: Sec, character size: 18
[Placement/size] X: 230 Y: 310 Width: 29 (Height: 18)

Next, create the display part of the set time. After clicking the "Object" tab ⇒ Numeric display/Input ⇒ Numerical Display, click the screen.

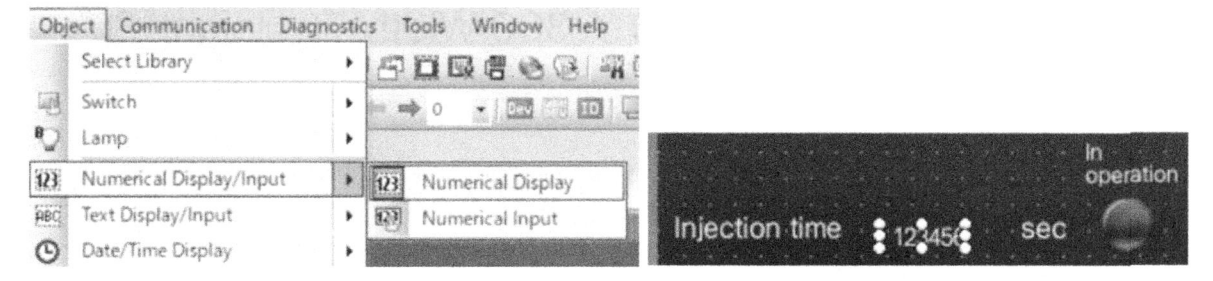

Double-click the part to make each setting. Regarding the number of display digits, since the timer on the PLC side is in units of 0.1 seconds, adjust the display on the touch panel side so that it is also in units of 0.1 seconds.

【device】
Device: D350, Number size: 20, Alignment: Centered, Display format: Real number (The data format is a signed BIN16 integer, with a decimal point only for appearance) Number of digits in integer part: 2, Number of digits in decimal part: 1, Preview value: 123

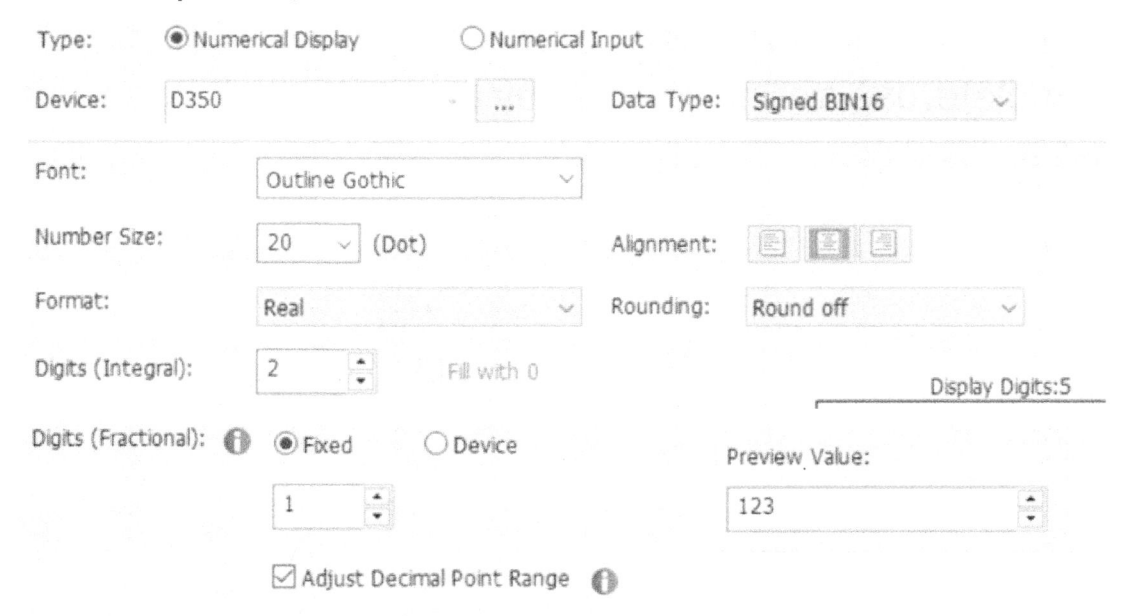

【style】

After clicking "Shape...", select number 7 of "71 Square_3D_Fixed Width" and press OK to close.
[Placement/Size]　X: 150 Y: 300 Width: 75 Height: 35

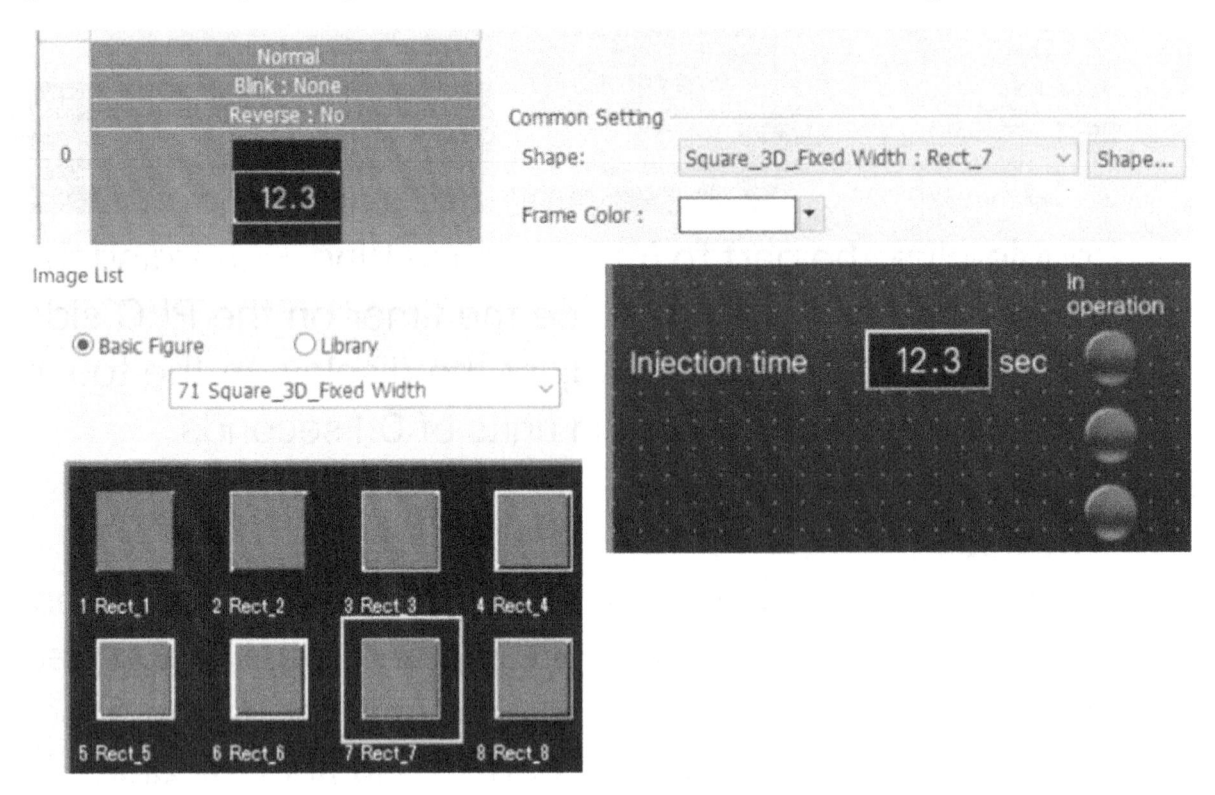

Now that the irrigation process set time display is complete, use a continuous copy to create each remaining set time display.

＜Washing / rinsing / dehydration process set time display＞

After selecting all the characters and display parts, select the "Edit" tab ⇒ Continuous copy. Then, the total number after copying: X direction: 1, Y direction: 4, check Include figure/object at interval, Y direction at interval: 46, check device number to be incremented, set to 1 at once, Press OK at the bottom. After that, change the characters of "water injection time" to each process name and the creation is completed.

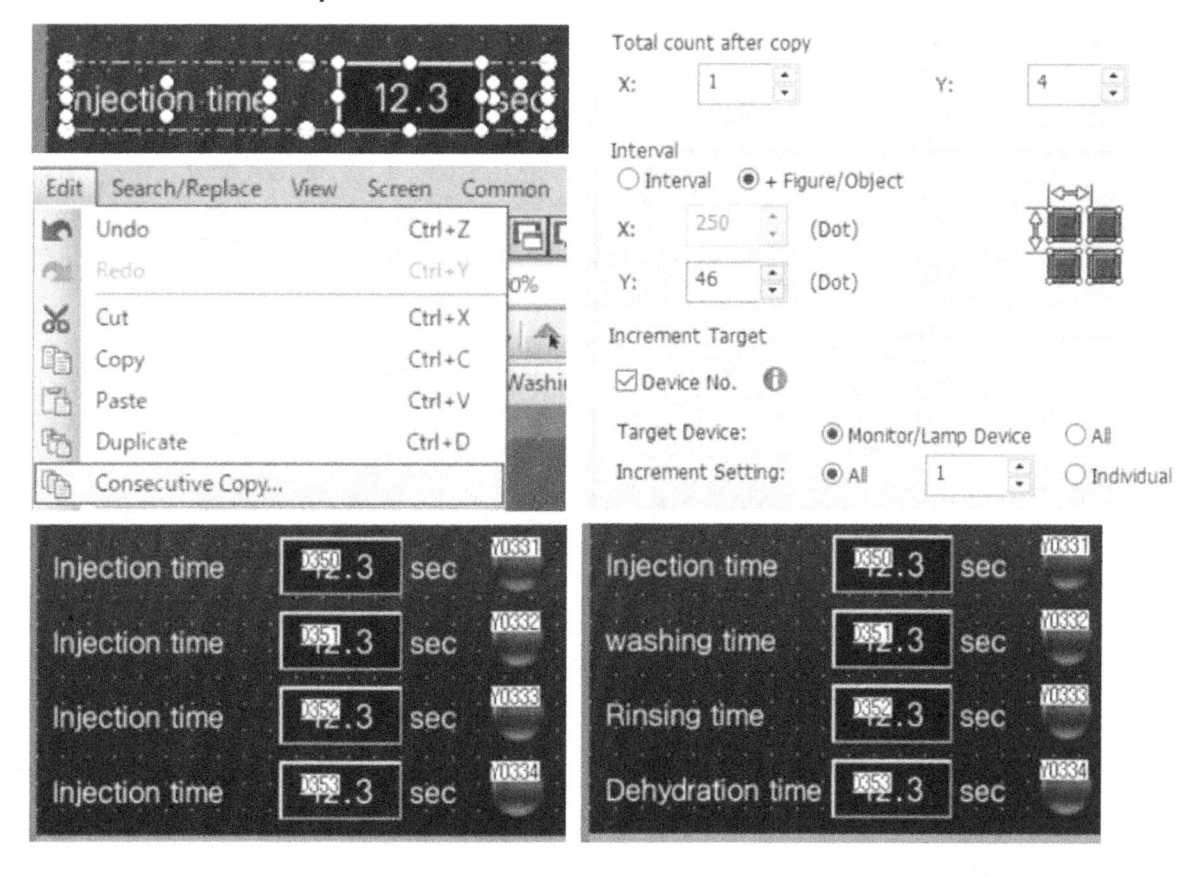

Finally, create the outer frame. After clicking the "Shape" tab ⇒ Rectangle, move the mouse while holding down the left click to create a rectangle. Then set the placement and size to X: 5 Y: 142 Width: 255 Height: 335 and it's complete.

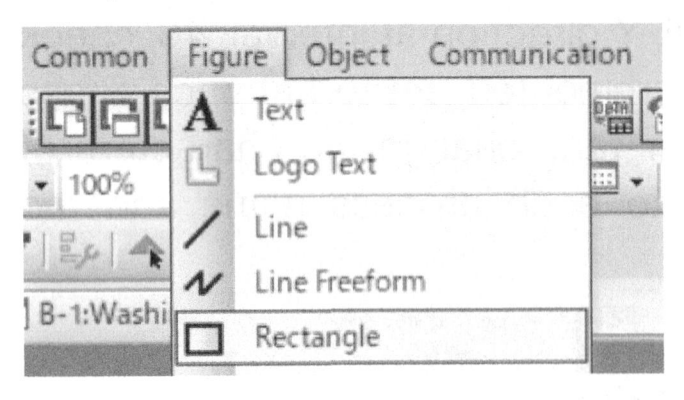

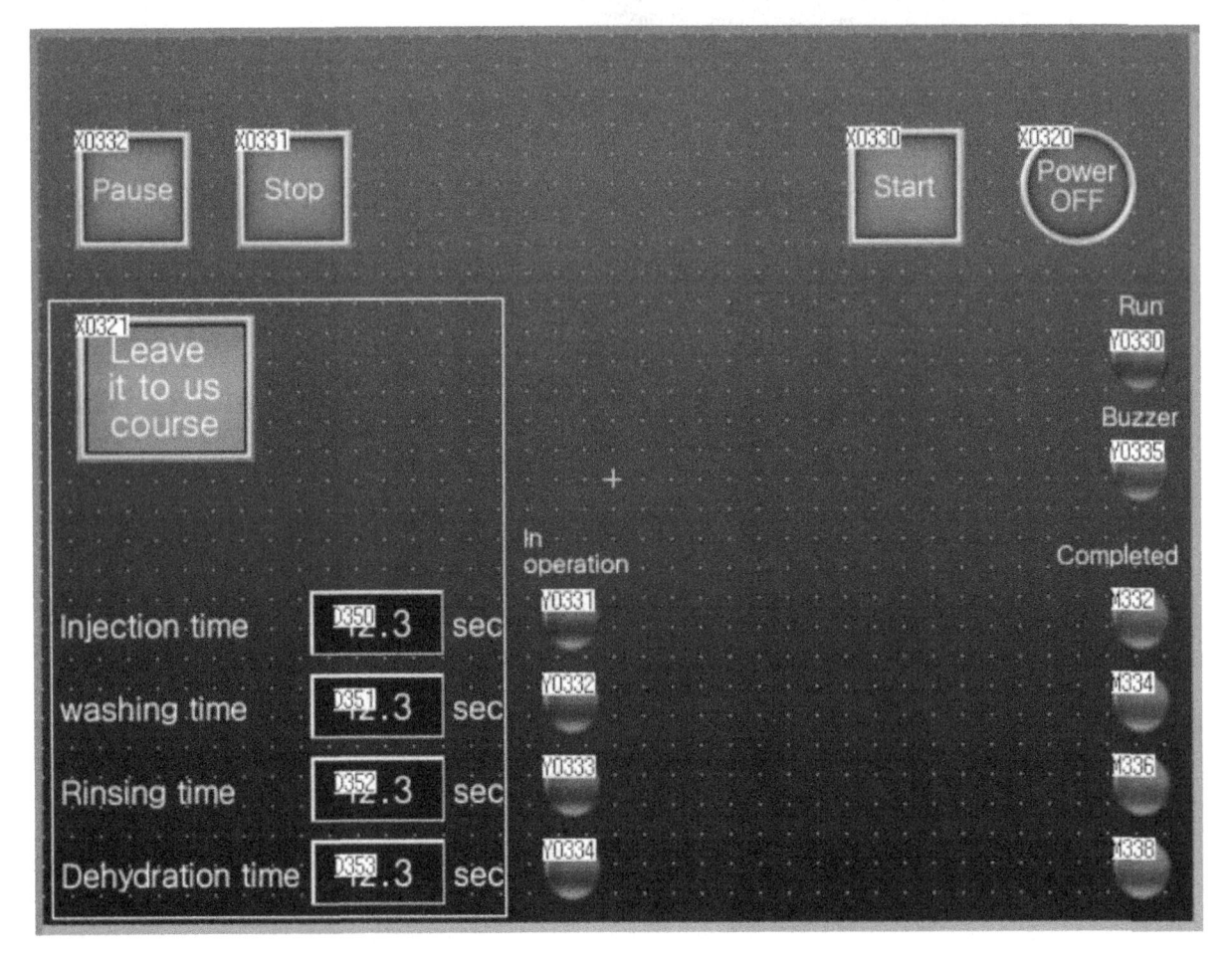

11. Next, create the remaining time to complete washing and the remaining time display for each process. First, create a remaining time display for each process.

First, create the PLC program side. First, regarding the device, create D370 remaining time for water filling, D371 remaining time for washing, D372 remaining time for rinsing, D373 remaining time for dehydration, and D374 remaining time for washing completion. Create a location under Washer Pause.

First, the remaining water injection time can be obtained by calculating the water injection time setting D350 - water injection execution time ST331, so create a program as follows. For the instruction part, press F8 and enter "-D350 ST331 D370".

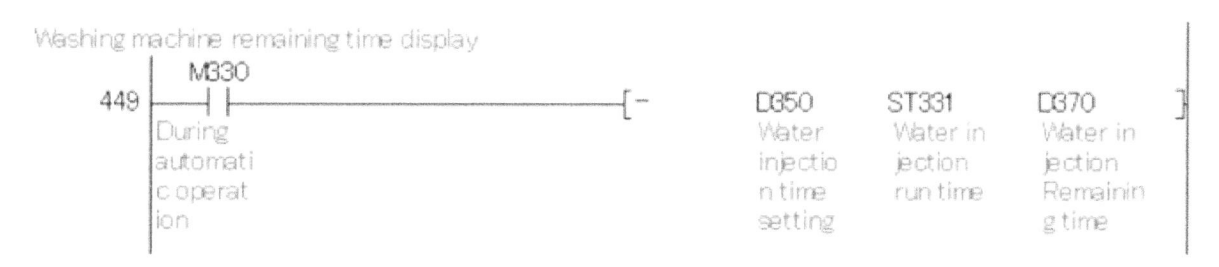

```
Washing machine remaining time display
           M330
 449  ──┤ ├──────────────────────[-   D350      ST331      D370   ]
         During                        Water      Water in    Water in
         automati                      injectio   jection     jection
         c operat                      n time     run time    Remainin
         ion                           setting                g time
```

Follow the same procedure to create other remaining time displays for each process.

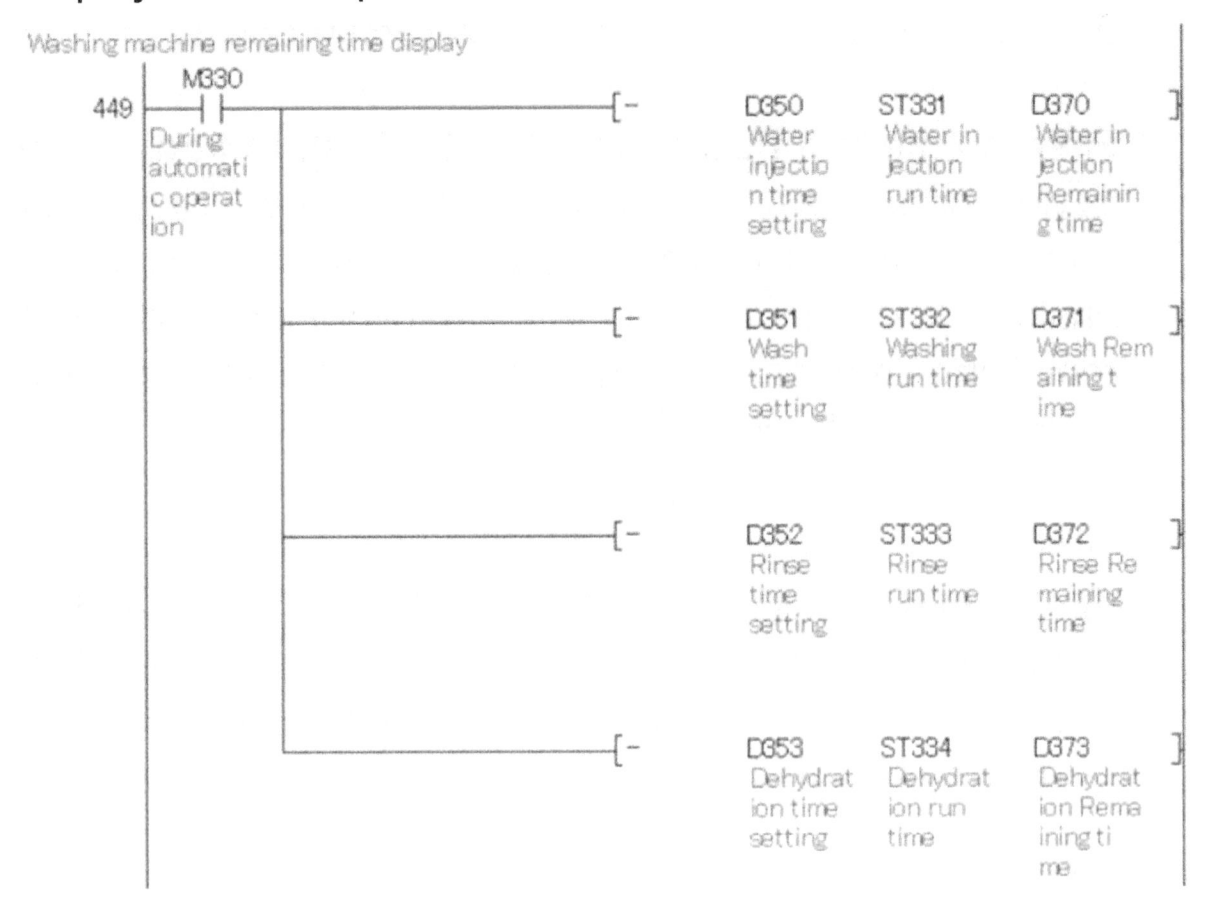

Washing machine remaining time display

```
         M330
449  ─────┤ ├──────────────────[- D350    ST331    D370  ]
         During                    Water   Water in Water in
         automati                  injectio jection jection
         c operat                  n time   run time Remainin
         ion                       setting           g time

                     ─────────────[- D351    ST332    D371  ]
                                    Wash    Washing  Wash Rem
                                    time    run time aining t
                                    setting          ime

                     ─────────────[- D352    ST333    D372  ]
                                    Rinse   Rinse    Rinse Re
                                    time    run time maining
                                    setting          time

                     ─────────────[- D353    ST334    D373  ]
                                    Dehydrat Dehydrat Dehydrat
                                    ion time ion run  ion Rema
                                    setting  time     ining ti
                                                      me
```

Next, create the remaining time for washing completion. It would be nice to display the sum of D370 to D373 in D374 but using the addition command (+) would make the circuit quite long.

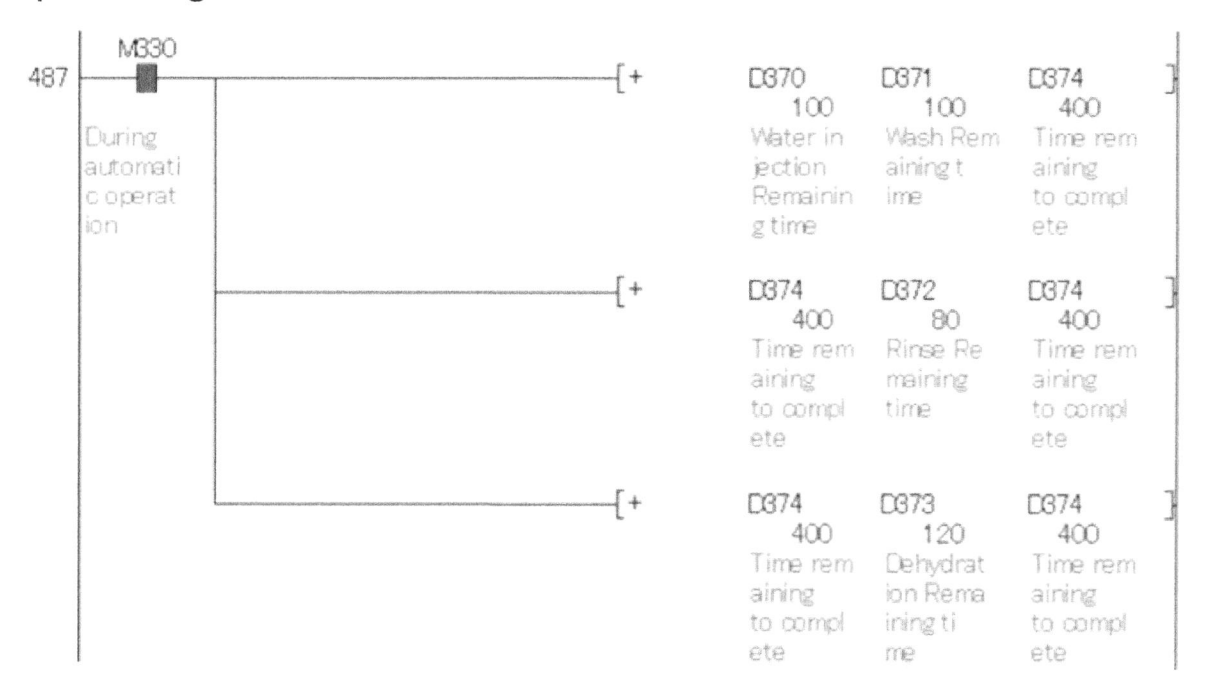

```
       M330
487 ────┤ ├──────────────────────────[+  D370    D371    D374  ]
        During                           100     100     400
        automati                         Water in Wash Rem Time rem
        c operat                         jection  aining t aining
        ion                              Remainin ime     to compl
                                         g time           ete

                                     [+  D374    D372    D374  ]
                                         400     80      400
                                         Time rem Rinse Re Time rem
                                         aining  maining aining
                                         to compl time    to compl
                                         ete              ete

                                     [+  D374    D373    D374  ]
                                         400     120     400
                                         Time rem Dehydrat Time rem
                                         aining  ion Rema aining
                                         to compl ining ti to compl
                                         ete      me      ete
```

So, this time **Total value calculation instruction (WSUM)**Use the. By using this, you can create a circuit with only one line. To write, press F8 and enter "WSUM D370 D374 K4". This means "Start with D370, add four words from there, and put them in D374". Please remember this as it is convenient to remember.

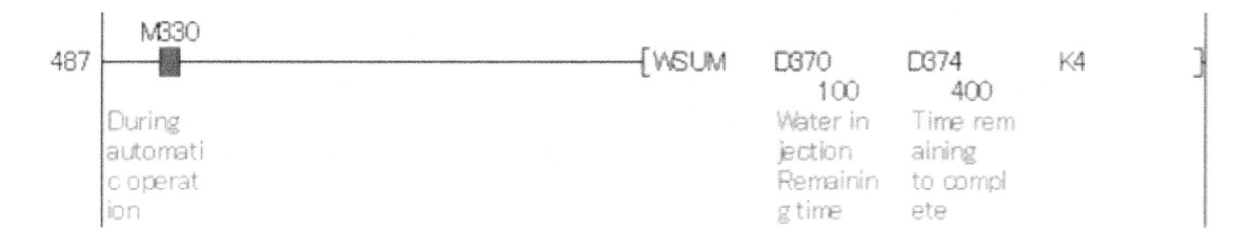

```
       M330
487 ────┤ ├──────────────────────[WSUM  D370    D374    K4  ]
        During                          100     400
        automati                        Water in Time rem
        c operat                        jection  aining
        ion                             Remainin to compl
                                        g time   ete
```

Finally, create a circuit to reset the remaining time of each process. Reset during automatic operation (M330) or when the power (X320) is turned off. Press F8 and enter "FMOV K0 D370 K5" for the command word.

```
        M330
492 ─────┤/├──────────────────────[FMOV   K0      D370        K5  ]
        During                                    Water in
        automati                                  jection
        c operat                                  Remainin
        ion                                       g time

        X320
    ─────┤/├──
        Washing
        machine
        power ON
```

This completes the creation of the PLC program. Now let's create the screen.

<Remaining time display for each process>
Copy ⇒ Paste the parts created in the Omakase Course. Currently, paste it so that it matches the upper surface of the numerical display part.

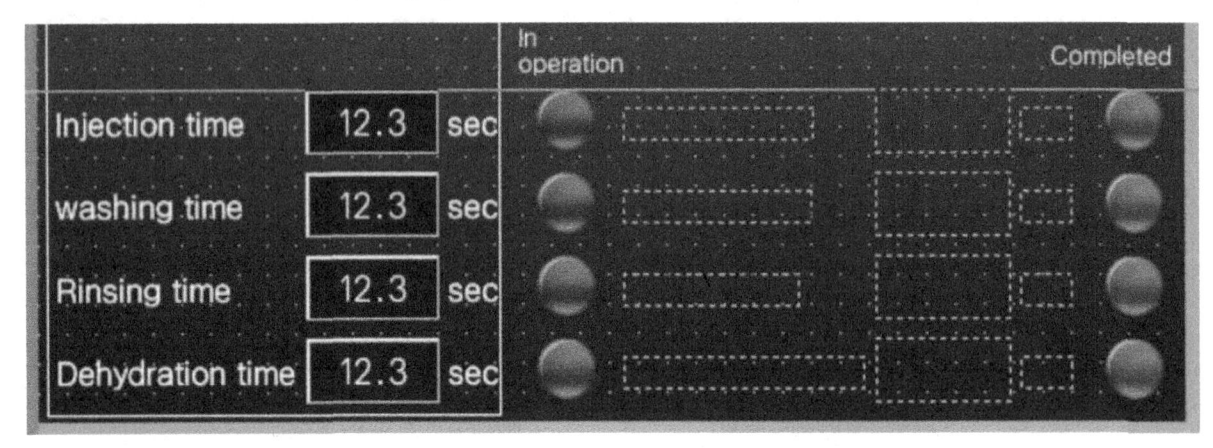

			In operation			Completed
Injection time	12.3	sec	●	[....]	[....]	●
washing time	12.3	sec	●	[....]	[....]	●
Rinsing time	12.3	sec	●	[....]	[....]	●
Dehydration time	12.3	sec	●	[....]	[....]	●

Change the device of the numeric display part. After selecting four numerical display parts, press Ctrl + F3 or right click ⇒ change all ⇒ select device. Then, after checking "Batch" for the display method on the display screen, set the device after change to D370 to D373 and press OK at the bottom right to complete the batch change of devices, so click "Close" at the bottom right. Push to close.

Display Type: ○ Individual ● Range
☐ Include the double word and quad word devices in the word devices

	Device	Before	After	Point
1	Word	D350~D353	D370~D373	4
2	Bit			1

After that, change the character and adjust the position.

remaining characters
: Change the characters as shown in the screen below.
Remaining time character position
: After selecting 4, set to X: 340
Position of numeric parts
: After selecting 4, set to X: 485
second character position
: After selecting 4, set to X: 565

And copy the text of "Injection time" ⇒ Paste ⇒ Click on the screen
　【letter】
Character string: Time Remaining, character size: 18
[Placement/size] X: 340 Y: 275 Width: 128 (Height: 18)

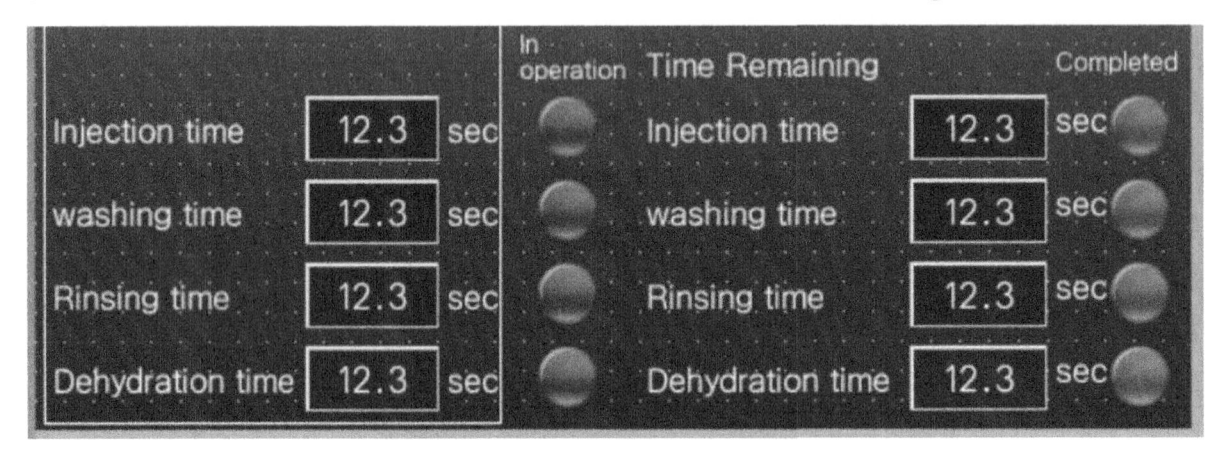

Next, create a display of the remaining time after washing is completed.

<Washing completion remaining time display>
Copy "Injection time" ⇒ After pasting and clicking, set Text: Completed time remaining, Text size: 18, Placement/Size to X: 270, Y: 170, Width: 117 (Height: 36).

Copy "Sec" ⇒ Paste, click, and set the placement and size to X: 490 Y: 180 Width: 29 (Height: 18).

Copy the remaining numerical display parts during injection ⇒ Paste, click,
【device】
Device: D374, Number size: 20, Number of digits in integer part: 3, Preview value: 1234
After changing to press OK at the bottom right.
[Placement/size]
X: 400 Y: 170 Width: 85 Height: 35

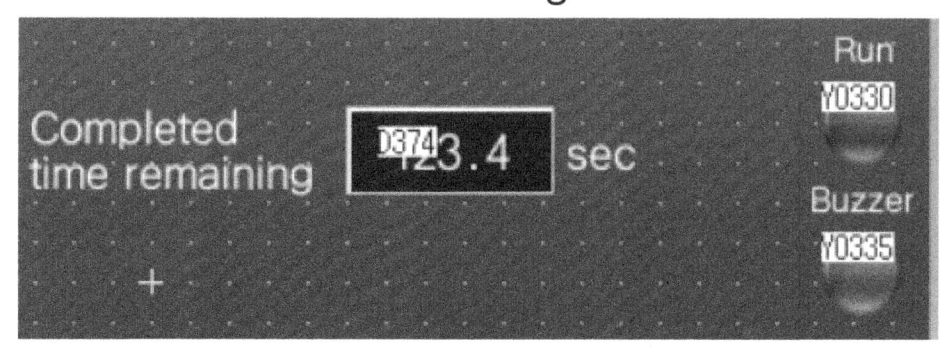

12. Next, create a monitor display.

First, we will create a PLC program. Device on the monitor display: Using D330 D330=1: Filling, D330=2: Washing, D330=3: Rinsing, D330=4: Spinning, D330=5: Washing complete, D330=6: Create a circuit that displays D330=90: Clogging error, D330=91: Leakage error during pause. Display only when the power (X320) is turned on.

Also, since it is not possible to know what to display depending on the state of the D330 from the circuit alone, we will use a notebook to make it possible to understand the display when each numerical value is entered.
Create a location under the washing machine remaining time display.

D330 = 1 at Y331 ON (filling), D330 = 2 at Y332 ON (during washing), D330 = 3 at Y333 ON (during rinsing)

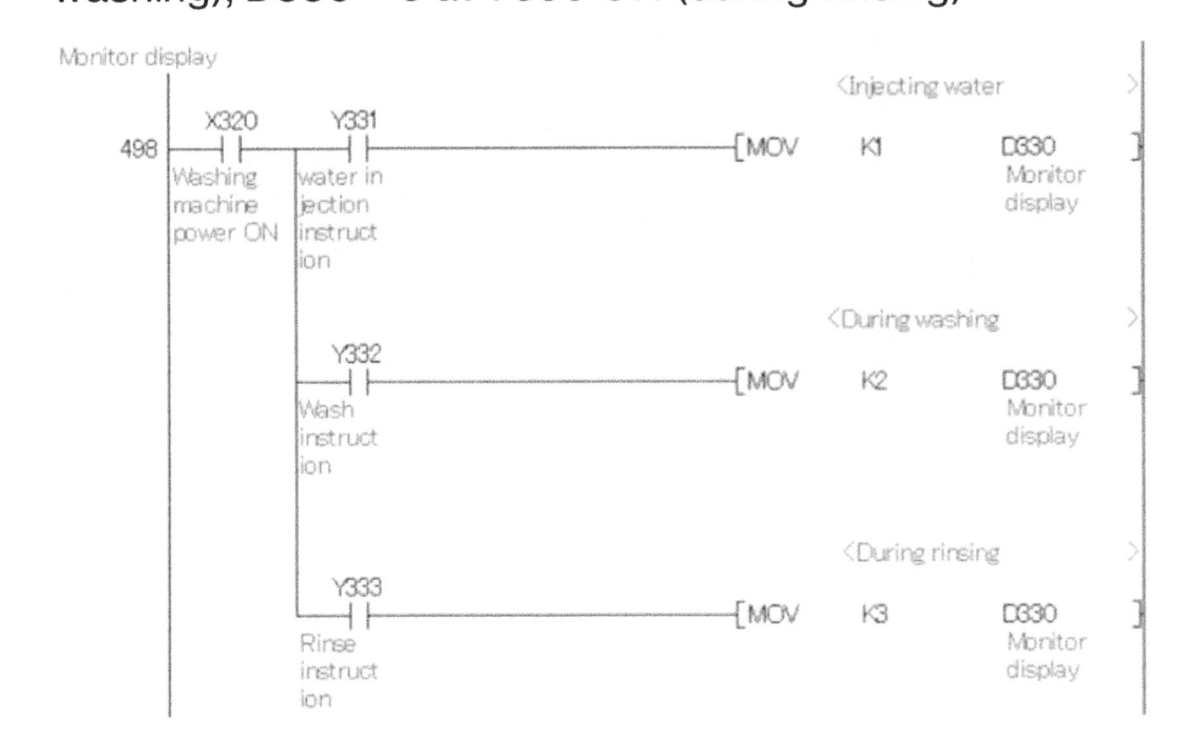

```
Monitor display
                                                          <Injecting water
       X320      Y331
 498 ──┤├───────┤├──────────────────────[MOV   K1       D330      ]
      Washing   water in                                 Monitor
      machine   jection                                  display
      power ON  instruct
                ion

                                                          <During washing
                Y332
        ────────┤├──────────────────────[MOV   K2       D330      ]
                Wash                                     Monitor
                instruct                                 display
                ion

                                                          <During rinsing
                Y333
        ────────┤├──────────────────────[MOV   K3       D330      ]
                Rinse                                    Monitor
                instruct                                 display
                ion
```

Y334 ON D330 = 4 (drying), M339 ON D330 = 5 (washing completed), M348 ON D330 = 6 (paused)

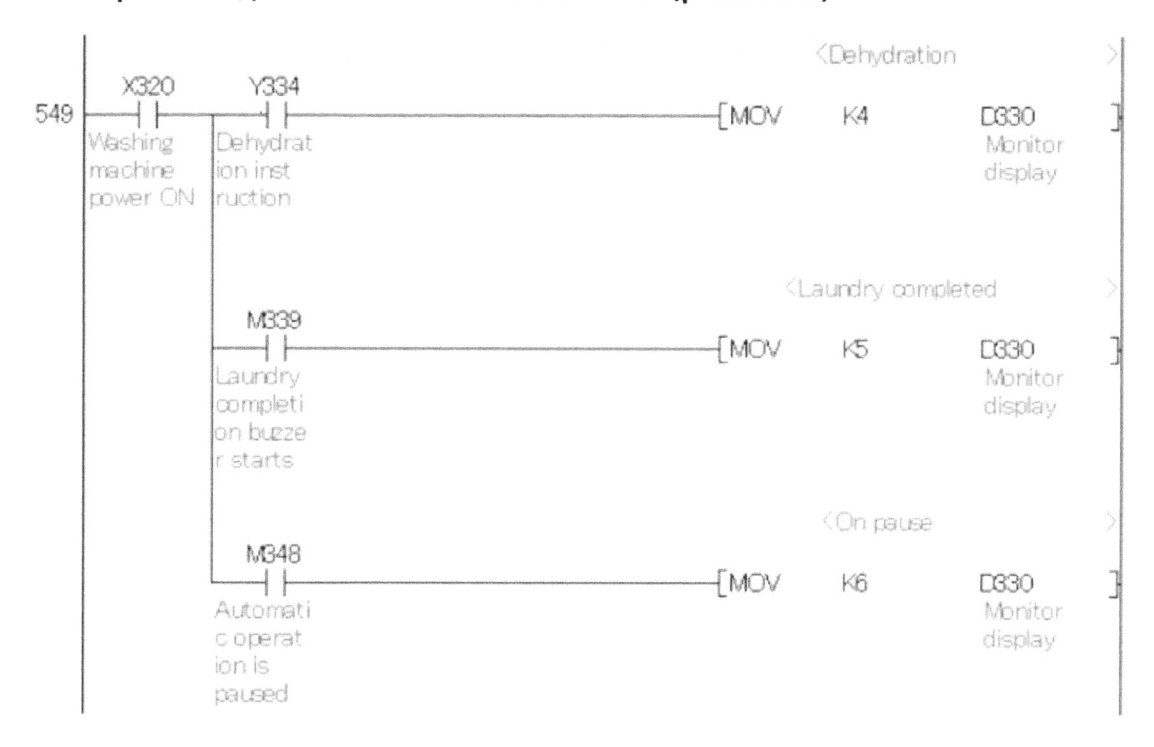

```
                                                        <Dehydration>
      X320      Y334
549 ──┤├───────┤├──────────────────────[MOV   K4    D330 ]
    Washing  Dehydrat                               Monitor
    machine  ion inst                               display
    power ON ruction

                                                     <Laundry completed>
               M339
          ─────┤├──────────────────────[MOV   K5    D330 ]
             Laundry                                Monitor
             completi                               display
             on buzze
             r starts

                                                     <On pause>
               M348
          ─────┤├──────────────────────[MOV   K6    D330 ]
             Automati                               Monitor
             c operat                               display
             ion is
             paused
```

D330=90 at X326ON (clogging error), D330=91 at X327ON (leakage error)

```
                                                     <Clogging Abnormality>
      X320      X326
587 ──┤├───────┤├──────────────────────[MOV   K90   D330 ]
    Washing  Filter                                 Monitor
    machine  clogging                               display
    power ON error

                                                     <Leakage Abnormality>
               X327
          ─────┤├──────────────────────[MOV   K91   D330 ]
             Leakage                                Monitor
             Abnormal                               display
             ity
```

The condition for resetting the value of D330 (to 0) is the same timing as the execution time of each process, so create a reset circuit for D330 as follows.

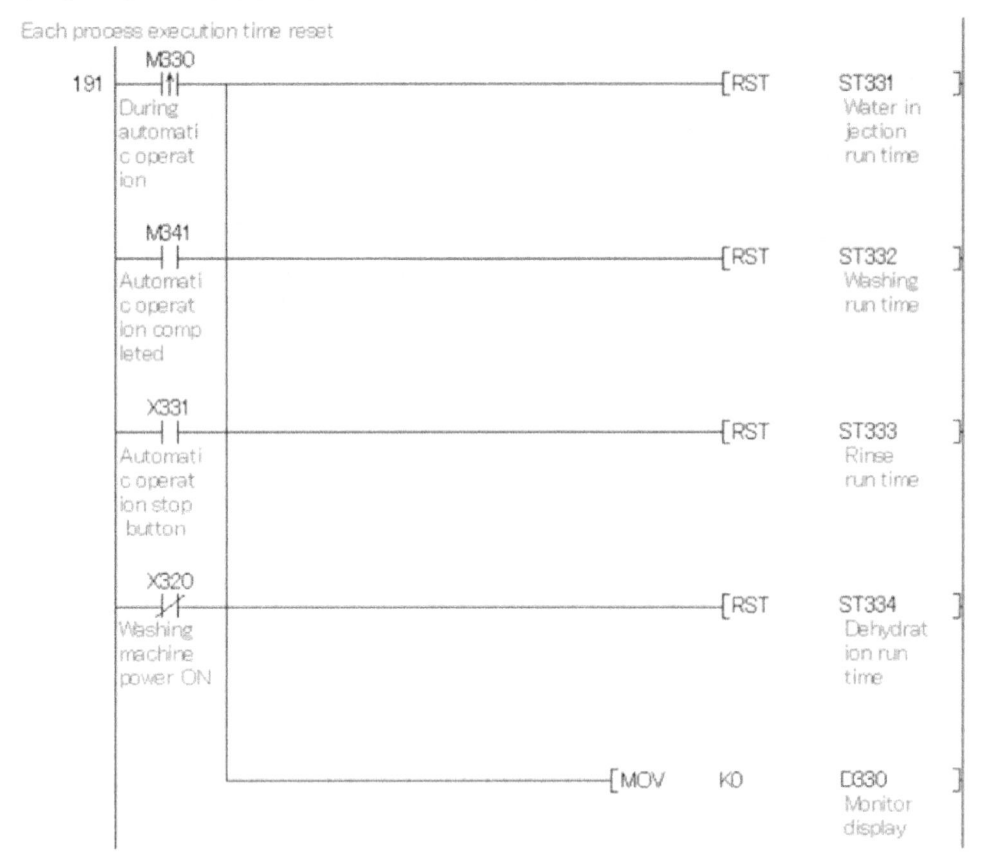

```
Each process execution time reset
         M330
         ─│↑│─                                    ─[RST   ST331  ]
 191    During                                            Water in
        automati                                          jection
        c operat                                          run time
        ion

         M341
         ─│ │─                                    ─[RST   ST332  ]
        Automati                                          Washing
        c operat                                          run time
        ion comp
        leted

         X331
         ─│ │─                                    ─[RST   ST333  ]
        Automati                                          Rinse
        c operat                                          run time
        ion stop
        button

         X320
         ─│↓│─                                    ─[RST   ST334  ]
        Washing                                           Dehydrat
        machine                                           ion run
        power ON                                          time

                                          ─[MOV   K0      D330   ]
                                                          Monitor
                                                          display
```

This time, we will also create a circuit for turning on the buzzer when an error occurs. The buzzer sounds intermittently when an error occurs, and the ON time (T336) is 5 seconds. Places are created below the monitor display.

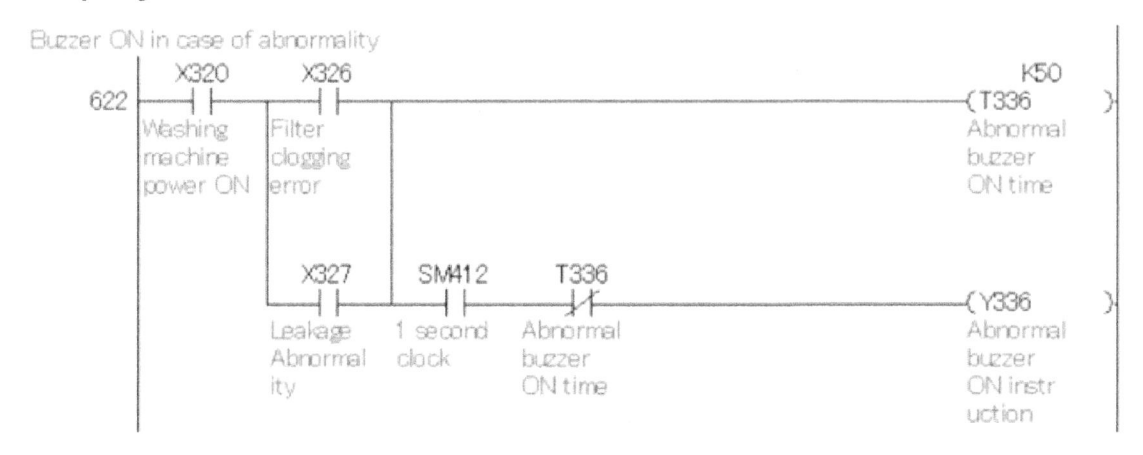

```
Buzzer ON in case of abnormality
         X320     X326                                           K50
 622    ─│ │─────│ │─                                       ─(T336  )─
        Washing  Filter                                          Abnormal
        machine  clogging                                        buzzer
        power ON error                                           ON time

                 X327     SM412    T336
                ─│ │─────│ │──────│↓│─                      ─(Y336  )─
                Leakage  1 second Abnormal                       Abnormal
                Abnormal clock    buzzer                         buzzer
                ity               ON time                        ON instr
                                                                 uction
```

Also, after creating the conditions for the screen washing machine buzzer lamp (Y337), change the screen washing machine buzzer lamp device to Y337. The place is created under the buzzer ON when an error occurs.

Now that the creation of the program is complete, let's create the screen. After selecting the "Object" tab ⇒ Comment display ⇒ Word comment, click the screen and double-click the placed part to make each setting.

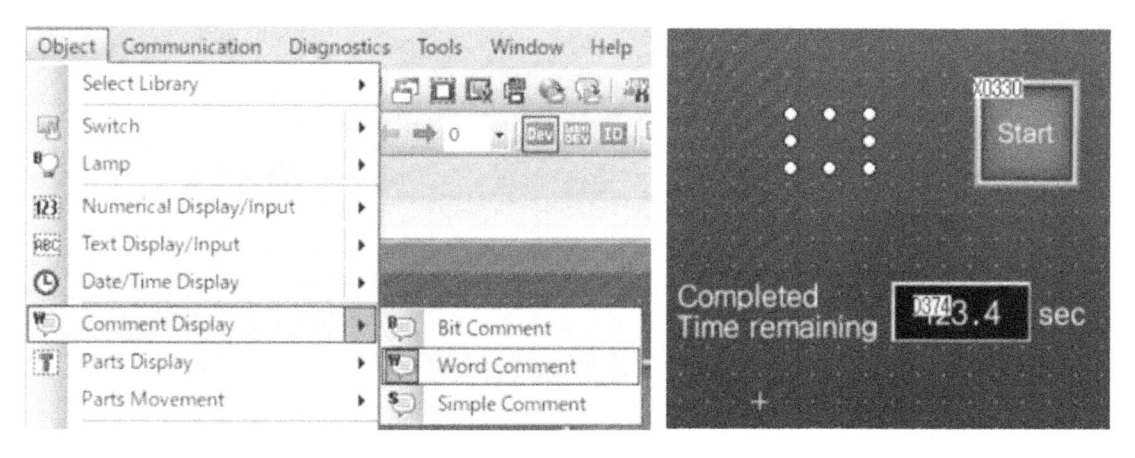

[Device/Style] Device: D330

Figure: After selecting "Shape...", select No. 3 of "71 Square_3D_Fixed Width"

Frame color: Dark white (No. 109)

Shape color: Black (No. 0)

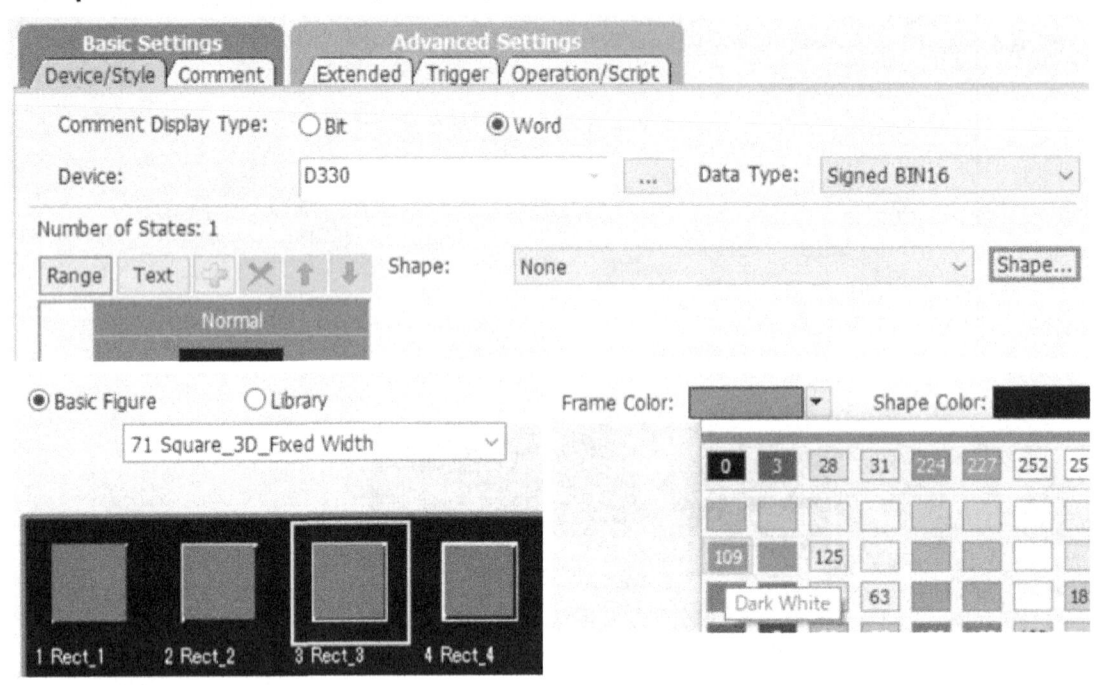

Next, create a condition when a numerical value is entered in D330. If you press the plus mark in the condition number, the following screen will appear. $V==1 has the same meaning as D330=1, so there is no need to change the setting.

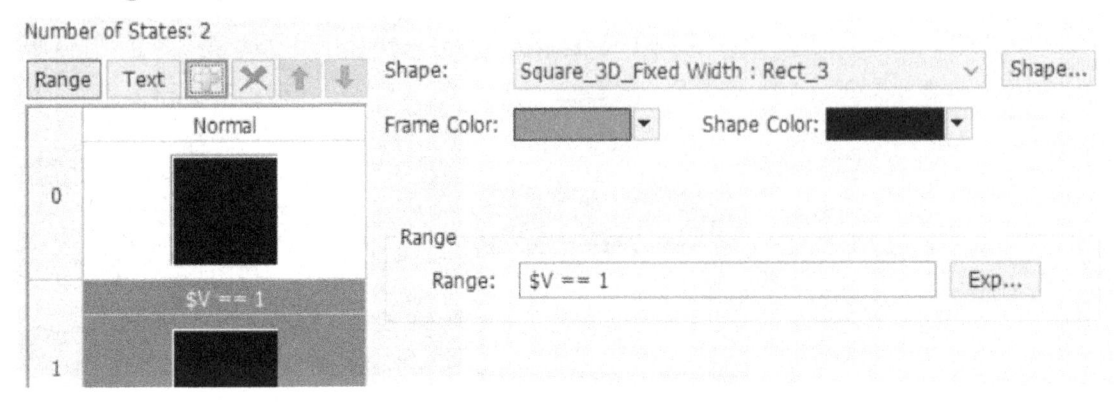

Create up to $V==6 in the same procedure.

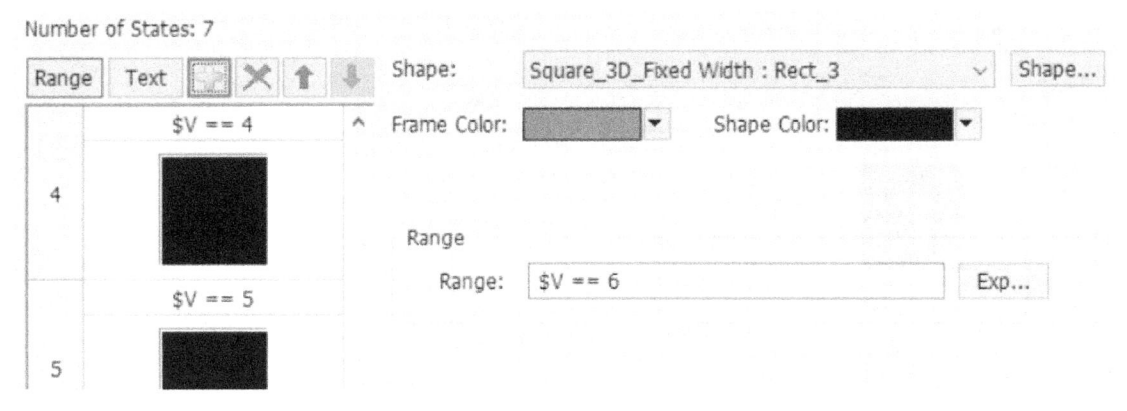

So far, the conditions from D330=1 to D330=6 have been created. Then create conditions for D330=90 and D330=91. After pressing the plus mark in the condition number, click "Range..." in the range. Then change the B constant to 90 on the range input screen and press OK. Also, change the figure color to dark red (No. 160) so that it can be identified as an abnormal display.

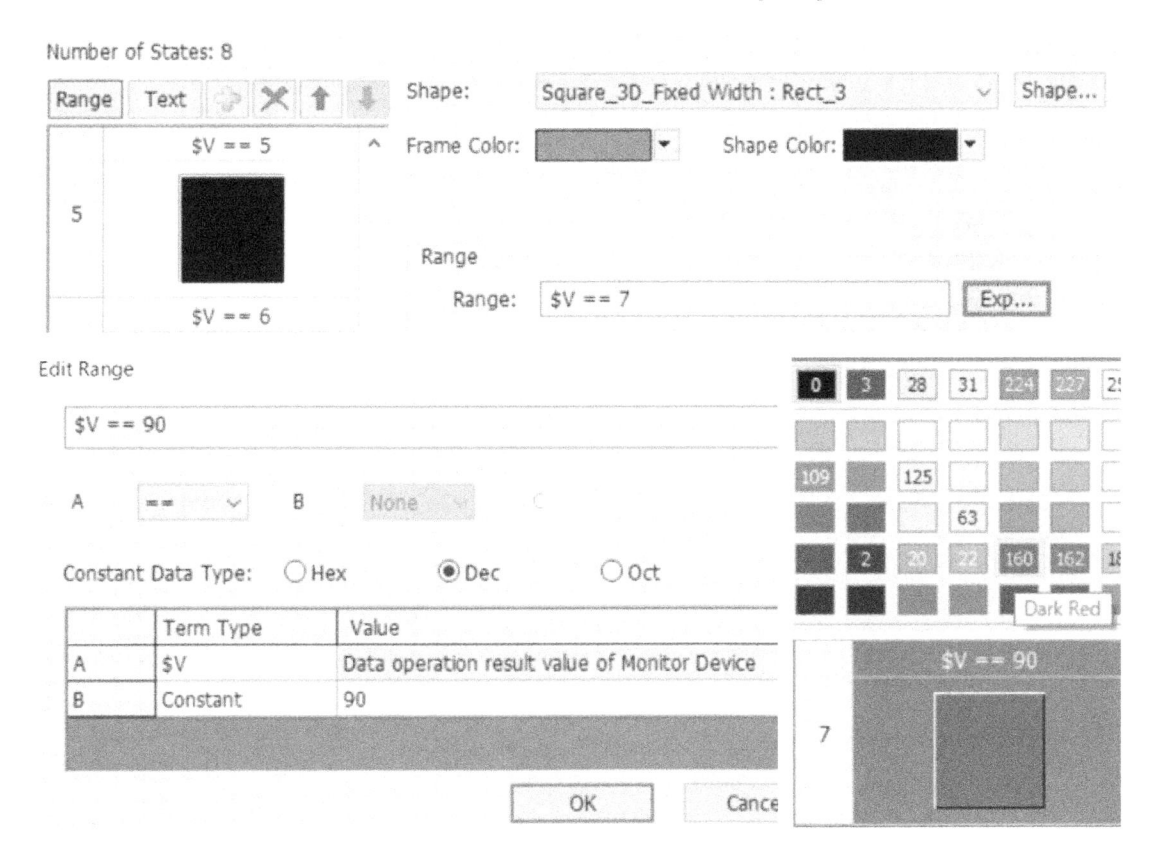

Create D330=91 in the same way.

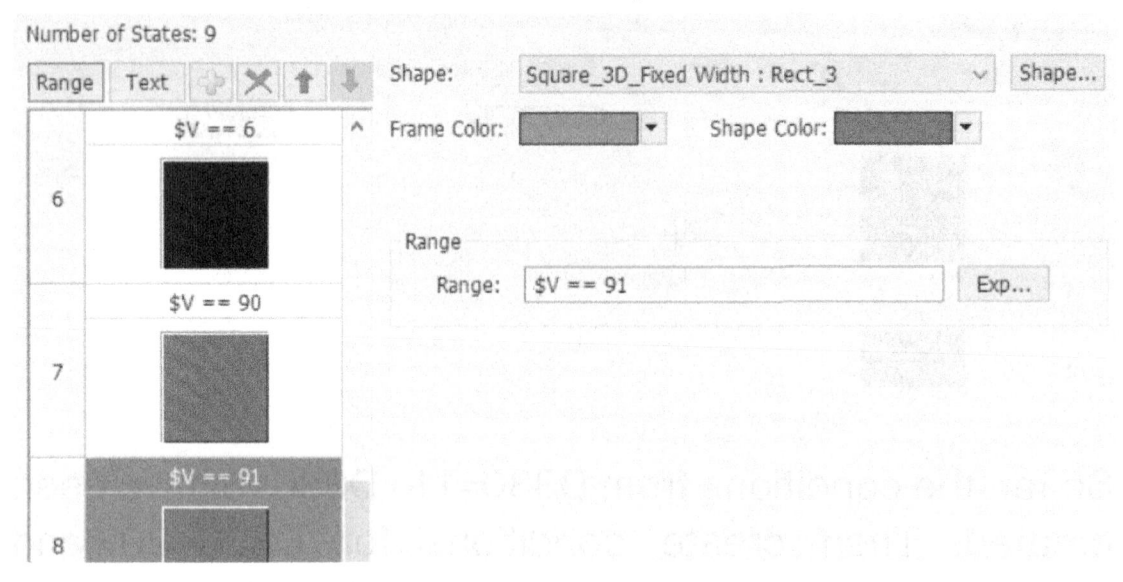

[Display comment] Since it is not necessary to display condition 0, select Comment: Hold. *Condition 0 is not D330 = 0 but is displayed when the set conditions are not met.

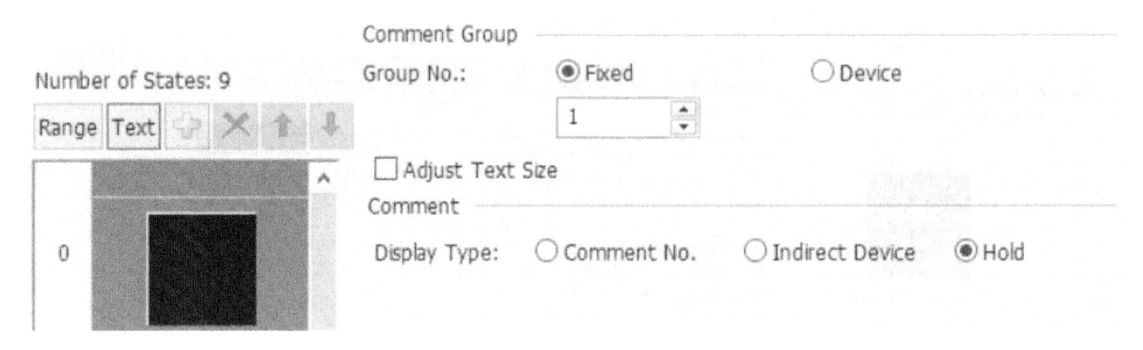

Next, after selecting Condition 1, press "Edit..." on the right side with Comment No. 1. Then, after entering "Injecting water" in the comment field, press OK and select "Yes"(はい) to confirm the comment. After that, change the font size to 20 and the setting of condition 1 will be completed.

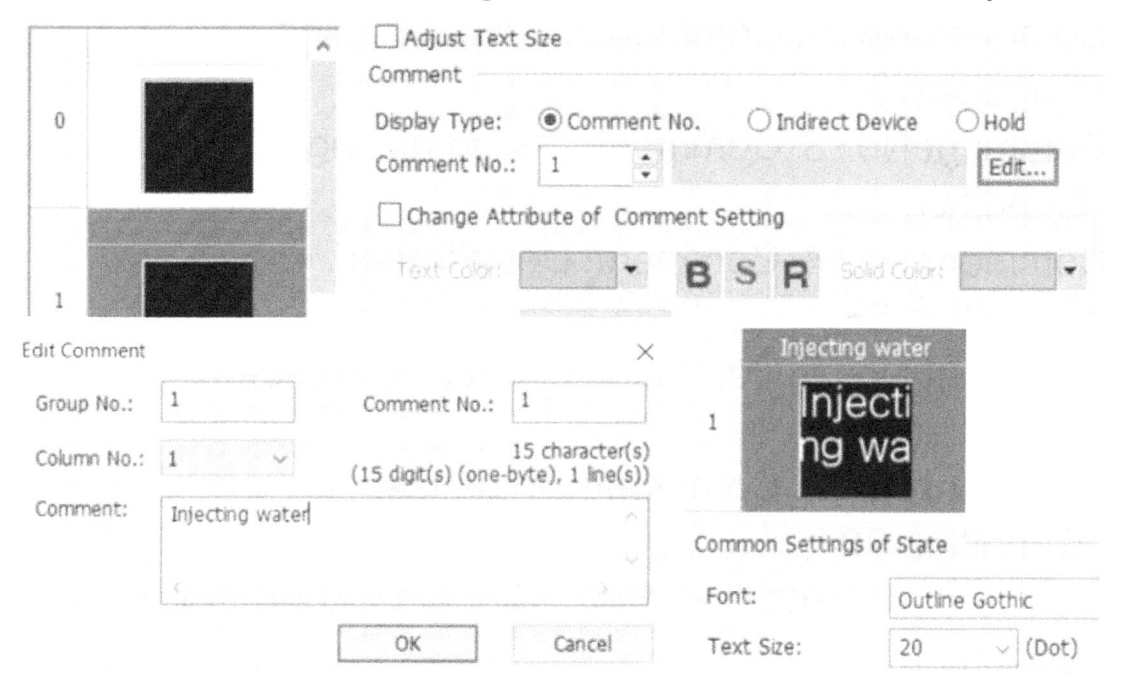

Set other conditions in the same way. *You can also enter the value of the comment number directly instead of using the arrow.

<Condition 2>
Comment No.: 2, Comment: During washing.
<Condition 3>
Comment No.: 3, Comment: During rinsing.
<Condition 4>
Comment No.: 4, Comment: Dehydration.
<Condition 5>
Comment No.: 5, Comment: Laundry completed.
<Condition 6>
Comment No.: 6, Comment: On pause.
<Condition 90>
Comment No.: 90, Comment: Clogging Abnormality.
<Condition 91>
Comment No.: 91, Comment: Leakage Abnormality.

0	■	3	During rinsing	6	On pause
1	Injecting water	4	Dehydration	7	Clogging Abnormality
2	During washing	5	Laundry completed	8	Leakage Abnormality

Adjust the placement and size.
[Placement/size]　X: 190 Y: 60 Width: 240 Height: 50
After creation, use the left and right arrows of the ON/OFF button to check whether each condition is displayed correctly. This completes the monitor display.

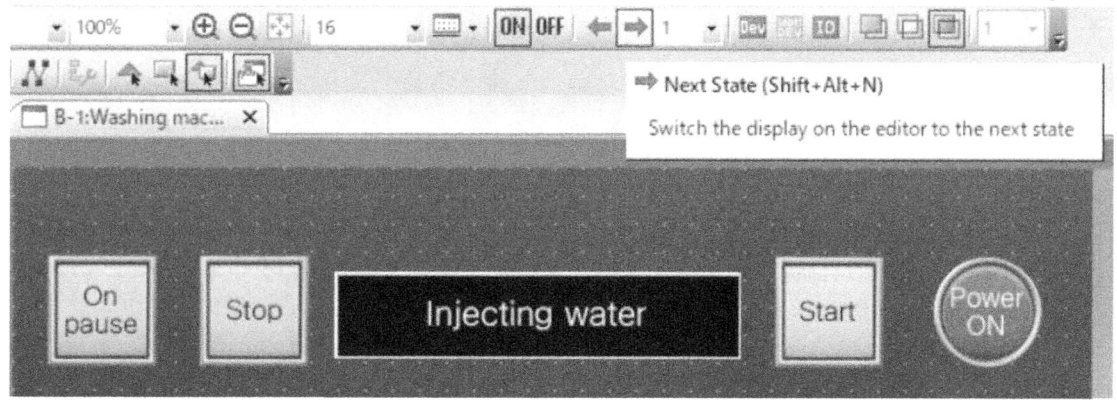

13. Create a current date and time display. After selecting "Object" tab ⇒ Date/Time Display ⇒ Date display, click the screen and double-click the placed part to make each setting.

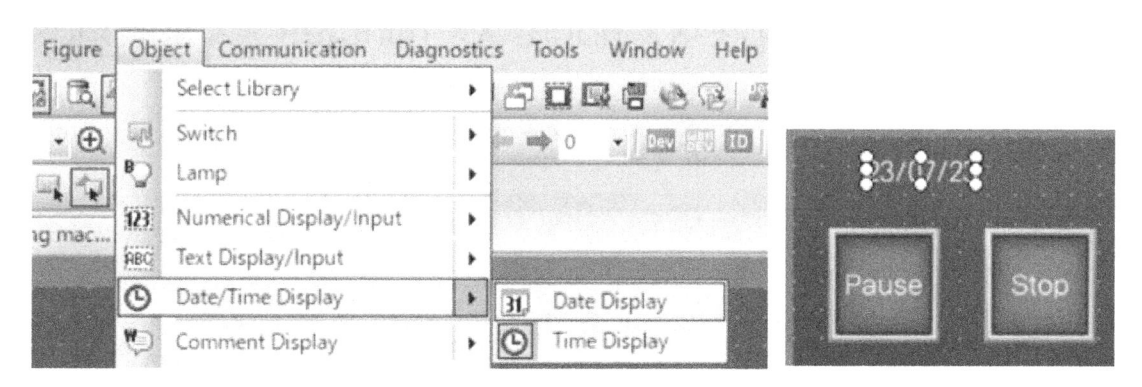

[Character/Style]

Type: Date, Sort: yy/mm/dd, Date Type: XXXX/XX/XX (day of week), Font size: 24

【Configuration】 X:5 Y:5

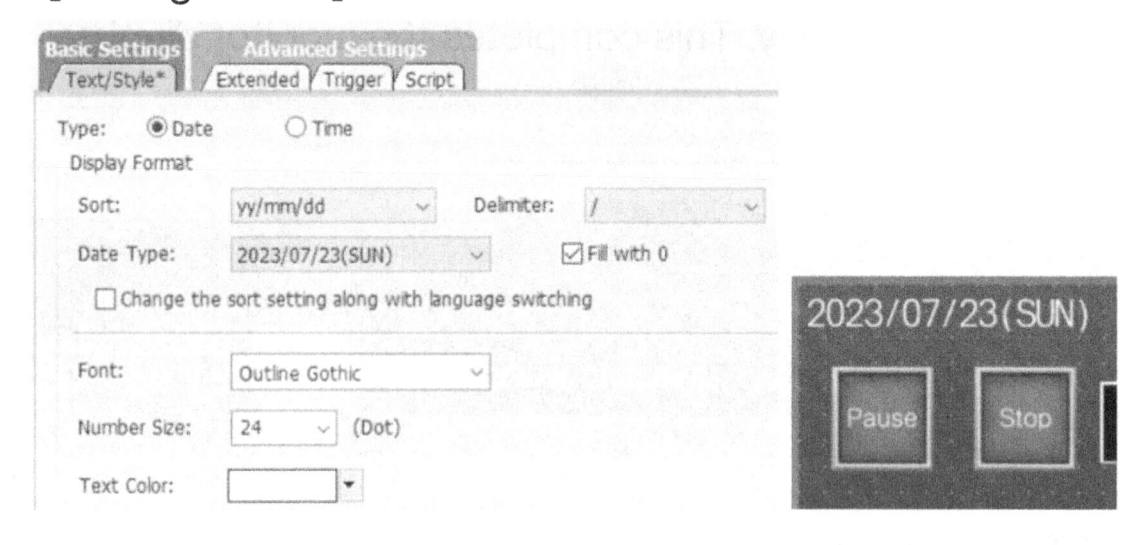

For the time, copy the date data ⇒ After pasting, change the settings.

[Character/Style]

Type: time, time type: XX hours XX minutes XX seconds, character size: 24

【Configuration】 X:200 Y:5

14. This completes the creation of the PLC program and screen. From now on, we will conduct a simulation that links the PLC program and the screen to check the operation.

First, on the PLC program side, press the "Debug" tab ⇒ Start/Stop Simulation to start the simulation.

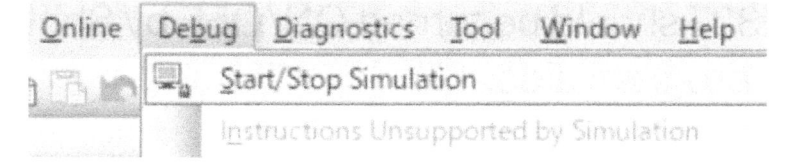

Next, press the "Tools" tab ⇒ Simulator ⇒ Activate on the touch panel side to open the simulation screen, so click each button on the screen with the cursor to turn it ON/OFF.

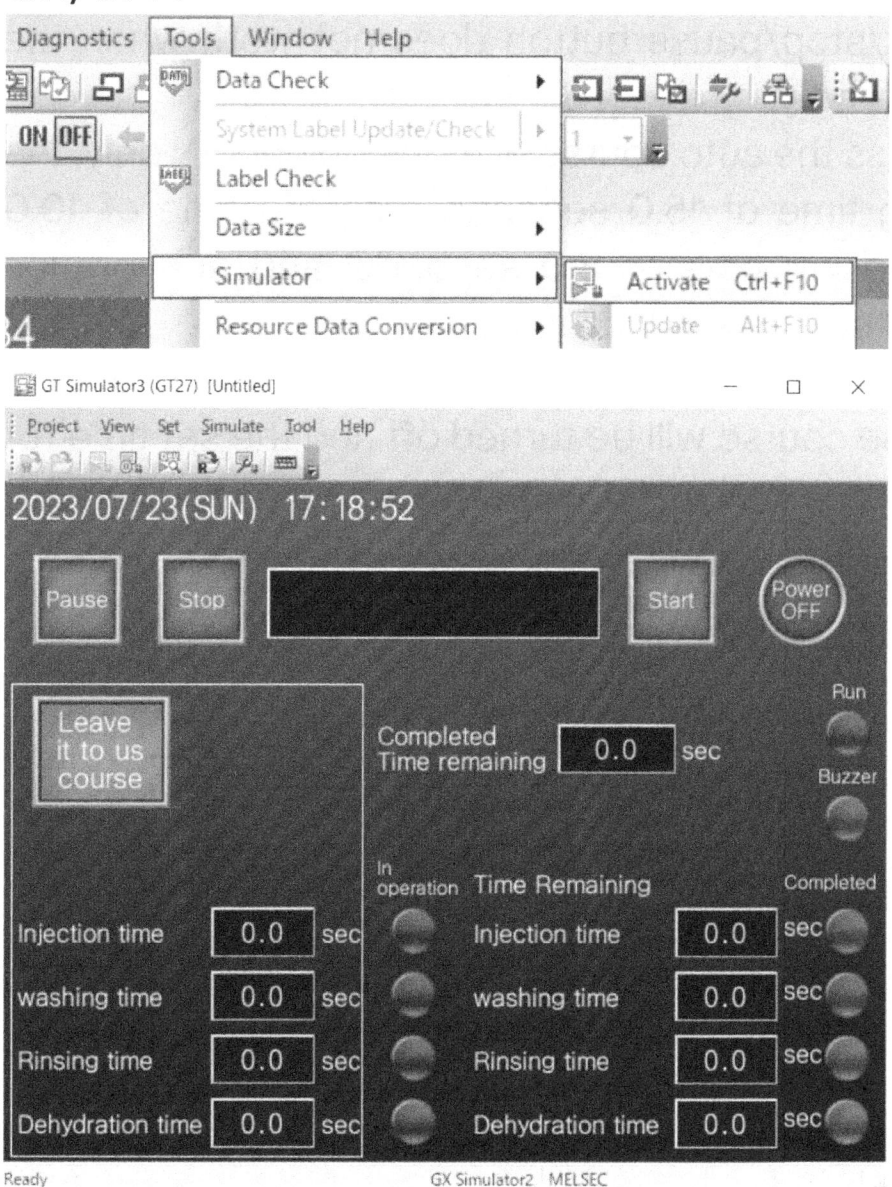

Now, please check the following operation using the simulation screen. However, clogging error X326 and short circuit error X327 should be turned ON/OFF by Shift + Enter on the PLC program side.

・The power can be turned on and off, and the date and time must be displayed correctly.
・Start/Stop/Pause/Omakase course buttons do not work when the power is off.
・The start/stop/pause button does not work when the power is ON only.
・If you press the auto course with the power ON only, the water filling time of 15.0 seconds, washing time of 10.0 seconds, rinsing time of 8.0 seconds, and dehydration time of 12.0 seconds will be set.
・If you turn off the power while the omakase course is on, the omakase course will be turned off and the set time for each process will all be 0.0 seconds.

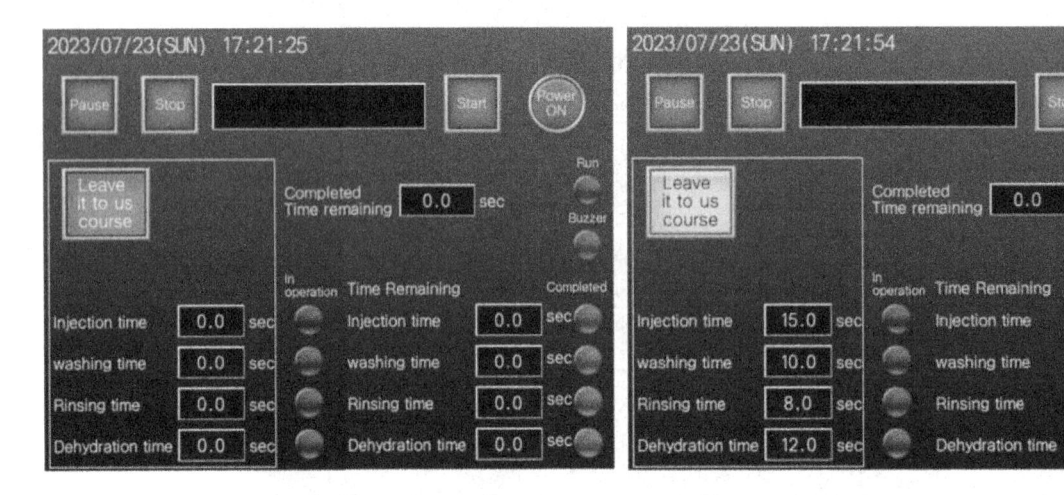

· If you press the start button with the power on and the auto-running course on, the washing machine will operate according to the sequence.

· The lamp display during automatic operation, each remaining time, and the monitor display are correct.

· The stop button and pause button work correctly.

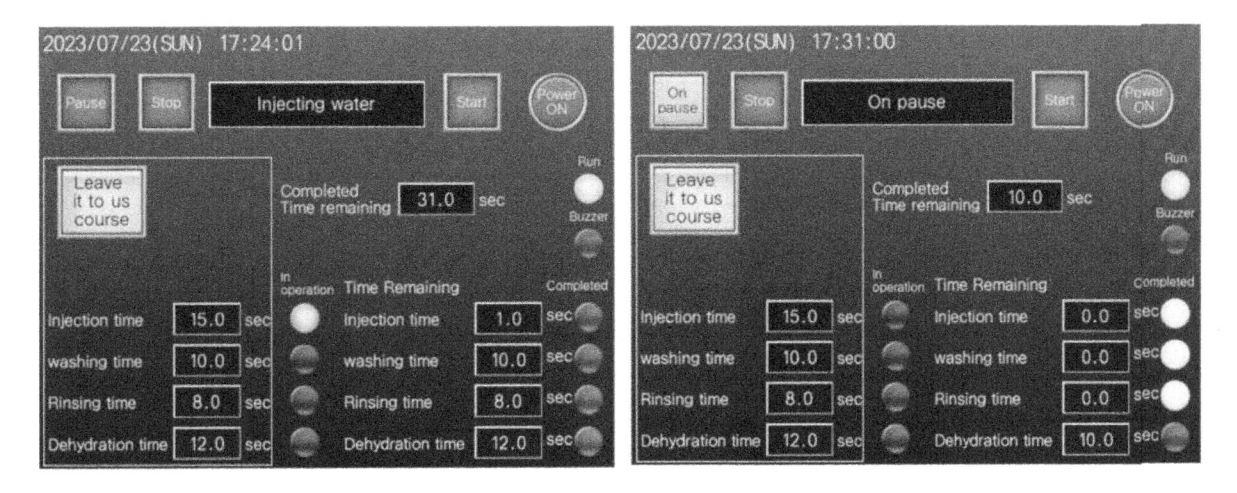

· When clogging error X326 or earth leakage error X327 is forcibly turned ON by the PLC program, the details of the error are displayed on the monitor with a red background, and the buzzer lamp blinks for 5 seconds.

· Automatic operation cannot be started when an abnormality occurs.

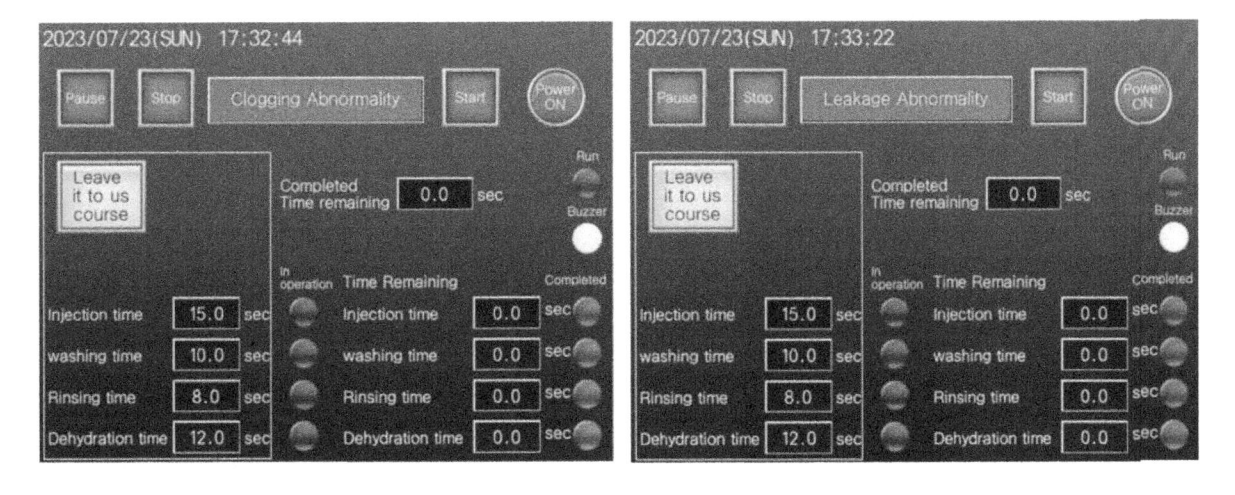

This completes the creation of the washing machine operation screen and the operation check by simulation. I used a washing machine, a familiar home appliance, for explanation, so I think it was easy to imagine the sequence operation.

This time, we entered a fixed time for each process in the auto course, but in the next step, we will create a manual course program and screen that can manually set the time for each process.

2-6 Summary

・To sum the values of multiple devices **Total value calculation instruction (WSUM)** is convenient.

・To write the total value calculation command (WSUM), press F8 and enter "WSUM D○○○D□□□K◇". this is **"Start with D○○○, add ◇ words from there, and put it in D□□□"** It means that・・・

2-7 Step 6 Washing machine manual course circuit/screen creation

In step 6, we will create a PLC program and screen for the manual course so that the operation time of each process can be freely set from the touch panel.

1. First, create it from the PLC program. Add a circuit to turn off washing machine manual course Y350 and turn on washing machine manual course Y351 when the washing machine manual course button X322 is pressed. Also, the washing machine will not be able to switch courses during automatic operation.

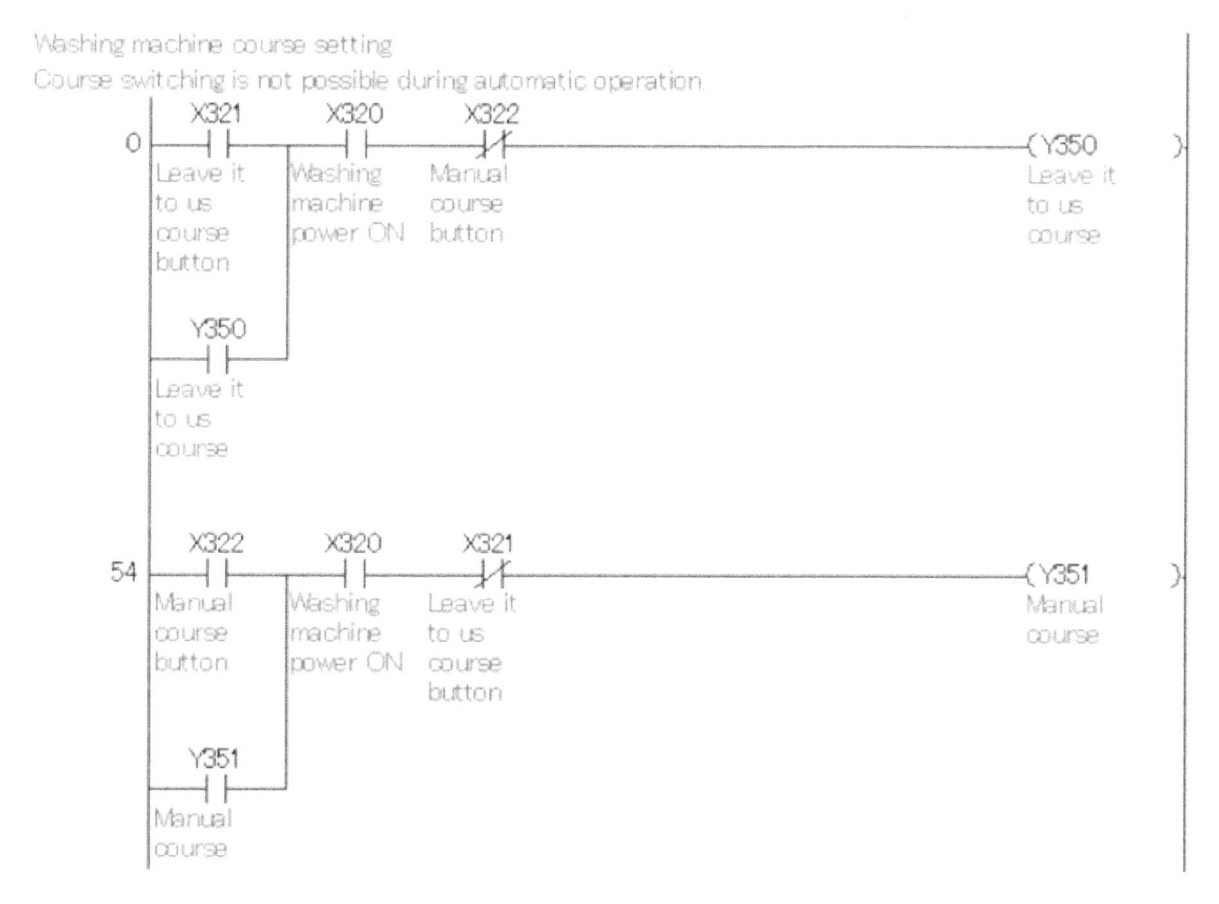

```
Washing machine course setting
Course switching is not possible during automatic operation.
         X321      X320      X322
      0 ──┤ ├──────┤ ├──────┤/├──────────────────────( Y350 )
         Leave it  Washing   Manual                    Leave it
         to us     machine   course                    to us
         course    power ON  button                    course
         button
         Y350
         ──┤ ├──
         Leave it
         to us
         course

         X322      X320      X321
     54 ──┤ ├──────┤ ├──────┤/├──────────────────────( Y351 )
         Manual    Washing   Leave it                  Manual
         course    machine   to us                     course
         button    power ON  course
                             button
         Y351
         ──┤ ├──
         Manual
         course
```

2. Next, add a condition to reset when manually selecting the course to the circuit that resets the set time for each process.

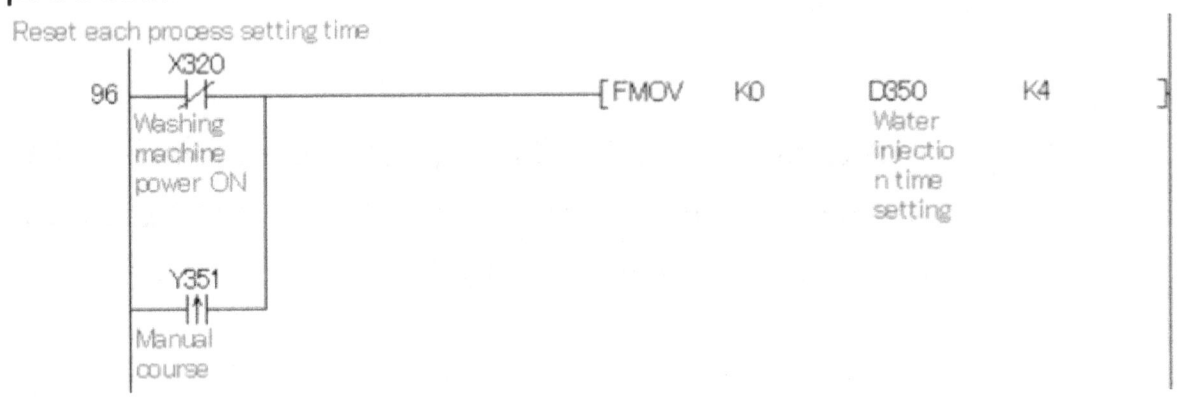

```
Reset each process setting time
        X320
96 ─────┤/├──────────────────────────[FMOV  K0   D350         K4  ]
        Washing                                  Water
        machine                                  injectio
        power ON                                 n time
                                                 setting
        Y351
   ─────┤↑├──────
        Manual
        course
```

And when the manual course is selected, automatic operation cannot be started unless the time for each process is entered. First, create a circuit that turns on the washing machine manual course setting completion M352 when all process times are set. For the compare instruction, press F8 and enter "<> K0 D350". This circuit consists of 2 lines, but if you enter it in the blue frame, it will automatically break into a new line. The location is created above "Washing machine automatic operation possible conditions".

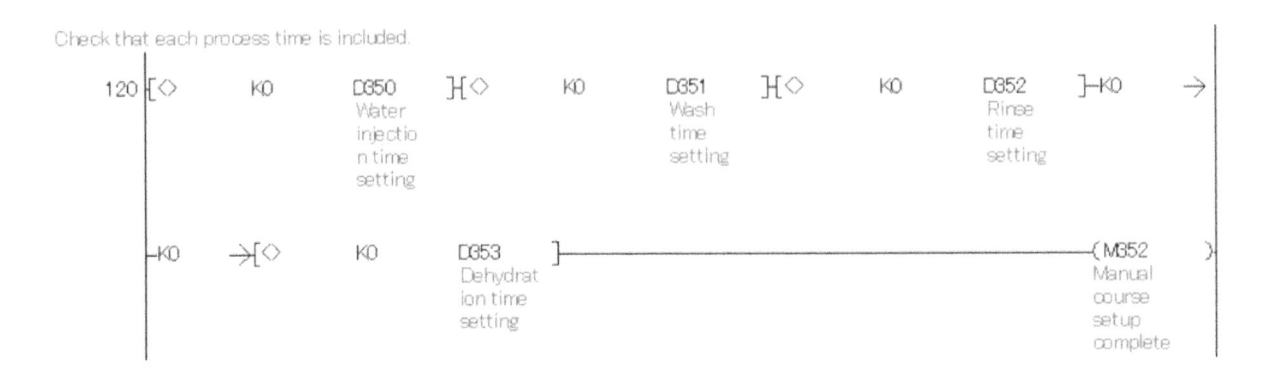

```
Check that each process time is included.
120 ─[<>  K0   D350   ]─[<>  K0   D351   ]─[<>  K0   D352   ]─K0 →
               Water            Wash             Rinse
               injectio         time             time
               n time           setting          setting
               setting

    ─K0  →[<>  K0   D353   ]─────────────────────────────(M352  )
                     Dehydrat                             Manual
                     ion time                             course
                     setting                              setup
                                                          complete
```

140

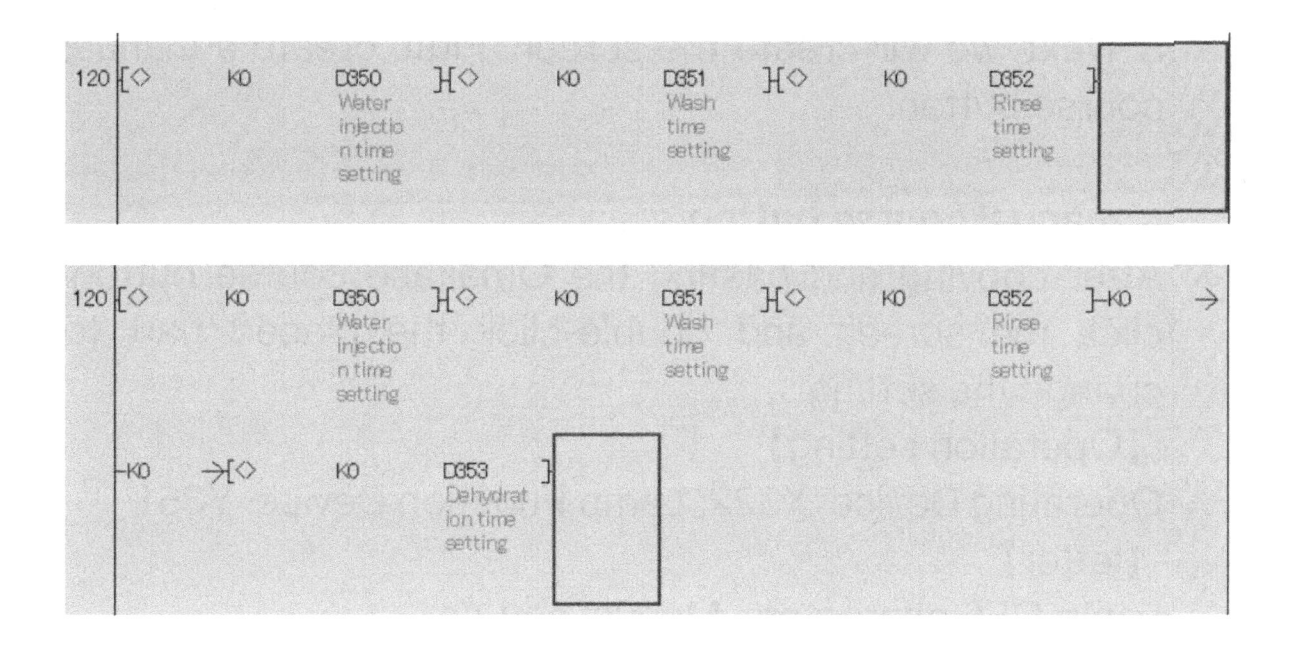

```
120─[◇  K0   D350   ]─◇   K0   D351   ]─◇   K0   D352   ]
             Water             Wash             Rinse
             injectio          time             time
             n time            setting          setting
             setting
```

```
120─[◇  K0   D350   ]─◇   K0   D351   ]─◇   K0   D352  ]─K0  →
             Water             Wash             Rinse
             injectio          time             time
             n time            setting          setting
             setting

 ─K0   →[◇   K0   D353   ]
                  Dehydrat
                  ion time
                  setting
```

Add the manual course Y351 and the created M352 to the automatic operation possible conditions.

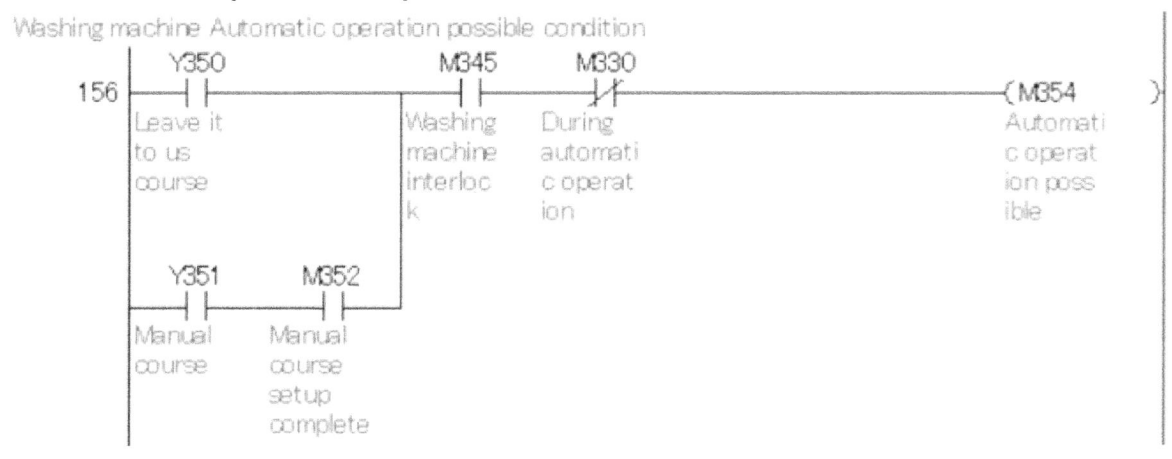

```
Washing machine Automatic operation possible condition
         Y350              M345      M330
  156 ───┤ ├────────────────┤ ├──────┤/├─────────────────(M354 )
         Leave it           Washing   During             Automati
         to us              machine   automati           c operat
         course             interloc  c operat           ion poss
                            k         ion                ible

         Y351     M352
        ─┤ ├──────┤ ├─
         Manual   Manual
         course   course
                  setup
                  complete
```

There are still parts to be created regarding PLC program creation, but it will be easier to understand if you create it with the screen as a set, so I will explain it later.

3. Next, we will create the screen. First, create a manual course button.

<**manual course button**>

After copying and pasting the Omakase course button, click the screen and double-click the placed part to change the setting.

【Operation setting】

Operating Device: X322, Lamp Function Device: Y351

【letter】

Lamp OFF characters: Manual course

Lamp ON characters: Manual course

[Placement/size]

X: 145 Y: 150 Width: 100 Height: 80

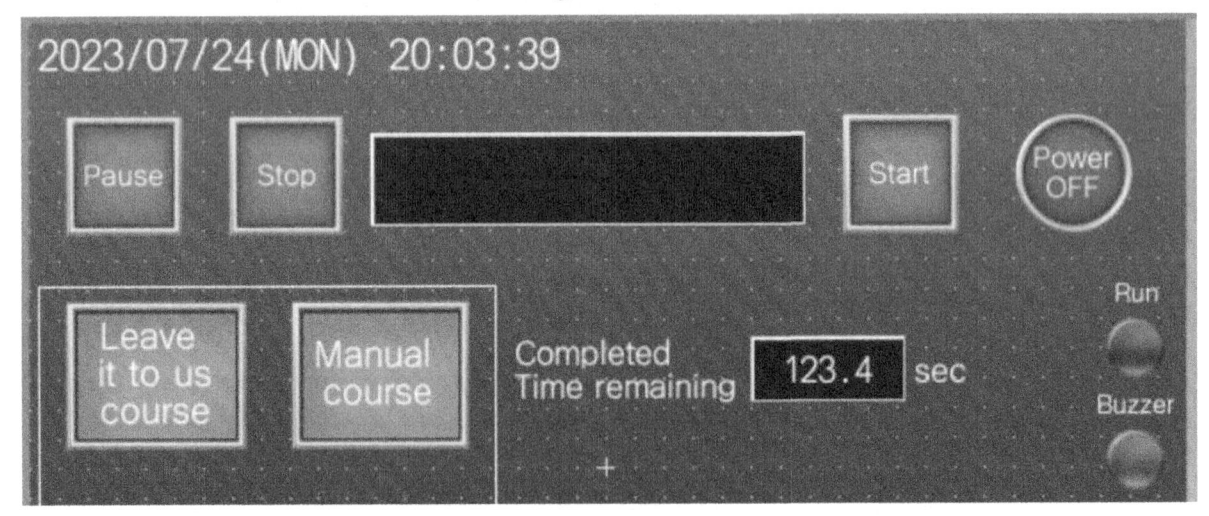

4. Next, enable the input of each process setting time.

＜Water injection time input＞

First, double-click the time display part of the water injection time, change the type from numerical display to numerical input, and press OK at the bottom right. Now you can enter the set time for the water filling time.

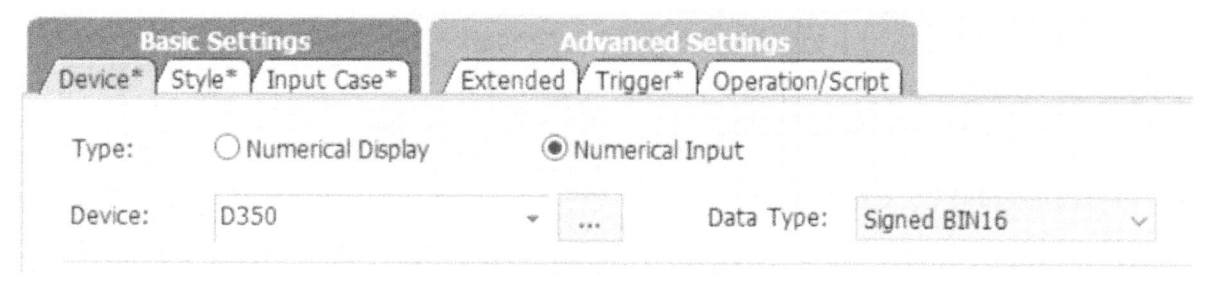

Basic Settings			Advanced Settings		
Device*	Style*	Input Case*	Extended	Trigger*	Operation/Script

Type: ◯ Numerical Display   ◉ Numerical Input

Device: D350   Data Type: Signed BIN16

However, if this setting time is changed during automatic operation, the operation will become strange. Also, in auto mode, the circuit continues to write a fixed value, so it cannot be changed, but it feels strange to be able to touch it and enter it. Therefore, here we will create a PLC program and change the screen settings so that input can only be made when the manual course is selected and not during automatic operation. First, create the conditions that can be operated on the PLC program side as M353, which can change the setting time for each process. Location "Conditions for automatic operation of washing machine Please create it on.

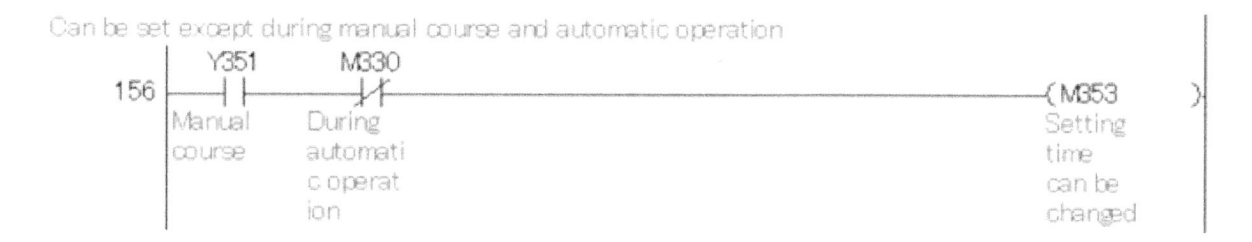

```
Can be set except during manual course and automatic operation
         Y351      M330
156 ─────┤ ├──────┤/├─────────────────────────────( M353 )
        Manual    During                                  Setting
        course    automati                                time
                  c operat                                can be
                  ion                                     changed
```

Double-click the time display part of the water injection time, click the "Display/Operating conditions" tab, set the trigger type to ON, and the trigger device to M353, then press OK at the bottom right. Now you can enter numerical values on the touch panel only while M353 is ON.

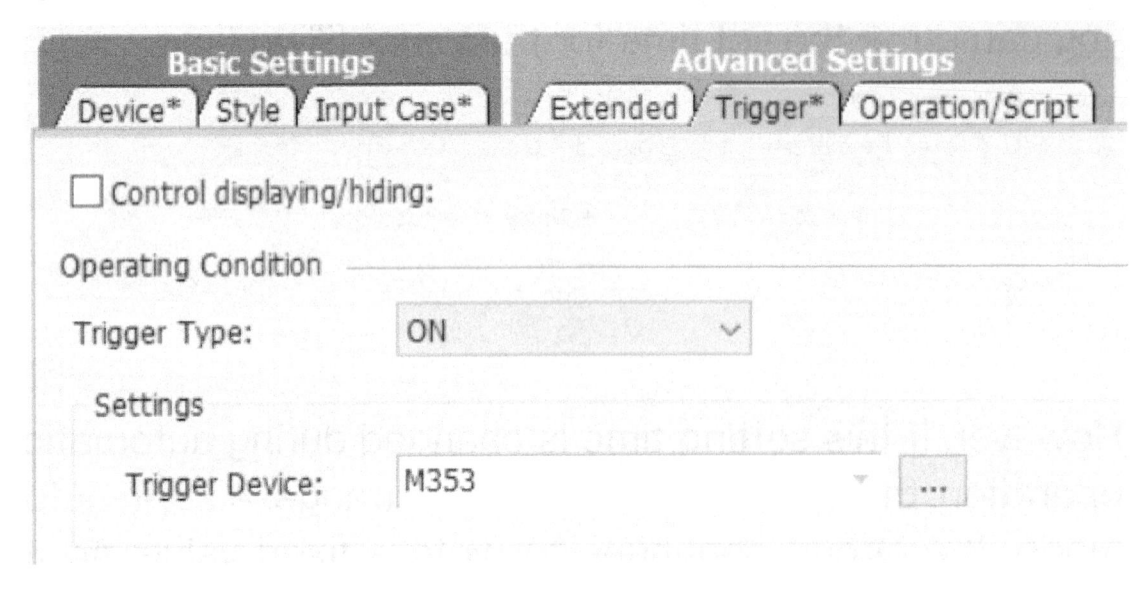

Basic Settings	Advanced Settings
Device* / Style / Input Case*	Extended / Trigger* / Operation/Script

☐ Control displaying/hiding:

Operating Condition

Trigger Type: ON

  Settings

  Trigger Device: M353

Also, in the current settings, you can enter from -99.9 seconds to 99.9 seconds, so you cannot enter negative values. This time, you can enter from 1 second to 99.9 seconds.

After selecting the "Input range" tab, press the plus mark next to the number of settings. Then, 0<=$W<=100 ($W refers to your own device) is displayed in the condition, so press "Range..." on the right side and change the constant of A to 1 and the constant of C to 99.9 Then press OK and press OK again to complete the setting.

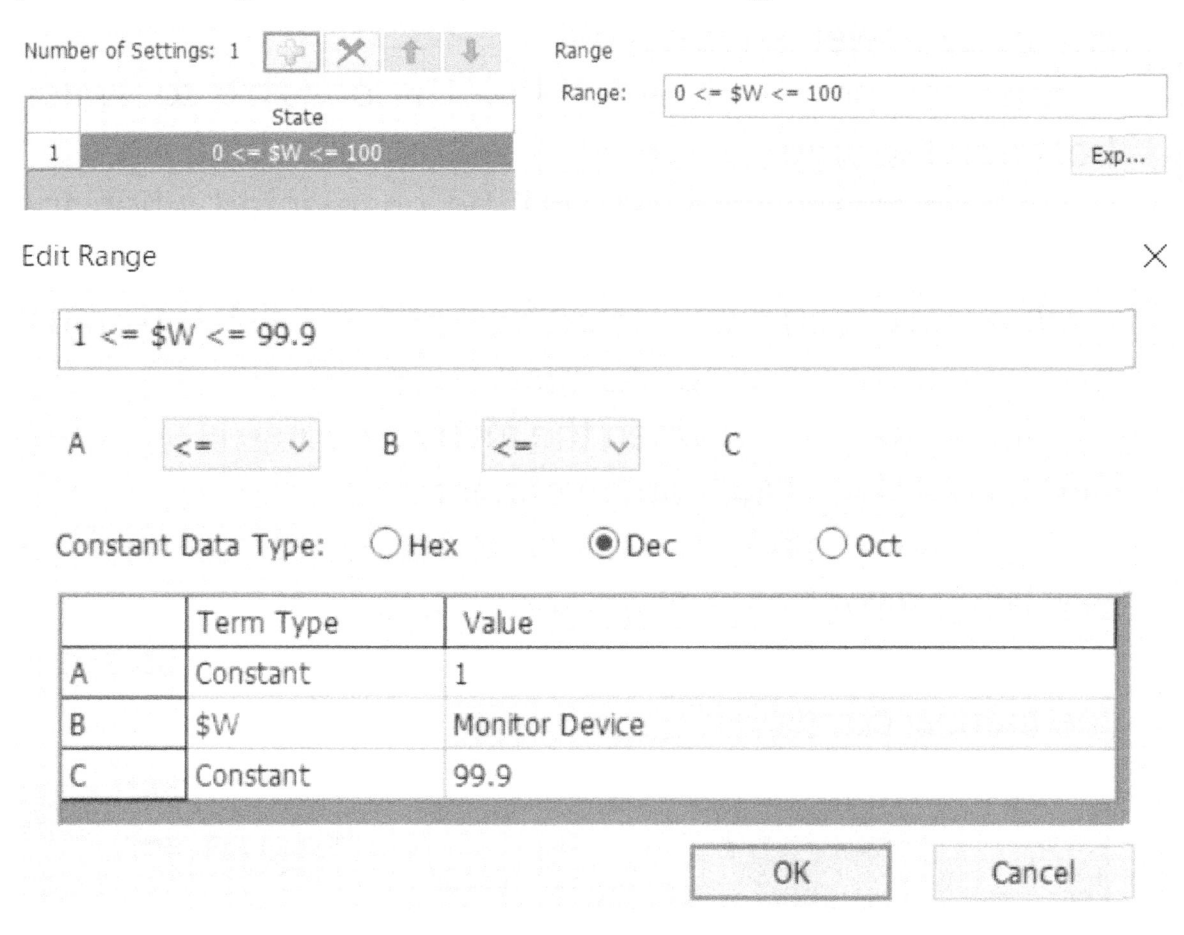

Use the same procedure to change the settings for washing time/rinsing time/dehydration time. This completes the creation of the screen side.

6. Now that the manual course has been created, we will perform a simulation that links the PLC program and the screen to check the operation. Check the following operations using the simulation screen.

・Course selection and time settings cannot be made when the power is turned off.
・After the power is turned on, it is possible to switch between the auto course and the manual course.
・Neither course selection will be unselected when the power is turned off.
・When selecting the Omakase course, the set value must be fixed and cannot be changed.
・Each value is reset when the manual course is selected, and the setting value can be changed.
・The setting value can only be changed from 1.0 to 99.9, and other values cannot be entered.
・The washing machine automatically operates as set in the manual course.

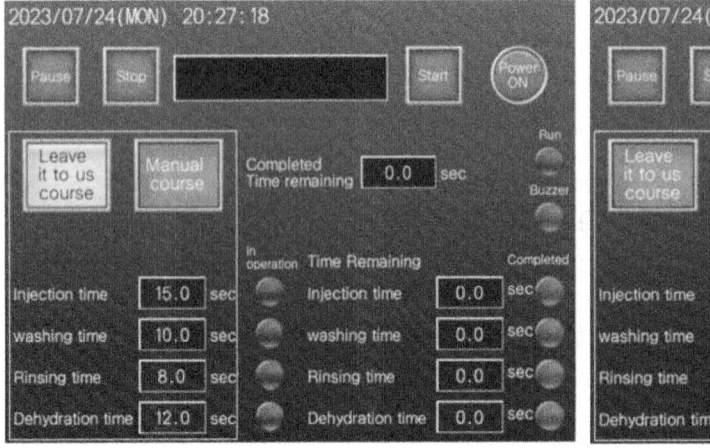

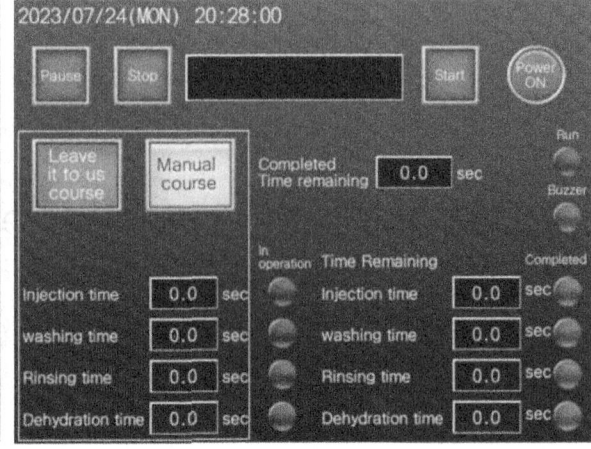

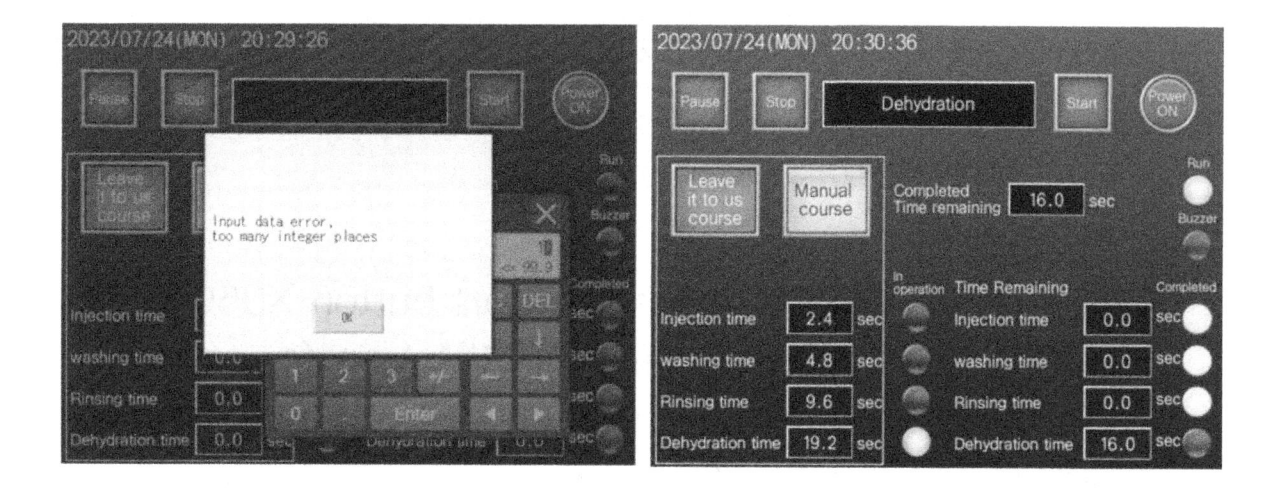

This completes the learning of sequence control using the washing machine. This time it was a PLC program with about 650 steps, but I hope you understood the basic form of sequence control.

As applications, there are robot control and servo motor control, but by knowing the basic form explained this time, you can create it by looking up the manual or asking the manufacturer if you do not understand anything. increase.

Next, let's create a PLC program and touch panel using what you learned in exercises 2 and 3.

Exercise 2 (Bottle transfer sequence control: PLC program)

When the automatic operation start button X350 is ON, M360 is ON during automatic bottle transfer operation, and when the automatic operation stop button X351 is ON, M360 is OFF during automatic bottle transfer operation. Create a circuit in which bottle transfer sequence control operates when a bottle flows under the transfer hand while M360 is ON during bottle transfer automatic operation and the bottle transfer execution conditions are met. (After creating new program data "Assignment 2" in the "PLC program creation" file, create it.) *Operation check using the touch panel will be performed in exercise 3

The transfer hand commands, and detection sensor devices are as follows. Down command Y360, Up command Y361, left move command Y370, Right move command Y371, Chuck close command Y380, Chuck open command Y381, left bottle detection sensor X355, Right bottle detection sensor X356, Down detection sensor X360, Up detection sensor X361, Left position detection sensor X370, Right position detection sensor X371, Chuck close detection sensor X380, Chuck open detection sensor X381.

Bottle transfer automatic operation start: X350 ON ⇒ M360 ON and hold

Bottle transfer flow activation conditions (M365): Down detection X360, left position detection X370, chuck close detection X380 are OFF, rise detection X361, right position detection X371, chuck open detection X381 are ON, right side bottle detection X356 is ON, left side bottle Detection X355 is OFF + bottle transfer flow not executed.

[Bottle transfer flow: M370 is ON during execution] * Flow = flow

1 Descent: Y360 (descent command) is ON ⇒ X361 (ascend detection) is OFF ⇒ X360 (descent detection) is ON ⇒ Y360 (descent command) is OFF

2 Chuck close: Y380 (chuck close command) is ON ⇒ X381 (chuck open detection) is OFF ⇒ X380 (chuck close detection) is ON ⇒ Y380 (chuck close command) is OFF

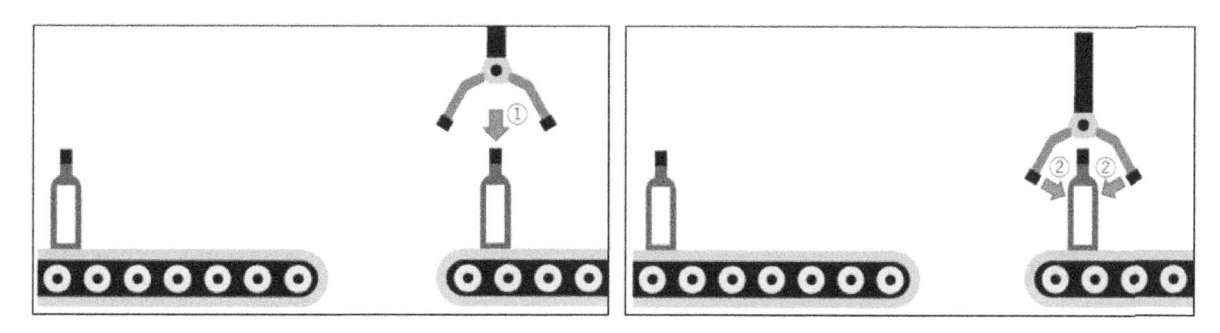

3 Rise: Y361 (Rise command) is ON ⇒ X356 (Right bottle detection) and X360 (Descent detection) are OFF ⇒ X361 (Rise detection) is ON ⇒ Y361 (Rise command) is OFF

4 Left movement: Y370 (left movement command) is ON ⇒ X371 (right position detection) is OFF ⇒ X370 (left position detection) is ON ⇒ Y370 (left movement command) is OFF

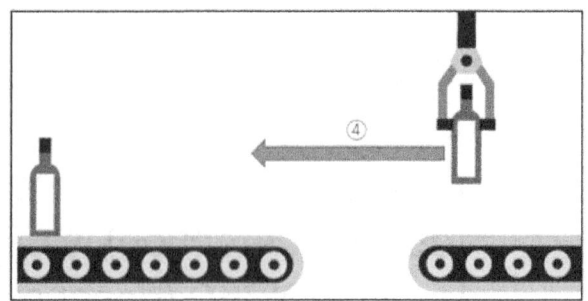

5 Descent: Y360 (descent command) is ON ⇒ X361 (ascend detection) is OFF ⇒ X355 (left bottle detection) and X360 (descent detection) are ON ⇒ Y360 (descent command) is OFF

6 Chuck open: Y381 (chuck open command) is ON ⇒ X380 (chuck close detection) is OFF ⇒ X381 (chuck open detection) is ON ⇒ Y381 (chuck open command) is OFF

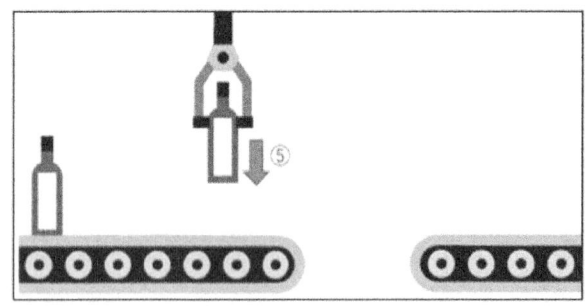

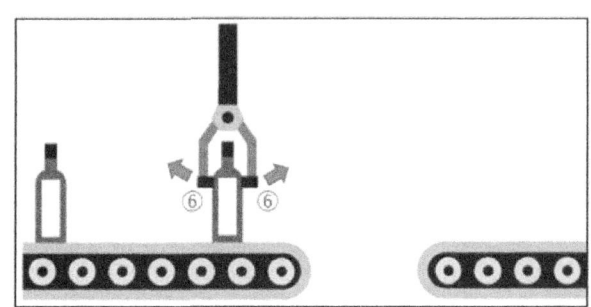

7 Rise: Y361 (Rise command) is ON ⇒ X360 (Descent detection) is OFF ⇒ X361 (Rise detection) is ON ⇒ Y361 (Rise command) is OFF

8 Right movement: Y371 (right movement command) is ON ⇒ X370 (left position detection) is OFF ⇒ X371 (right position detection) is ON ⇒ Y371 (right movement command) is OFF

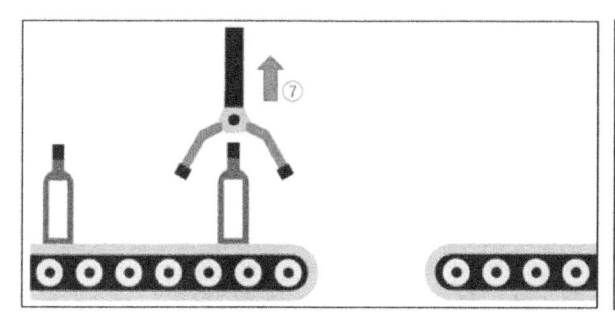

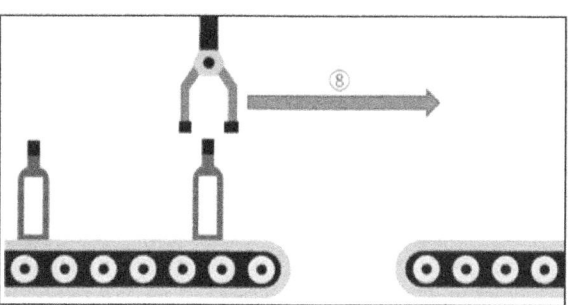

Practice Question 2 Answers

1. First, right-click the program in the navigation ⇒ select Create New, enter "Task 2" in the data name, and click OK at the bottom right to create a new program data "Task 2".

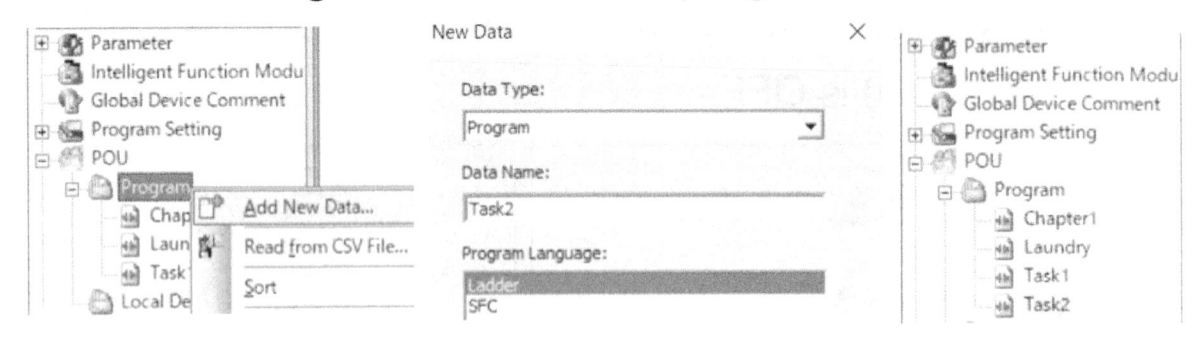

2. First, create a circuit that turns on M360 during automatic bottle transfer operation when the bottle transfers automatic operation start button X350 is ON, and turns off M360 during bottle transfer automatic operation when the bottle transfers automatic operation stop button X351 is ON.

3. Next, create the execution conditions for the bottle transfer flow as follows. Malfunctions are prevented by ensuring that the conditions are not met while Flow Execution (M370) is ON.

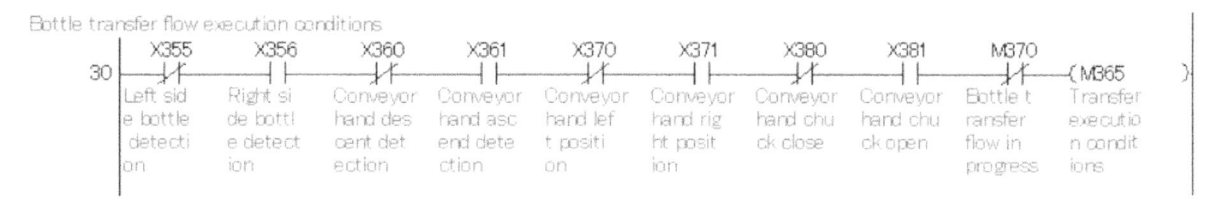

Bottle transfer flow execution conditions

```
     X355    X356    X360    X361    X370    X371    X380    X381    M370
30 ──┤/├────┤ ├────┤/├────┤ ├────┤/├────┤ ├────┤/├────┤ ├────┤/├────(M365)
   Left sid  Right si  Conveyor  Conveyor  Conveyor  Conveyor  Conveyor  Conveyor  Bottle t  Transfer
   e bottle  de bottl  hand des  hand asc  hand lef  hand rig  hand chu  hand chu  ransfer   executio
   detecti   e detect  cent det  end dete  t positi  ht posit  ck close  ck open   flow in   n condit
   on        ion       ection    ction     on        ion                          progress  ions
```

4. Create a condition for bottle transfer flow running (M370). When the conditions are met and M370 turns ON, M365 will not turn ON until M370 turns OFF, so the conditions for turning ON M370 again during the bottle transfer flow will not be met.

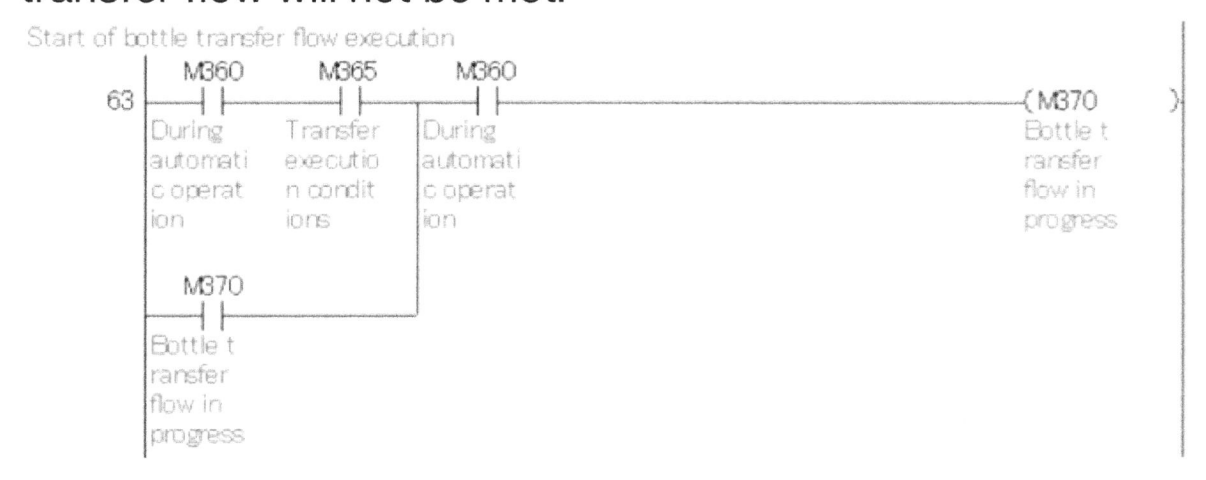

Start of bottle transfer flow execution

```
     M360    M365    M360
63 ──┤ ├────┤ ├────┤ ├──────────────────────────────(M370)
   During   Transfer  During                         Bottle t
   automati executio  automati                       ransfer
   c operat n condit  c operat                       flow in
   ion      ions      ion                            progress

     M370
   ──┤ ├──
   Bottle t
   ransfer
   flow in
   progress
```

153

5. Let's consider how to create a flow circuit here. This time, the transfer hand will rise and fall twice in the flow. If the descent command Y360 and the rise command Y361 are used in each step, it will become a double coil and correct operation will not be possible. In such a case, use M (auxiliary relay).

This time, we will create a coil using M (auxiliary relay) like this.

M371: STEP1 transfer hand start descending
M372: STEP1 transfer hand lowering complete.
M373: STEP2 transfer hand chuck closing start
M374: STEP2 transfer hand chuck closing completion
M375: STEP3 Transfer hand start rising
M376: STEP3 transfer hand rise complete.
M377: STEP4 Transfer hand left movement start
M378: STEP4 Transfer hand left movement complete
M379: STEP5 Transfer hand start descending
M380: STEP4 Transfer hand lowering complete.
M381: STEP6 Transfer hand chuck opening start.
M382: STEP6 transfer hand chuck open completion
M383: STEP7 Transfer hand start rising
M384: STEP7 transfer hand rise complete.
M385: STEP8 transfer hand right movement start
M386: STEP8 transfer hand right movement complete
M387: Bottle transfer flow completed

6. First, let's create the lowering movement of the transfer hand in STEP1. When M370 is ON during execution of the transfer flow, M371 to start lowering the transfer hand is turned ON. We will create the turning on of the descent command Y360 later.

Then, while M371 is ON, the rise detection X361 is OFF, and the descent detection X360 is ON, and the transfer hand descent completion M372 is turned ON and held. The condition for M372 to turn on can be just turning on descent detection X360, but if there is a change, adding it will improve accuracy.

Also, when the stop button is pressed, M370 turns OFF, so M371 is OFF because M370 is included in the condition, and M372 is OFF because M370 is included in the condition to turn off the hold, so all operations are performed. can be stopped.

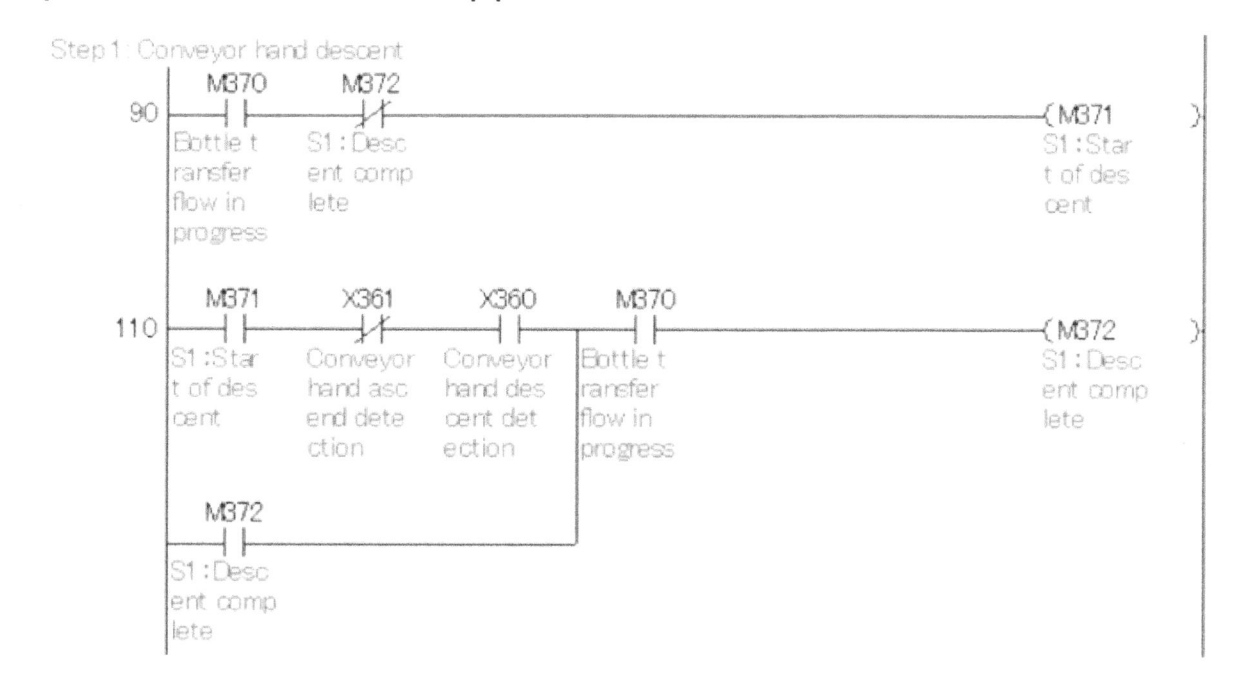

```
Step 1: Conveyor hand descent
         M370      M372
   90 ───┤ ├──────┤/├──────────────────────────────(M371)
         Bottle t  S1:Desc                          S1:Star
         ransfer   ent comp                         t of des
         flow in   lete                             cent
         progress

         M371      X361      X360      M370
  110 ───┤ ├──────┤/├──────┤ ├──────┤ ├────────────(M372)
         S1:Star   Conveyor  Conveyor  Bottle t     S1:Desc
         t of des  hand asc  hand des  ransfer      ent comp
         cent      end dete  cent det  flow in      lete
                   ction     ection    progress

         M372
        ─┤ ├──
         S1:Desc
         ent comp
         lete
```

There are a wide variety of ways to create a program depending on the person, but I think this is the basic form when creating steps for automatic driving. The best way to improve your skills is to first learn the basics and then apply them in your own way.

7. Create other steps in the same way as the transfer hand descending motion in STEP1.

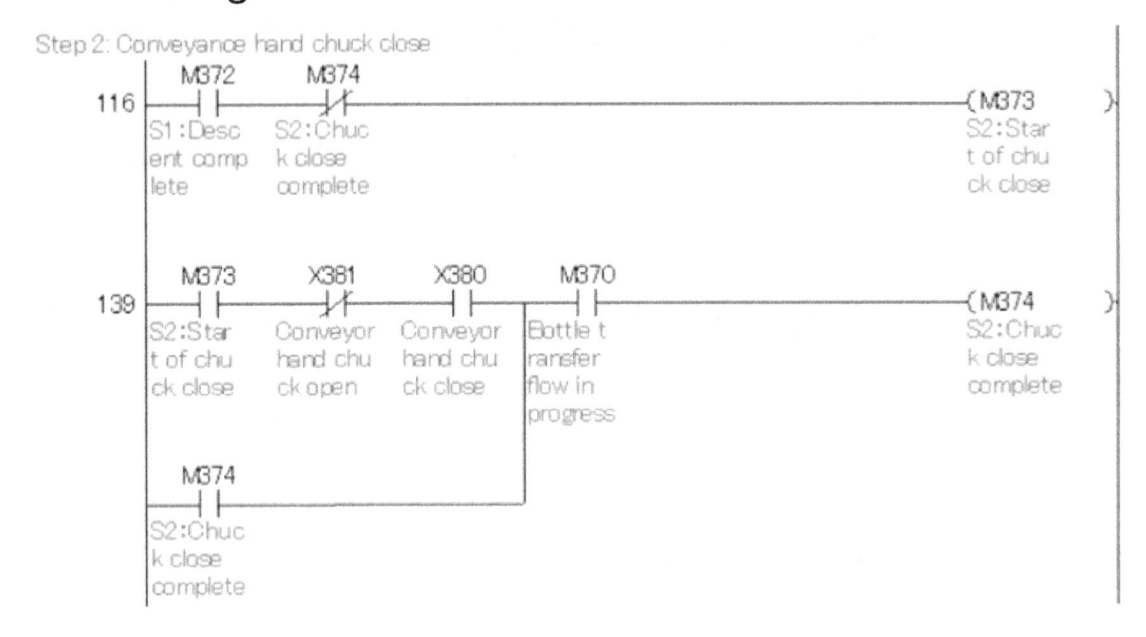

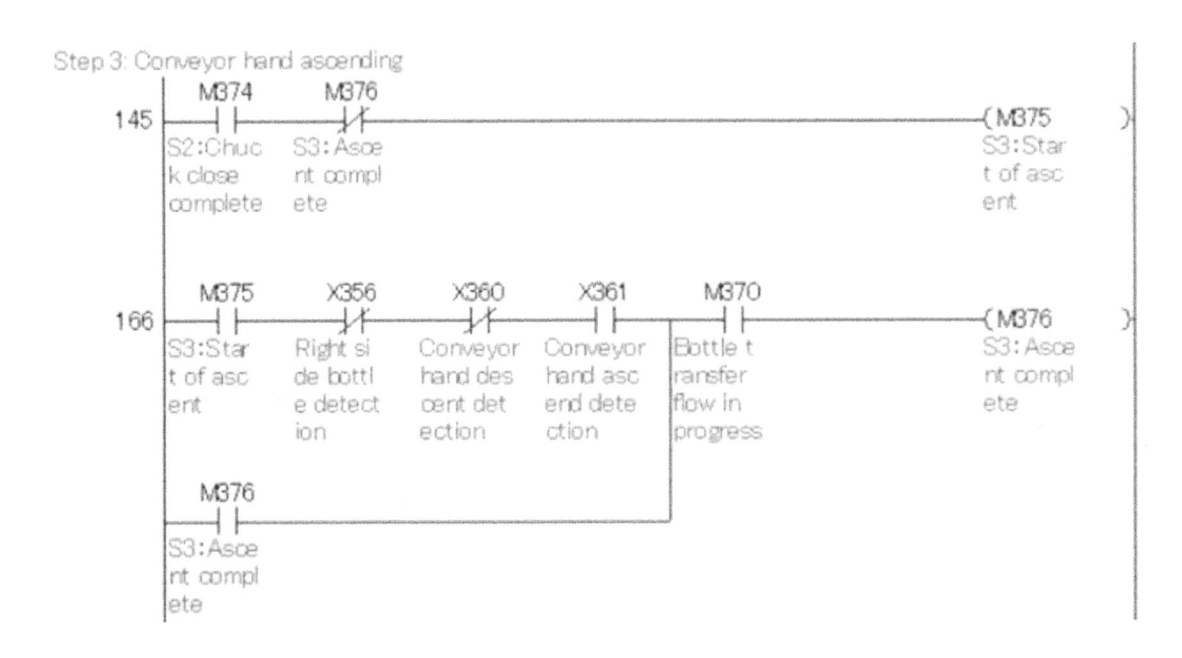

Step 2: Conveyance hand chuck close

```
        M372       M374                                                    (M373)
116     ─┤├────────┤/├─────────────────────────────────────────────────────
        S1:Desc    S2:Chuc                                                  S2:Star
        ent comp   k close                                                  t of chu
        lete       complete                                                 ck close

        M373       X381      X380      M370                                 (M374)
139     ─┤├────────┤/├───────┤├────────┤├──────────────────────────────────
        S2:Star    Conveyor  Conveyor  Bottle t                             S2:Chuc
        t of chu   hand chu  hand chu  ransfer                              k close
        ck close   ck open   ck close  flow in                              complete
                                       progress

        M374
        ─┤├──
        S2:Chuc
        k close
        complete
```

Step 3: Conveyor hand ascending

```
        M374       M376                                                    (M375)
145     ─┤├────────┤/├─────────────────────────────────────────────────────
        S2:Chuc    S3:Asce                                                  S3:Star
        k close    nt compl                                                 t of asc
        complete   ete                                                      ent

        M375       X356      X360      X361      M370                      (M376)
166     ─┤├────────┤/├───────┤/├───────┤├────────┤├─────────────────────────
        S3:Star    Right si  Conveyor  Conveyor  Bottle t                   S3:Asce
        t of asc   de bottl  hand des  hand asc  ransfer                    nt compl
        ent        e detect  cent det  end dete  flow in                    ete
                   ion       ection    ction     progress

        M376
        ─┤├──
        S3:Asce
        nt compl
        ete
```

Step 4: Conveyor hand left move

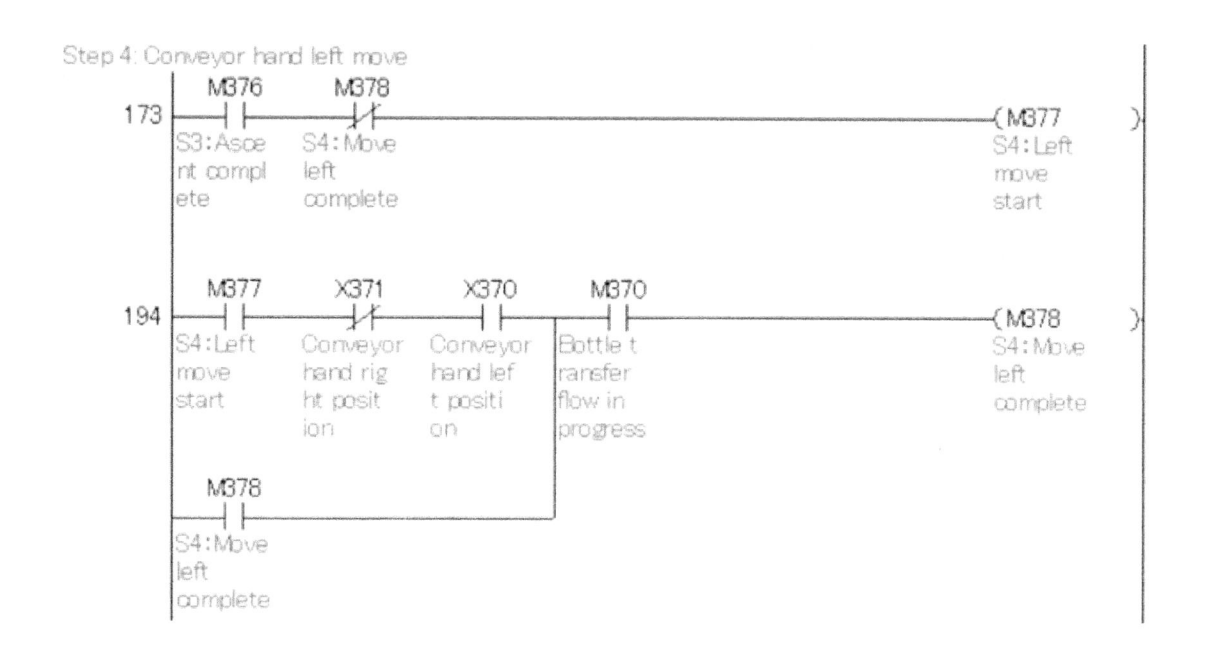

```
        M376      M378                                                    (M377)
173     ─┤├──────┤/├──────────────────────────────────────────────────────
        S3:Asce  S4:Move                                                  S4:Left
        nt compl left                                                     move
        ete      complete                                                 start


        M377     X371     X370     M370                                   (M378)
194     ─┤├─────┤/├──────┤├──────┤├───────────────────────────────────────
        S4:Left  Conveyor Conveyor Bottle t                                S4:Move
        move     hand rig hand lef ransfer                                 left
        start    ht posit t positi flow in                                 complete
                 ion      on       progress

        M378
        ─┤├─
        S4:Move
        left
        complete
```

Step 5: Conveyor hand descent

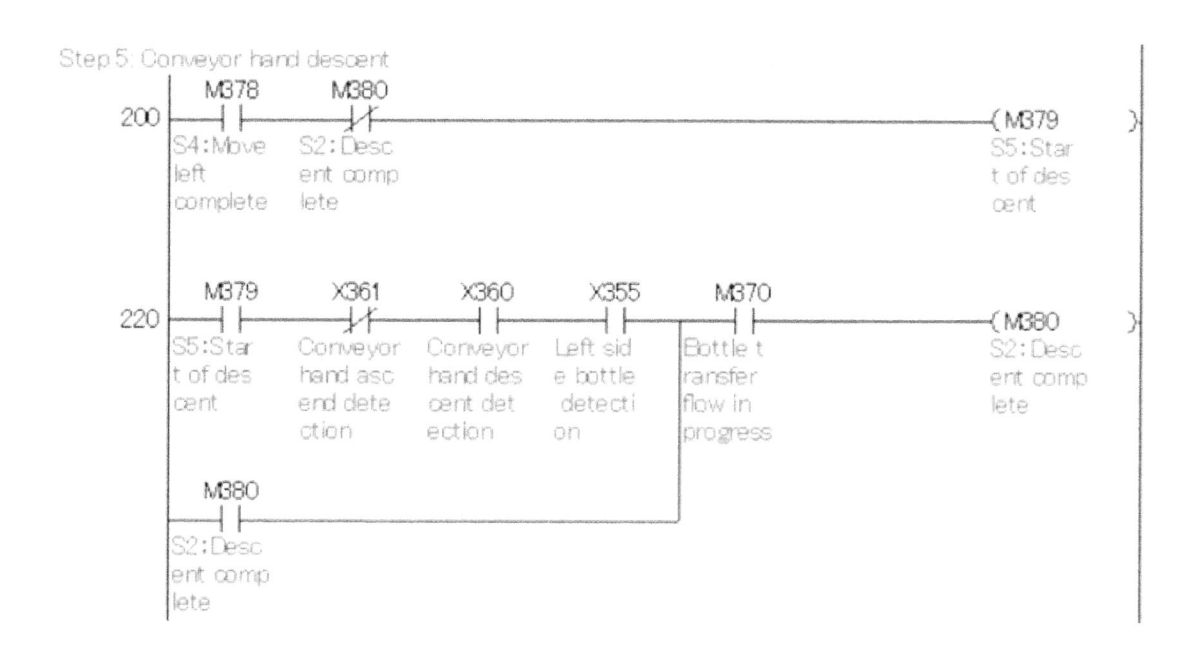

```
        M378     M380                                                     (M379)
200     ─┤├─────┤/├──────────────────────────────────────────────────────
        S4:Move  S2:Desc                                                   S5:Star
        left     ent comp                                                  t of des
        complete lete                                                      cent


        M379    X361     X360     X355     M370                            (M380)
220     ─┤├────┤/├──────┤├──────┤├───────┤├──────────────────────────────
        S5:Star Conveyor Conveyor Left sid Bottle t                        S2:Desc
        t of des hand asc hand des e bottle ransfer                        ent comp
        cent    end dete cent det detecti  flow in                         lete
                ction    ection   on       progress

        M380
        ─┤├─
        S2:Desc
        ent comp
        lete
```

157

Step 6: Conveyor hand chuck open

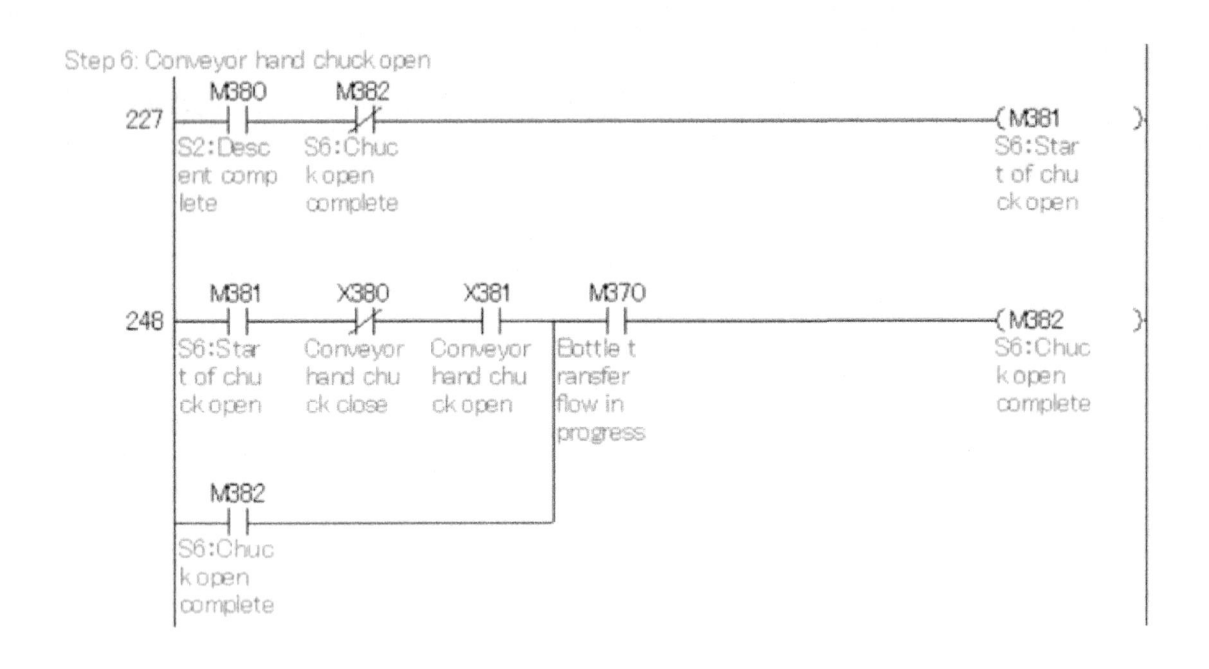

```
       M380      M382                                                    (M381)
227    ─┤├──────┤/├──────────────────────────────────────────────────────( )
       S2:Desc  S6:Chuc                                                  S6:Star
       ent comp k open                                                   t of chu
       lete     complete                                                 ck open


       M381     X380     X381     M370                                   (M382)
248    ─┤├──────┤/├──────┤├──────┤├───────────────────────────────────────( )
       S6:Star  Conveyor Conveyor Bottle t                                S6:Chuc
       t of chu hand chu hand chu ransfer                                 k open
       ck open  ck close ck open  flow in                                 complete
                                  progress

       M382
       ─┤├──
       S6:Chuc
       k open
       complete
```

Step 7: Conveyor hand ascending

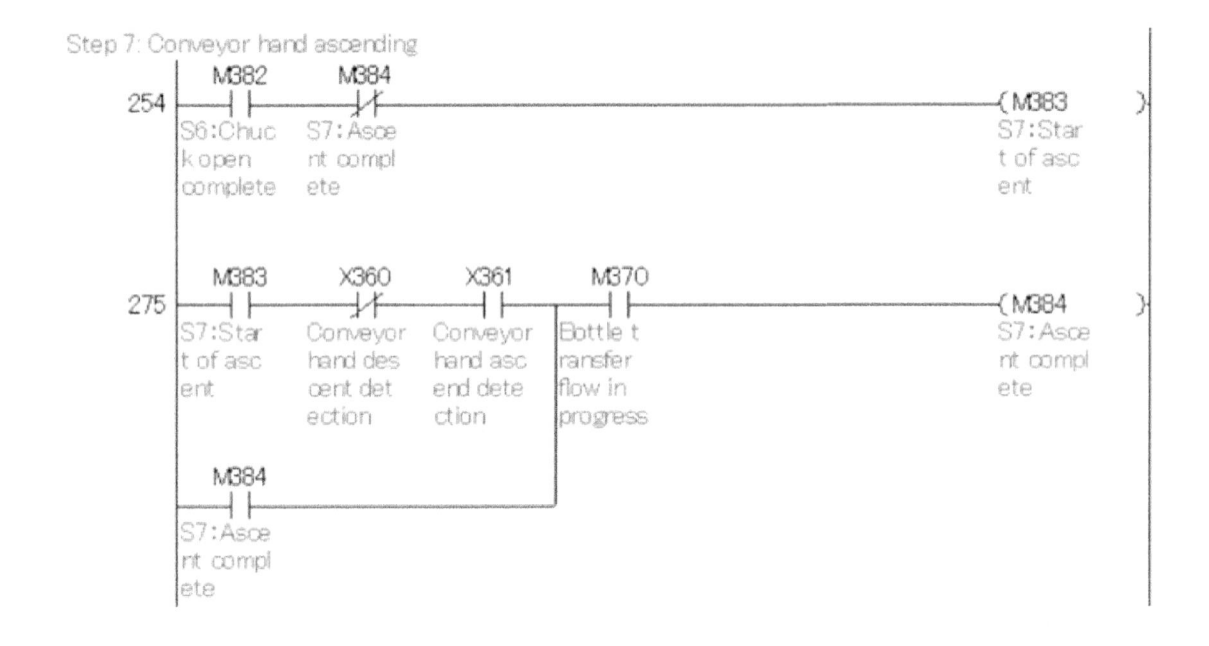

```
       M382     M384                                                     (M383)
254    ─┤├──────┤/├──────────────────────────────────────────────────────( )
       S6:Chuc  S7:Asce                                                  S7:Star
       k open   nt compl                                                 t of asc
       complete ete                                                      ent


       M383     X360     X361     M370                                   (M384)
275    ─┤├──────┤/├──────┤├──────┤├───────────────────────────────────────( )
       S7:Star  Conveyor Conveyor Bottle t                                S7:Asce
       t of asc hand des hand asc ransfer                                 nt compl
       ent      cent det end dete flow in                                 ete
                ection   ction    progress

       M384
       ─┤├──
       S7:Asce
       nt compl
       ete
```

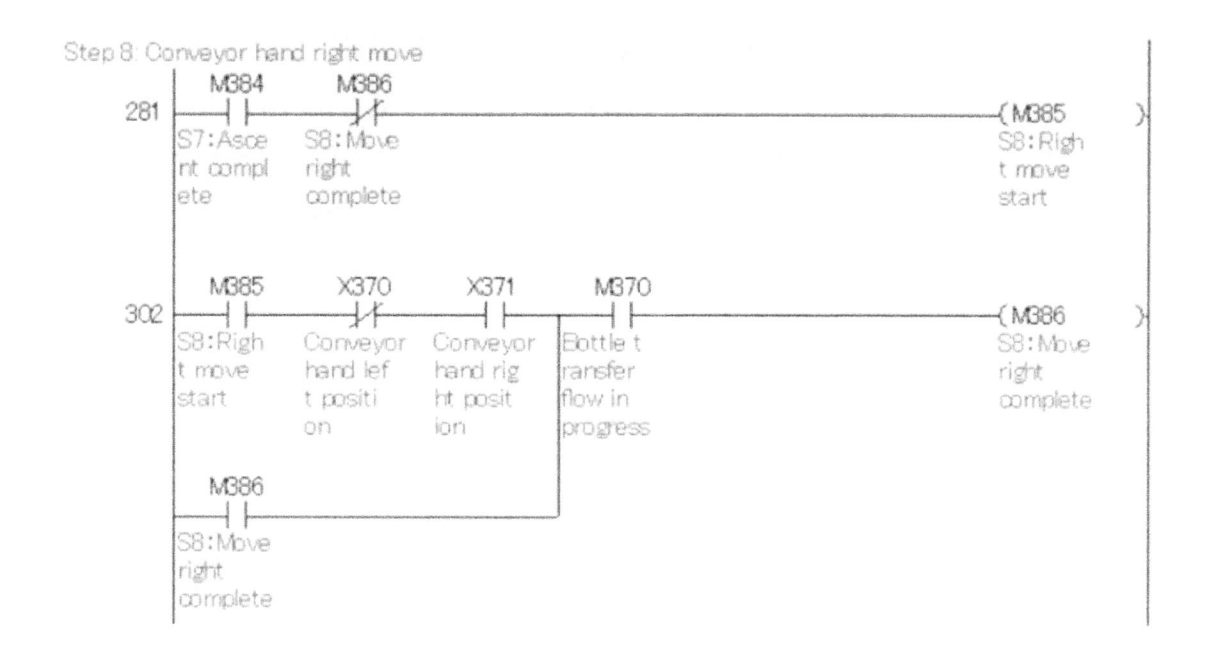

```
Step 8: Conveyor hand right move
          M384    M386
281       ─┤ ├────┤/├─────────────────────────────(M385)
          S7:Asce  S8:Move                        S8:Righ
          nt compl right                          t move
          ete      complete                       start

          M385    X370    X371    M870
302       ─┤ ├────┤/├────┤ ├─────┤ ├──────────────(M386)
          S8:Righ Conveyor Conveyor Bottle t      S8:Move
          t move  hand lef hand rig ransfer       right
          start   t positi ht posit flow in       complete
                  on       ion      progress
          M386
          ─┤ ├
          S8:Move
          right
          complete
```

8. Turn on M387, which completes bottle transfer flow, when M386, which completes right movement of the transfer hand in STEP8, turns ON. Also, add M387 as a condition to turn off the hold during execution of the bottle transfer flow (M370).

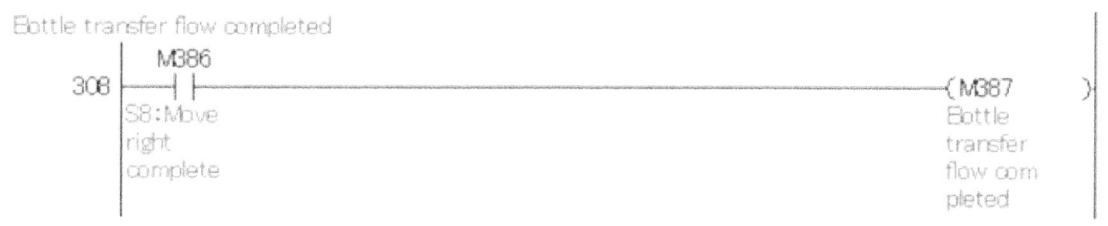

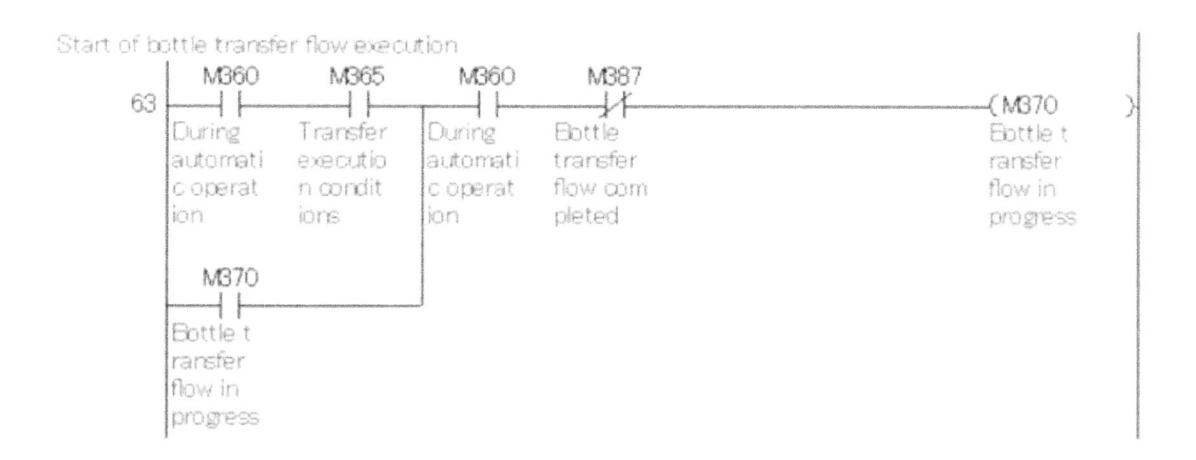

```
Bottle transfer flow completed
          M386
308       ─┤ ├──────────────────────────────────(M387)
          S8:Move                                Bottle
          right                                  transfer
          complete                               flow com
                                                 pleted


Start of bottle transfer flow execution
          M360    M365    M360    M387
63        ─┤ ├────┤ ├──┬──┤ ├────┤/├─────────────(M370)
          During  Transfer During  Bottle         Bottle t
          automati executio automati transfer    ransfer
          c operat n condit c operat flow com    flow in
          ion      ions     ion      pleted      progress
          M370
          ─┤ ├───────┘
          Bottle t
          ransfer
          flow in
          progress
```

9. Each operation output is turned ON by the operation start flag of each step. The descent command of the transfer hand operates in steps 1 and 5, and the up command operates in steps 3 and 7, so the circuit is as follows.

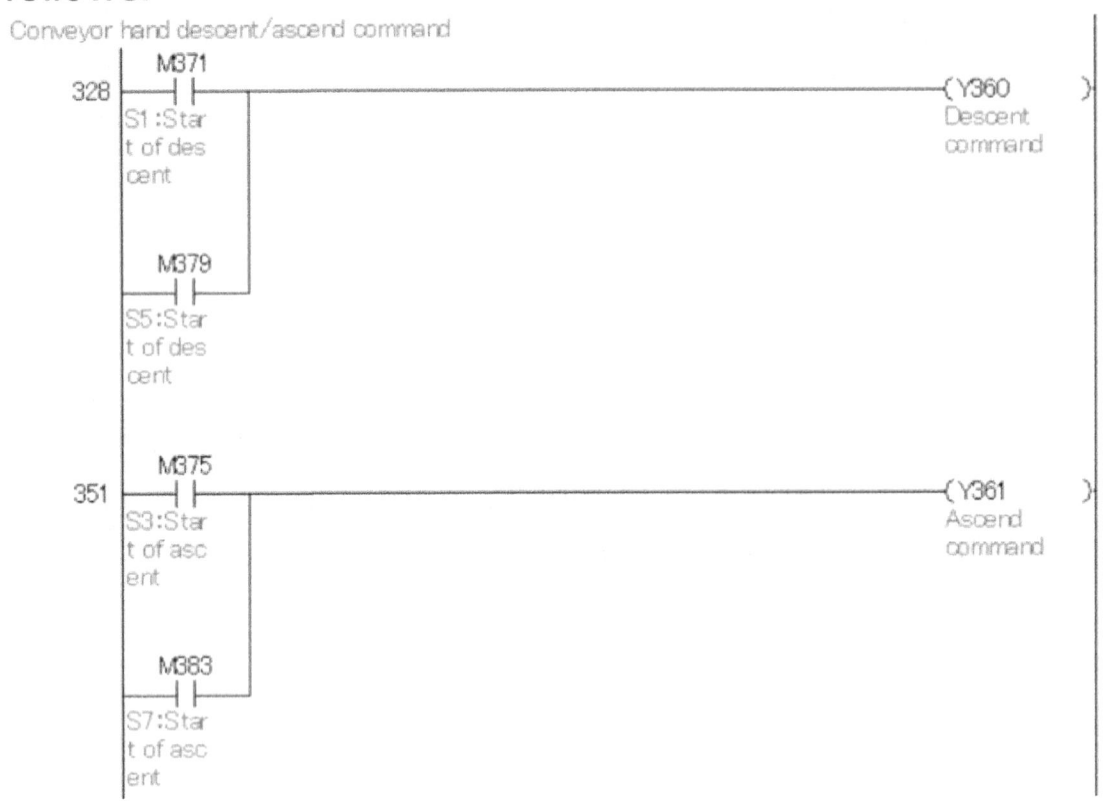

```
Conveyor hand descent/ascend command
             M371
328   ──┤├──────────────────────────────(Y360)
        S1:Start                         Descent
        of descent                       command

             M379
        ──┤├──
        S5:Start
        of descent

             M375
351   ──┤├──────────────────────────────(Y361)
        S3:Start                         Ascend
        of ascent                        command

             M383
        ──┤├──
        S7:Start
        of ascent
```

Left movement, right movement, chuck close, and chuck open commands are created in the same procedure.

```
Conveyor hand left/right movement command
             M377
354   ──┤├──────────────────────────────(Y370)
        S4:Left                          Move Left
        move start                       command

             M385
379   ──┤├──────────────────────────────(Y371)
        S8:Right                         Move Right
        move start                       command
```

```
Conveyor hand Chuck close/chuck open command
        M373
449 ─────┤ ├───────────────────────────────(Y380 )
       S2:Star                              Chuck
       t of chu                             close
       ck close                             command


        M381
475 ─────┤ ├───────────────────────────────(Y381 )
       S6:Star                              Chuck
       t of chu                             open
       ck open                              command
```

10. Double-click "Parameter" in the navigation, then double-click "PLC Parameter" just below it. Then press the "Program " tab, click "Task 2" in the program, press Insert, and press Finish Settings at the bottom right. (This setting is required during simulation.) Also, if you want to change the order of the programs, change the program order on the right side.

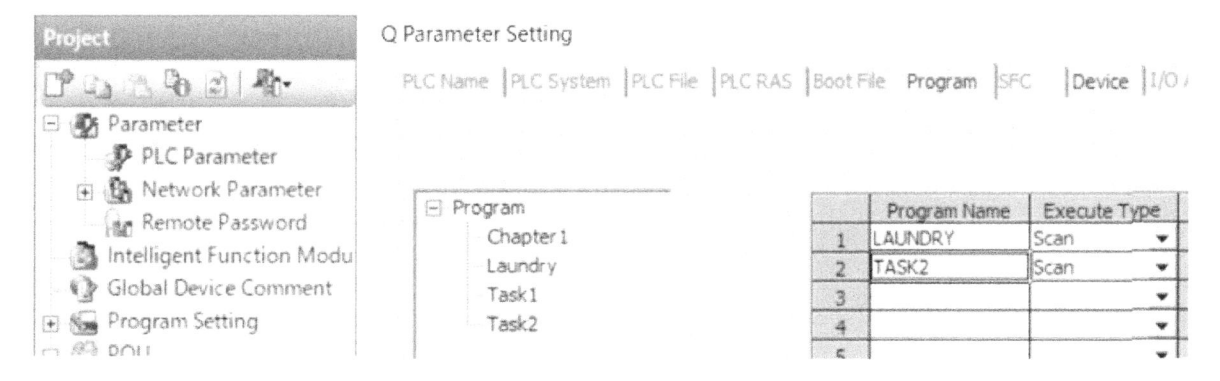

This completes the bottle transfer sequence circuit.

Regarding the operation check, we will create a monitor screen for the bottle transfer sequence in the next task, so after creating it, we will use the simulation function to check the operation.

Exercise 3 (Bottle transfer sequence control: touch panel)

After creating the following touch panel screen to check the operation of the bottle transfer sequence circuit created in Exercise 2, please check that each operation of the PLC program is correct in the simulation operation. Also, for each detection sensor, please create it using switch parts so that you can check the operation on the touch panel. (Arrangement and size are free and OK) Also, please add a button to move between the washing machine operation screen and the bottle transfer monitor screen.

Exercise Question 3 Answers

1. Open the screen created in Chapter 2 and double-click the new button on the left. After that, after inputting Screen number: 2, Title: Bottle transfer monitor screen, press OK at the bottom right to create Screen 2: Bottle transfer monitor screen.

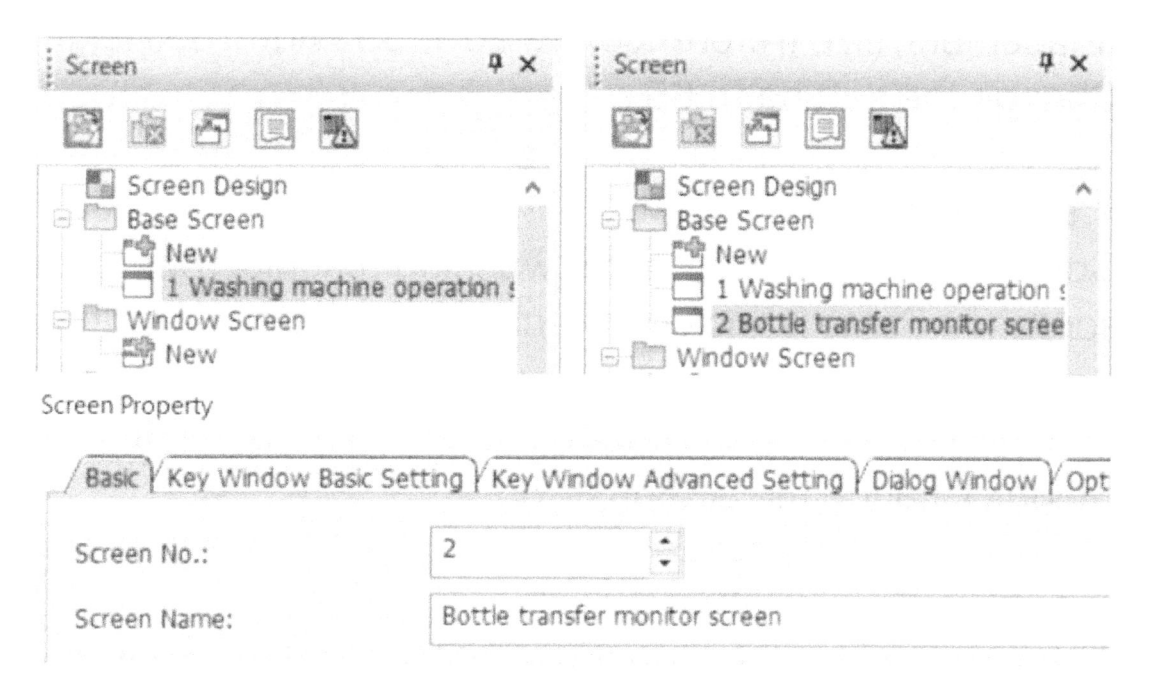

2. First, create a start button, a stop button, an automatic operation lamp, and a bottle transfer start condition OK lamp.

<start button>

Copy the start button of the washing machine operation screen ⇒ Paste it and double click it, [Operation settings] Device: X350, Lamp function device: X350, [Placement/size (reference)] X: 20 Y: 35 Width: 65 Height: Change the setting to 65.

<stop button>

Copy the stop button on the washing machine operation screen ⇒ Paste it and double-click it, [Operation settings] Device: X351, Lamp function device: X351, [Placement/size (reference)] X: 110 Y: 35 Width: 65 Height: Change the setting to 65.

<Automatic operation lamp>

Copy the running lamp on the washing machine operation screen ⇒ Paste it and double-click it, [Operation settings] Device: M360, [Placement/size (reference)] X: 230, Y: 65, Width: 33, Height: 33 Change settings.

Copy and paste the text "Injection time" on the washing machine operation screen ⇒ After double-clicking, and change the text to "Run", [Placement/Size (reference)] X: 230 Y: 40 Width: 32 (Height: Change the setting to 18).

<Bottle transfer start condition OK lamp>

Copy the lamp during automatic operation ⇒ Paste it, double-click it, and then [Operation settings] Device: M365

[Placement/size (reference)] Change the settings to X: 340, Y: 65, width: 33, height: 33.

Copy the text "Run" ⇒ paste it, double-click it, and change the text to "Condition OK", [Arrangement/size (reference)] X: 305 Y: 40 Width: 106 (Height : 18) to change the setting.

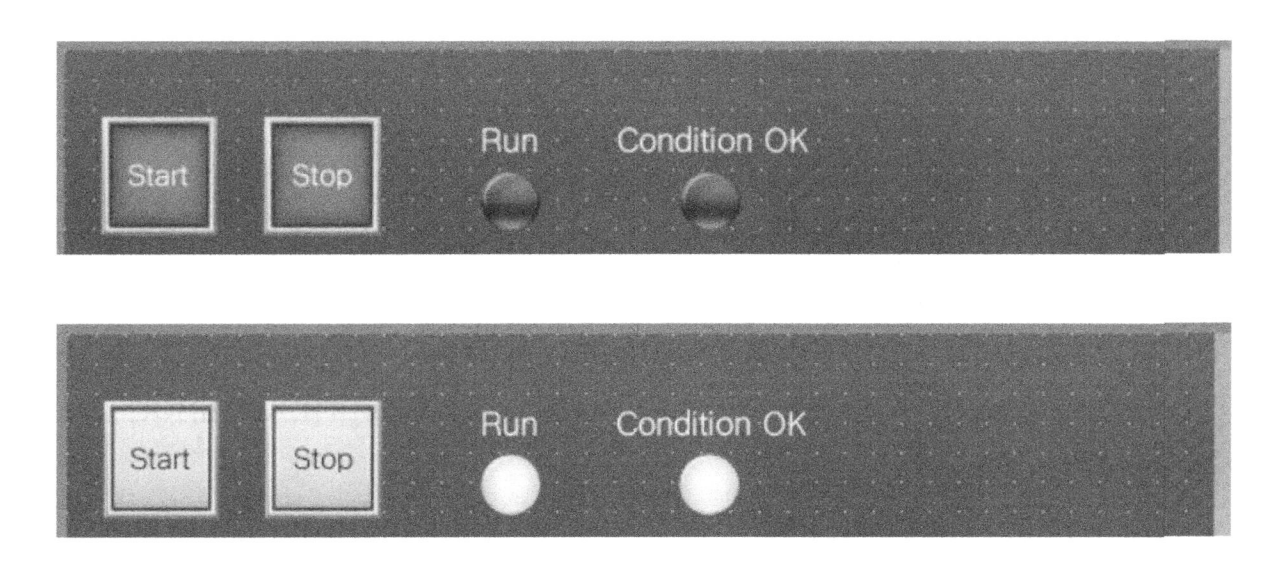

3. Next, create each running lamp and each completed lamp. First step 1: create a descending ramp.

<Step 1: In operation lamp>
Copy one of the operating lamps on the washing machine operation screen ⇒ Paste and double-click, [Operation settings] Device: M371, [Placement/size (reference)] X: 310 Y: 130 Width: 33 Height : Change the setting to 33.

Copy the text "Run" ⇒ paste it, double-click it, change the text to "In operation", set the text color to green (28), [placement/size (reference)] X: 280 Y: 90 width : Change the setting to 76 (height: 36).

<Step 1: Completed lamp>
Copy one of the completion lamps on the washing machine operation screen ⇒ Paste and double-click, [Operation settings] Device: M372, [Placement/size (reference)] X: 370, Y: 130, Width: 33, Height: Change the setting to 33.

Copy the "Working" text ⇒ Paste it, double-click, check the text string is "Done", the text color is green (28), [Placement/Size (reference)] X: 370 Y: 110 Width : Change the setting to 54 (height: 18).

4. Other In operation lamp and completed lamp are created using continuous copy.

After selecting the running lamp and completed lamp created earlier, select the "Edit" tab ⇒ Consecutive copy.

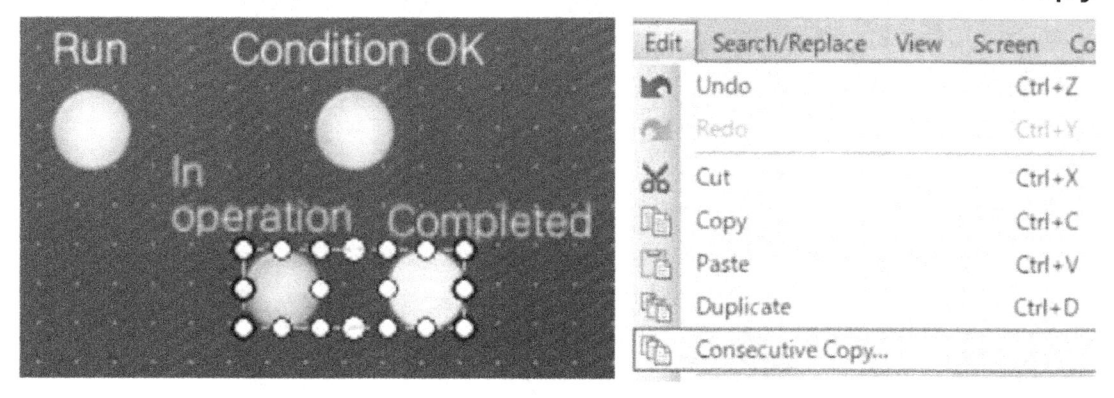

On the continuous copy screen, Y direction: 8 * Enter the number including the lamps that have already been created. Spacing: Check Include Figure/Object, Y direction: 46 * Enter the number for the spacing you want to open +1. Increment target: Check the device number, Increment setting: After entering 2 at once, press OK at the bottom right.

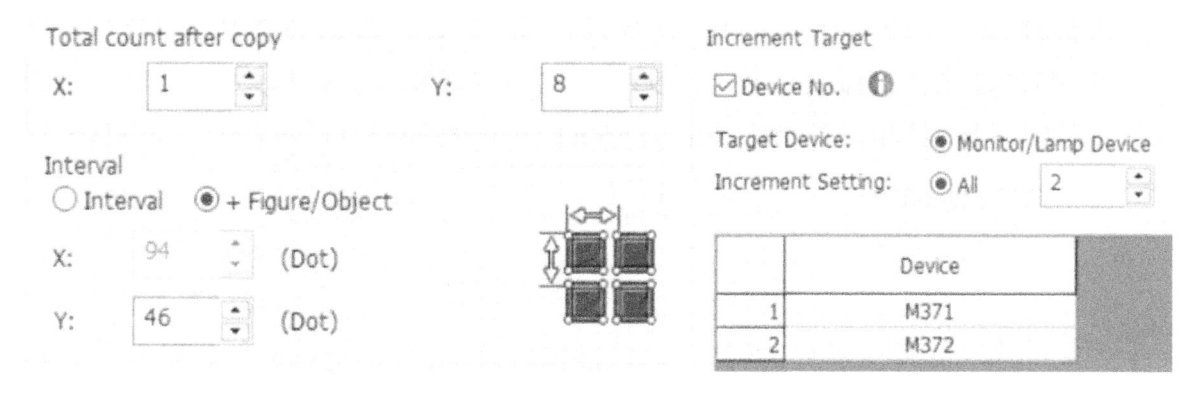

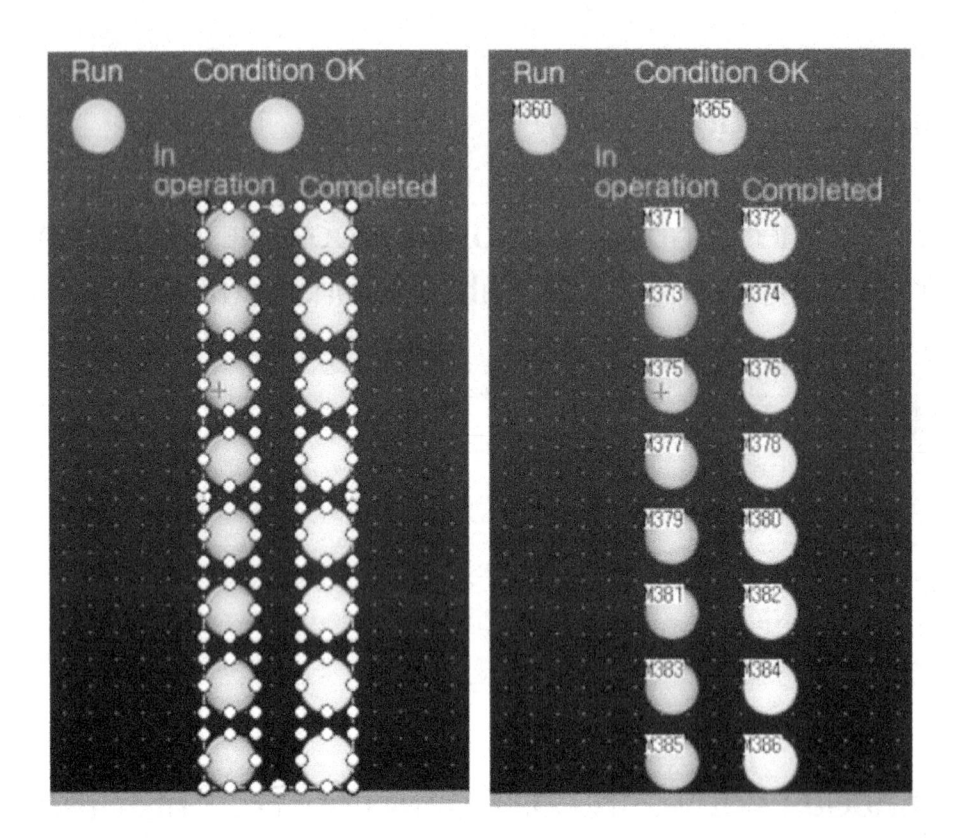

5. Next, create each detection sensor for operation confirmation using switch parts. First, copy and paste one of the completion lamps, double-click it, and press "Convert to switch..." at the bottom of the setting screen to change it to a switch part. And after clicking "bit" of operation addition, after setting to device: X355, operation setting: bit reversal, lamp function device: X355, press OK at the bottom right. Now you can turn on/off the X355 on the screen.

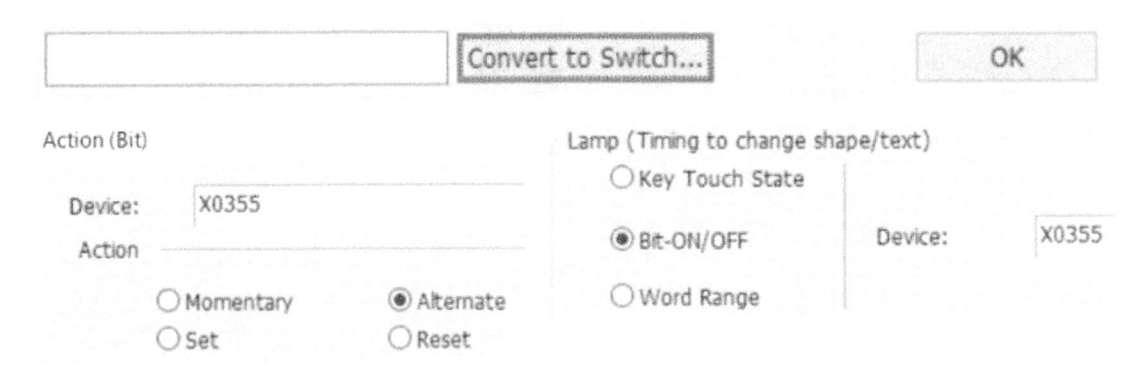

After selecting the created switch, change the settings to [Placement/Size (Reference)] X: 595 Y: 130 Width: 33 Height: 33.

Copy and paste the text "Completed" ⇒ After double-clicking, confirm that the text string is "Operation check", the text color is green (28), [placement / size (reference)] X: 500 Y: 110 Width: Change the setting to 135 (Height: 18).

Then, in the same way as the operating lamp and completion lamp, use continuous copy to create switches for checking the operation of each other detection sensor. Since the devices are different this time, uncheck the device numbers to be incremented, copy them continuously, double-click each switch, and select devices and lamp function devices in order from the top: Change to X355、X356、X360、X361、X370、X371、X380、X381.

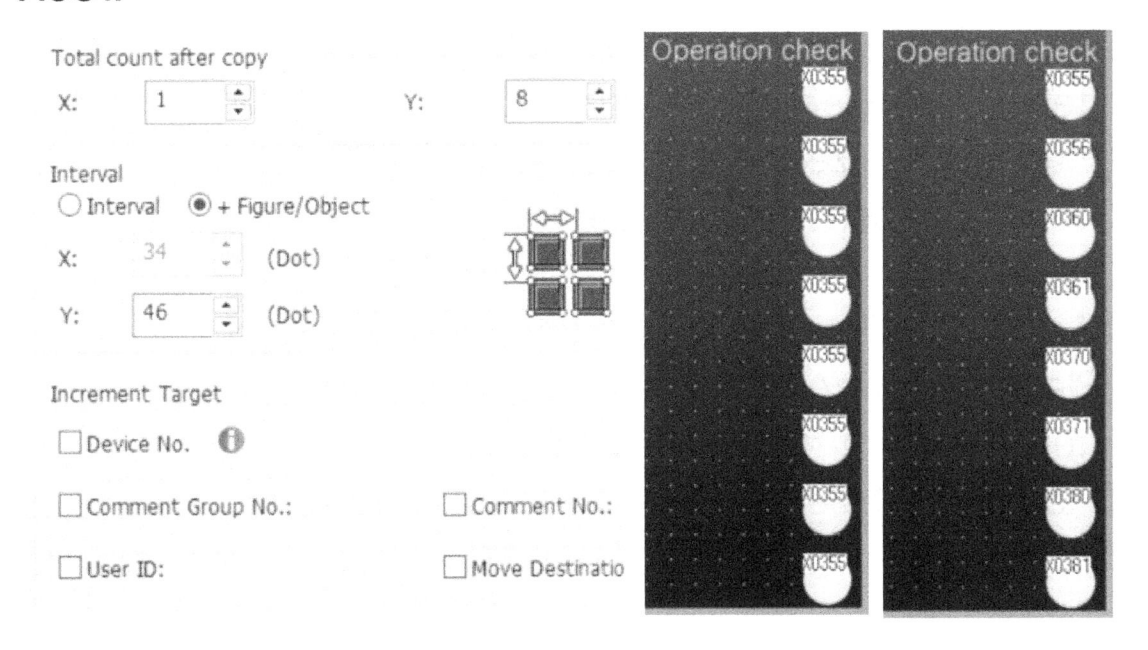

6. Create the upper left date and time display and each character string.

<Date and time display on the upper left>
Copy the date and time displayed on the washing machine operation screen ⇒ Paste

<each string>
Step ⇒ Character size 18
[Placement/size (reference)] X: 10 Y: 110
Conveyor hand ⇒ Character size 18
[Placement/size (reference)] X: 105 Y: 110

Step 1: Descent ⇒ Font size 26
[Placement/size (reference)] X: 10 Y: 135
Step 2: Close chuck ⇒ Character size 26
[Placement/size (reference)] X: 10 Y: 180
Step 3: Ascent ⇒ Font size 26
[Placement/size (reference)] X: 10 Y: 225
Step 4: Move left ⇒ Font size 26
[Placement/size (reference)] X: 10 Y: 270
Step 5: Descent ⇒ Font size 26
[Placement/size (reference)] X: 10 Y: 315
Step 6: Chuck open ⇒ Character size 26
[Placement/size (reference)] X: 10 Y: 360
Step 7: Ascent ⇒ Font size 26
[Placement/size (reference)] X: 10 Y: 405
Step 8: Move right ⇒ Font size 26
[Placement/size (reference)] X: 10 Y: 450

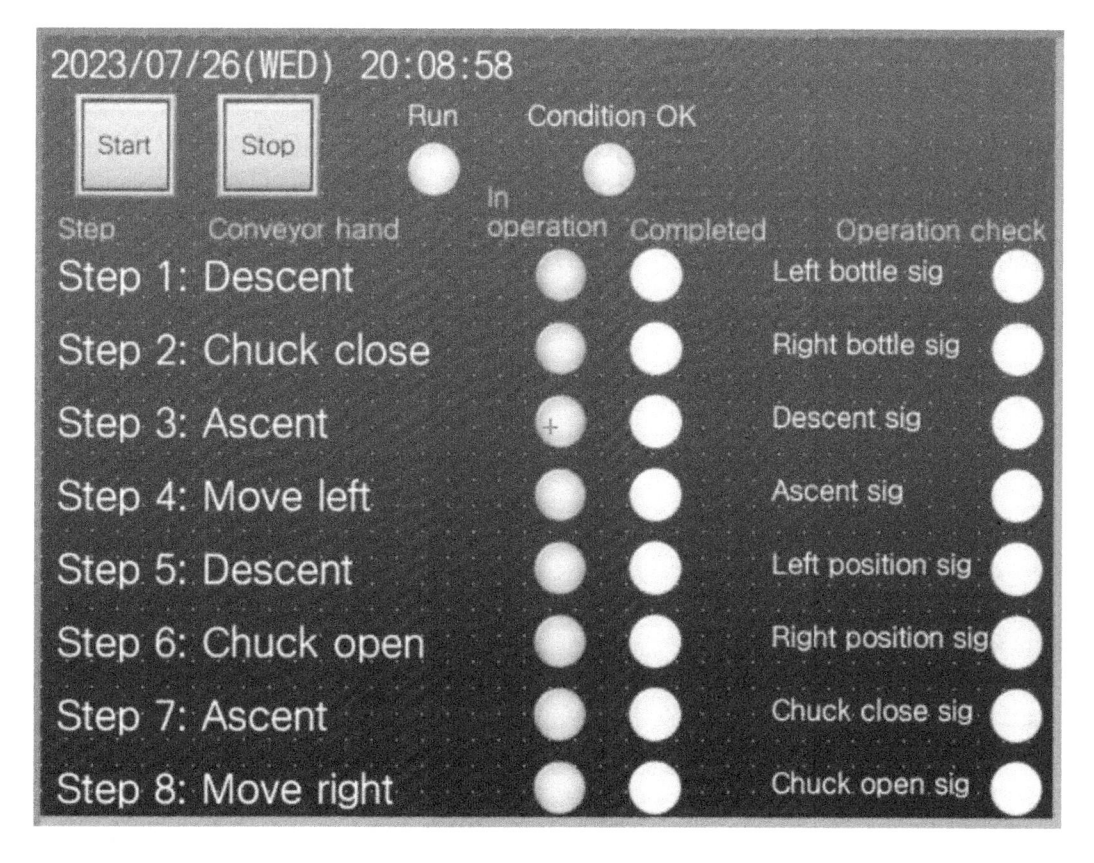

Left bottle sig ⇒ Character size 18
[Placement/size (reference)] X: 460 Y: 135
Right bottle sig ⇒ Character size 18
[Placement/size (reference)] X: 460 Y: 180
Descent sig ⇒ Character size 18
[Placement/size (reference)] X: 460 Y: 225
Ascent sig ⇒ Character size 18
[Placement/size (reference)] X: 460 Y: 270
Left position sig ⇒ Character size 18
[Placement/size (reference)] X: 460 Y: 315
Right position sig ⇒ Character size 18
[Placement/size (reference)] X: 460 Y: 360
Chuck close sig ⇒ Character size 18
[Placement/size (reference)] X: 460 Y: 405
Chuck open sig ⇒ Character size 18
[Placement/size (reference)] X: 460 Y: 450

*Regarding the placement of this string, you can align it neatly without entering the placement in the lower left by using the "Edit" tab ⇒ Align well. For each method of alignment, see the previous book "BASIC PLC PROGRAMMING FOR BEGINNERS (Mitsubishi Electric GX Works2)", so I will omit it.

7. When the simulation starts, the washing machine operation screen will be displayed, so create a button that allows you to switch between the washing machine operation screen and the bottle transfer monitor screen.

<**"Next" button on the washing machine operation screen**> After clicking the "Object" tab ⇒ Switch ⇒ Go To Screen Switch, click the screen to place the part. Then double-click to make each setting.

[Switch destination setting] Screen number: 2
 【style】 After clicking "Figure...", change both key touch OFF/ON lamps to 33 SW_02_0_B.
 【letter】 Character size: 12 Characters: next
[Placement/size] X: 580 Y: 0 Width: 60 Height: 40

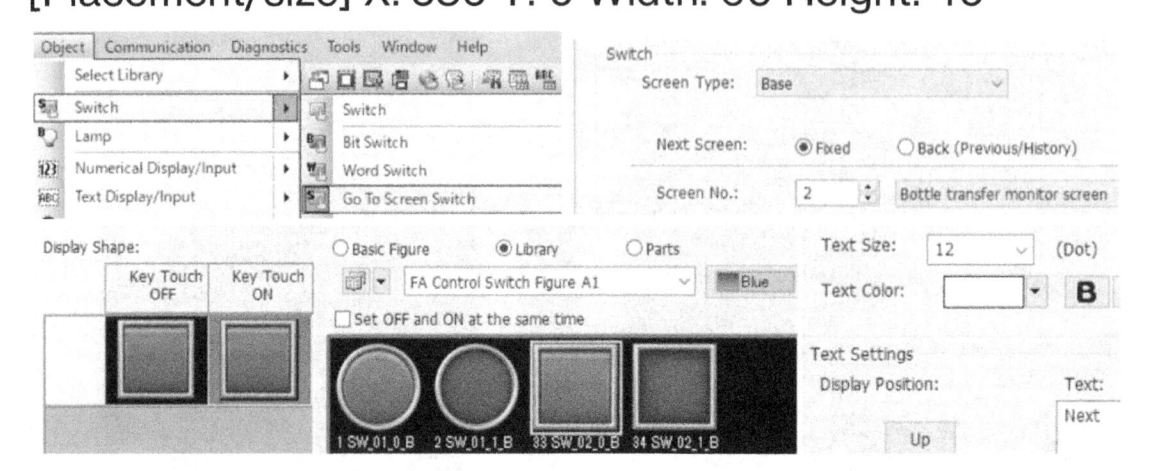

<" Prev." button on the bottle transfer monitor screen>

After copying and pasting the "Next" button on the washing machine operation screen, double-click to make the following settings.
[Switch destination setting] Screen number: 1.
【letter】
Character size: 12 Characters: Prev.
[Placement/size (reference)]
X: 580 Y: 0 Width: 60 Height: 40

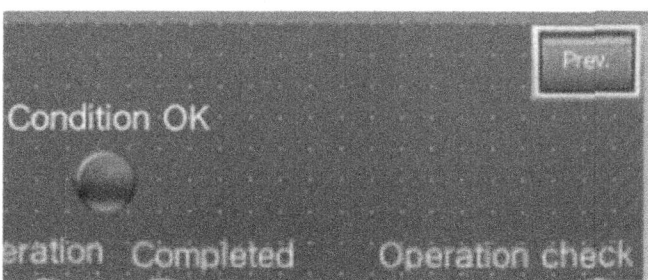

8. Perform a simulation that links the PLC program and the screen to check the operation. Check the following operations using the simulation screen.
・You can move between screens with the "Next" button and "Previous" button.
・When the start button is pressed, the automatic operation lamp turns on.
・When the stop button is pressed, the automatic operation lamp turns off.
・The detection switch for each operation check can be turned ON/OFF.
・When the lamp is off during automatic operation, the right side bottle detection, rise detection, right position

detection, and chuck open detection are all on, and the bottle transfer start condition OK lamp is on.

・If you press the start button while the bottle transfer start condition OK lamp is ON, the operation lamp in step 1 lights up and the start condition OK lamp turns OFF.

・Proceed to the next step by aligning the conditions of each step

・After completing all the steps, the screen on the lower right should be displayed.

・When the left side bottle detection is turned off and the right side bottle detection is turned on from the lower right state, the operation lamp in step 1 lights up.

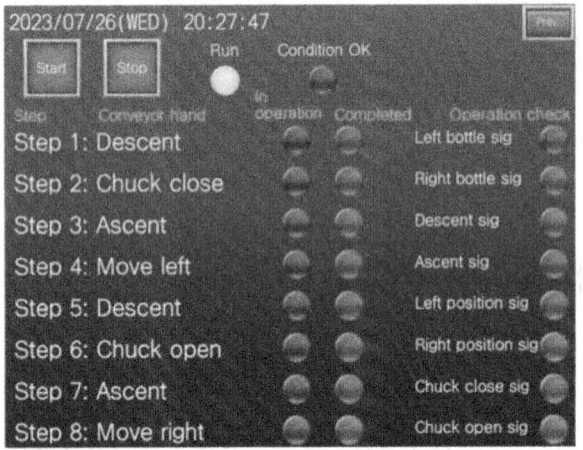

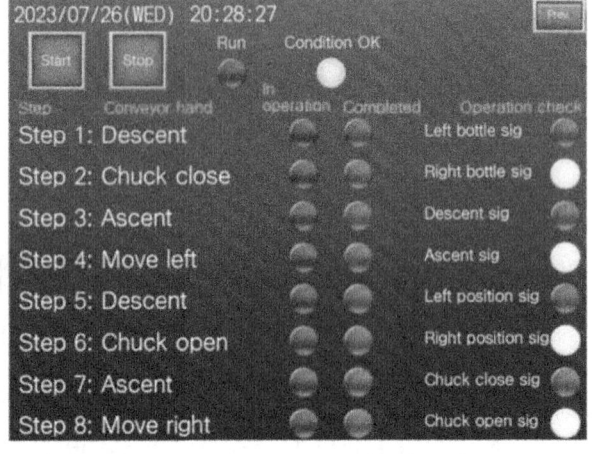

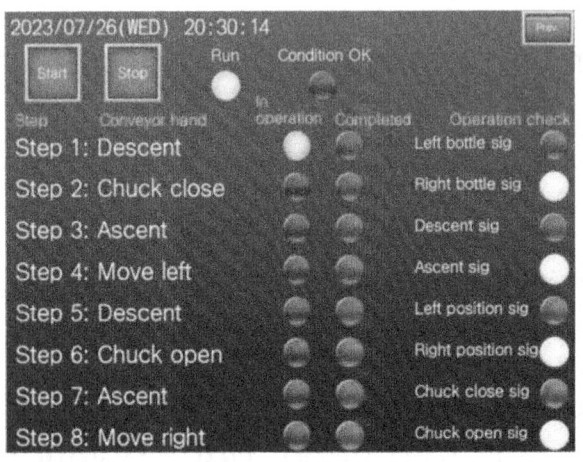

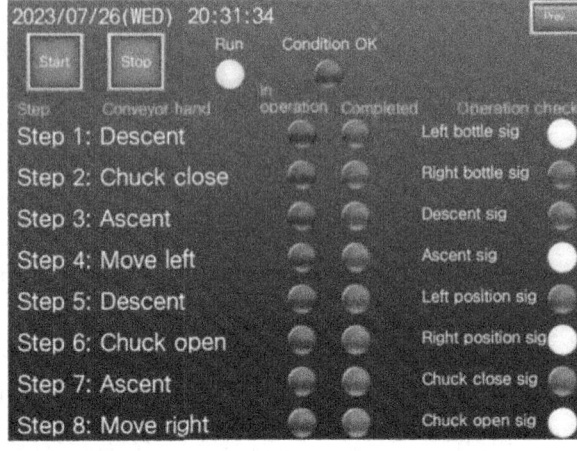

174

Chapter 3 Specific examples of PLC/GOT improvement.

In this chapter, we would like to introduce specific PLC/GOT improvement examples that can be used in actual factories.

3-1 Improvement example 1: Creation of energy-saving operation circuits for equipment/machinery

First, I will explain the recent SDGs (Sustainable Development Goals), carbon neutrality, and the energy-saving operation of equipment and machinery, for which there is an increasing demand for improvement due to soaring electricity bills.

This time, we will explain the energy-saving operation of a facility that uses robots and conveyors (equipment that transports objects in one direction at a constant speed) to transport products that flow continuously every 10 seconds from the upstream as an example.

As for robots, since most robots operate only when a workpiece can be detected under the robot hand from upstream equipment, they are not covered by the energy-saving operation circuit this time.

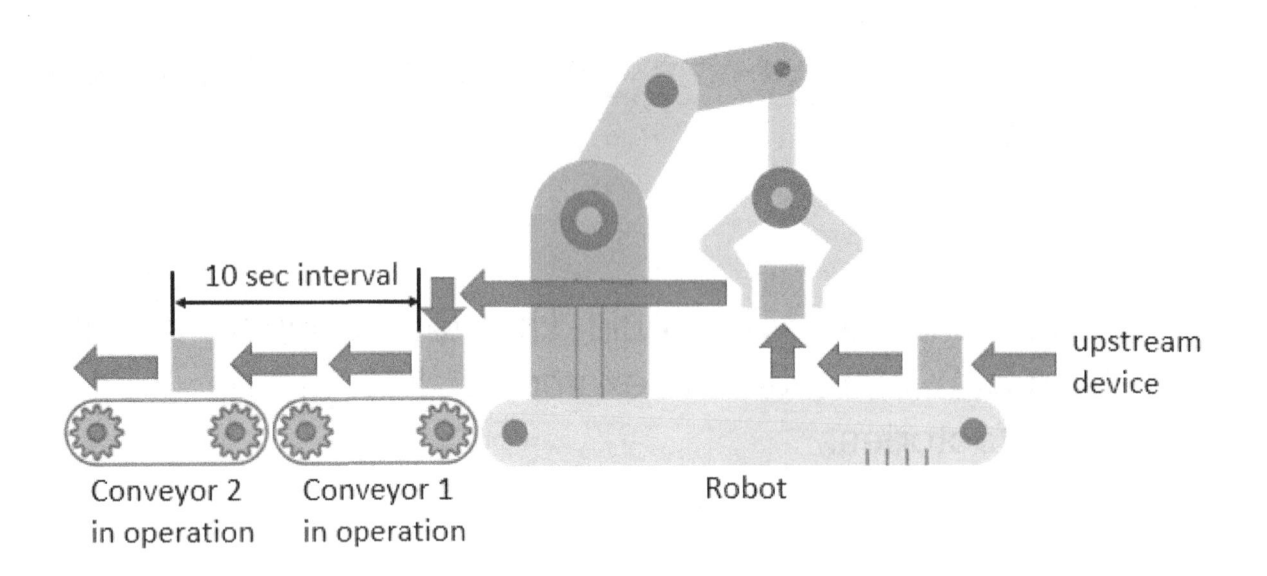

Normally, the conveyor is in constant motion, as the products are continuously transferred at 10-second intervals. However, even if trouble occurs upstream and the product does not flow, the conveyor continues to operate, in which case energy is wasted.

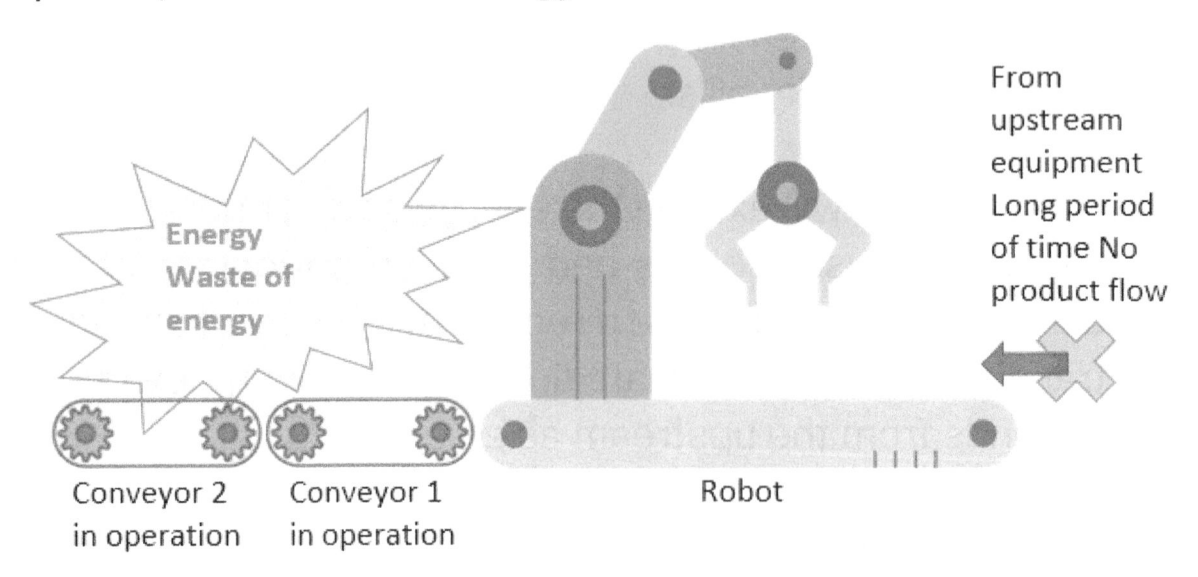

This time, I would like to explain how to perform energy-saving operation of conveyors 1 and 2 while creating a program.

1. First, create new data in the program created in the previous chapter. Right-click the program ⇒ Click Create New Data, then set the data name to "Conveyor" and press OK. Also add "Conveyor" in the program settings.

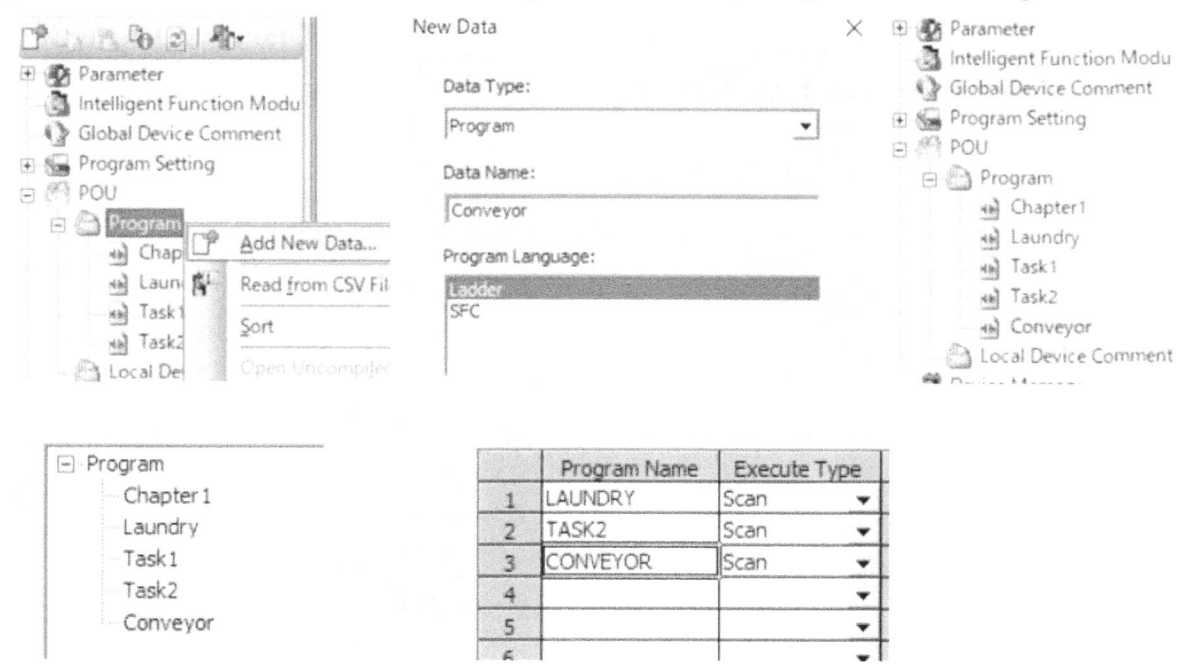

2. Set the operation outputs of conveyors 1 and 2 to Y500 and Y501 on the created "conveyor", and basically create the following circuit so that it will remain ON when the PLC power is turned on. (SM400 is a special relay that is always ON)

As an improvement for energy saving this time, we first installed two product detection sensors, product detection sensor 1 (X500) where the product is transferred from the upstream device to the robot, and product detection sensor 2 (X501) where the robot places the product on the conveyor 1. Add a sensor.

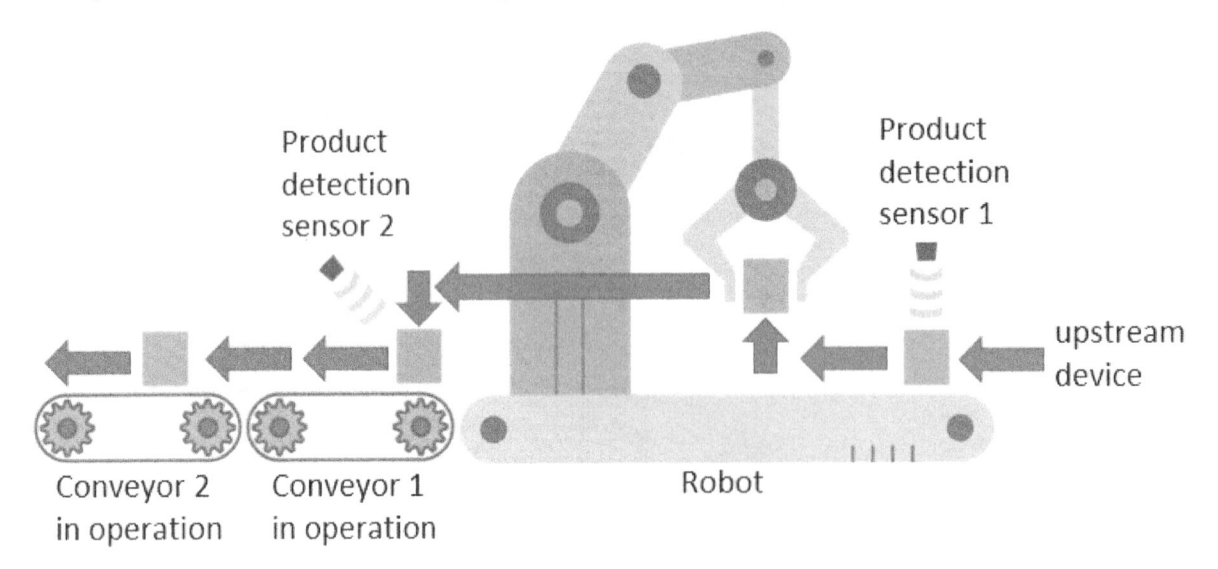

And if each sensor is OFF for 60 seconds, it will be judged that the product is not flowing from the upstream device, and the conveyor will stop. However, if you stop the part where the sensor is located, the product will not flow, so the next conveyor will be stopped.

3. Create an energy-saving operation circuit for conveyor 1 using product detection sensor 1 (X500) where products are transferred from the upstream device to the robot as follows.

```
Conveyor 1,2 operation output
      SM400      X500                                              K600
0 ─────┤ ├───────┤/├──────────────────────────────────────────────(T500)─
      Always    Product                                          Sensor 1
      ON       detectio                                          OFF time
               n sensor
               1
               T500
               ─┤/├──────────────────────────────────────────────(Y500)─
               Sensor 1                                          Conveyor
               OFF time                                          1 operat
                                                                 ion comm
                                                                 and
```

In this circuit, when X500 is OFF for 60 seconds, T500 is turned ON and the output Y500 of conveyor 1 is turned OFF.

```
Conveyor 1,2 operation output
      SM400      X500                                              K600
0 ─────┤ ├───────┤/├──────────────────────────────────────────────(T500)─
                                                                   600
      Always    Product                                          Sensor 1
      ON       detectio                                          OFF time
               n sensor
               1
               T500
               ─┤/├──────────────────────────────────────────────(Y500)─
               Sensor 1                                          Conveyor
               OFF time                                          1 operat
                                                                 ion comm
                                                                 and
```

When the product flows and X500 turns ON, T500 turns OFF, so output Y500 of conveyor 1 turns ON.

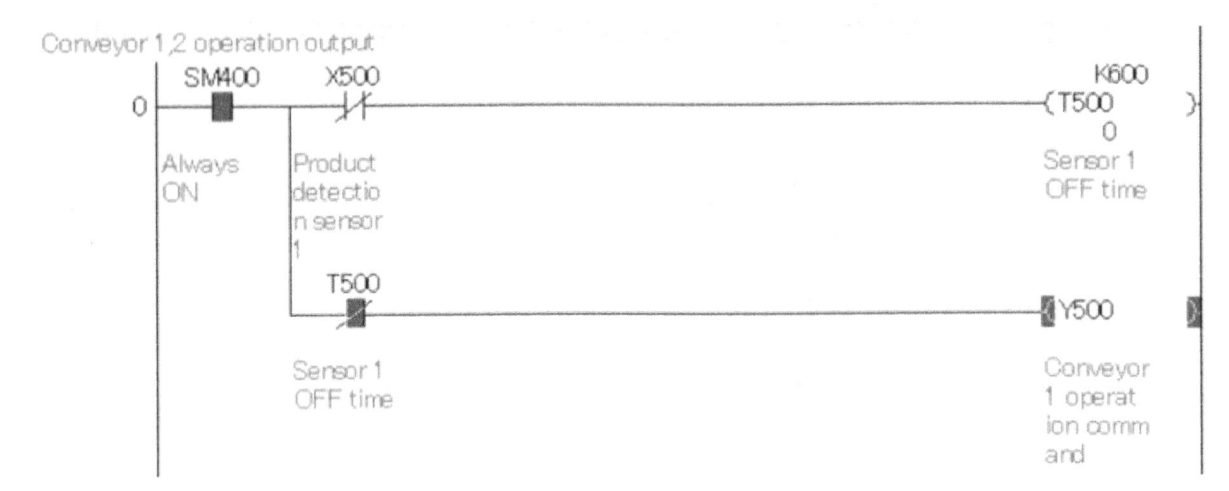

```
Conveyor 1,2 operation output
       SM400        X500                                            K600
  0 ─────┤├────────┤/├──────────────────────────────────────────────(T500)─
         Always    Product                                          0
         ON        detectio                                         Sensor 1
                   n sensor                                         OFF time
                   1
                   T500
                   ┤/├──────────────────────────────────────────────(Y500)─
                   Sensor 1                                         Conveyor
                   OFF time                                         1 operat
                                                                    ion comm
                                                                    and
```

Create Conveyor 2 in the same way.

```
       SM400        X501                                            K600
 27 ─────┤├────────┤/├──────────────────────────────────────────────(T501)─
         Always    Product                                          Sensor 2
         ON        detectio                                         OFF time
                   n sensor
                   2
                   T501
                   ┤/├──────────────────────────────────────────────(Y501)─
                   Sensor 2                                         Conveyor
                   OFF time                                         2 operat
                                                                    ion comm
                                                                    and
```

In this way, you can reduce power consumption by adding a product detection sensor and stopping the conveyor when the sensor is turned off for a specified time. This is not limited to conveyors, and it is possible to practice energy saving with the same procedure for machines that continue to operate normally.

Conversely, if product detection sensor 1 continues to be ON for 10 seconds, it is possible to determine that the equipment has stopped due to a problem and stop conveyor 1. In many cases, robots and conveyors stop due to trouble, so adding such a circuit is often not necessary. If you want to add it, please create it as follows. (This circuit is not added in the following explanation)

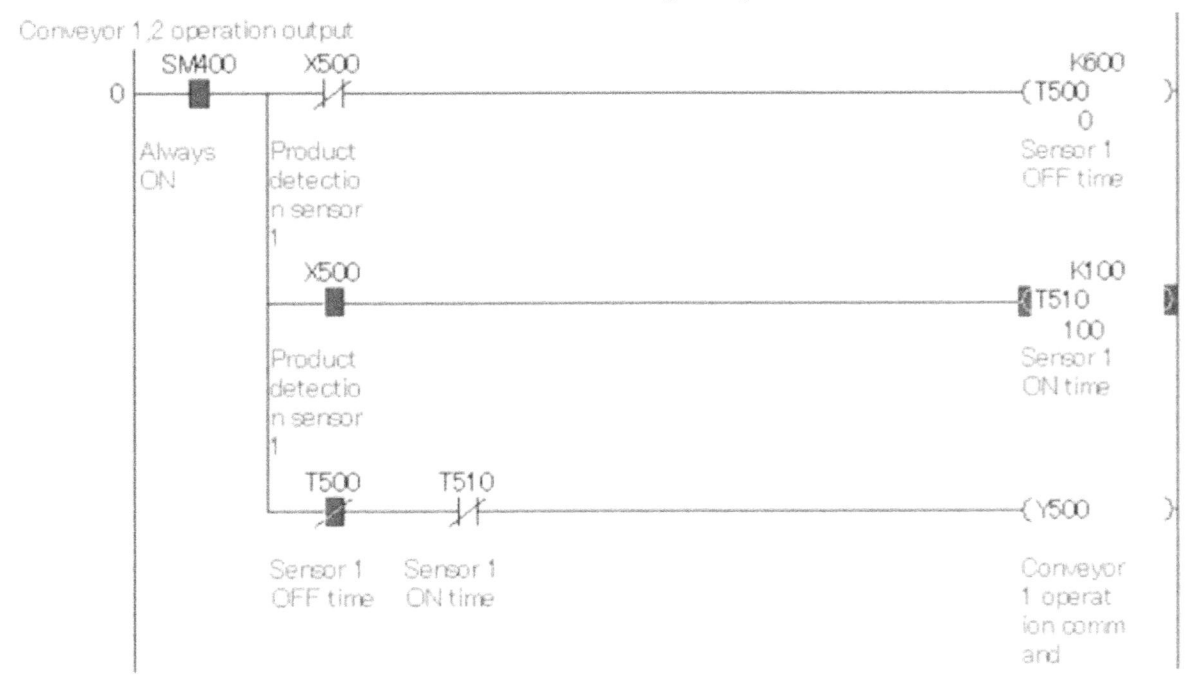

```
Conveyor 1,2 operation output
     SM400      X500                                              K600
0 ────┤├────────┤/├─────────────────────────────────────────────(T500 )
      Always    Product                                           0
      ON        detectio                                          Sensor 1
                n sensor                                          OFF time
                1
                X500                                              K100
                ─┤├───────────────────────────────────────────────(T510 )
                                                                  100
                Product                                           Sensor 1
                detectio                                          ON time
                n sensor
                1
                T500       T510
                ─┤├────────┤/├────────────────────────────────────( Y500 )
                Sensor 1   Sensor 1                               Conveyor
                OFF time   ON time                                1 operat
                                                                  ion comm
                                                                  and
```

4. In addition, if it is not possible to check the operation of the created circuit because the equipment does not stop for a long time, in addition to changing the PLC program, by adding a valid / invalid function, it is possible to check the operation by looking at the timing.

This time I am using a latching relay L500 to create a valid/invalid flag. A latch relay is a device that retains its state even if the power to the PLC is turned off.

The circuit with valid/invalid flag added is as follows. If L500 is turned off (disabled), even if X500 is off for 60 seconds, T500 will not turn on, so Y500 will remain on.

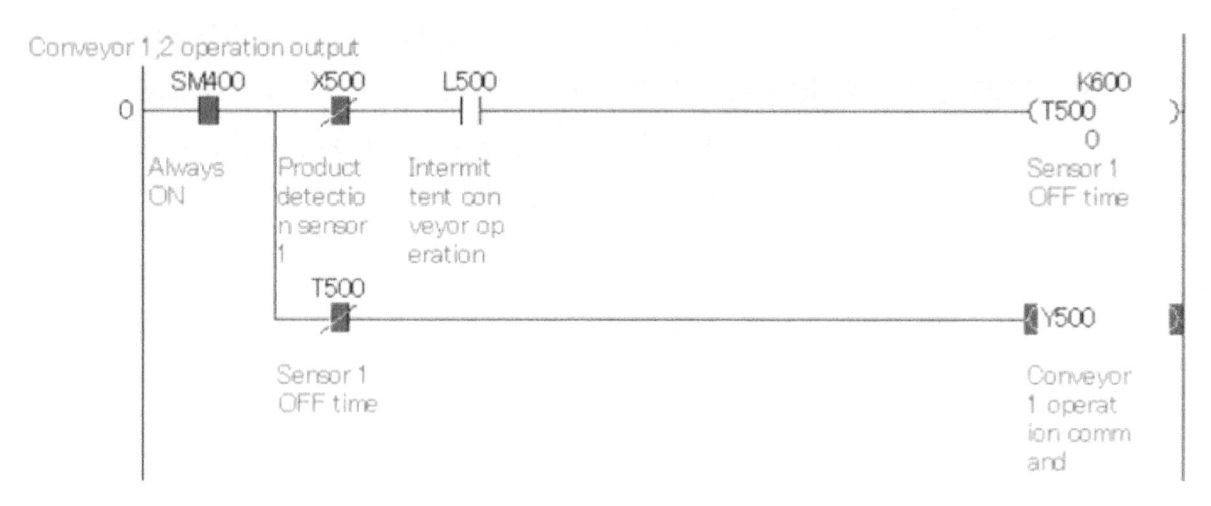

```
Conveyor 1,2 operation output
    SM400      X500      L500                                    K600
0───┤├────┬───┤/├──────┤ ├─────────────────────────────────────(T500 )
    Always │  Product   Intermit                                  0
    ON     │  detectio  tent con                                  Sensor 1
           │  n sensor  veyor op                                  OFF time
           │  1         eration
           │  T500
           └──┤/├──────────────────────────────────────────────── Y500
              Sensor 1                                            Conveyor
              OFF time                                            1 operat
                                                                  ion comm
                                                                  and
```

When L500 is turned ON (enabled), T500 turns ON and Y500 turns OFF after X500 is OFF for 60 seconds.

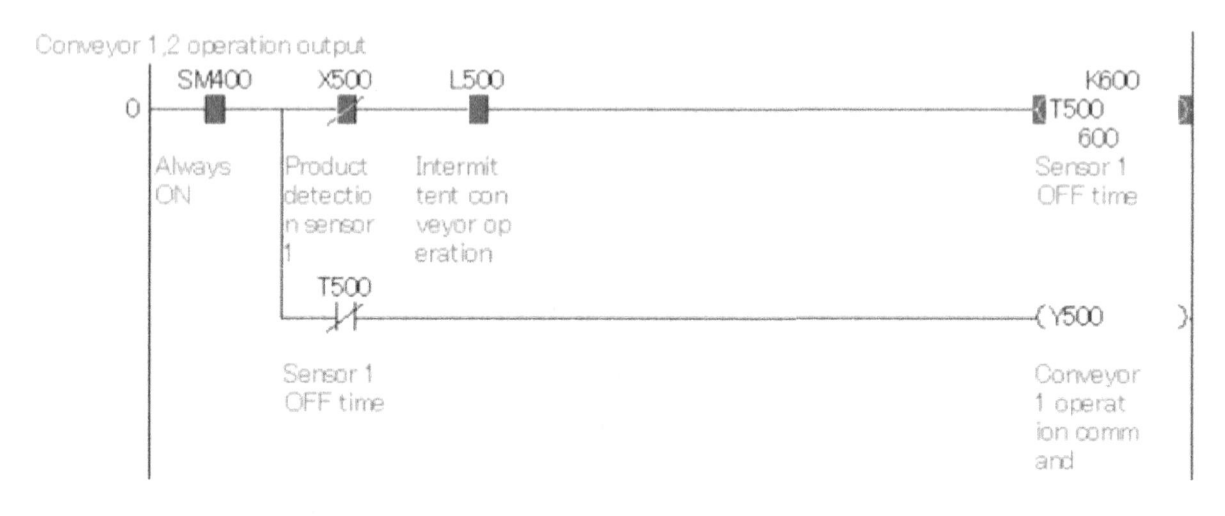

```
Conveyor 1,2 operation output
    SM400      X500      L500                                    K600
0───┤├────┬───┤/├──────┤ ├─────────────────────────────────────(T500 )
    Always │  Product   Intermit                                  600
    ON     │  detectio  tent con                                  Sensor 1
           │  n sensor  veyor op                                  OFF time
           │  1         eration
           │  T500
           └──┤/├──────────────────────────────────────────────(Y500 )
              Sensor 1                                            Conveyor
              OFF time                                            1 operat
                                                                  ion comm
                                                                  and
```

Add L500 to the conveyor 2 side in the same way.

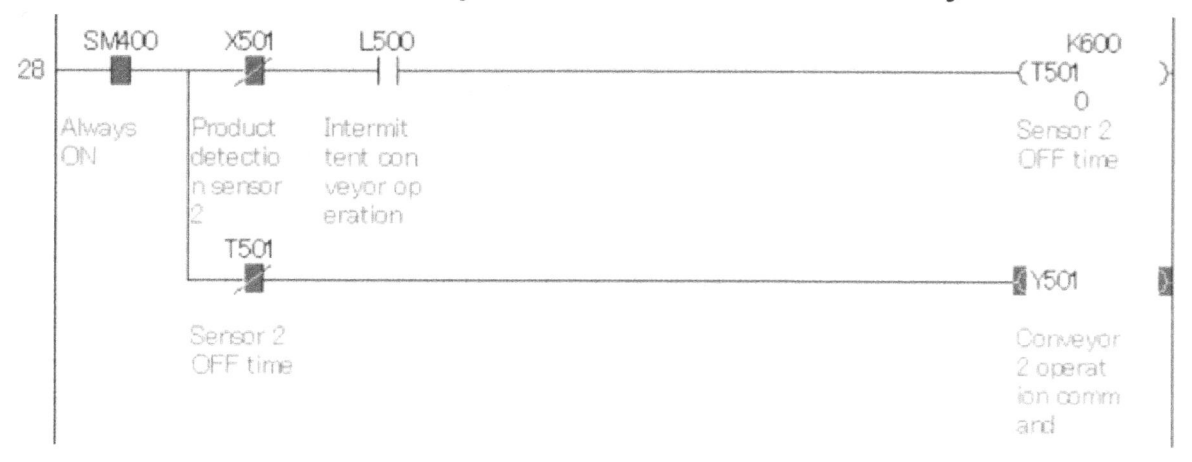

```
      SM400      X501      L500                                              K600
28 ────┨┠────────┨/┠───────┨┠─────────────────────────────────────────────(T501  )
       Always   Product   Intermit                                           0
       ON       detectio  tent con                                           Sensor 2
                n sensor  veyor op                                           OFF time
                2         eration
                T501
                ─┨/┠───────────────────────────────────────────────────────────[Y501]
                Sensor 2                                                     Conveyor
                OFF time                                                     2 operat
                                                                             ion comm
                                                                             and
```

5. Also, if you have a touch panel, you can make further fine adjustments by adding the enable/disable button introduced earlier and setting the sensor OFF time so that you can adjust the sensor OFF time for each conveyor.

Assuming that there is a touch panel in the future, we will create the necessary PLC program according to the addition of enable/disable buttons, the display of the sensor OFF time for each conveyor, and the set time until the conveyor stops, and then carry out the simulation.

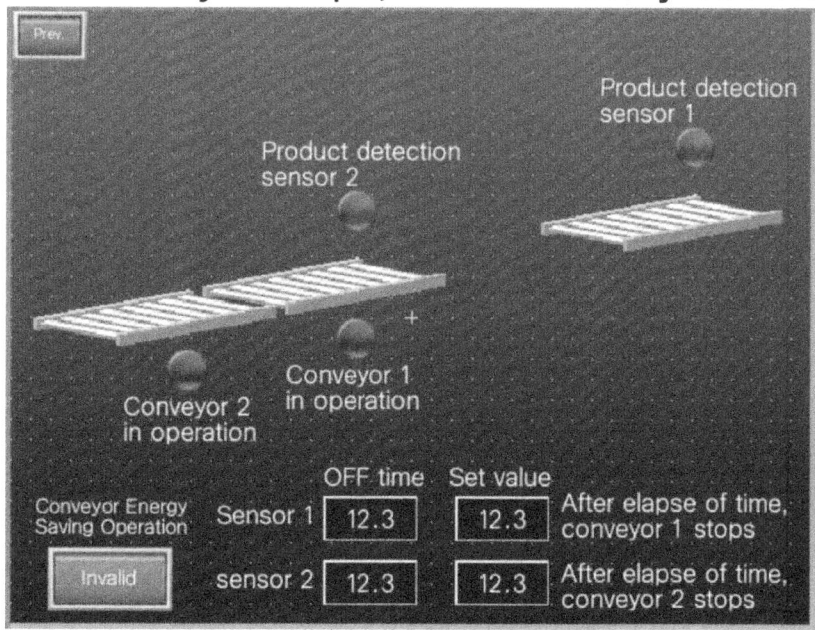

6. First, change the PLC program.

In the previous program, the time of T500 and T501 was fixed at 60 seconds but change K600 to a device so that the time can be adjusted. This time, D500 (product detection sensor 1 OFF setting time) is used for T500, and D501 (product detection sensor 2 OFF setting time) is used for T501.

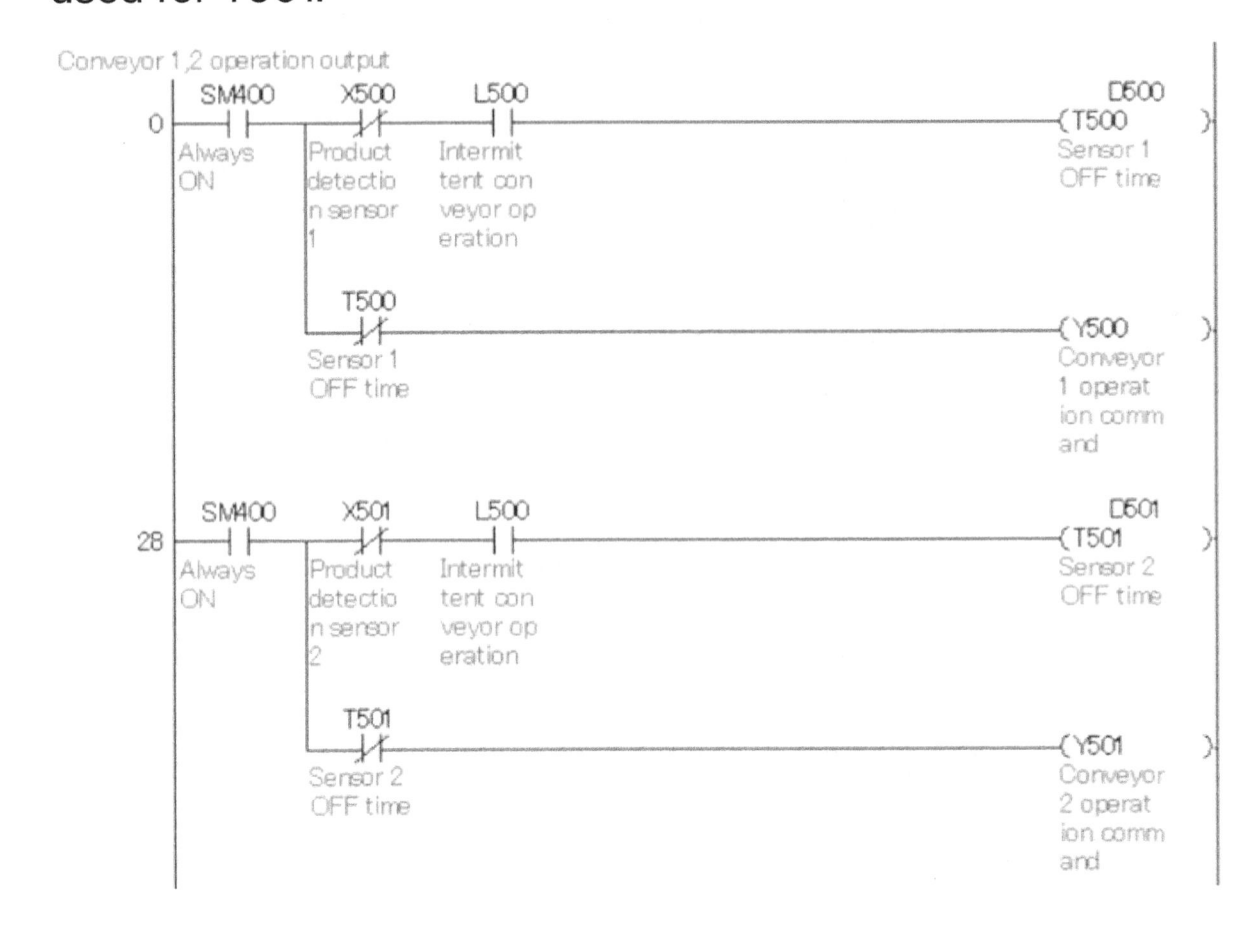

```
Conveyor 1,2 operation output
         SM400      X500       L500                                    D500
    0 ───┤ ├───────┤/├────────┤ ├─────────────────────────────────────(T500 )─
         Always    Product    Intermit                                 Sensor 1
         ON        detectio   tent con                                 OFF time
                   n sensor   veyor op
                   1          eration

                   T500
                  ─┤/├───────────────────────────────────────────────(Y500 )─
                   Sensor 1                                           Conveyor
                   OFF time                                           1 operat
                                                                      ion comm
                                                                      and

         SM400      X501       L500                                    D501
   28 ───┤ ├───────┤/├────────┤ ├─────────────────────────────────────(T501 )─
         Always    Product    Intermit                                 Sensor 2
         ON        detectio   tent con                                 OFF time
                   n sensor   veyor op
                   2          eration

                   T501
                  ─┤/├───────────────────────────────────────────────(Y501 )─
                   Sensor 2                                           Conveyor
                   OFF time                                           2 operat
                                                                      ion comm
                                                                      and
```

7. Next, create a screen. Open the screen created in Chapter 2 and double-click the new button on the left. After that, after entering screen number: 3, title: Conveyor energy saving setting, press OK at the bottom right to create screen 3: Conveyor energy saving setting screen.

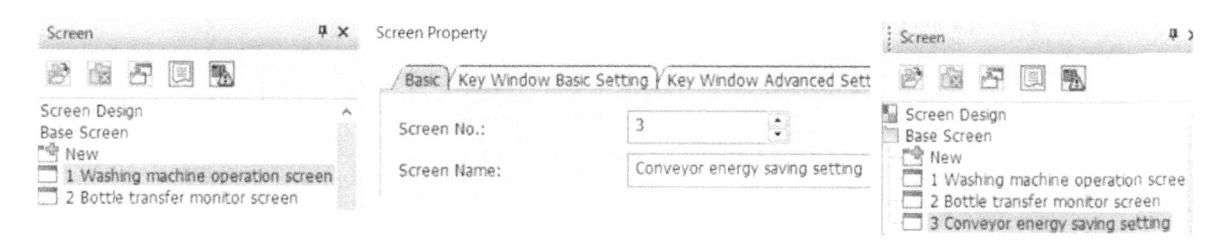

8. First, place the display parts of the conveyor. "Object" tab ⇒ Select a library ⇒ Click the library list or press F9 to display the library on the right side of the screen. System Library in the Library ⇒ Search By Subject ⇒ Illustration ⇒ Illustration After selecting "10 Conv04_" in Illustration parts_3, click the screen to place the conveyor parts, so set the placement and size to X: 420 Y: 140 Width: 200 Height: Set to 50.

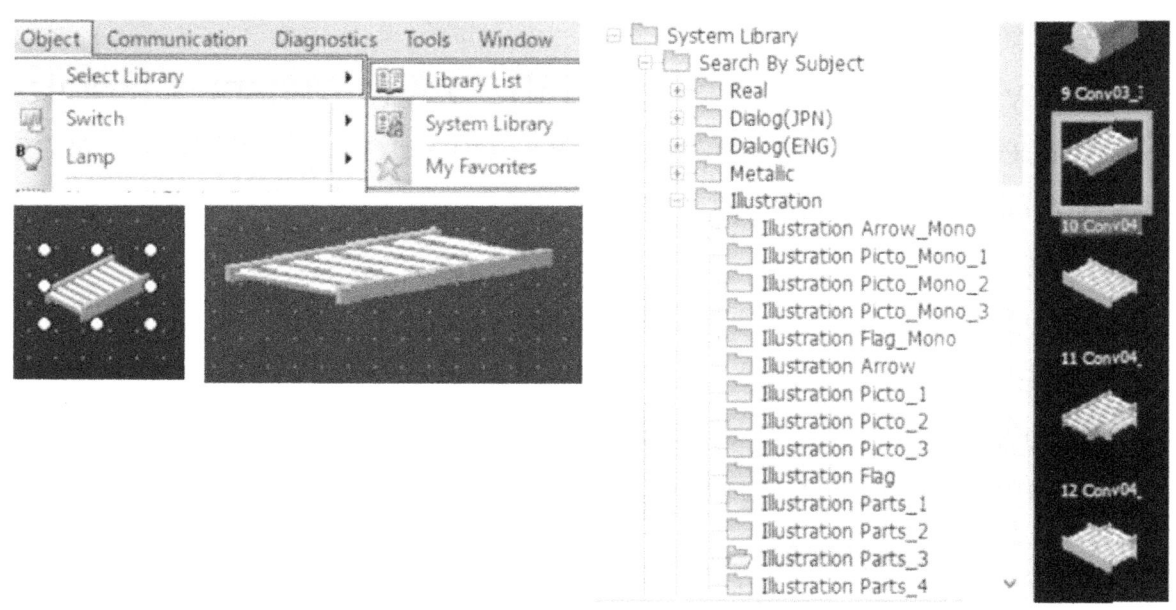

Copy the created conveyor part ⇒ Paste it twice, and
[Placement/size]　X: 150 Y: 190 Width: 200 Height: 50
[Placement/Size]　　X: 15 Y: 215 Width: 200 Height: 50

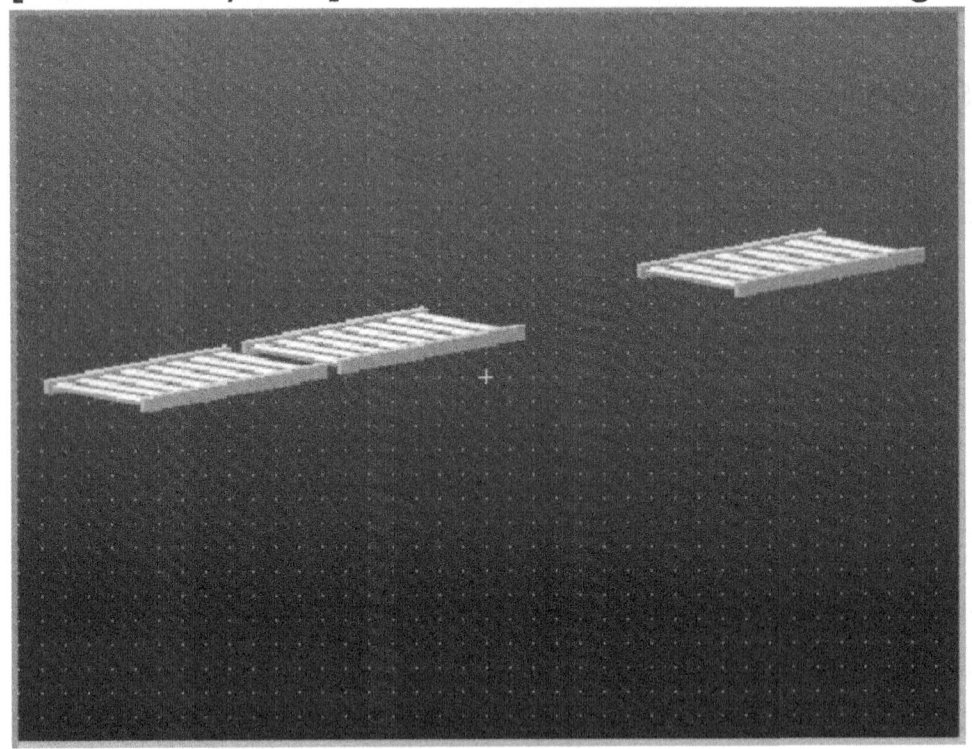

9. Next, create a conveyor running lamp and a product detection sensor.

Copy the operating lamp on the bottle transport monitor screen created in the previous chapter ⇒ Paste it twice, double-click each part, and
　【device】 Y500
[Placement/size]　X: 260 Y: 240 Width: 33 Height: 33
　【device】 Y501
[Placement/size]　X: 125 Y: 265 Width: 33 Height: 33
Change the setting to

As for the characters, copy one of the characters on the bottle transport monitor screen ⇒ Paste twice, double-click each part, and

【letter】

Character string: Conveyor 1 in operation Text size: 20
[Placement/size]　X: 220 Y: 275 Width: 107(Height: 40)

【letter】

Character string: Conveyor 2 in operation Text size: 20
[Placement/size]　X: 90 Y: 300 Width: 107 (Height: 40)
Change the setting to

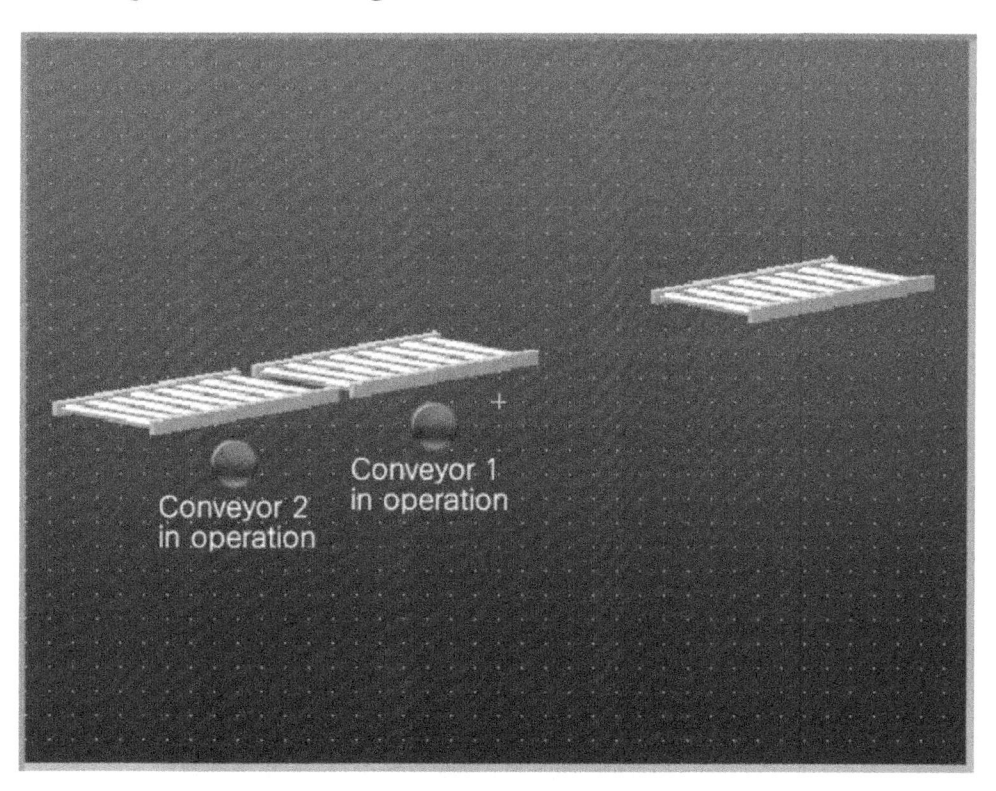

10. Create a product detection sensor. This time, the product detection sensor is created as a switch so that it can be easily debugged (operation check) on the touch panel. Copy the operation confirmation lamp on the bottle transfer monitor screen ⇒ Paste it twice, double-click each part, and
  【device】　Device: X500 Lamp function device: X500
[Placement/size]　X: 530 Y: 90 Width: 33 Height: 33
  【device】　Device: X501 Lamp function device: X501
[Placement/size]　X: 260 Y: 140 Width: 33 Height: 33

For the characters, copy the characters during conveyor 1 operation ⇒ paste and double-click each part,
  【letter】　String: Product detection sensor 1
[Placement/size]　X: 470 Y: 50 Width: 159 (Height: 40)
  【letter】　String: Product detection sensor 2
[Placement/size]　X: 200 Y: 100 Width: 159 (Height: 40)

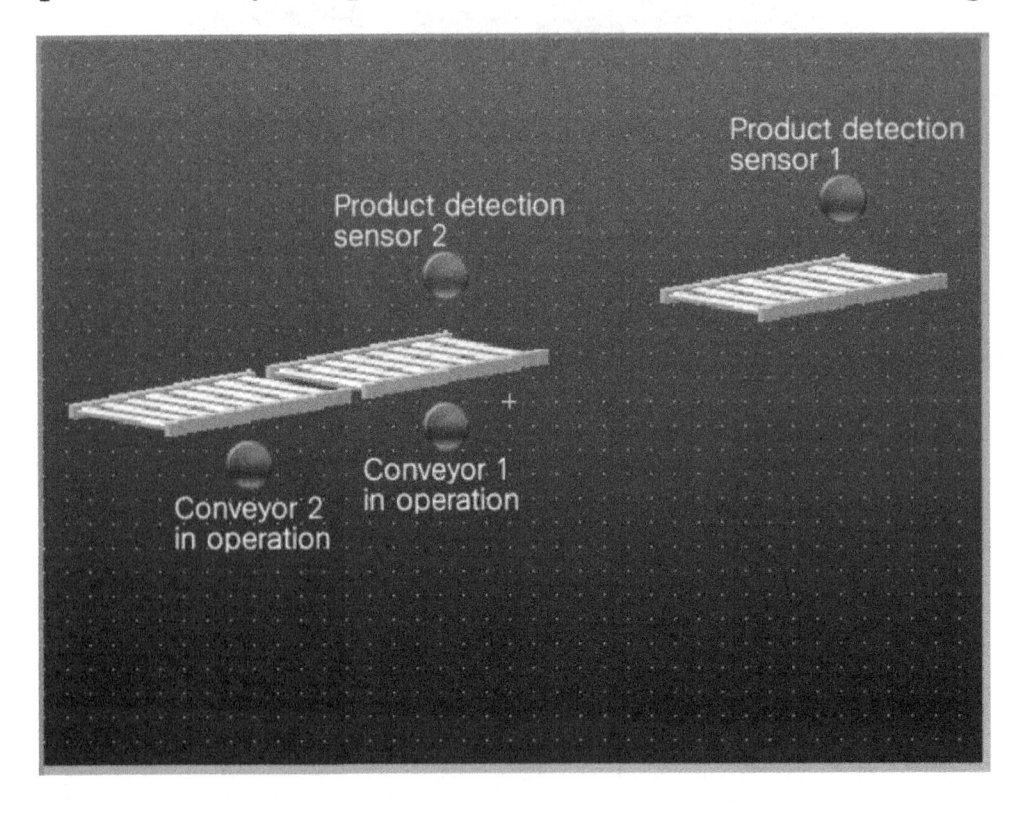

11. Create an enable/disable button. Copy the start button on the bottle transfer monitor screen ⇒ Paste it, and after double-clicking,
【Operation setting】
Device: L500 Operation settings: Bit inversion, ramp function Device: L500
【style】
Figure color when lamp is off: blue. Figure color when lamp is on green.
【letter】
Lamp OFF text color: White Lamp OFF text: Invalid
Lamp ON text color: White Lamp ON text: Validity
[Placement/size]   X: 30 Y: 420 Width: 100 Height: 50
Change the setting to

For characters, copy one of the characters ⇒ paste, double-click,
【letter】
Character string: Conveyor energy-saving operation
Text Size:16
[Placement/size]
X: 20 Y: 380 Width: 122 (Height: 32)
Change the setting to

12. Regarding this Conveyor energy-saving operation enable/disable button, if D500 (product detection sensor 1 OFF setting time) is set to 0.0 seconds, the conveyor will stop immediately. To prevent this from happening, D500 and D501 must be set for 15 seconds or more to enable them. First, create the flags used for the button operating conditions in the PLC program. Set M500 to ON when the value of D500 and D501 is 150 (15 seconds) or more. Press F8 and enter the comparison instruction like ">= D500 K150".

Conveyor energy-saving operating conditions

```
0─[>= D500 K150]─[>= D501 K150]──(M500)
    Sensor 1        Sensor 2        energy-s
    OFF             OFF             aving op
    setting         setting         eration
    time            time            possible
```

Then, set the condition created above as the operating condition for the enable/disable button: Trigger type: ON Trigger device: M500. With this, the enable/disable button will not work unless D500 and D501 are set for 15 seconds or more.

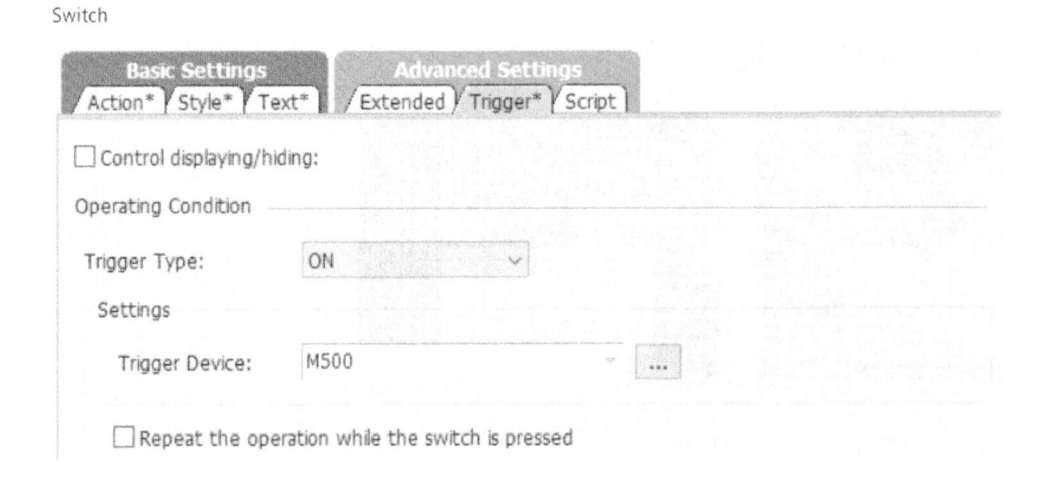

Switch

Basic Settings	Advanced Settings
Action* / Style* / Text*	Extended / Trigger* / Script

☐ Control displaying/hiding:

Operating Condition

Trigger Type: ON

Settings

Trigger Device: M500

☐ Repeat the operation while the switch is pressed

Similarly, by setting the time from when the sensor is turned off to when the conveyor stops, it is possible to input only 15 seconds or more, so that the conveyor cannot be stopped by mistake during normal production. This will be explained in the next creation.

13. Next, create the current time display for each sensor OFF time and the time setting from when the sensor is OFF until the conveyor stops.

First, create a current time display for the OFF time of sensor 1. Copy and paste the remaining time display on any of the washing machine operation screens, double-click, and then set the device to TN500. (If you use a timer device with a touch panel, it will be TN) And set the placement and size to X: 250 Y: 380 Width: 75 Height: 35.

Copy the sensor 1 OFF time display ⇒ paste it, double-click it, change the device to TN501, and create the current time display of the sensor 2 OFF time. Then set the placement and size to X: 250 Y: 430 Width: 75 Height: 35.

For setting the time from sensor OFF to conveyor stop, copy the sensor 1 OFF time display twice ⇒ paste, double click,

[Sensor 1 device]　Type: Numeric Input, Device: D500
[Sensor 1 input range]　15 seconds to 90 seconds
[Sensor 1 placement and size]
X: 355 Y: 380 Width: 75 Height: 35
[Sensor 2 device]　Type: Numeric Input, Device: D501
[Sensor 2 input range]　15 seconds to 90 seconds
[Sensor 2 placement/size]
X: 355 Y: 430 Width: 75 Height: 35
Change the setting to

The input range settings explained earlier are performed here. This time, set so that only the range of 15 seconds to 90 seconds can be entered. Click the Input Range tab, click "Exp...," enter 15 in the A constant and 90 in the C constant, and press OK.

Numerical Input

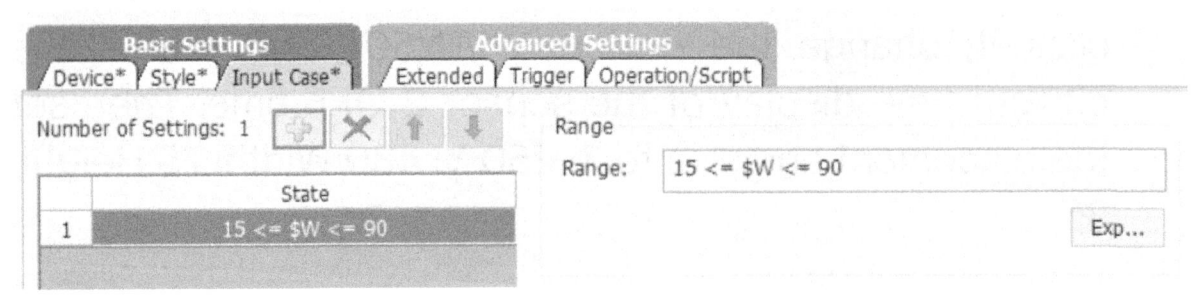

	Basic Settings			Advanced Settings		
Device*	Style*	Input Case*	Extended	Trigger	Operation/Script	

Number of Settings: 1

Range

Range: 15 <= $W <= 90

	State
1	15 <= $W <= 90

Exp...

Copy and paste each character to create the following.
[Character] Sensor 1　　Text Size:20
[Placement/size]　　X: 175 Y: 385 Frame: 71
[Character] Sensor 2　　Text Size:20
[Placement/size]　　X: 175 Y: 435 Frame: 71
[Character] OFF time　　Text Size:20
[Placement/size]　　X:250 Y:355 Frame: 77
[Character] Set value.　　Text Size:20
[Placement/size]　　X:365 Y:355 Frame: 60
[Character] After elapse of time, conveyor 1 stops
Text Size:20
[Placement/size]　　X: 440 Y: 385 Frame: 171
[Character] After elapse of time, conveyor 2 stops
Text Size:20
[Placement/size]　　X: 440 Y: 435 Frame: 171

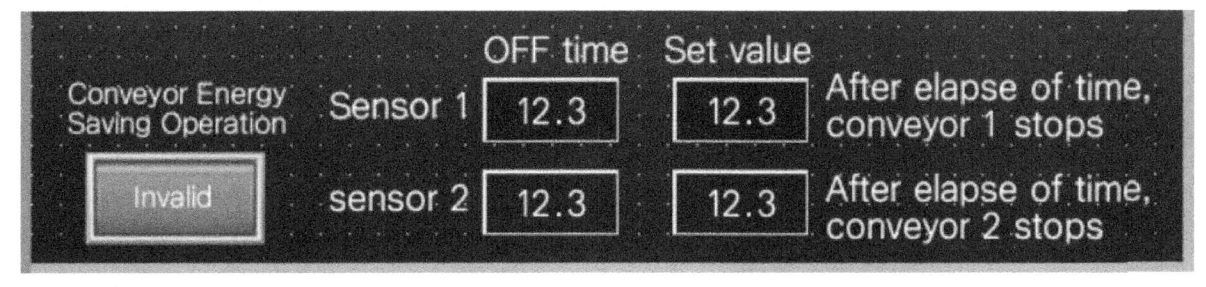

14. Regarding the set time until the conveyor stops, at present the value of each device is cleared to 0 when the PLC power is turned off. To prevent this from happening, use the parameters on the PLC side latch setting to hold. When set to latch, the value of the setting device is retained even if the power of the PLC is turned off.

In addition, there are latch (1) and latch (2) in the setting, but latch (1) clears the data when the latch clear process is performed on the PLC side, but latch (2) clears the latch. There is a difference that the This time we use a stronger latch (2) to set the parameter.

After double-clicking parameter ⇒ PLC parameter in the PLC program navigation, click the "Device" tab, enter 500 at the beginning of latch (2) and 599 at the end of latch (2) in the data register row and press OK . D500 to D599 will now retain their values even if the PLC power is turned off.

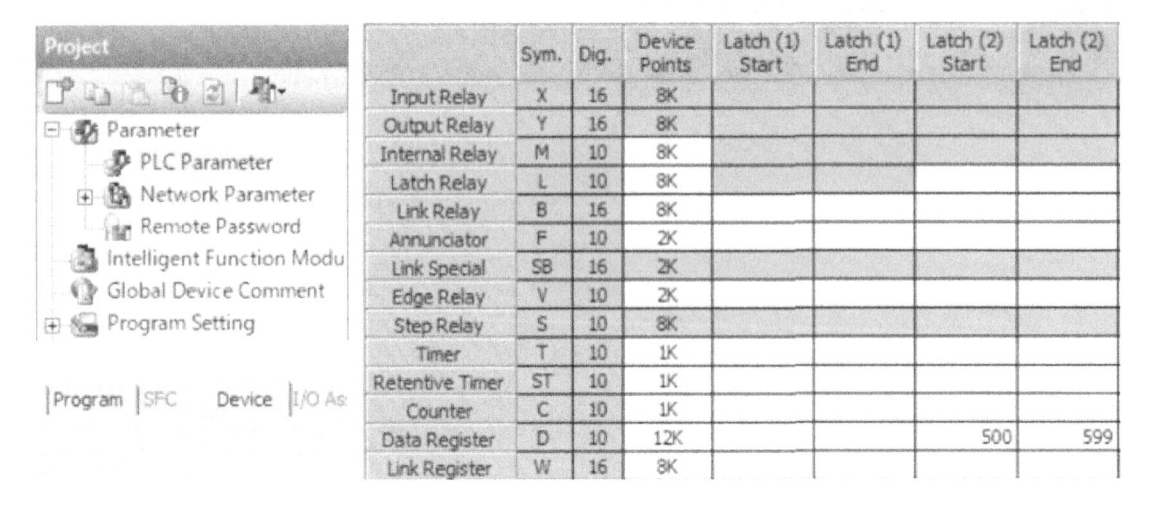

Device	Sym.	Dig.	Device Points	Latch (1) Start	Latch (1) End	Latch (2) Start	Latch (2) End
Input Relay	X	16	8K				
Output Relay	Y	16	8K				
Internal Relay	M	10	8K				
Latch Relay	L	10	8K				
Link Relay	B	16	8K				
Annunciator	F	10	2K				
Link Special	SB	16	2K				
Edge Relay	V	10	2K				
Step Relay	S	10	8K				
Timer	T	10	1K				
Retentive Timer	ST	10	1K				
Counter	C	10	1K				
Data Register	D	10	12K			500	599
Link Register	W	16	8K				

15. Add a move button so that you can move from the bottle transfer monitor screen to the conveyor energy saving setting screen during simulation.

＜"Next" button on the bottle transfer monitor screen＞
First, change the placement of the original "previous" button.
[Placement/size]　X: 510 Y: 0 Width: 60 Height: 40

After copying and pasting the "Next" button on the washing machine operation screen, double-click to make the following settings.
[Switch destination setting]　Screen number: 3
[Placement/size]　X: 580 Y: 0 Width: 60 Height: 40

＜"Previous" button on the conveyor energy saving setting screen＞
Copy the "Previous" button on the bottle transfer monitor screen ⇒ After pasting, click the screen and double-click the placed part to change each setting.
[Switch setting]　Screen number: 2
[Placement/size]　X: 580 Y: 0 Width: 60 Height: 40

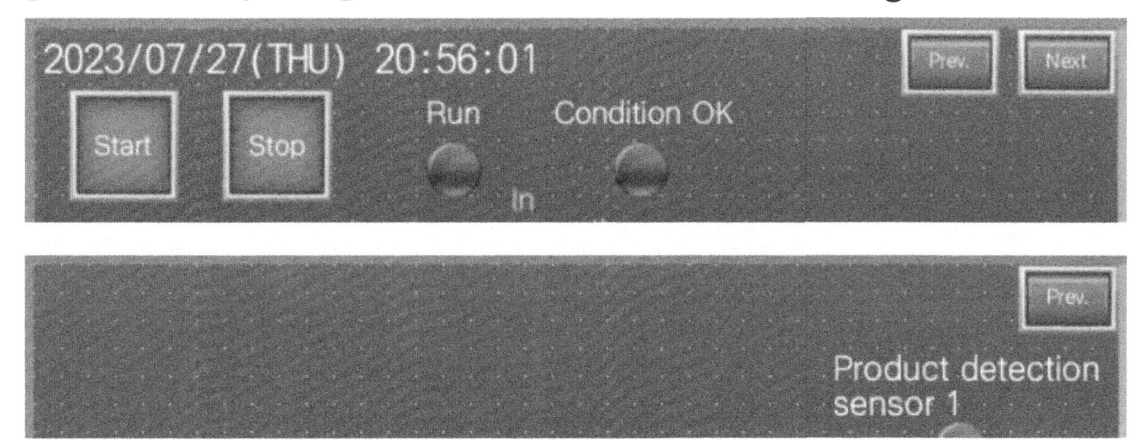

16. The creation of the touch panel screen and PLC program is now complete. Perform a simulation that links the PLC program and the screen to check the operation. Please check the following operation.

・The screen can be moved between the bottle transport monitor screen and the conveyor energy saving setting screen.
・Sensors 1 and 2 can be turned ON/OFF, and the operating lamp must be ON.
・The enable/disable button does not work unless both setting values are entered for 15 seconds or more.
・Each set value cannot be set other than 15 to 90 seconds.
・The enable/disable button works when both setting values are in for 15 seconds or longer.
・When disabled, the OFF time display must remain 0.0 seconds even if sensors 1 and 2 are OFF.
・When enabled, sensors 1 and 2 are ON and each OFF time is reset to 0.0 seconds.
・When enabled, each operating lamp turns off after the set time has elapsed with each sensor turned off.

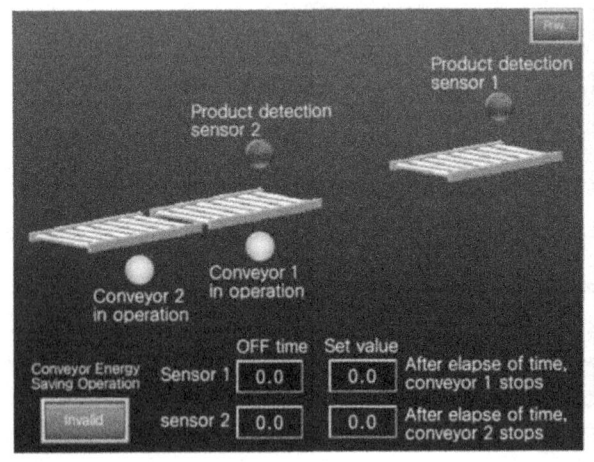

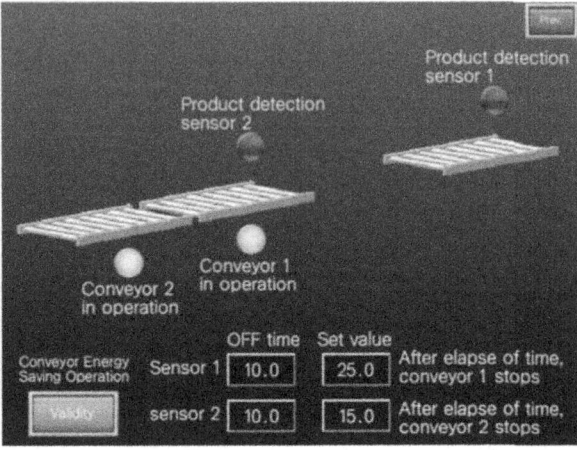

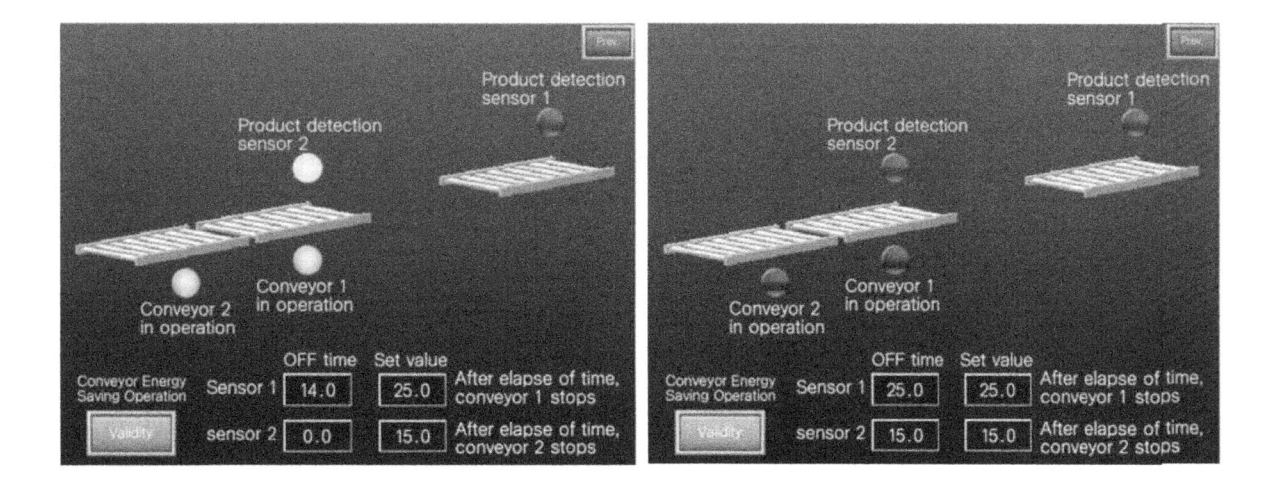

The above is the explanation of the conveyor energy saving circuit. It can also be used for other than conveyors, so please try to save energy at your site.

3-2 Improvement example 2: Creating a maintenance alarm circuit and screen based on the number of operations.

Next, we will explain how to create a circuit/screen that issues a maintenance alarm when the number of operations of equipment/machine exceeds a certain number of times. For example, let's say that there is a mechanism in which, when a defective product is detected on a conveyor that transports products, the dispensing device advances and retreats to eject the defective product into the defective product box.

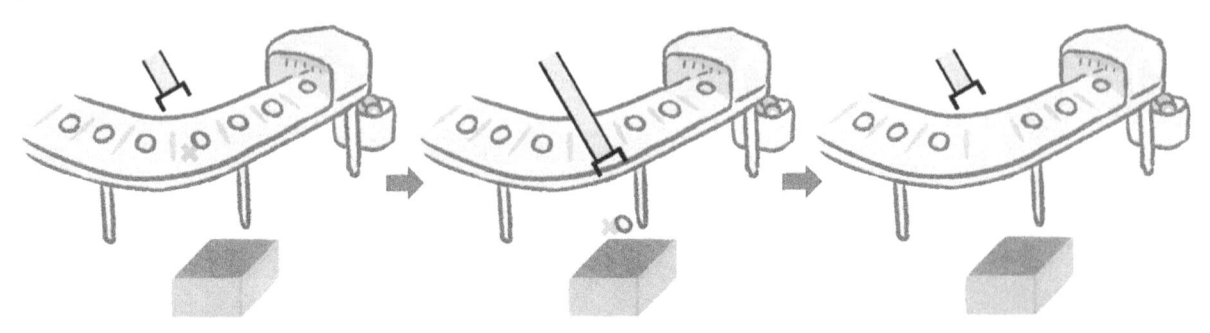

This dispensing device operates only when a defective product occurs, so the number of production and the number of operations is not equal. For example, if you want to perform maintenance (part replacement, etc.) after one million operations, you need to count the number of operations of the dispensing device separately from the number of productions.

This time, we will create a PLC program and a touch panel screen that will issue a maintenance warning when the number of operations of this dispensing device reaches the set number of times.

1. First, create a PLC program for the dispenser. The devices related to the operation of the dispensing device are as follows.

・Forward command Y610, backward command Y611, forward detection sensor X610, backward detection sensor X611
・Press the production start button X600 to turn on M600 during product production.
・Press the production stop button X601 to turn off M600 during product production.
・Forward detection sensor X610 is OFF, backward detection sensor X611 is ON, dispensing operation flow execution M610 is OFF, dispensing operation start condition M605 is ON
・If NG judgment X620 turns ON when M600 during product production is ON and dispensing operation start condition M605 is ON, M610 during dispensing operation flow is ON.
・Flags used for the flow are forward start M611, forward complete M612, backward start M613, backward complete M614, payout operation flow complete M615

[Dispensing operation flow: M610 is ON during execution]
(1) Forward: M611 (forward start) is ON ⇒ Y610 (forward command) is ON ⇒ X611 (backward detection) is OFF, X610 (forward detection) is ON ⇒ M612 (forward complete) is ON, Y610 (forward command) is OFF

②Reverse: M613 (Reverse start) is ON ⇒ Y611 (Reverse command) is ON ⇒ X610 (Forward detection) is OFF, X611 (Reverse detection) is ON ⇒ M614 (Reverse complete) is ON, Y611 (Reverse command) is OFF , M614 (backward complete) is ON, M615 (Dispensing operation flow complete) is ON, and M610 (dispensing operation flow is in progress) is OFF.

This is the same as the procedure created in the previous chapter, so only the PLC program will be described. Create a new program data "Device", insert "dispensing device" in the program setting of the PC parameter, and then create it in order from the top with reference to the following.

[Products in production]

```
Products in production
       X600        X601
0 ─────┤ ├────────┤/├──────────────────────────(M600)
       Producti   Stop Pro                      In produ
       on start   duction                       ction
       button     button

       M600
       ─┤ ├─
       In produ
       ction
```

[Condition for starting extrusion movement]

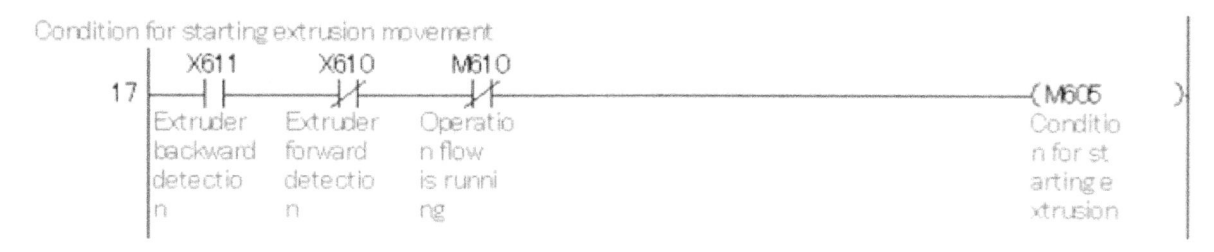

```
Condition for starting extrusion movement
         X611        X610        M610
17       ─┤├─────────┤/├─────────┤/├──────────────────────────( M605 )
         Extruder    Extruder    Operation                    Condition
         backward    forward     flow                         for starting
         detection   detection   is running                   extrusion
```

[Start of push-out operation flow]

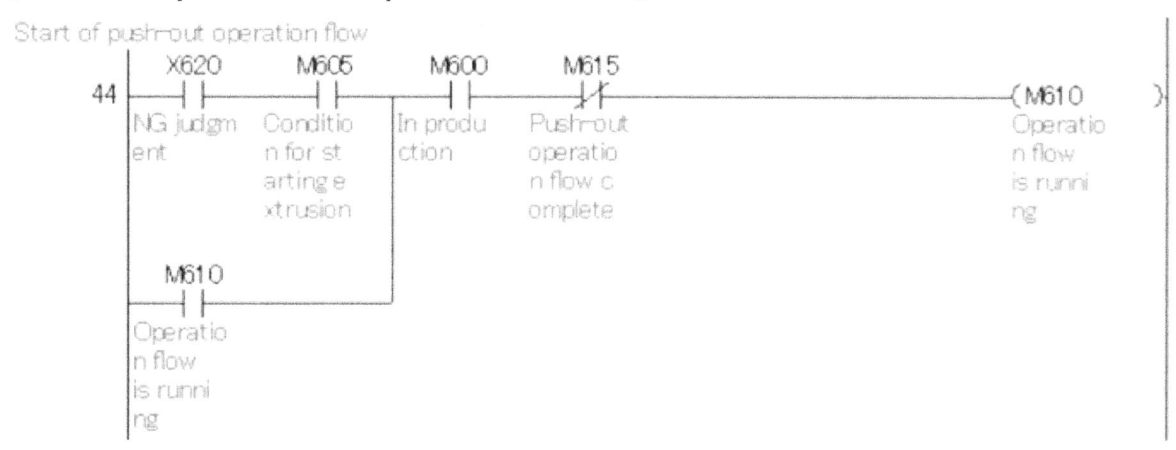

```
Start of push-out operation flow
         X620        M605        M600        M615
44       ─┤├─────────┤├──────────┤├──────────┤/├───────────────( M610 )
         NG judgment Condition   In          Push-out          Operation
                     for starting production operation         flow
                     extrusion               flow complete     is running
         M610
         ─┤├──┐
         Operation
         flow
         is running
```

[Step 1: Extruder advance]
*The forward command circuit will be created later.

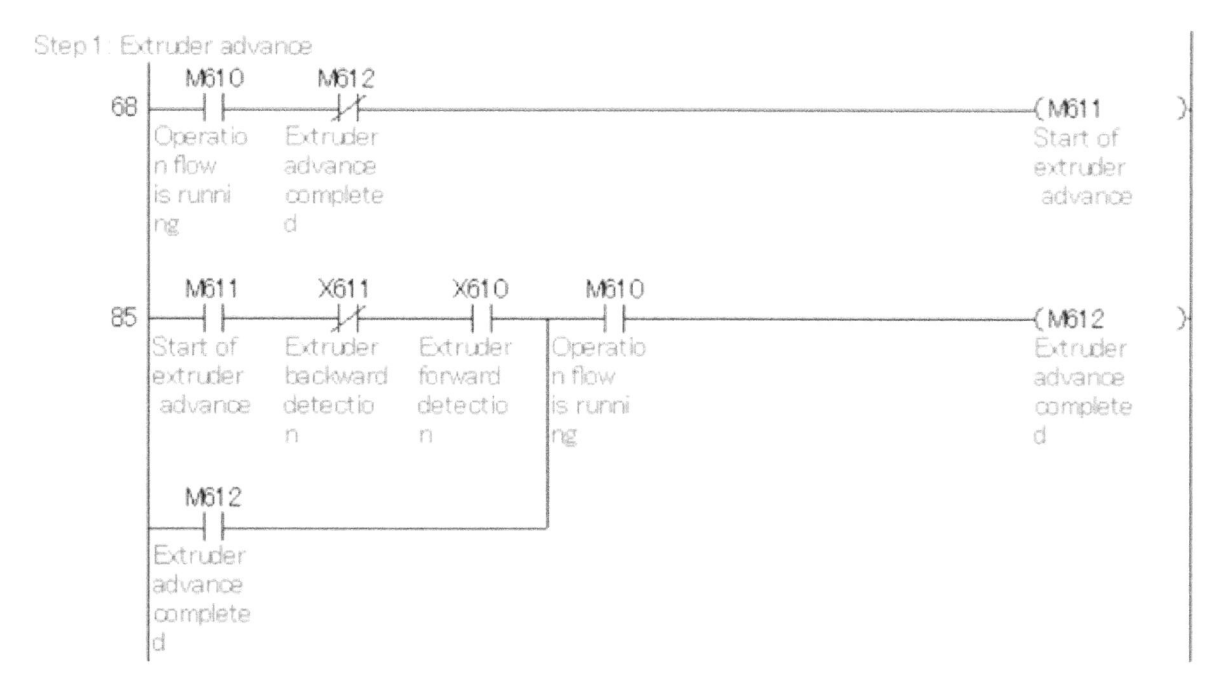

```
Step 1: Extruder advance
         M610        M612
68       ─┤├─────────┤/├──────────────────────────────────────( M611 )
         Operation   Extruder                                  Start of
         flow        advance                                   extruder
         is running  completed                                 advance

         M611        X611        X610        M610
85       ─┤├─────────┤/├─────────┤├──────────┤├────────────────( M612 )
         Start of    Extruder    Extruder    Operation         Extruder
         extruder    backward    forward     flow              advance
         advance     detection   detection   is running        completed
         M612
         ─┤├──┐
         Extruder
         advance
         completed
```

[Step 2: Extruder retracts]
*The reverse command circuit will be created later.

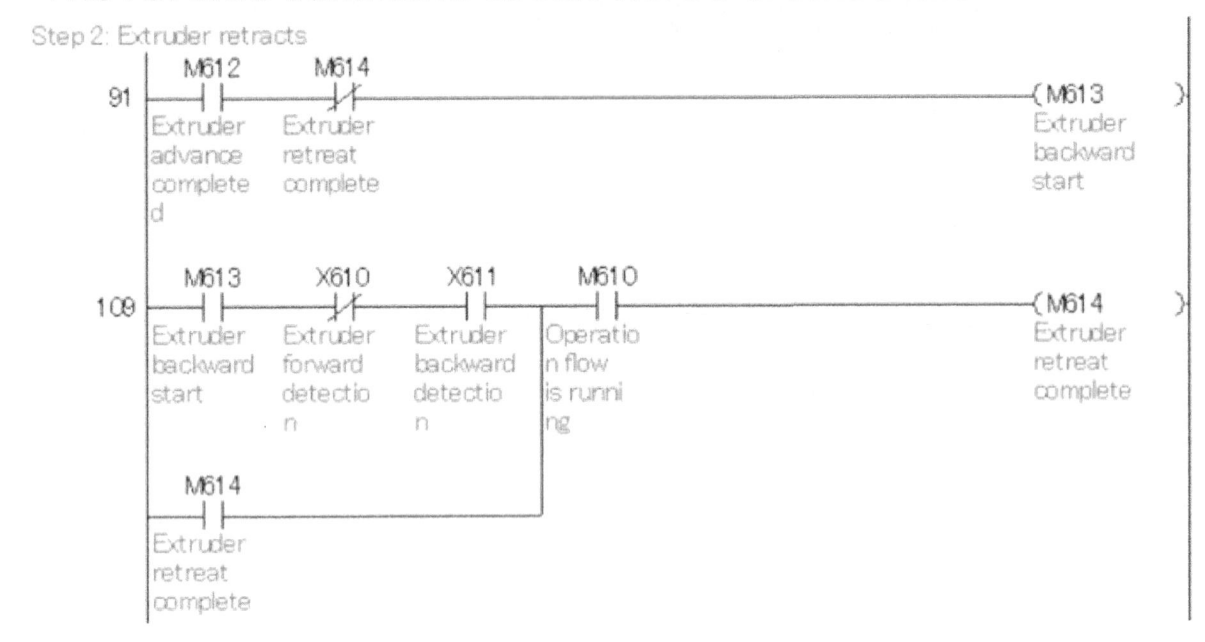

```
Step 2: Extruder retracts
       M612      M614
  91 ──┤ ├──────┤/├─────────────────────────────────(M613)
      Extruder  Extruder                            Extruder
      advance   retreat                             backward
      completed complete                            start

       M613      X610      X611      M610
 109 ──┤ ├──────┤/├──────┤ ├──────┤ ├──────────────(M614)
      Extruder  Extruder  Extruder  Operation       Extruder
      backward  forward   backward  flow            retreat
      start     detection detection is running      complete

       M614
      ──┤ ├──
      Extruder
      retreat
      complete
```

[Push-out operation flow complete]

```
Push-out operation flow complete
       M614
 115 ──┤ ├─────────────────────────────────────────(M615)
      Extruder                                      Push-out
      retreat                                       operation
      complete                                      flow complete
```

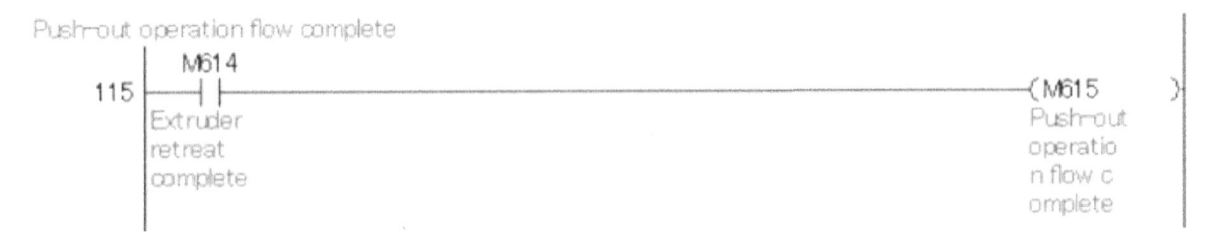

[Extruder Forward/backward command]

```
Extruder Forward/backward command
       M611
 135 ──┤ ├─────────────────────────────────────────(Y610)
      Start of                                      Extruder
      extruder                                      Forward
      advance                                       command

       M613
 156 ──┤ ├─────────────────────────────────────────(Y611)
      Extruder                                      Extruder
      backward                                      Backward
      start                                         command
```

2. Next, create a touch panel screen for the dispenser.

Open the screen you created earlier and double-click the new button on the left. After that, after inputting Screen number: 4, Title: Device monitor screen, press OK on the lower right to create Screen 4: Dispensing device monitor screen.

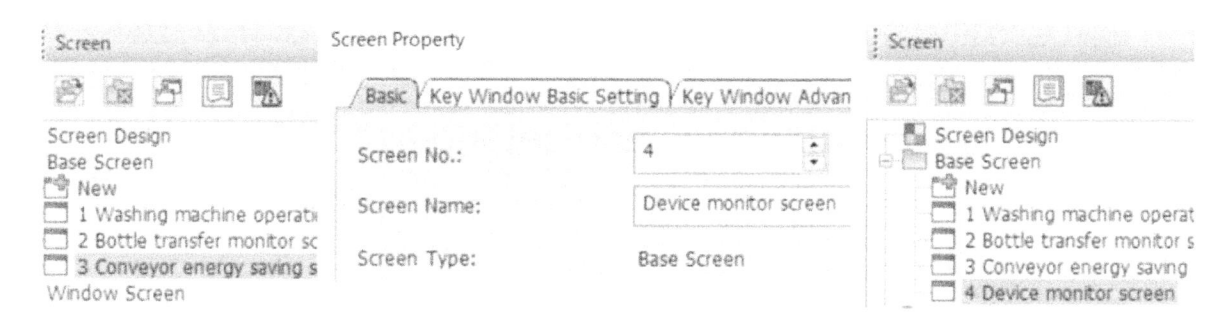

Screen 2: Enclose the following image from the top of the bottle transfer monitor screen to step 2 while left clicking, copy with Ctrl + C, open screen 4, paste with Ctrl + V, press Enter to make it the same as screen 2 Paste it in place.

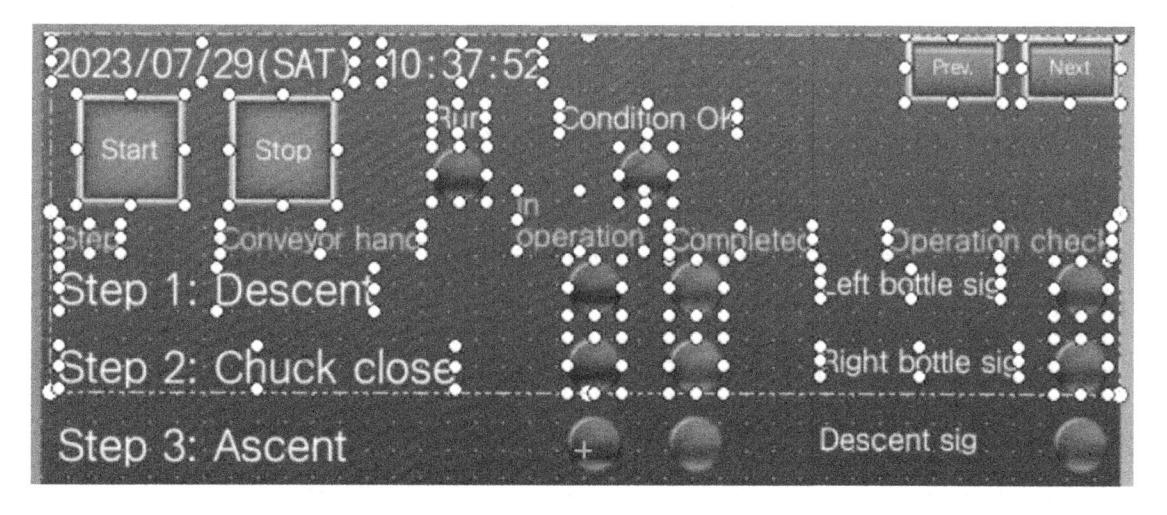

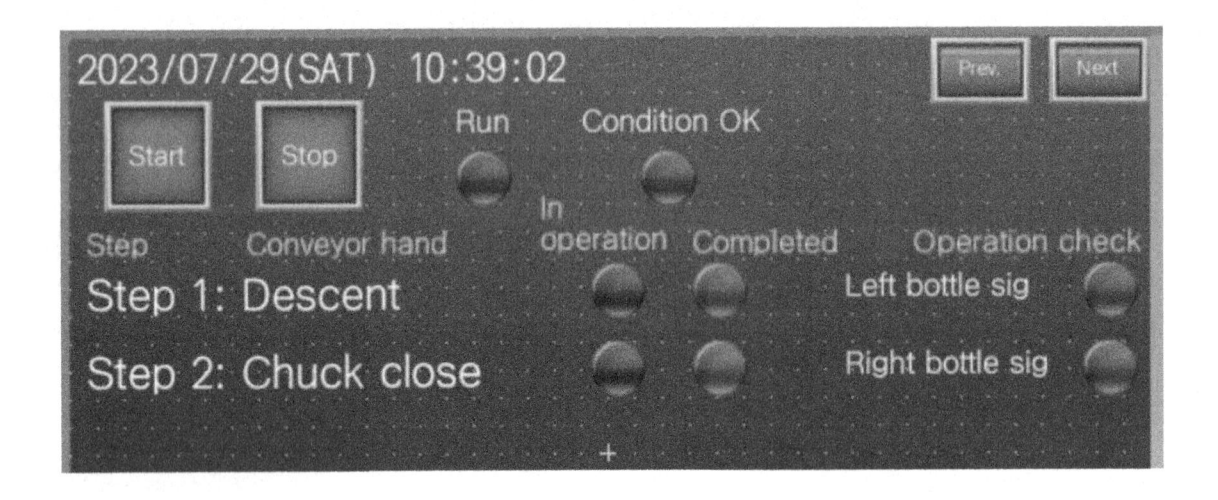

![Screen showing: 2023/07/29(SAT) 10:39:02, Start, Stop, Run, Condition OK, Prev, Next, Step, Conveyor hand, In operation, Completed, Operation check, Step 1: Descent, Left bottle sig, Step 2: Chuck close, Right bottle sig]

And change each device and setting as follows.

・Start button
⇒ Change the operating device and lamp device to X600
・Stop button
⇒ Change the operating device and lamp device to X601
・ Characters during automatic operation
⇒ Change during product production
・Lamp during automatic operation
⇒ Change lamp device to M600
・Condition OK ⇒ Change to NG product judgment
・Lamp indicating bottle transfer start conditions OK
⇒ After changing to the switch at the bottom of the setting screen, press the operation addition bit and change to device: X620, operation setting: bit reversal, lamp device: X620
・Characters on the Conveyor hand ⇒ Changed to device
・Step 1: Descent ⇒ Step 1: Change to Advance
・Step 2: Chuck close ⇒ Step 2: Change to Retreat
・Devices in operation and completed: M371 to M374
⇒ Changed to M611 to M614

- Left bottle sig character ⇒ Change to Advance sig
- Right bottle sig character ⇒ Change to Retreat sig
- Operation check device, lamp device: X355, X356
⇒ Changed to X610, X611

- "Prev." and "Next" buttons
⇒ After selecting and copying "Prev." and "Next" on screen 4, delete "Prev." on screen 3, paste it on screen 3, switch to "Prev.": screen 2, "Next": Change to screen 4. After that, delete "Prev." on screen 4, change the character string of "Next" to "Prev.", and confirm that the destination is screen 3.

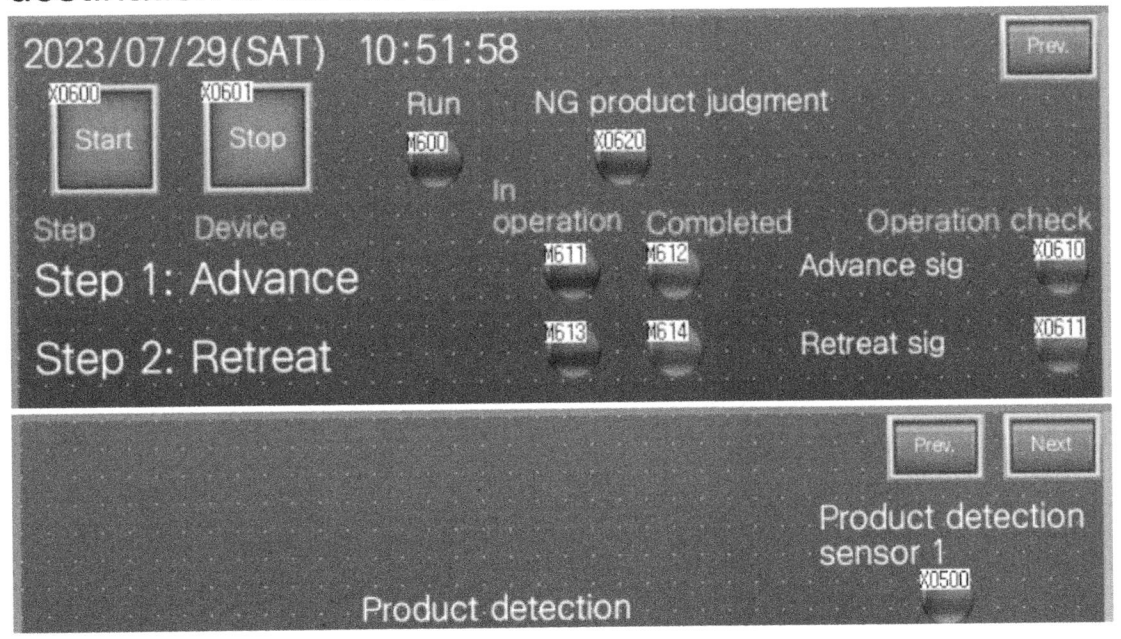

3. Now that the PLC program and screen for the dispensing device have been created, we will create a PLC program and touch panel screen that will issue a maintenance warning when the number of operations of the dispensing device reaches the set number, which is the main theme.

First, create a PLC program. D600 is the dispensing operation count, D610 is the dispensing operation alarm set count, and when the D600 count exceeds the set value of D610, the dispensing device maintenance alarm M650 is turned ON. Also, if the setting value of D610 is 0, it is not set, so the alarm is disabled. (Alarm setting count and alarm display are created on the screen)

Use the increment command to count the number of times M615 (dispensing operation flow complete) turns ON. DINCP means that a double word (D) increment command (INC) is executed with a pulse (P). A single word can only handle numbers from -32768 to 32767. For example, if you want to exchange for 1 million operations, the number of digits is insufficient, so double word (32bit) is used. By making it a double word, you will be able to handle numbers from -2147483648 to 2147483647. For DINCP, press F8 and enter "DINCP D600". For the compare instruction, press F8 and enter "D<> K0 D610" and "D>= D600 D610" respectively.

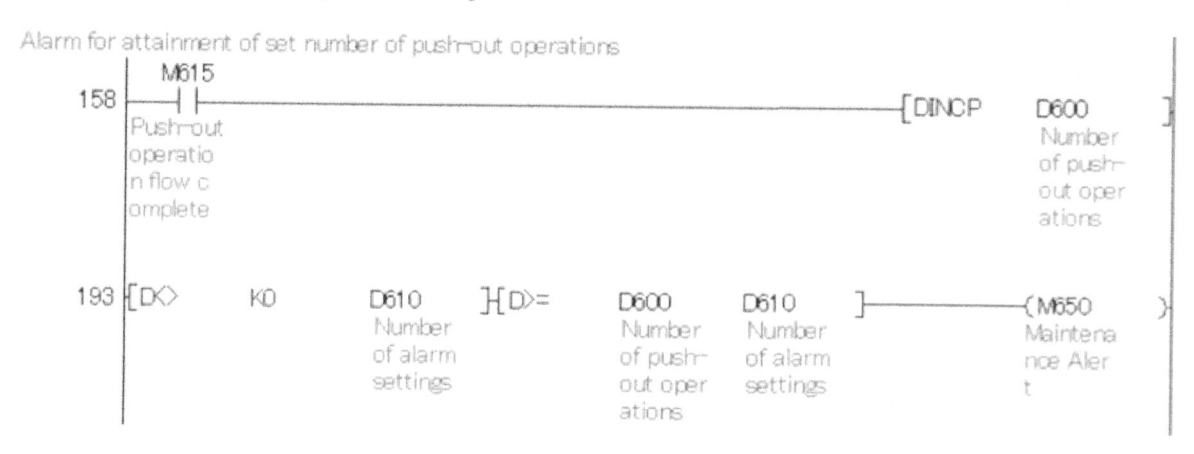

Alarm for attainment of set number of push-out operations

```
158 ──┤M615├──────────────────────────[DINCP  D600 ]
       Push-out                                Number
       operatio                                of push-
       n flow c                                out oper
       omplete                                 ations

193 ──[D<>  K0   D610  ]─[D>=  D600   D610 ]──────(M650)
             Number            Number Number        Maintena
             of alarm          of push- of alarm    nce Aler
             settings          out oper settings    t
                               ations
```

Next, create a touch panel screen. Screen 3: On the Conveyor Energy Saving Setting, enclose the OFF time and set value characters, and the numerical display parts and numerical input parts below them with Ctrl + C while left clicking, then paste them on screen 4.

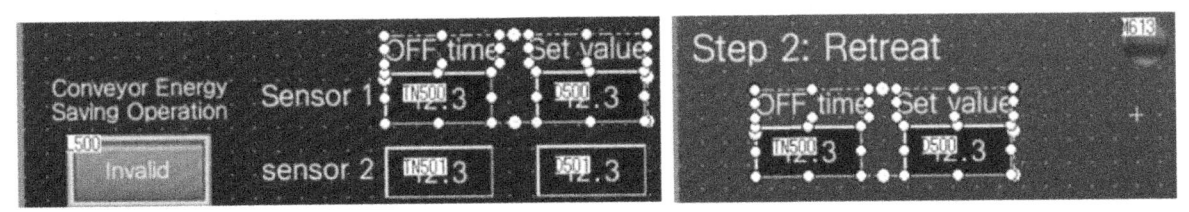

Change each device and setting of each part pasted on Screen 4.

・OFF time characters
⇒ Changed to Device operation count
[Placement/size (reference)]
X: 10 Y: 230 Width: 152 (Height: 40)
・Set value characters
⇒ Change to Device alarm count setting
[Placement/size (reference)]
X: 180 Y: 230 Width: 117 (Height: 40)

• Numerical display parts under device operation count
⇒ [Device] Device: D600, Data format: Unsigned BIN32, Display format: Unsigned decimal, Number of digits in integer part: 8, Preview value: 12345678
[Placement/size]　X: 10 Y: 280 Width: 105 Height: 35

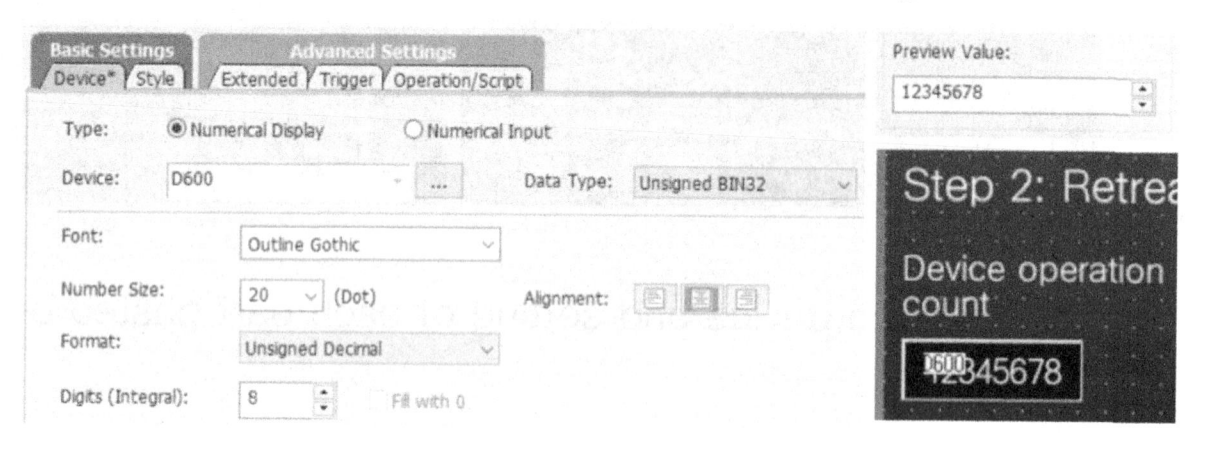

• Numerical value input part under Dispensing device alarm frequency setting
⇒ [Device] Device: D610, Data format: Unsigned BIN32, Display format: Unsigned decimal, Number of digits in integer part: 8, Preview value: 12345678
【Input range】Delete condition by pressing x.
【Operation setting】
Trigger type: OFF、Trigger device: M600
[Placement/size]　X: 180 Y: 280 Width: 105 Height: 35

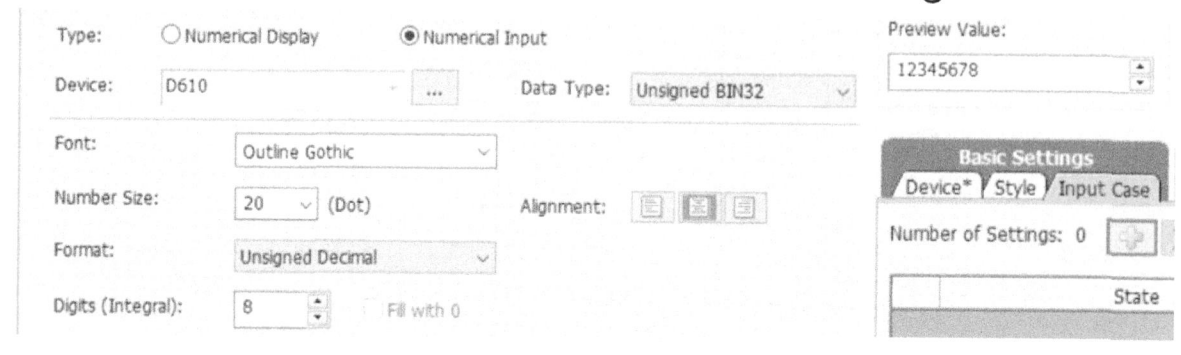

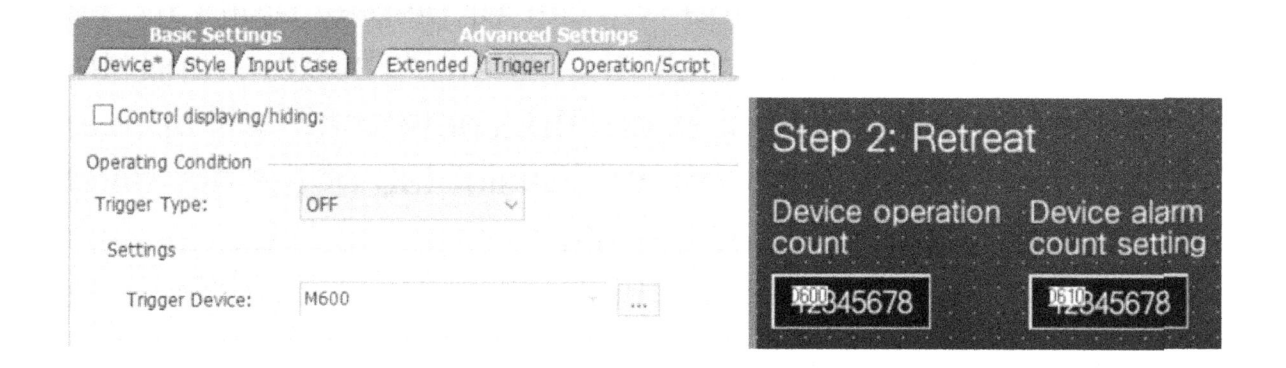

Next, create an alarm screen that displays an alarm. After selecting "Object" tab ⇒ Alarm Display ⇒ Alarm Display (User), click the screen to place an alarm part.

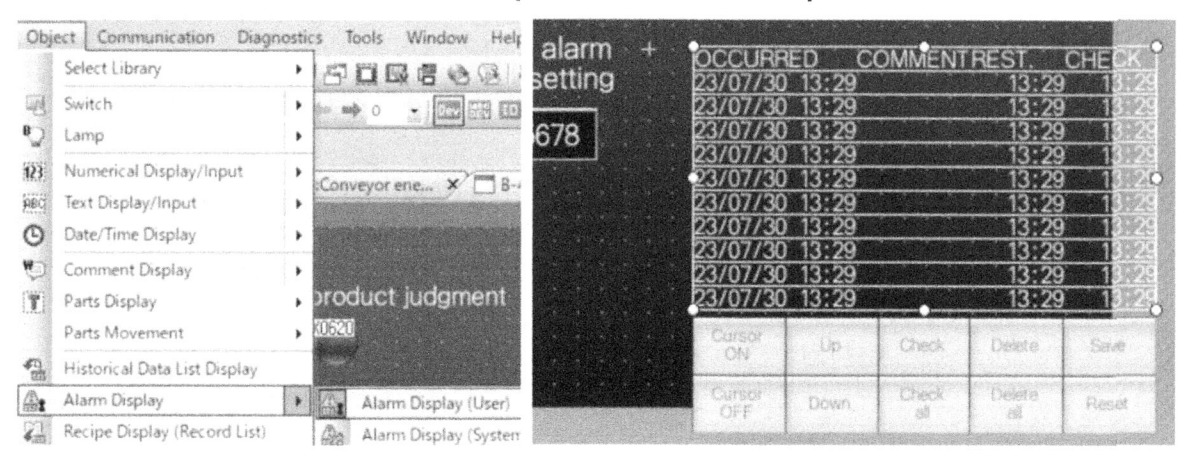

Since the "cursor display" under the alarm display is not used, click it to delete it, then double-click the alarm part to make each setting.

First, after changing the number of display digits to 5 in the alarm settings, click the "Edit..." button, and the message "Do you want to create a new one?" will appear, so select "Yes". Then, on the "Basic" tab of the displayed user alarm screen, set the alarm name to "Maintenance alarm display" and the history collection method to "Occurring alarm only".

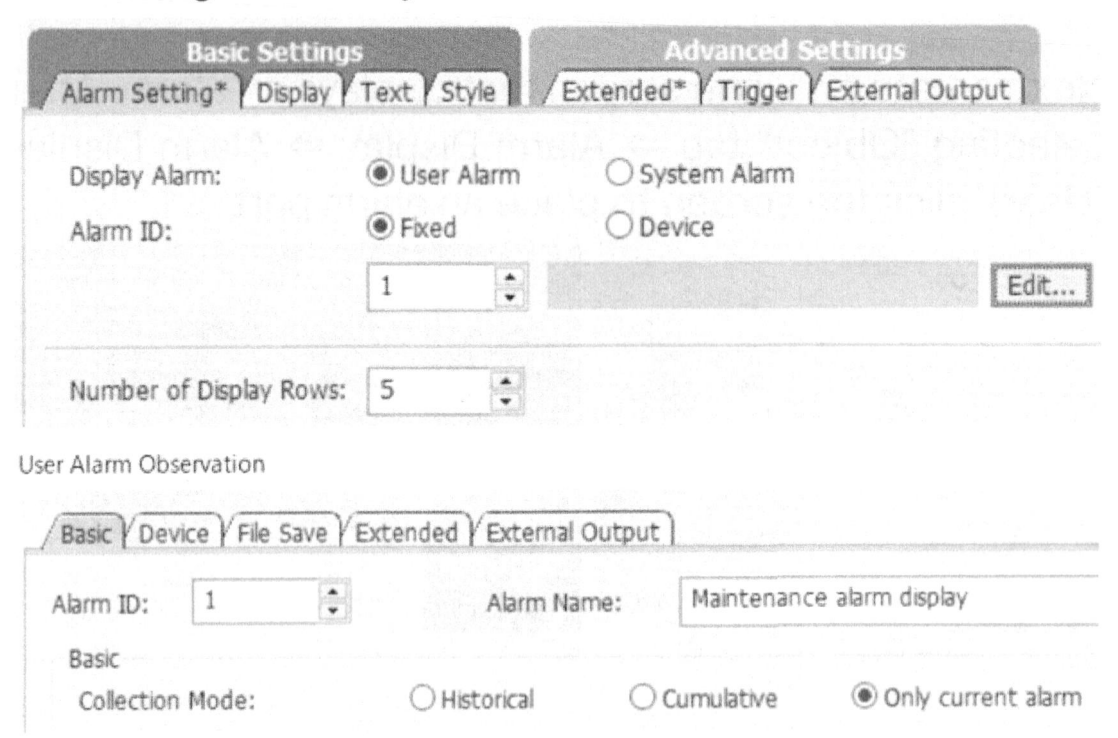

Next, select the "Device" tab, enter M650 in the device, change the basic alarm comment No. to 100, and press the "Edit..." button. The comment editing screen will be displayed. After entering "Device maintenance alarm", press OK at the bottom of the comment editing screen. A message "Are you sure?" will appear, so press "Yes" to reflect the comment. After that, press OK on the lower right to return to the alarm display (user) screen.

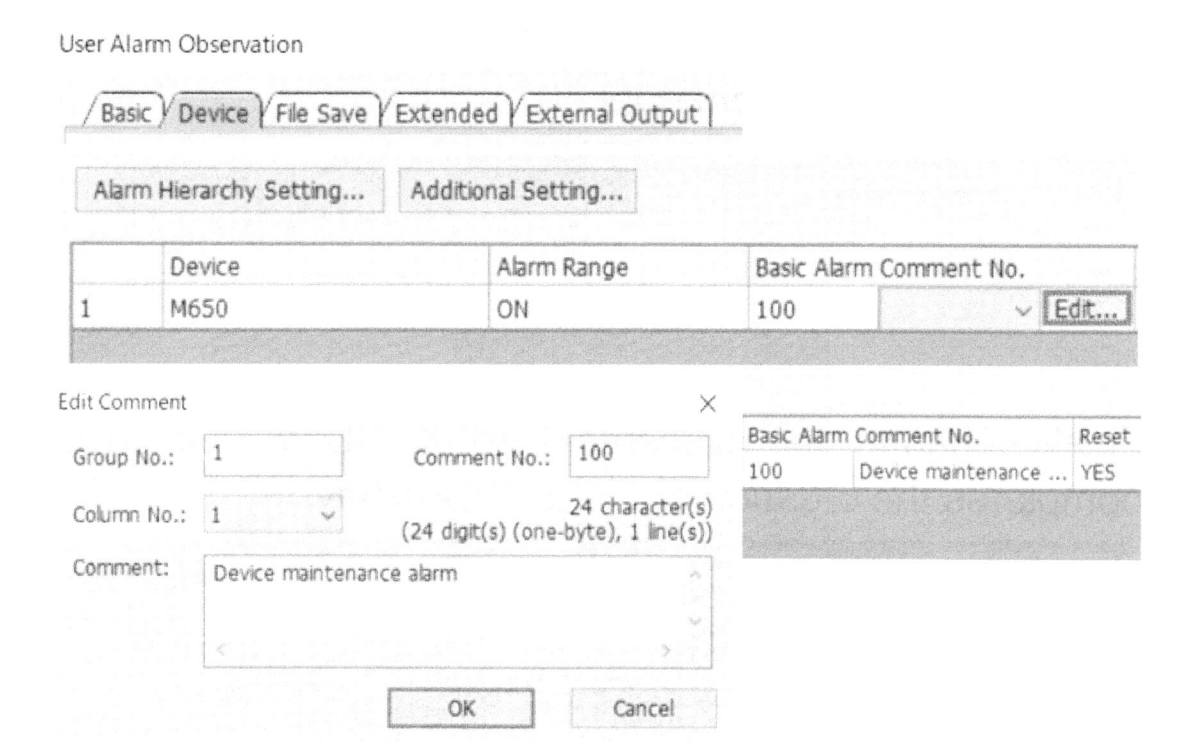

User Alarm Observation

	Device	Alarm Range	Basic Alarm Comment No.	
1	M650	ON	100	Edit...

Edit Comment

Group No.: 1   Comment No.: 100

Column No.: 1   24 character(s) (24 digit(s) (one-byte), 1 line(s))

Comment: Device maintenance alarm

Basic Alarm Comment No.		Reset
100	Device maintenance ...	YES

Select the "Display items" tab and uncheck the recovery date and time and confirmation date and time. Then change the number of digits for the comment to 30 and the title to "ALARM NAME".

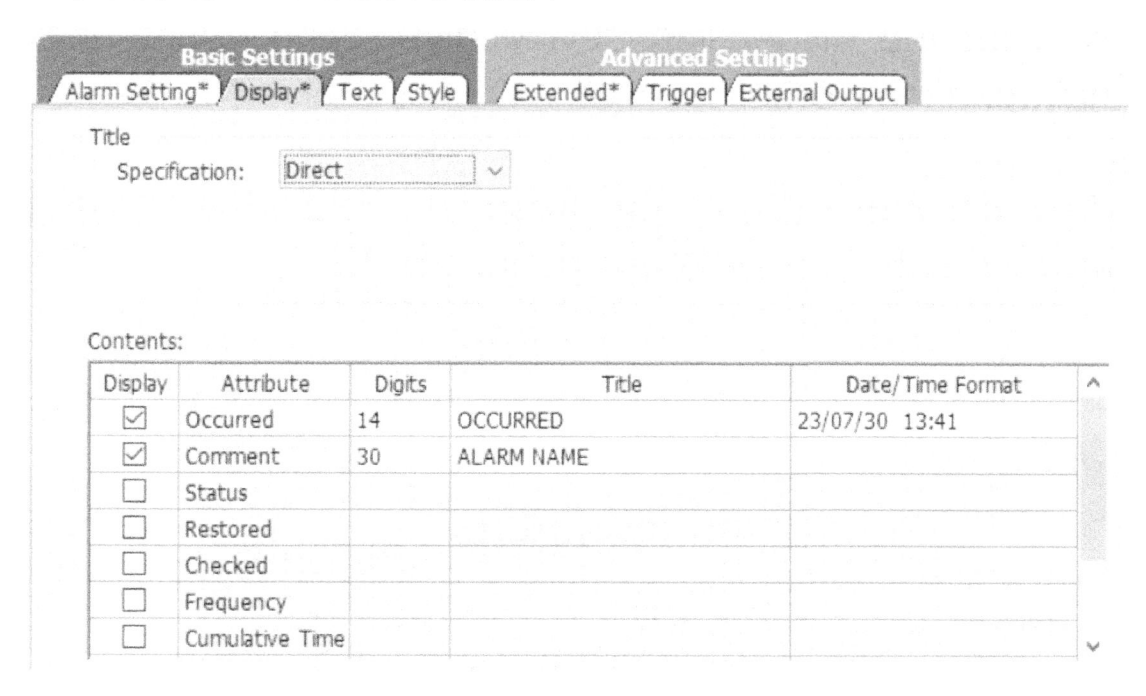

Basic Settings: Alarm Setting* / Display* / Text / Style
Advanced Settings: Extended* / Trigger / External Output

Title
Specification: Direct

Contents:

Display	Attribute	Digits	Title	Date/Time Format
☑	Occurred	14	OCCURRED	23/07/30 13:41
☑	Comment	30	ALARM NAME	
☐	Status			
☐	Restored			
☐	Checked			
☐	Frequency			
☐	Cumulative Time			

Select the "Text" tab, change the font size to 20, and press OK at the bottom right.

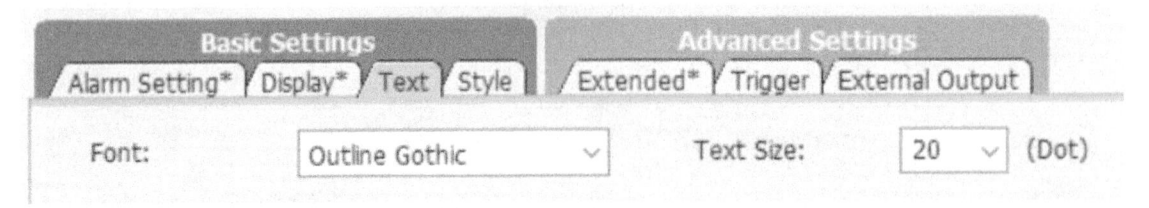

Finally change the placement to X: 30 Y: 345. This completes the creation of the alarm display.

4. Next, we will add a reset button because it is necessary to reset the dispensing device dispensing count after maintenance work.

<PLC program> (This time, press and hold for 3 seconds will be created on the touch panel side.)

<Touch panel>

Copy the enable/disable button and conveyor energy-saving operation characters on Screen 3 to Screen 4 ⇒ After pasting, change each setting.

・Conveyor Energy Saving Operation characters

⇒ Changed to Operation count reset

[Placement/size]　X: 335 Y: 230 Width: 146 (Height: 40)

・Copy the characters for Retreat sig

⇒ After pasting, change the character to ※Long press for 3 sec

[Placement/size]　X: 440 Y: 290 Width: 183 (Height: 18)

・Invalid/ Validity button

【Operation setting】

Device: M620, Operation setting: Bit momentary, Lamp device: Changed to M620

【letter】

Change to OFF character: Reset, ON character: Reset complete.

[Extension]

Delay: ON, Delay time: 3 seconds ⇒ Press and hold for 3 seconds to set the delay on the touch panel side. By doing this setting, pressing, and holding for 3 seconds will turn on the M620.

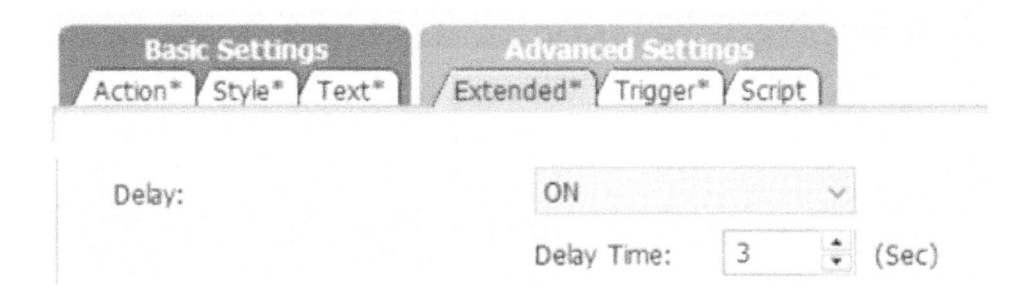

[Operating conditions]
Trigger type: OFF, Trigger device: M600
[Placement/size (reference)]
X: 330 Y: 275 Width: 100 Height: 50

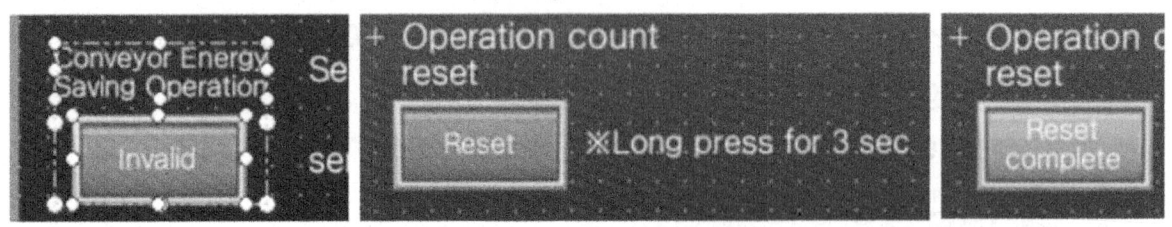

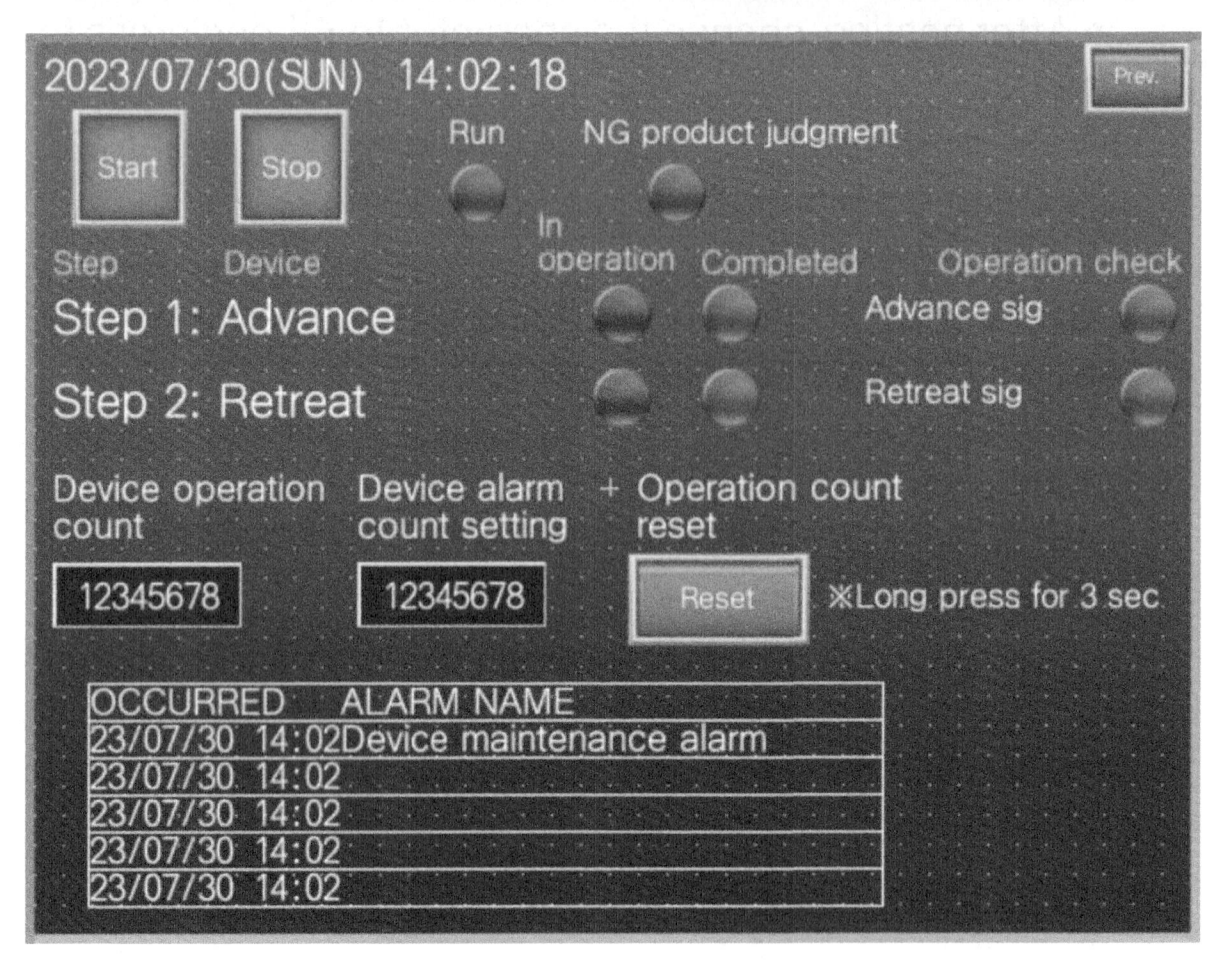

5. This completes the creation, so please perform a simulation that links the PLC program and the screen and check the operation below.

　・It is possible to move between screens 1 to 4 using the "next" and "previous" buttons.
　・Press the start/stop button to turn on/off the product production lamp.
　・The dispensing device alarm frequency setting cannot be entered during product production.
　・Can be set to 0 or more for the dispensing device alarm frequency setting during production stop
　・NG product judgment, forward detection, and backward detection can be turned ON/OFF.
　・During product production, it is in forward motion with backward detection ON and NG product judgment ON.
　・Reverse detection is OFF during forward movement, forward movement is completed when forward detection is ON, and backward movement is in progress.
　・Reversing is completed by NG judgment OFF, forward detection OFF, backward detection ON during backward movement, and the number of payouts increases by 1.
　・ Repeat the dispensing operation in the above procedure, and when the number of dispensing reaches the set number of times, "Dispensing device maintenance warning" is displayed on the alarm display.
　・ The payout count cannot be reset during product production.
　・Press and hold reset for 3 seconds to clear the number of payouts to 0 and the alarm will disappear.

216

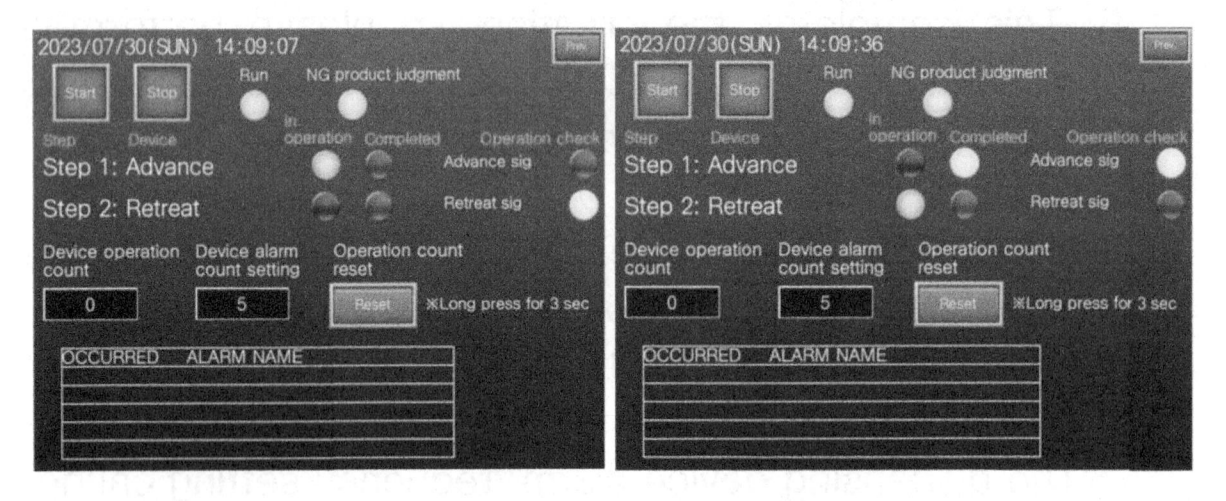

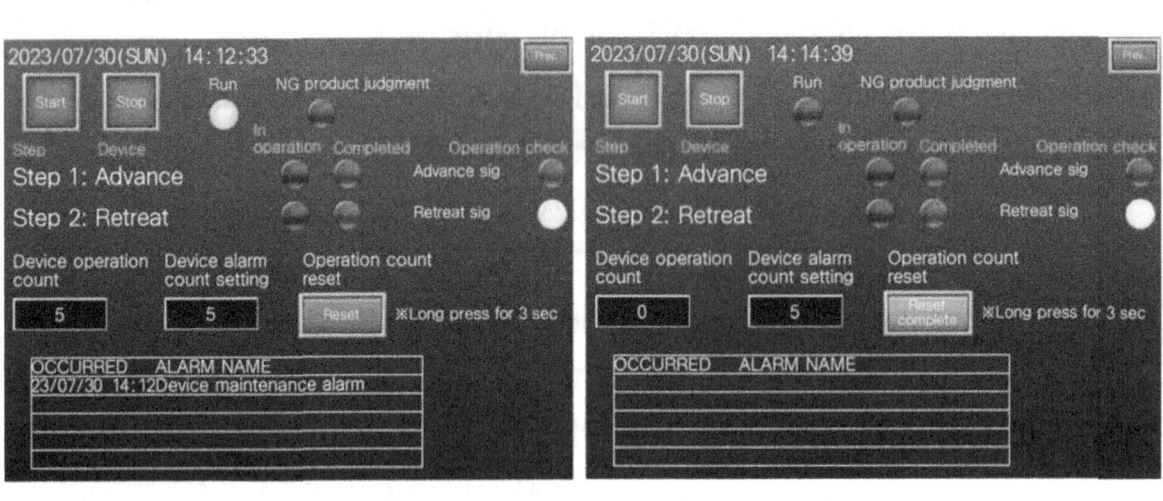

In the above simulation, the NG product judgment, forward detection, and backward detection were turned ON/OFF manually, but turning ON/OFF is troublesome and there is a possibility of incorrect operation.

Therefore, we will create a debug (operation check) circuit that operates ON/OFF NG product judgment, forward detection, and backward detection according to the conditions, and a debug enable/disable button (L600: Enable when ON) on the screen.

First, create a PLC program for debugging (operation check). This time, the forward detection X610, backward detection X611, and NG product judgment X620 are turned ON/OFF by the debug circuit but SET (set instruction) / RST (reset instruction) is used for ON/OFF each signal.

SET (set command): command to set the device to the ON state.
RST (reset command): Command to reset the device to the OFF state.

Now let's create a PLC program for debugging (operation check).

1. When the debug mode is enabled or disabled, the forward detection X610 and NG judgment X620 are turned OFF, and the backward detection X611 is turned ON when the stop button is pressed. Doing so has the advantage of making it easier to debug (check the operation) because the dispensing operation will start when the NG product judgment X620 is turned ON in the state where the dispensing operation is possible when enabled/disabled, and after the stop.

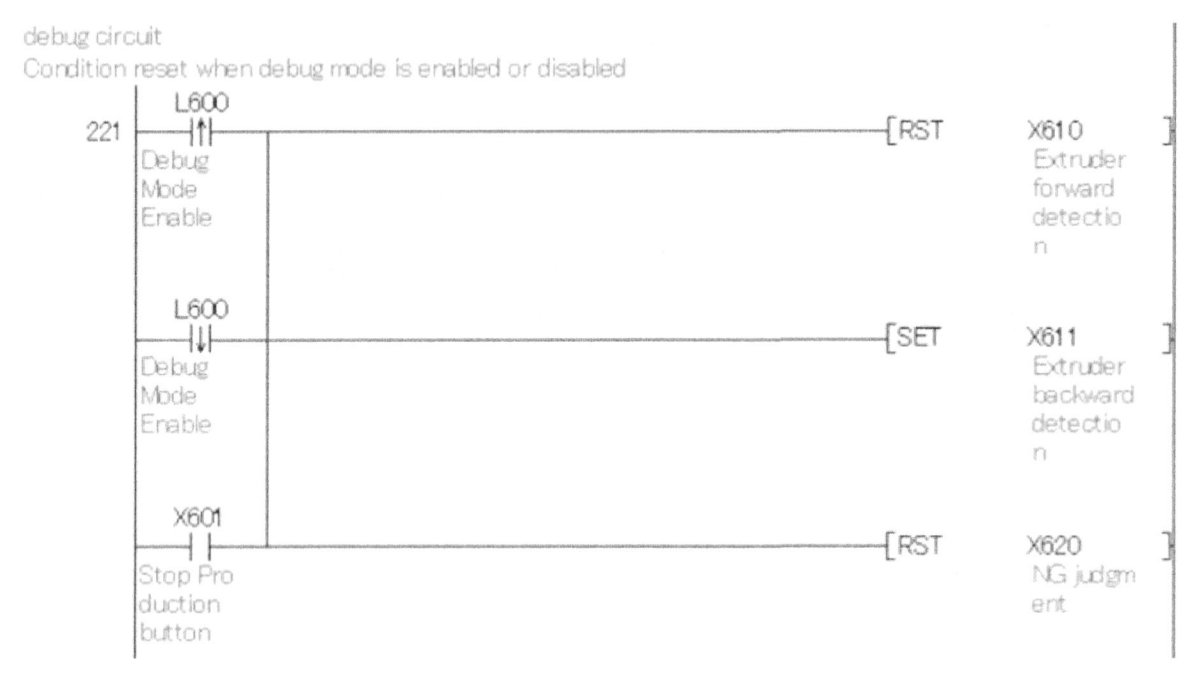

```
debug circuit
Condition reset when debug mode is enabled or disabled

        L600
221    ─┤↑├─────────────────────────────[RST   X610  ]
        Debug                                   Extruder
        Mode                                    forward
        Enable                                  detectio
                                                n

        L600
       ─┤↓├─────────────────────────────[SET   X611  ]
        Debug                                   Extruder
        Mode                                    backward
        Enable                                  detectio
                                                n

        X601
       ─┤ ├──────────────────────────────[RST  X620  ]
        Stop Pro                                NG judgm
        duction                                 ent
        button
```

2. When the debug mode L600 is ON (enabled) and the start button is pressed to turn on M600 during product production, NG judgment X620 is turned on after 3 seconds. With this, the payout operation flow will start 3 seconds after pressing the start button.

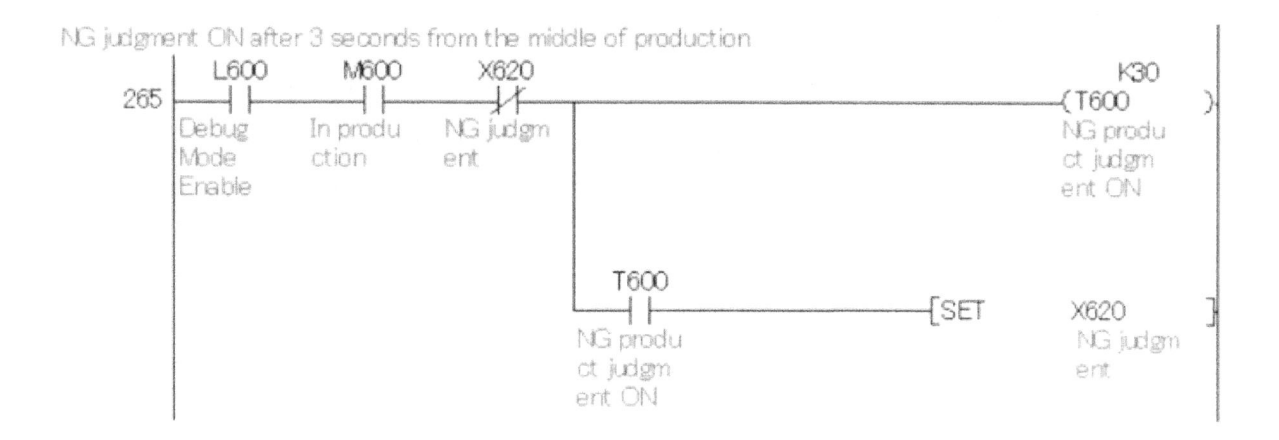

NG judgment ON after 3 seconds from the middle of production

```
      L600      M600      X620                                  K30
265 ───┤├───────┤├────────┤/├─────────────────────────────────(T600)───
      Debug     In produ  NG judgm                              NG produ
      Mode     ction      ent                                   ct judgm
      Enable                                                    ent ON

                          T600
                         ───┤├──────────────────────[SET    X620       ]
                          NG produ                          NG judgm
                          ct judgm                          ent
                          ent ON
```

3. Dispensing operation flow starts, Step 1: When forward command Y610 turns ON, reverse detection X611 turns OFF after 1 second, and forward detection X610 turns ON after 3 seconds. This completes the forward movement and advances to the next step.

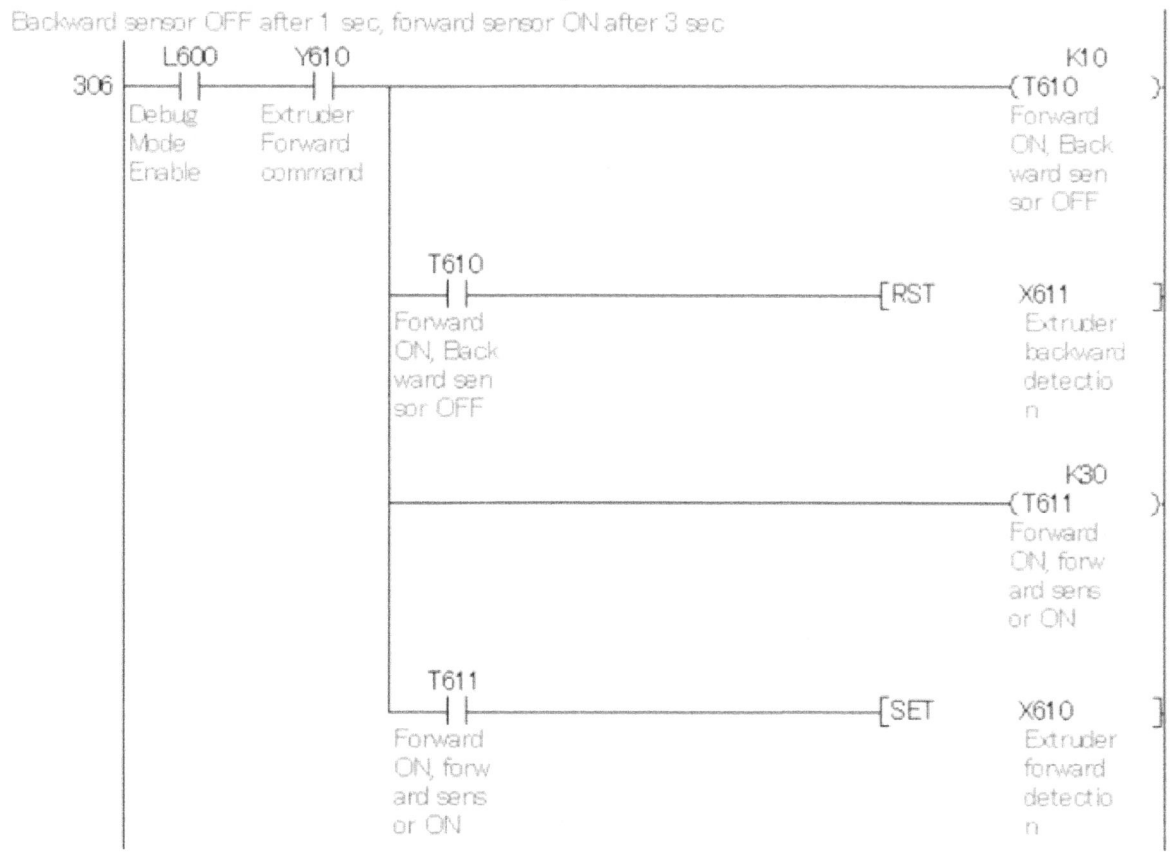

Backward sensor OFF after 1 sec, forward sensor ON after 3 sec

```
      L600      Y610                                            K10
306 ───┤├───────┤├───────────────────────────────────────────(T610)───
      Debug    Extruder                                         Forward
      Mode     Forward                                          ON, Back
      Enable   command                                          ward sen
                                                                sor OFF

                T610
               ───┤├──────────────────────────────[RST   X611          ]
                Forward                                  Extruder
                ON, Back                                 backward
                ward sen                                 detectio
                sor OFF                                  n

                                                                K30
                                                             (T611)───
                                                                Forward
                                                                ON, forw
                                                                ard sens
                                                                or ON

                T611
               ───┤├──────────────────────────────[SET   X610          ]
                Forward                                  Extruder
                ON, forw                                 forward
                ard sens                                 detectio
                or ON                                    n
```

4. Step 1 is completed, step 2: When backward command Y611 is turned ON, forward detection X610 is turned OFF after 1 second, and backward detection X611 is turned ON after 3 seconds. This completes the backward movement.

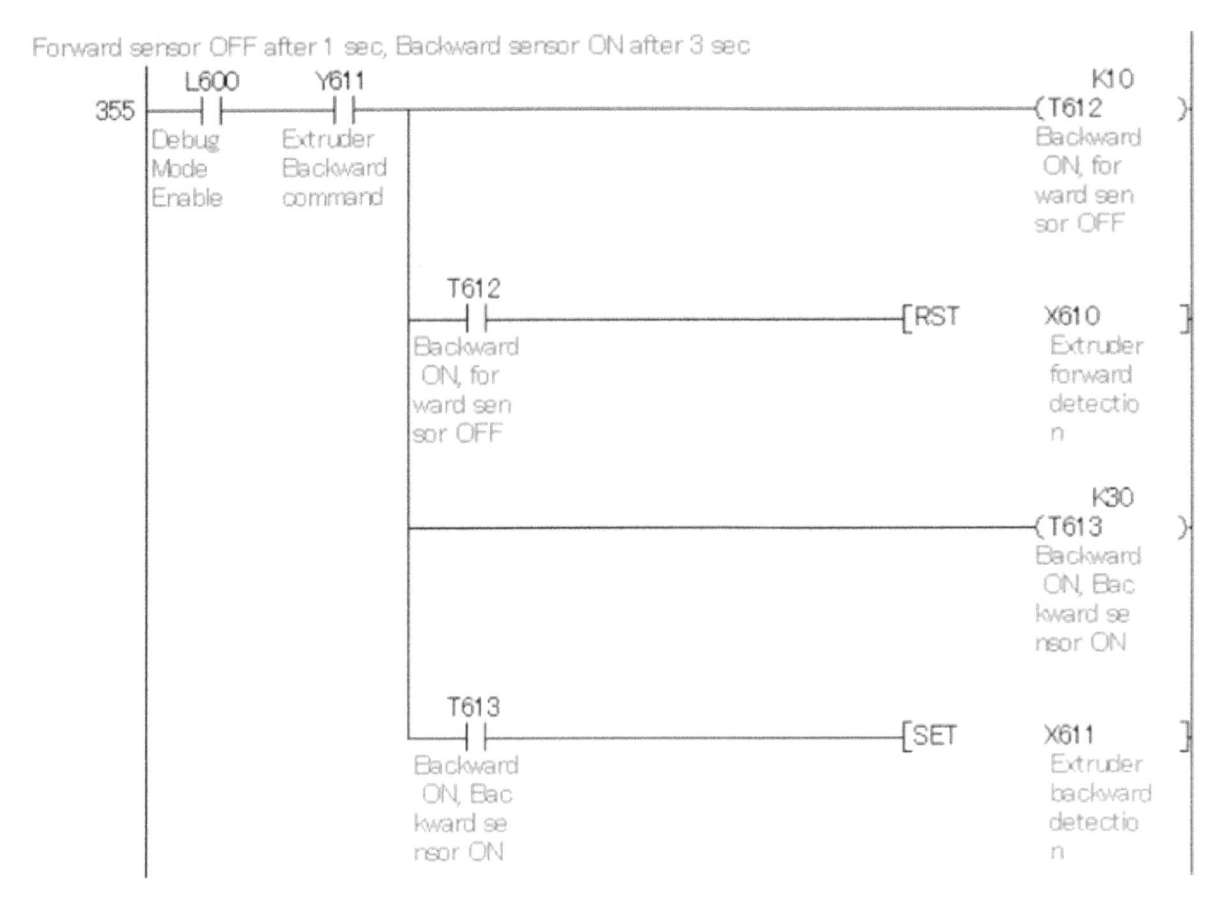

```
Forward sensor OFF after 1 sec, Backward sensor ON after 3 sec
          L600      Y611                                            K10
   355    ─┤ ├──────┤ ├────────────────────────────────────────────(T612)
          Debug    Extruder                                        Backward
          Mode     Backward                                        ON, for
          Enable   command                                         ward sen
                                                                   sor OFF

                            T612
                            ─┤ ├─────────────────────────[RST    X610    ]
                            Backward                             Extruder
                            ON, for                              forward
                            ward sen                             detectio
                            sor OFF                              n

                                                                   K30
                            ─────────────────────────────────────(T613)
                                                                 Backward
                                                                 ON, Bac
                                                                 kward se
                                                                 nsor ON

                            T613
                            ─┤ ├─────────────────────────[SET    X611    ]
                            Backward                             Extruder
                            ON, Bac                              backward
                            kward se                             detectio
                            nsor ON                              n
```

5. When Step 2 is completed and Dispensing operation flow completion M615 turns ON, NG judgment X620 turns OFF. Then, the conditions for T600 created at the beginning are completed, and after 3 seconds, NG judgment X620 turns ON and the dispensing operation flow starts again.

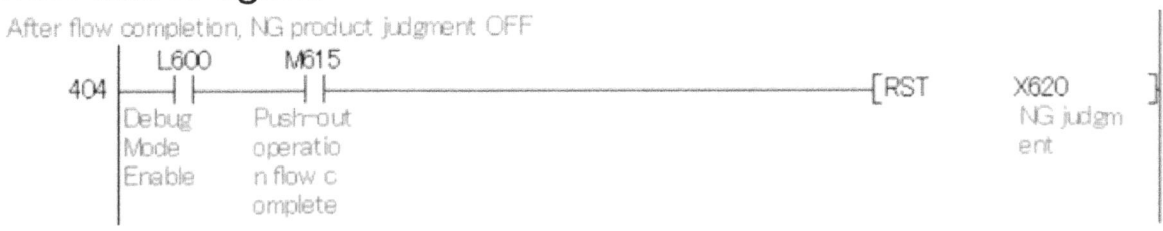

```
After flow completion, NG product judgment OFF
          L600      M615
   404    ─┤ ├──────┤ ├─────────────────────────────────[RST    X620    ]
          Debug    Push-out                                     NG judgm
          Mode     operatio                                     ent
          Enable   n flow c
                   omplete
```

220

6. Next, create an enable/disable button on the touch panel. Change each setting after copying and pasting the button and characters for resetting the number of payouts.

・Characters for Operation count reset
⇒ Change to Debug mode
[Placement/size]　X: 530 Y: 370 Width: 58 (Height: 40)

・Reset button
【Operation setting】
Device: L600, Operation setting: Alternate
Lamp device: Changed to L600
【letter】
OFF character: Invalid, ON character: Validity.
[Extension]
Delay: Change to None
[Operating conditions]
Trigger type: OFF, trigger device: M600 OK
⇒The debug mode cannot be turned ON/OFF during product production.
[Placement/size]　X: 510 Y: 415 Width: 100 Height: 50

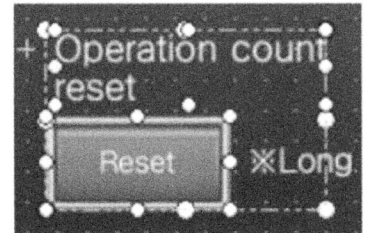

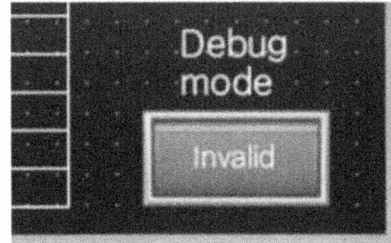

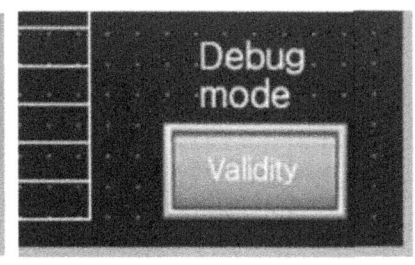

7. Each signal of the touch panel (defective product judgment, forward detection, backward detection) is changed so that it cannot be turned ON / OFF for the purpose of preventing erroneous operation when debug mode is enabled.

[Operating conditions]
Trigger type: OFF Trigger device: L600

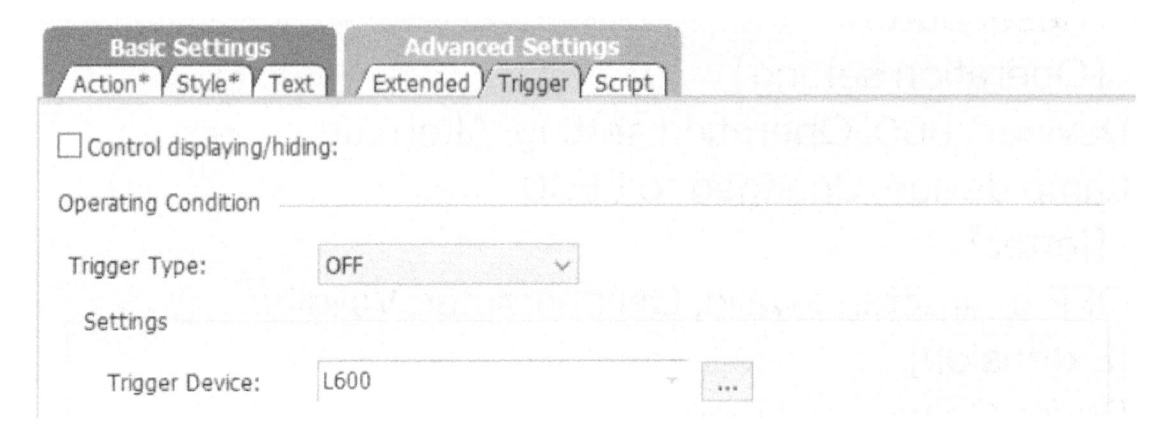

Basic Settings	Advanced Settings
Action* / Style* / Text	Extended / Trigger / Script

☐ Control displaying/hiding:

Operating Condition

Trigger Type: OFF

Settings

Trigger Device: L600

8. This completes the creation of the circuit and screen for debugging (operation check), so please perform a simulation that links the PLC program and the screen and check the operation.

・When the lamp is off during product production, the debug mode must be enabled/disabled.
・When the debug mode is enabled/disabled, when the stop button is pressed, forward detection X610 and NG product judgment X620 should be OFF, and backward detection X611 should be ON.
・When the debug mode is enabled, pressing the start button repeats the payout operation flow.

・Each signal cannot be turned ON/OFF when debug mode is enabled.

・Each signal can be turned ON/OFF when debug mode is disabled.

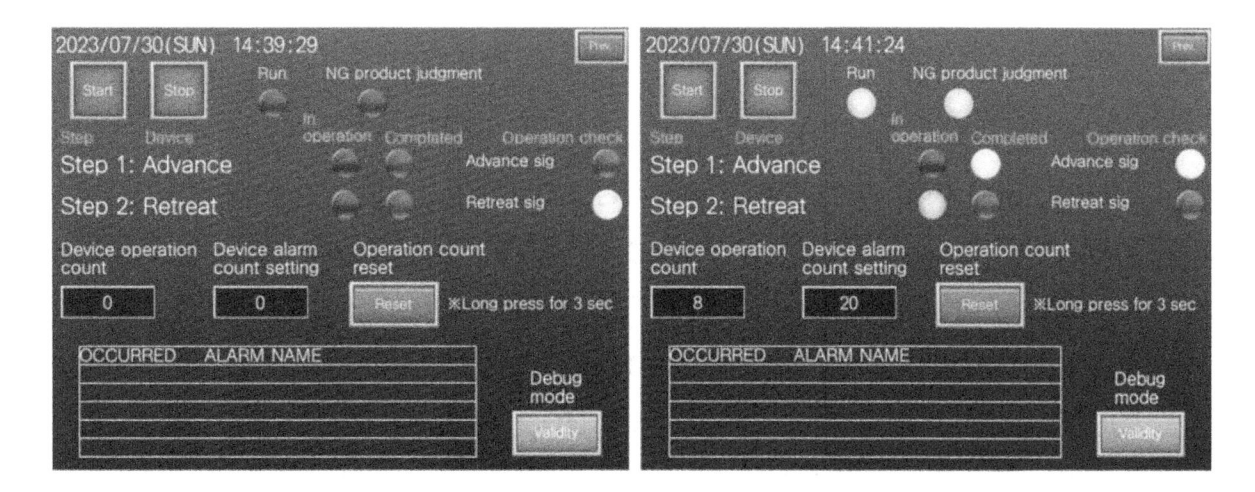

By creating a debug circuit and screen like this, you can check the operation without manually turning ON/OFF each sensor.

The above is an explanation of how to create a circuit/screen that issues a maintenance alarm when the number of operations of equipment/machine exceeds a certain number of times.

If you repair a machine after it breaks down, the equipment will stop, and productivity will drop. Before that happens, let's improve the equipment by adding the circuit introduced this time so that we can perform regular maintenance.

3-3 Improvement example 3: Alarm circuit/screen creation due to reduced operating time.

Next, we will explain how to create a circuit/screen that issues a warning when the operating time of equipment/machines is slower than the set time. Equipment machines include those that operate electrically, such as motors, and those that operate with air, such as air cylinders. * Air cylinder: Actuator (operating device) driven by air pressure. In the case of a motor, the operation may be slowed down due to equipment failure, or in the case of an air cylinder, due to air leaks. Speed monitoring is a very important factor because slowing down the operation of each piece of equipment can lead to a drop in the number of production units per hour.

By adding the circuit introduced this time, an alarm will be issued when the operation time is slower than the set time, so you will be able to notice when the number of production drops and quickly take countermeasures and responses. Here, as an example, display each operation time of the bottle transfer sequence control created in exercises 2 and 3, and the time until all operations are completed. When the time until all operations are completed exceeds the set time, create a circuit/screen that issues a transfer sequence operation delay alarm.

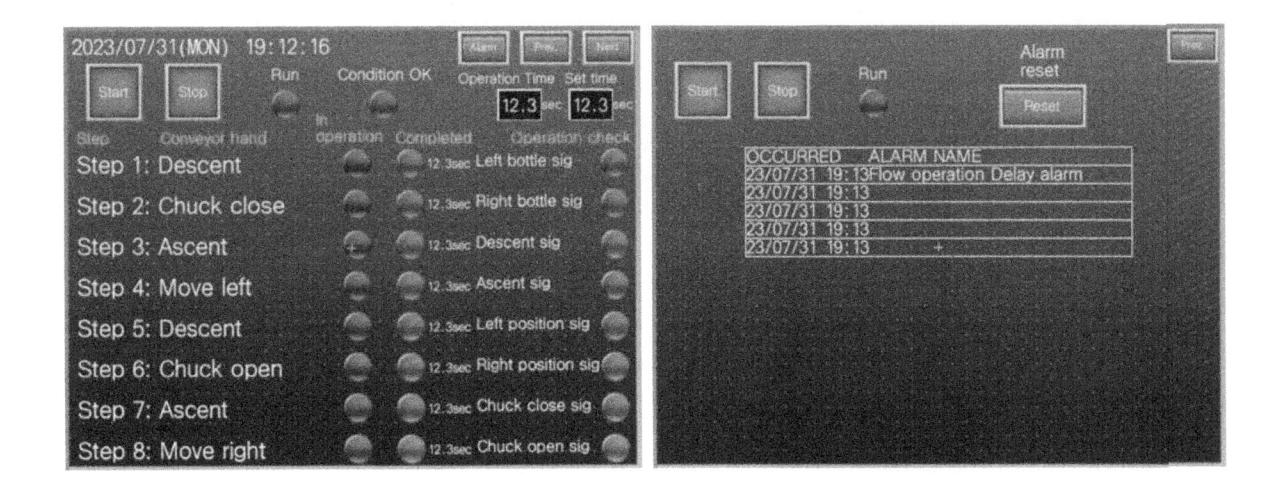

As for devices, devices T700 to T707 and D700 to D707 are used for each operation time display of steps 1 to 8. D710 is a device for displaying the completion time of all bottle transfer sequence operations, D720 is a time setting device for a bottle transfer sequence operation delay alarm, and when D710 exceeds D720, the bottle transfer flow operation delay alarm M700 is turned ON and the alarm screen is displayed. Switch the screen to and display the "bottle transfer flow operation delay alarm" on the alarm screen. Alarm reset is M750.

So, this time, we will create from the touch panel side first.

1. First, create the operation time display in step 1. Screen 1: Copy the numerical parts on the right side of "Remaining water filling" on the washing machine operation screen ⇒ After pasting, perform each setting.

【device】
Device: D700, Number size: 14
Format string: ##. # sec
⇒By setting this, the unit will be displayed.

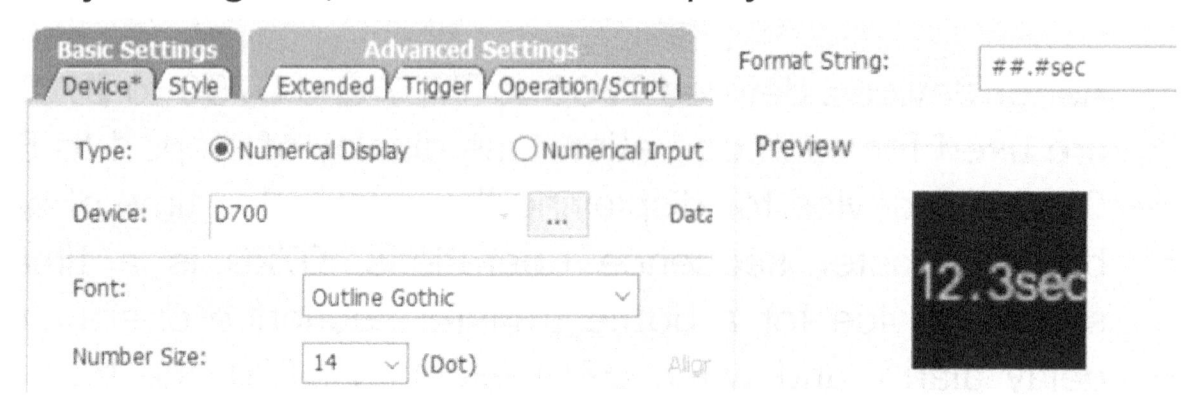

【style】
Shape: Select None
[Placement/size]　X: 405 Y: 140 Width: 49 (Height: 14)

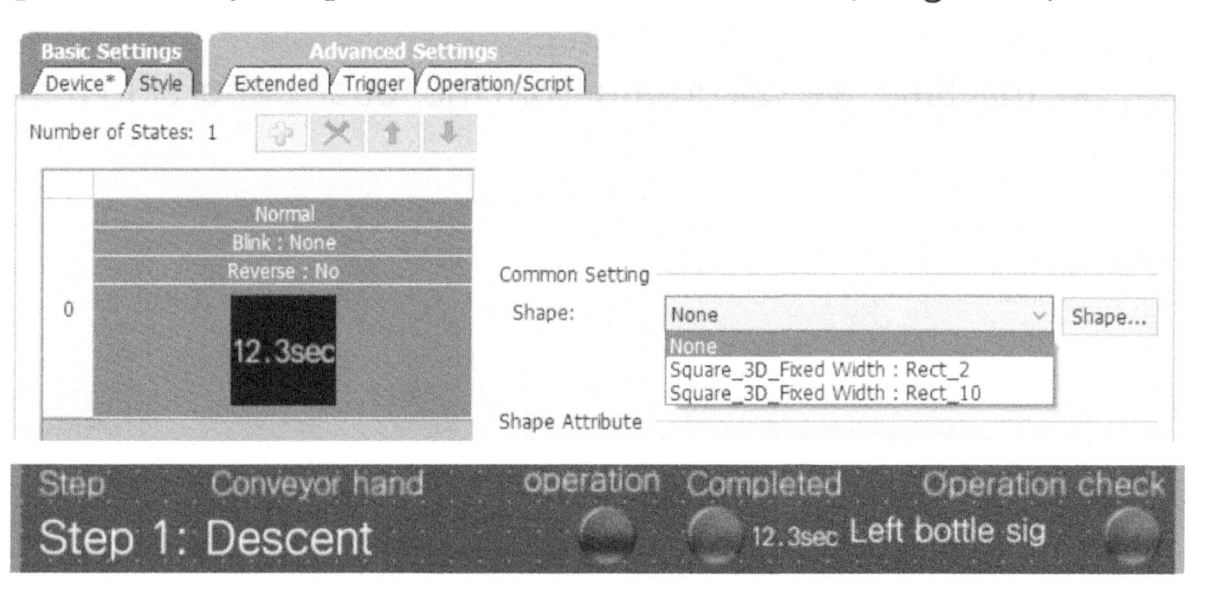

Continuously copy the time display from step 1 to step 8. After clicking the time display in step 1, press the continuous copy on the "Edit" tab, check the Y direction of the total number after copying: 8, Spacing: Include figures/objects, Y direction of spacing: 46, Increment target Check the device number, check the batch of increment settings, set the number to 1, and press OK at the bottom right to execute continuous copying. This completes the time display for steps 1-8.

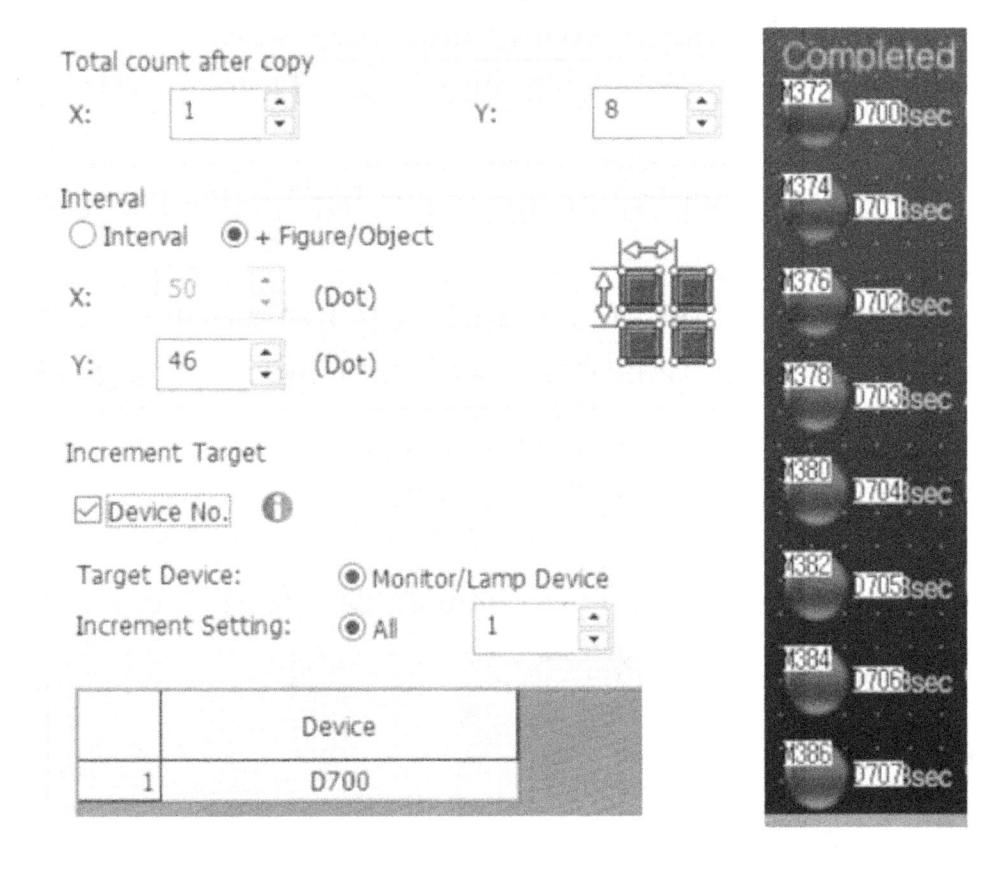

2. Create time settings for bottle transfer sequence operation completion time display and bottle transfer sequence operation delay alarm.

< **Transfer sequence all operation completion time display** >

・Character of operation time

Copy the text of "Run" ⇒ After pasting, double-click and text string: operation time, text size: 16

[Placement/size]　X: 440 Y: 45 Width: 109 (Height: 16)

・Second characters

Copy the operation time characters ⇒ After pasting, double-click the character string: sec, text size: 14

[Placement/size]　X: 535 Y: 75 Width: 23 (Height: 14)

・Completion time display component for bottle transfer sequence

Screen 1: Copy the numerical parts on the right side of "Injection time" on the washing machine operation screen ⇒ After pasting, perform each setting.

　【device】

Device: D710

[Placement/size]　X: 485 Y: 65 Width: 50 Height: 35

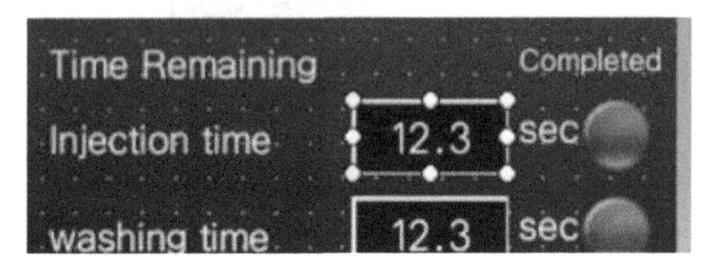

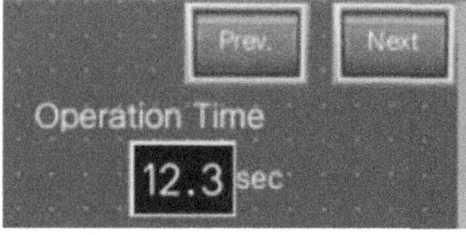

<Time setting for bottle transfer sequence operation delay alarm>

・Set time characters

Copy the operation time characters ⇒ After pasting, double-click

Text: Set time

[Placement/size]　X: 560 Y: 45 Width: 59 (Height: 16)

・Second characters

Copy the sec next to the operation time ⇒ After pasting,

[Placement/size]　X: 615 Y: 75 Width: 23 (Height: 14)

・Time setting component for bottle transfer sequence operation delay alarm

After copying and pasting the numerical display part of the operation time, perform each setting.

[Device] Type: Numeric input, Device: D720

[Input parts] Press the plus mark next to the number of settings. Then, 0<=$W<=100 ($W refers to your own device) is displayed in the condition, so press "Range..." on the right side and change the constant of A to 0 and the constant of C to 99.9 Then press OK and press OK again to complete the setting.

Constant Data Type:　○ Hex　　　● Dec　　　○ Oct

	Term Type	Value
A	Constant	0
B	$W	Monitor Device
C	Constant	99.9

【Display and operating conditions】
Trigger type: OFF, Trigger device: M360 (during automatic operation)
[Placement/size] X: 565 Y: 65 Width: 50 Height: 35

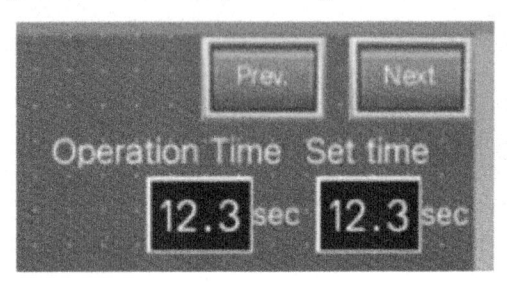

3. Next, create a bottle transport alarm screen. Open the screen you created earlier and double-click the new button on the left. Then, after inputting Screen No. 5, Title: Bottle Conveyance Alarm Screen, press OK at the bottom right to create Screen 5: Bottle transfer alarm screen.

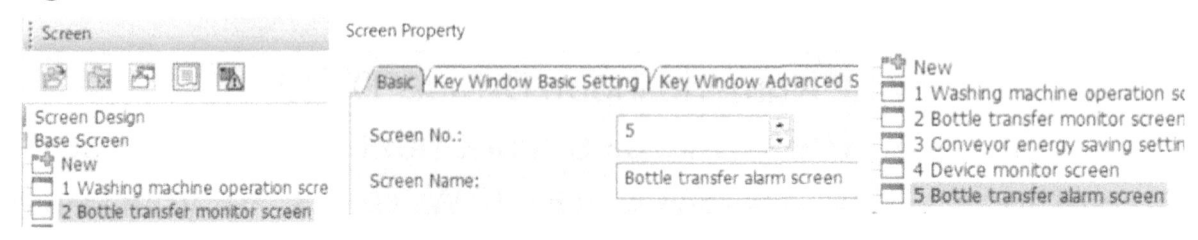

4. Create an alarm display part. Screen 4: Copy the alarm display part of the dispensing device monitor screen ⇒ After pasting, double-click to make each setting.
[Alarm setting]
Alarm ID: After changing to 2, click "Edit..." and the message "Do you want to edit?" will appear, so press "Yes".

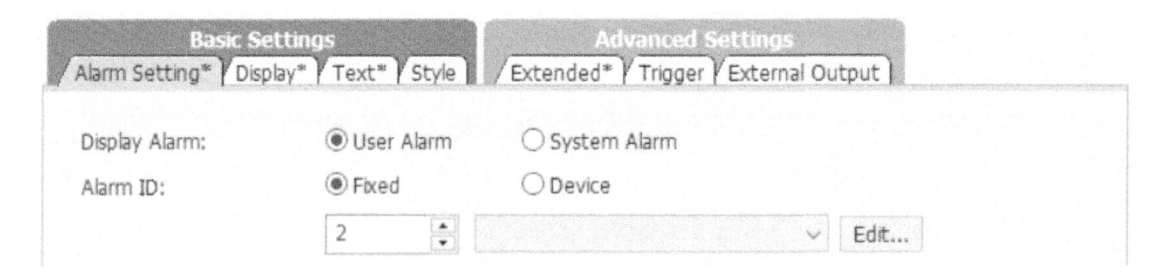

Change each setting on the displayed user alarm monitoring screen.

【Basic】

Alarm name: bottle transport alarm, history collection method: active alarm only

【device】

Device: M700, Basic Alarm Comment No.: 120

Press "Edit..." and add "Flow operation delay alarm" to the comment, then press OK on the bottom right, and then press OK on the bottom right again.

[Placement/size]   X: 100 Y: 130 (width: 441 heights: 121)

5. Next, create an alarm reset button. Screen 4: Copy the characters for resetting the number of dispensing and the reset button on the dispensing device monitor screen ⇒ After pasting, double-click to make each setting.

・Alarm reset character
String: Alarm reset
[Placement/size]　X: 415 Y: 15 Width: 50 (Height: 40)

・Reset button
【Operation setting】
Device: M750, Lamp Device: M750
[Extension]
Delay: Change to None
[Operating conditions]
Trigger type: OFF, Trigger device: M360
　(It is set so that it cannot be reset during automatic operation)
[Placement/size]　X: 390 Y: 60 Width: 100 (Height: 50)

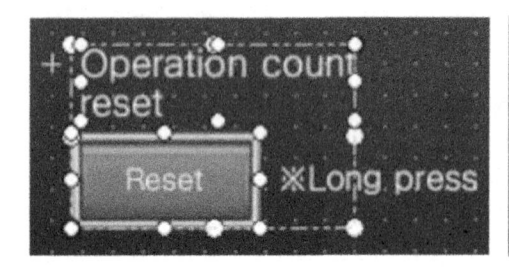

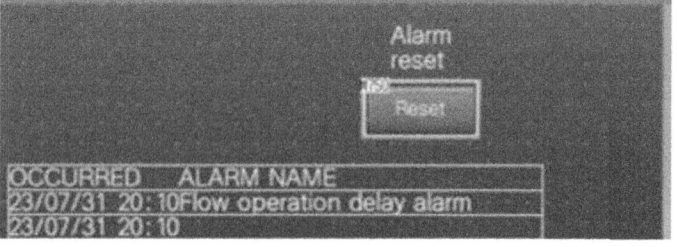

6. Add a button that allows you to move between screens 2 and 5, an automatic operation start/stop button for operation confirmation, and an automatic operation lamp.

・"Alarm screen" move button on screen 2

Copy the "Prev." button on screen 2 ⇒ After pasting, double-click to make each setting.

[Switch destination setting]

Screen number: 5

【letter】

Text column: Alarm

[Placement/size]　X: 440 Y: 0 Width: 60 Height: 40

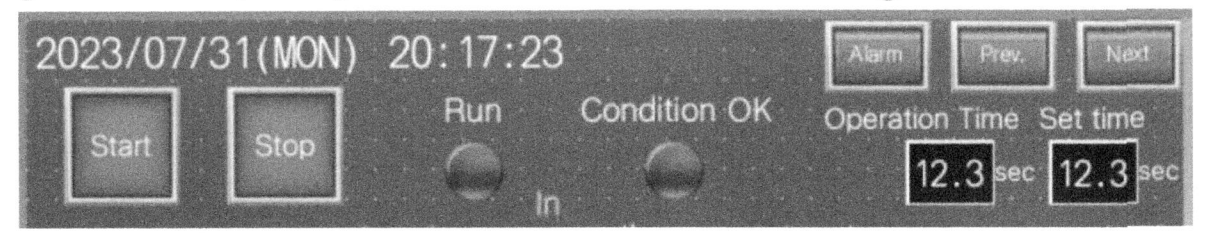

・"Prev." button on screen 5

Copy the "Previous" button on screen 4 ⇒ After pasting, double-click to make each setting.

[Switch destination setting]

Screen number: 2

　【letter】 text: Prev.

[Placement/size]　X: 580 Y: 0 Width: 60 Height: 40

・Automatic operation start/stop button, automatic operation lamp

Just copy from screen 2 ⇒ paste is OK.

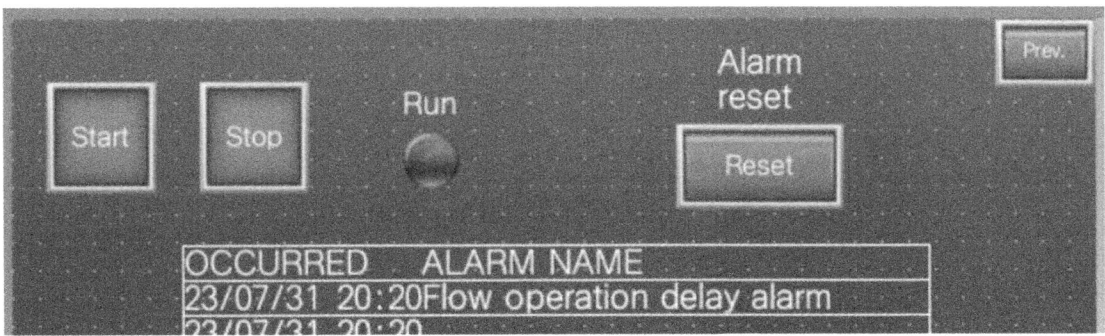

7. Change the GOT environment settings so that the screen can be switched from the PLC program to the alarm screen when the bottle transfer flow operation delay alarm M700 turns ON.

Select the "Common " tab ⇒ GOT environmental setting ⇒ Screen switching/windows, change the base screen of the setting screen to D1000, and press OK at the bottom right. By doing this setting, you can move to screen 5 by writing 5 to D1000 in the PLC program. Also, if you want to make the same settings in the overlap window (popup screen), you can do so by changing the device of GD101.

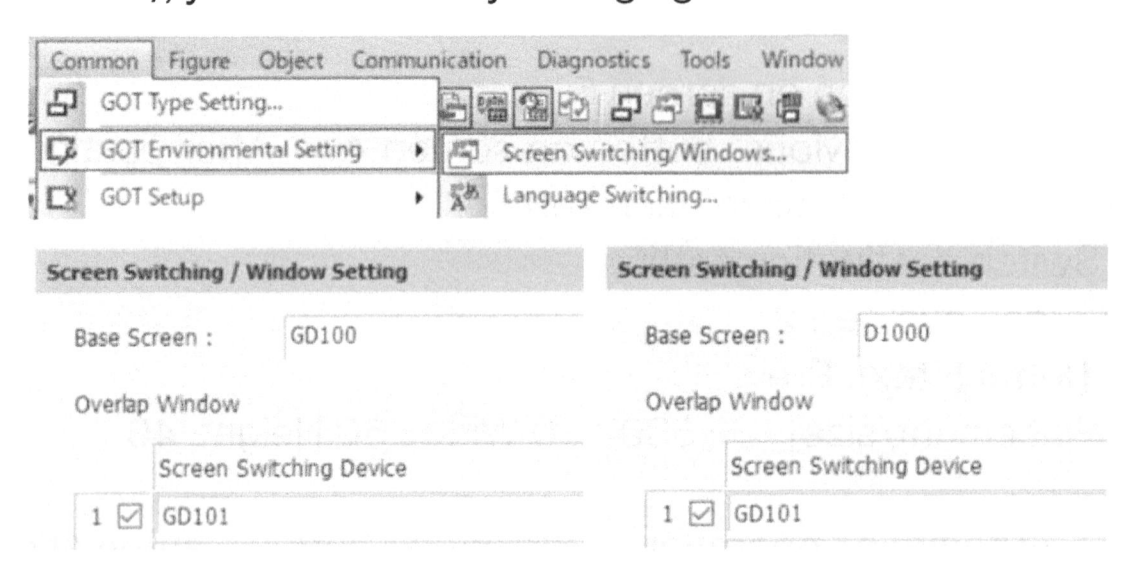

This completes the creation and setting of the touch panel.

8. Next, we will create a PLC program. First, create a time display circuit for each operation from step 1 to step 8.

Step 1: Create an operation time display for lowering the transfer hand under M371. By adding this circuit, the T700 time count starts from the start of the transfer hand descent, and the operation time is displayed on the screen by entering the T700 count in D700. Then, when transfer hand descent completion M372 turns ON, the condition expires, so the time from the start of processing to the completion of descent remains in D700. Also, K999 of T700 can count to 99.9 seconds. If it takes a long time to operate, it is OK to use K9999.

Step 1: Transfer hand lowering operation time (using T700, D700)

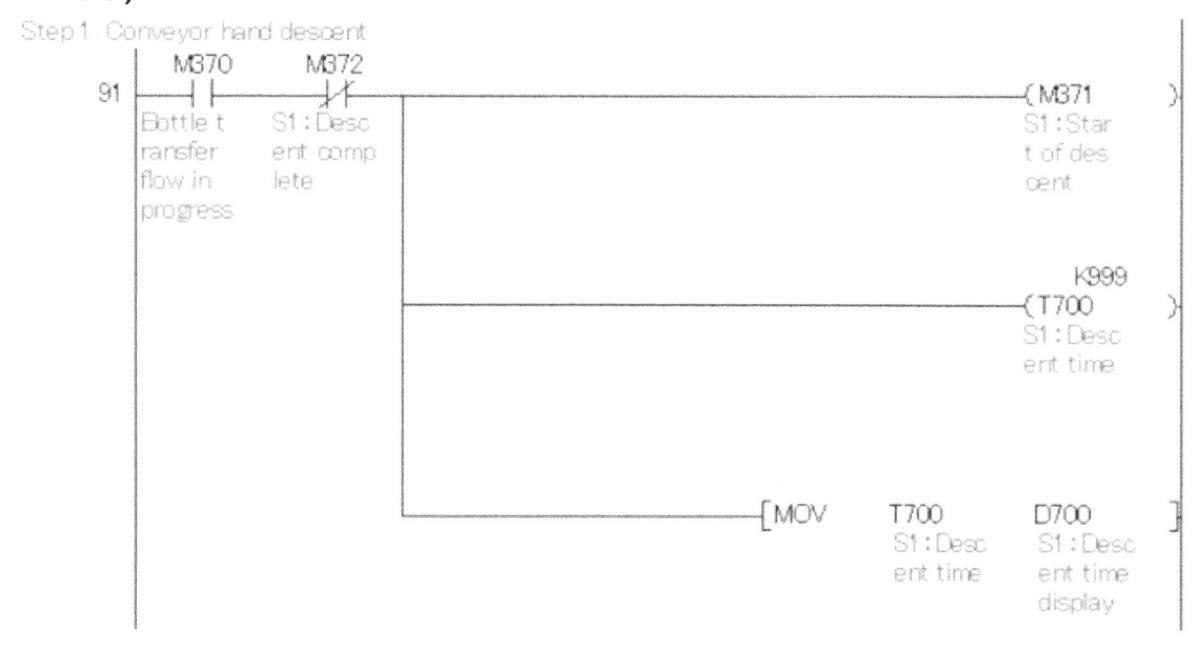

```
Step 1: Conveyor hand descent
        M370      M372
 91 ────┤├────────┤/├─────────────────────────────(M371)
        Bottle t  S1:Desc                          S1:Star
        ransfer  ent comp                          t of des
        flow in   lete                             cent
        progress

                                                   K999
                                                 ─(T700)─
                                                   S1:Desc
                                                   ent time

                                   ─[MOV   T700      D700  ]
                                          S1:Desc   S1:Desc
                                          ent time  ent time
                                                    display
```

Add a circuit below the operation start output in steps 2 to 8 in the same way.

Step 2: Transfer hand chuck closing operation time (using T701, D701)

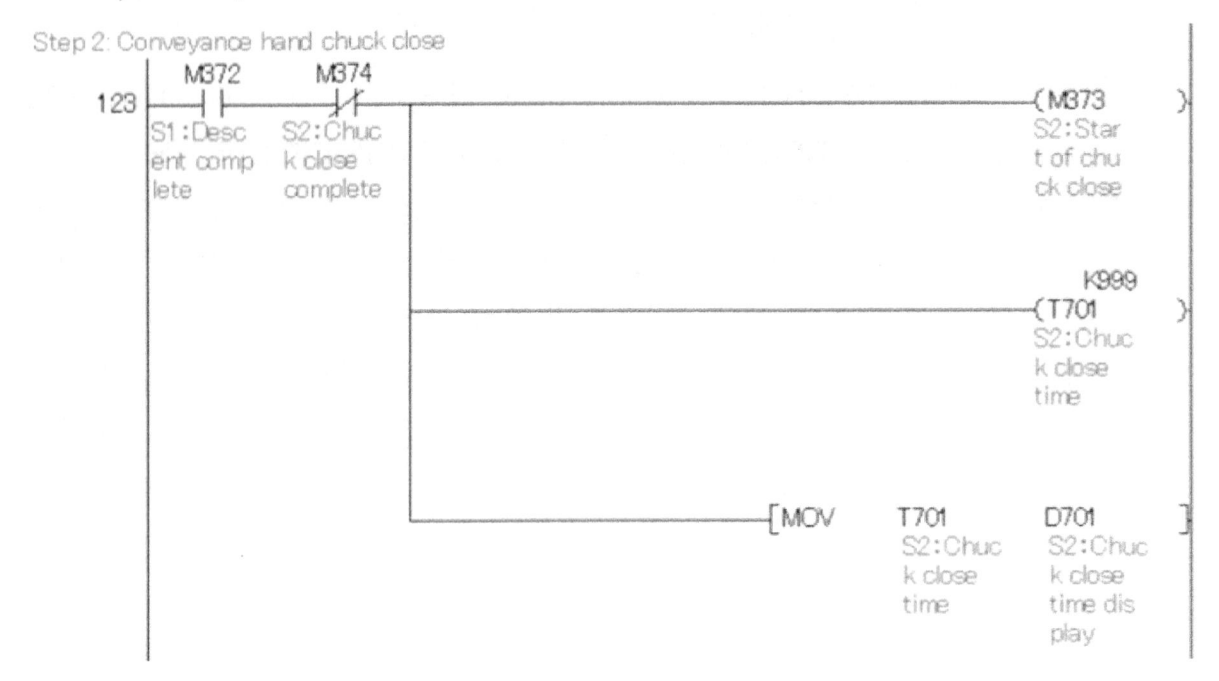

```
Step 2: Conveyance hand chuck close
        M372    M374
123 ─────┤├──────┤/├─────────────────────────────(M373)─
       S1:Desc  S2:Chuc                          S2:Start
       ent comp k close                          of chuck
       lete    complete                          close

                                                  K999
                                            ─────(T701)─
                                                 S2:Chuck
                                                 close
                                                 time

                              ─[MOV   T701        D701  ]─
                                      S2:Chuck    S2:Chuck
                                      close       close
                                      time        time display
```

Step 3: Transfer hand rising operation time (using T702, D702)

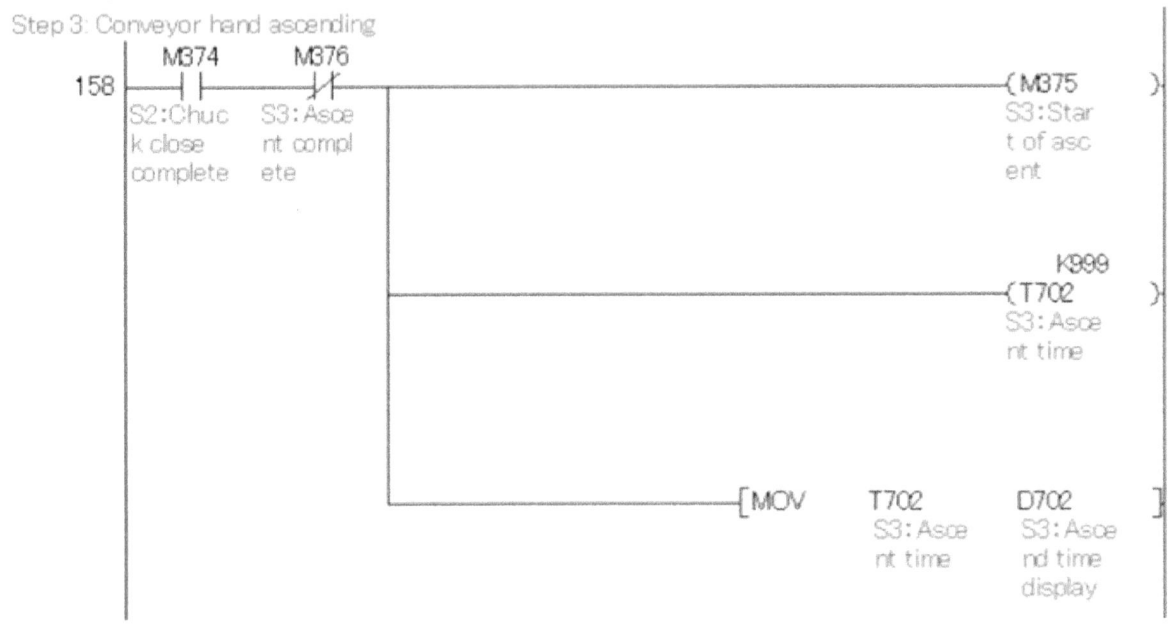

```
Step 3: Conveyor hand ascending
        M374    M376
158 ─────┤├──────┤/├─────────────────────────────(M375)─
       S2:Chuck S3:Ascent                        S3:Start
       k close  complete                         of ascent
       complete  ete

                                                  K999
                                            ─────(T702)─
                                                 S3:Ascent
                                                 time

                              ─[MOV   T702        D702  ]─
                                      S3:Ascent   S3:Ascend
                                      time        time display
```

Step 4: Transfer hand left movement operation time (using T703, D703)

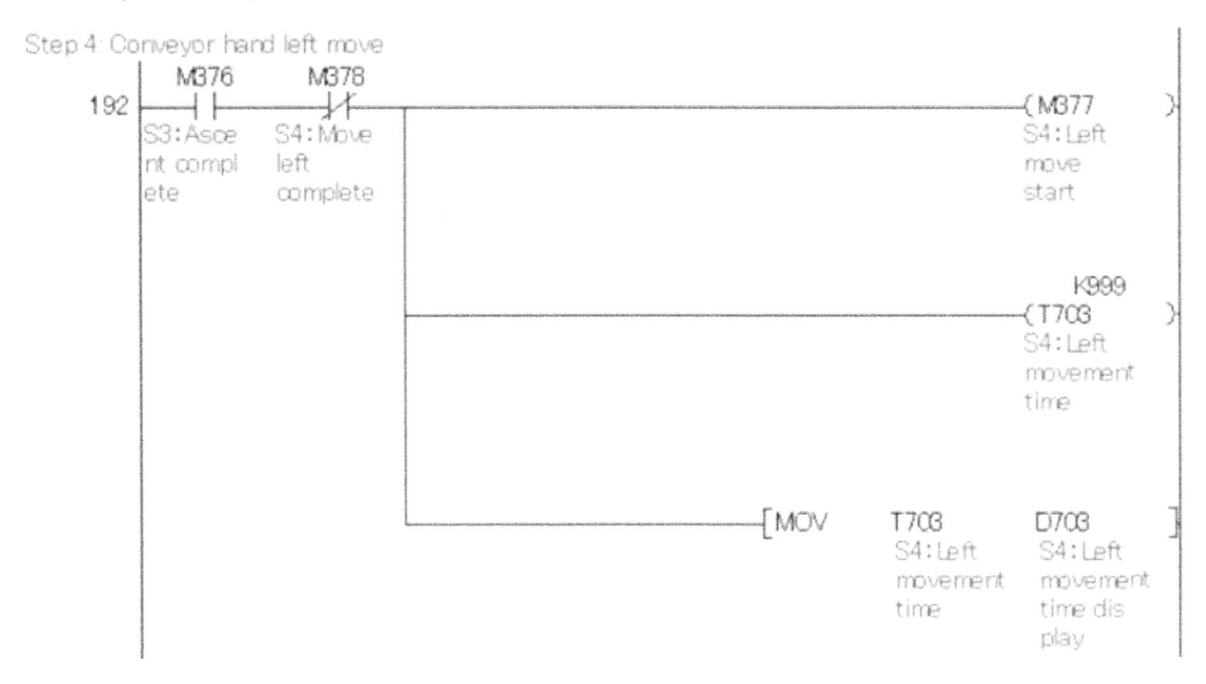

```
Step 4: Conveyor hand left move
        M376    M378                                              (M377)
  192   ─┤├─────┤/├─────────────────────────────────────────────
        S3:Asce  S4:Move                                          S4:Left
        nt compl left                                             move
        ete      complete                                         start

                                                                  K999
                                                                ─(T703)
                                                                  S4:Left
                                                                  movement
                                                                  time

                                         ─[MOV   T703       D703 ]
                                                 S4:Left    S4:Left
                                                 movement   movement
                                                 time       time dis
                                                            play
```

Step 5: Transfer hand lowering operation time (using T704, D704)

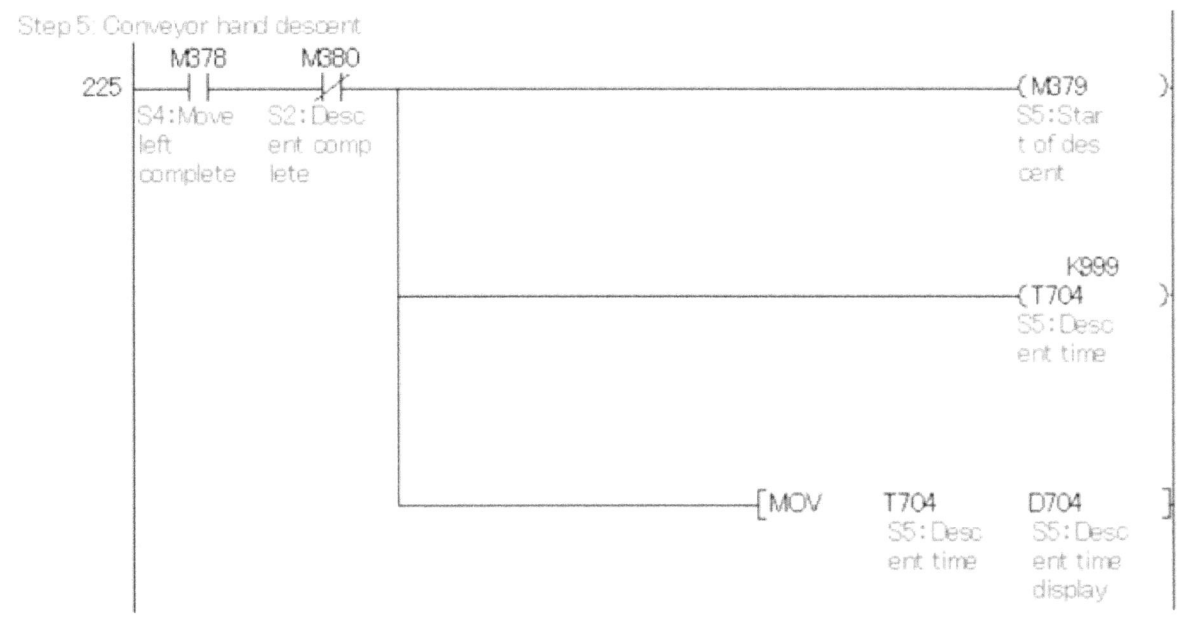

```
Step 5: Conveyor hand descent
        M378    M380                                              (M379)
  225   ─┤├─────┤/├─────────────────────────────────────────────
        S4:Move  S2:Desc                                          S5:Star
        left     ent comp                                         t of des
        complete lete                                             cent

                                                                  K999
                                                                ─(T704)
                                                                  S5:Desc
                                                                  ent time

                                         ─[MOV   T704       D704 ]
                                                 S5:Desc    S5:Desc
                                                 ent time   ent time
                                                            display
```

Step 6: Transfer hand chuck opening operation time (using T705, D705)

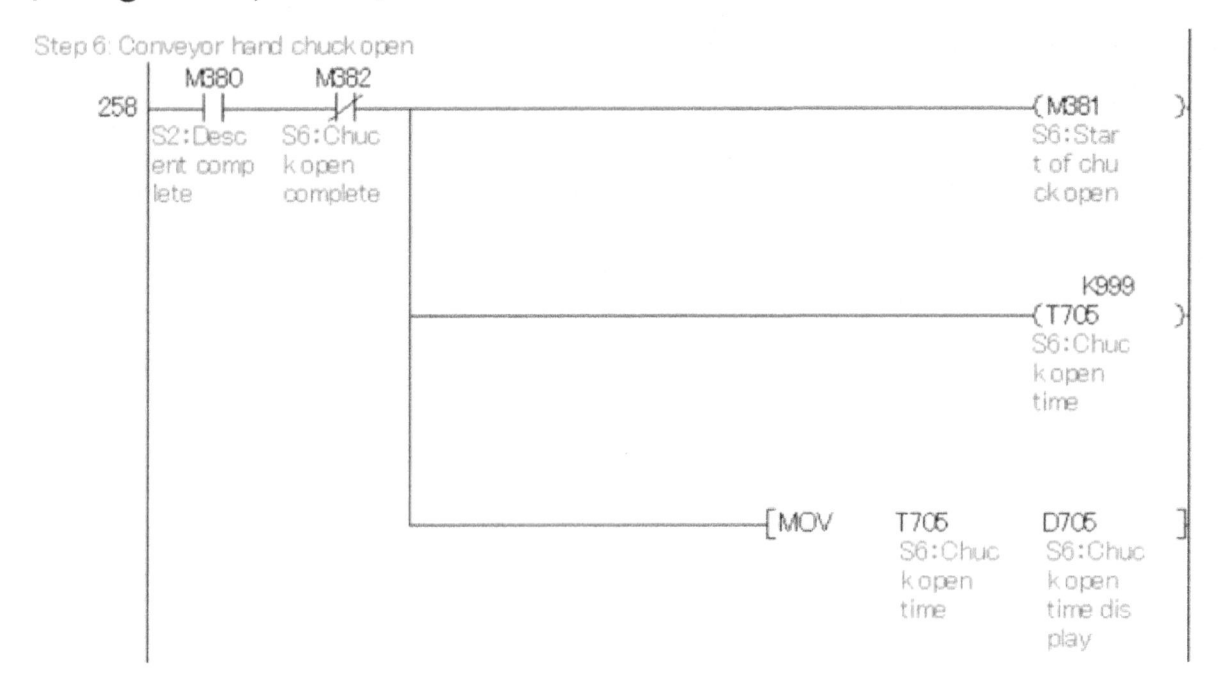

```
Step 6: Conveyor hand chuck open
        M380    M382                                              (M381)
258     ─┤├──── ─┤/├─                                             S6:Start of chuck open
        S2:Desc  S6:Chuck
        ent comp k open
        lete     complete

                                                                  K999
                                                                 (T705)
                                                                  S6:Chuck
                                                                  open time

                                          ─[MOV    T705    D705]
                                                   S6:Chuc  S6:Chuc
                                                   k open   k open
                                                   time     time display
```

Step 7: Transfer hand rising operation time (using T706, D706)

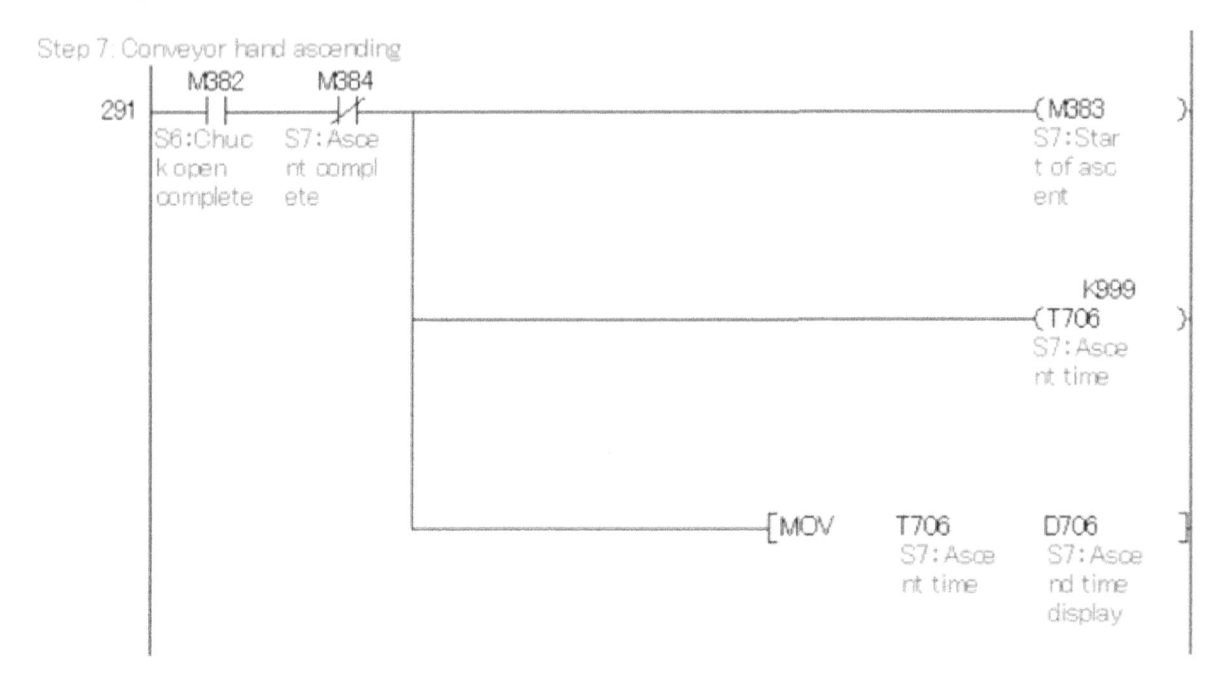

```
Step 7: Conveyor hand ascending
        M382    M384                                              (M383)
291     ─┤├──── ─┤/├─                                             S7:Start of ascent
        S6:Chuck S7:Ascent
        k open   complete
        complete

                                                                  K999
                                                                 (T706)
                                                                  S7:Ascent
                                                                  time

                                          ─[MOV    T706    D706]
                                                   S7:Ascent S7:Ascend
                                                   time      time display
```

Step 8: Transfer hand movement time to the right (using T707 and D707)

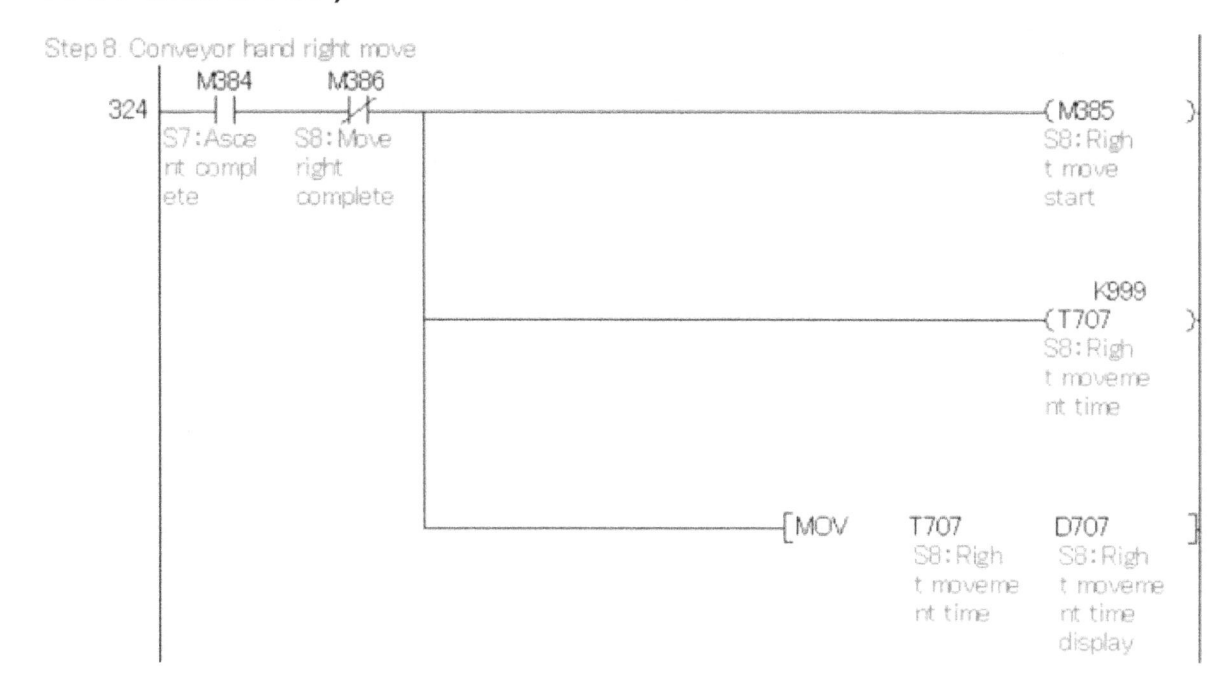

```
Step 8 Conveyor hand right move
       M384    M386
324 ───┤ ├────┤/├──────────────────────────────(M385)
       S7:Asce  S8:Move                         S8:Right
       nt compl right                           move
       ete     complete                         start

                                                 K999
                                                (T707)
                                                 S8:Right
                                                 movement
                                                 time

                                    ─[MOV  T707      D707]
                                           S8:Right  S8:Right
                                           movement movement
                                           time     time
                                                    display
```

Then, create a circuit that resets the operation time of all steps at the start of bottle transfer flow execution. This is built on top of the circuit from step 1.

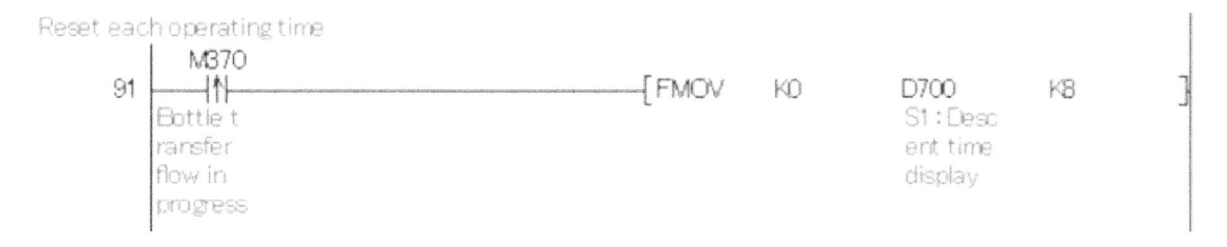

```
Reset each operating time
       M370
91 ────┤↑├─────────────────[FMOV  K0    D700     K8]
       Bottle t                         S1:Desc
       ransfer                          ent time
       flow in                          display
       progress
```

9. Next, create an operation time display for the entire bottle transfer flow. It would be nice to display the sum of D700 to D707 on D710 but using the addition command (+) would make the circuit quite long.

Therefore, **Total value calculation instruction (WSUM)** Use the. To write, press F8 and enter "WSUM D700 D710 K8". This means "starting with D700, totaling 8 words from there and putting them in D710". Also, SM400 is a special device that is always ON.

Create the location under "Conveyor hand Chuck close/chuck open command".

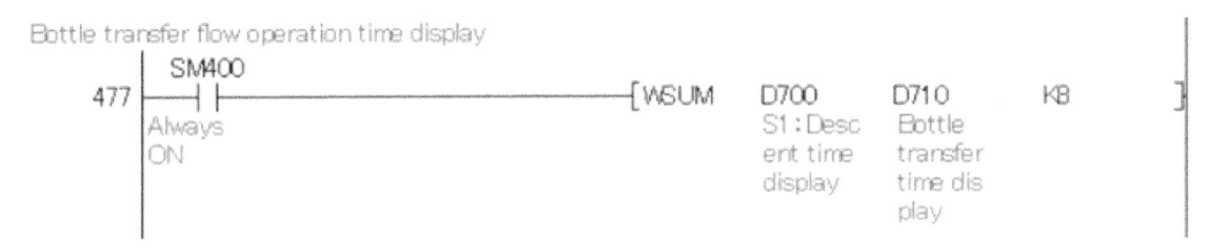

```
Bottle transfer flow operation time display
        SM400
477 ────┤ ├────────────────[WSUM   D700      D710      K8 ]
        Always                    S1:Desc    Bottle
        ON                        ent time   transfer
                                  display    time dis
                                             play
```

10. Next, create a circuit to display the bottle transfer flow operation delay alarm.

As a condition for issuing an alarm this time,
   · M370 is ON during bottle transfer flow execution,
   · Alarm setting time other than 0 (confirm that it is set)
   · The operating time is longer than the alarm setting time.

When the above conditions are met, the bottle transfer flow operation delay alarm M700 is turned ON and held. Also, turn off the retention by turning on the alarm reset M750. Create the location under "Bottle transfer flow operation time display".

```
Bottle transfer flow operation delay alarm
        M370                                                          M750
506 ────┤ ├──[<>  K0    D720 ]──[>=  D710     D720  ]──┤/├──────────(M700)
        Bottle t      Operatio        Bottle   Operatio  Alarm        Transpor
        ransfer       n alarm         transfer n alarm   reset        t operat
        flow in       setting         time dis setting                ion dela
        progress      time            play     time                   y alarm

        M700
     ───┤ ├───
        Transpor
        t operat
        ion dela
        y alarm
```

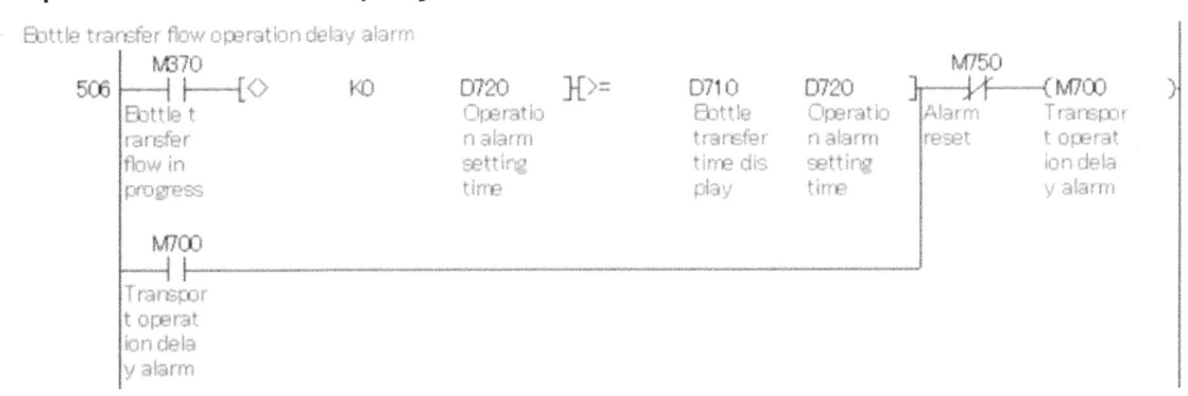

11. Finally, create a circuit to switch to Screen 5: Bottle transportation alarm screen when an alarm occurs. This is created to move to screen 5 with the rising signal of M700. (Because it will not be possible to switch screens while the alarm is active if it is set to a contact.) Create the location under the "Bottle transfer flow operation delay alarm".

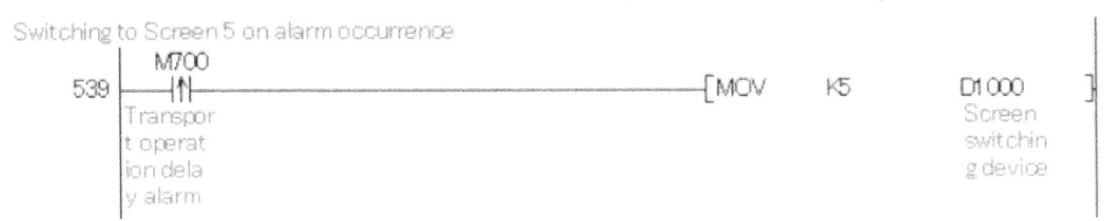

```
Switching to Screen 5 on alarm occurrence
           M700
539 ──────┤↑├─────────────────────[MOV   K5    D1000 ]
         Transpor                               Screen
         t operat                               switchin
         ion dela                               g device
         y alarm
```

This completes the creation of the program.

12. Perform a simulation that links the PLC program and the screen to check the operation.

・After turning ON the right bottle detection, rise detection, right position detection, and chuck open detection to set the automatic operation conditions, press the start button to start automatic operation, and the operation time of the entire flow and the operation time of step 1 will be counted. to be done
・If you press the stop button during automatic operation and press the start button again, the operation time of the entire flow and the operation time of step 1 will be counted from 0.
・When the last step is completed while pressing the operation confirmation button, the time of each step and the total will be displayed in the operation time of the entire flow.

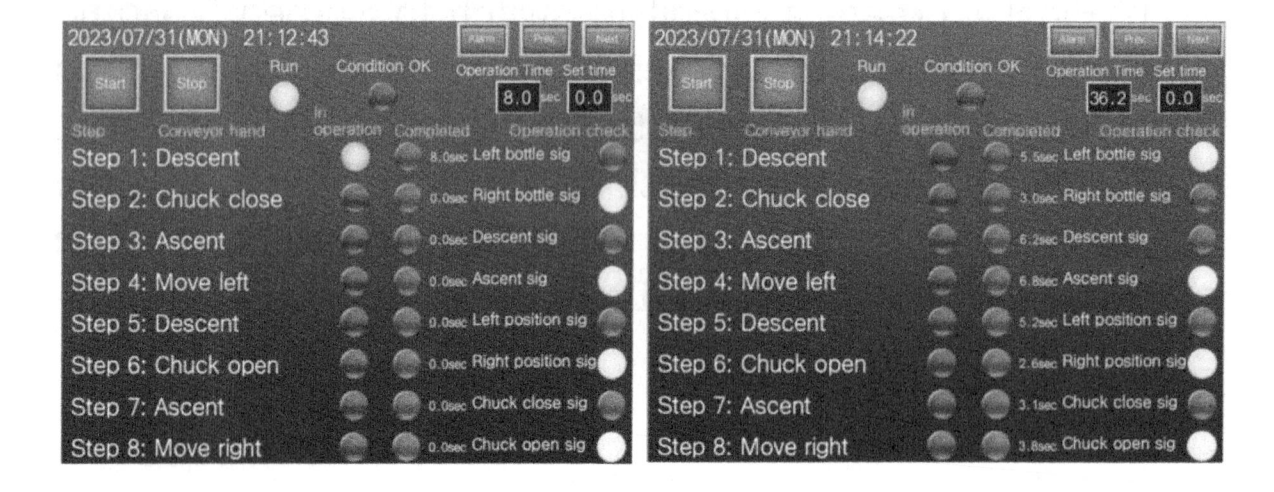

- The set time cannot be changed during automatic operation.
- The set time can be entered within the range of 0 to 99.9 while automatic operation is stopped.
- Even if you enter a set time that is less than the operation time during automatic operation stop, no alarm will be issued.
- When the conditions are met and automatic operation is started, and the operation time exceeds the set time, the screen will switch to screen 5 and an alarm will be displayed.

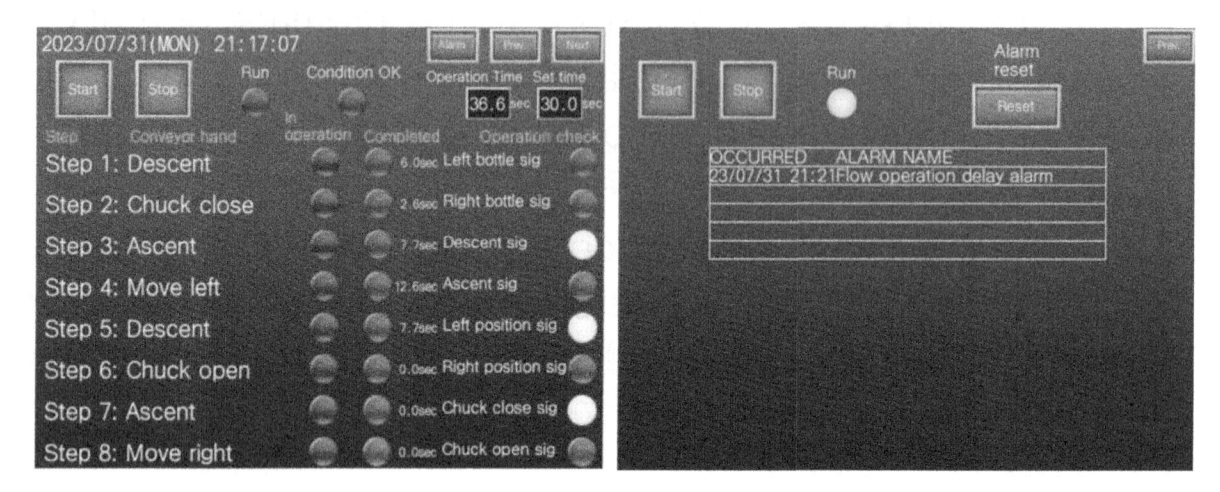

・Do not stop automatic operation even if an alarm is issued.
・If an alarm is issued during automatic operation, the alarm cannot be reset.
・If an alarm is issued for automatic operation stop, the alarm can be reset.
・Able to move between screen 2 and screen 5
・If all operations are completed within the set time, no alarm will be issued and the screen will not change.

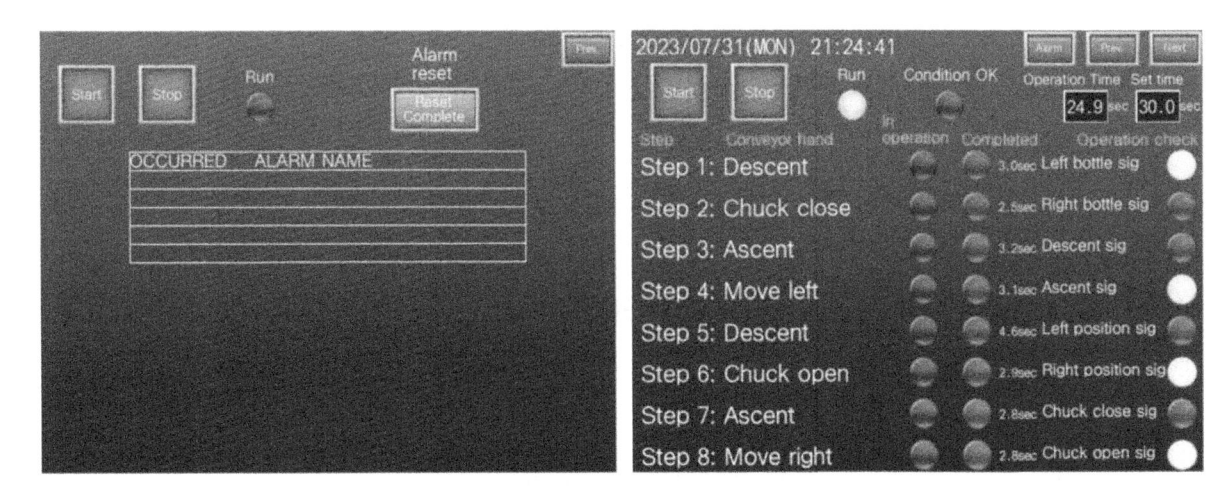

The above is how to create a circuit/screen to issue a warning when the operating time of equipment/machines is slower than the set time. As machines and equipment are used, their operation may slow down due to the deterioration of parts and the deterioration of the environment. By adding the circuits and screens introduced this time, you will be able to quickly notice such cases. Please try to improve the equipment and machines at the site by learning how to create the circuits and screens introduced.

3-4 Improvement example 4: Creating a circuit and screen that acquires each operation time as a log.

Next, we will explain how to create a circuit and screen that acquires and records each operation time as a log.

By learning how to create circuits and screens introduced this time,
　・Acquisition of necessary device logs when trouble occurs
　・Comparison between normal and abnormal conditions will be possible.

In addition to the above method, as a method of log acquisition, you can acquire the log of the setting device at a certain interval or trigger by setting the "Common settings" tab ⇒ logging on the touch panel, but this time We will create by imagining how to respond to time and visualization on the touch panel.

This time, I would like to create the following screen and circuit to display one log of the operation time of each step when an alarm occurs in the bottle transfer flow and three times of the log of the operation time of each step during normal operation.

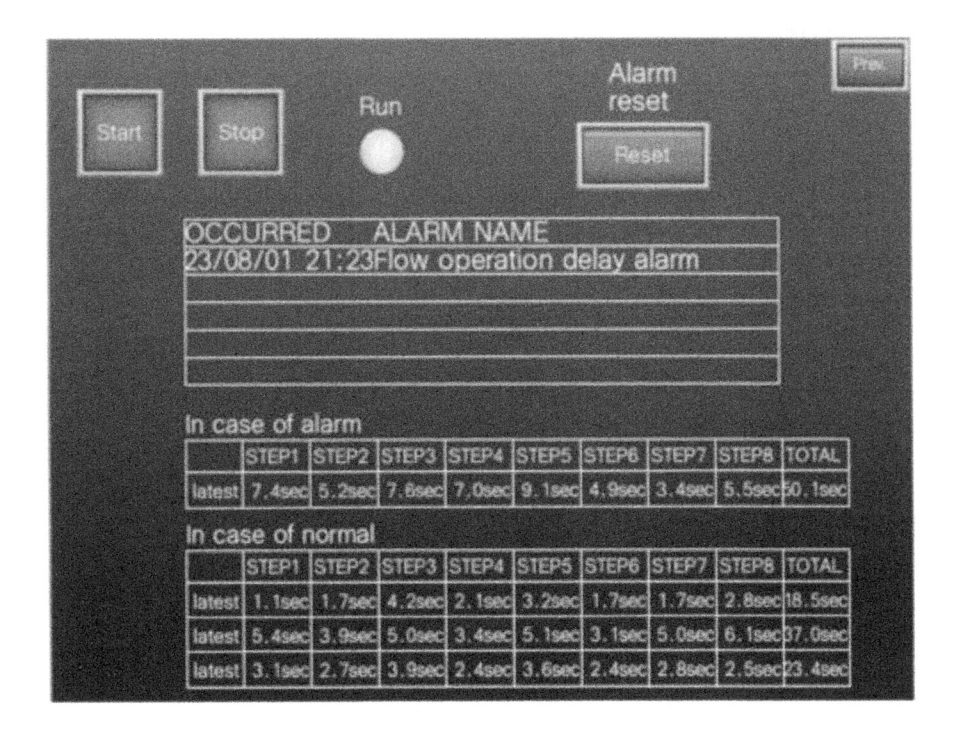

In addition, the device uses D800 to D808 for the latest log when an alarm occurs, D850 to D858 for the latest log for normal times, D860 to D868 for the first log before normal times, and D870 to D878 for the second log before normal times.

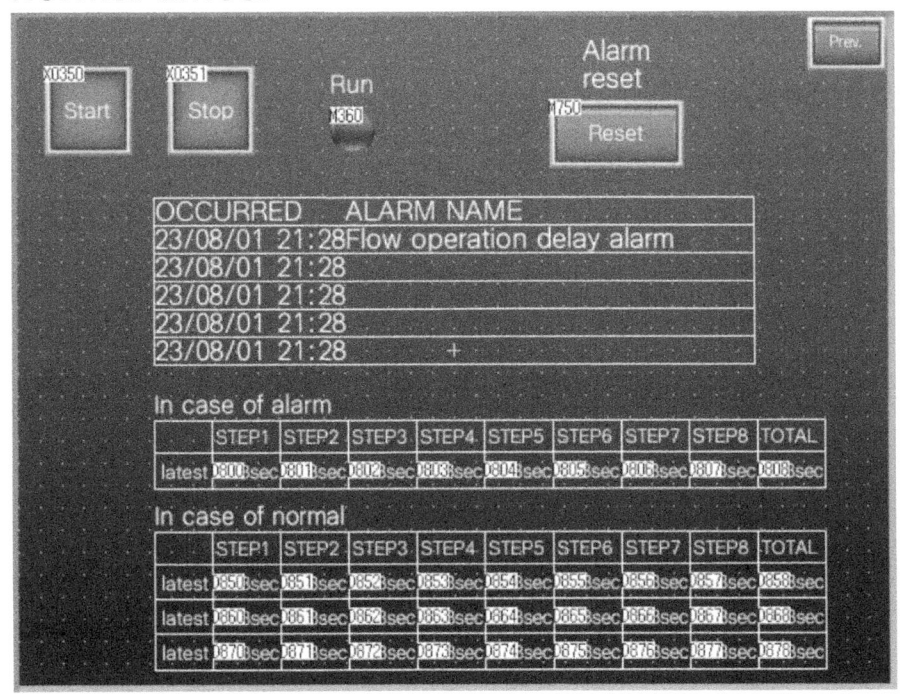

First, let's create the screen.

1. First, create a log acquisition display when an alarm occurs. Create the following screen part first, and then create other parts by continuous copying.

・Operation time log display of STEP1
After copying and pasting the step 1 operating time display on screen 2, double-click to make each setting.
　【device】 Device: D800
[Placement/size]　X: 142 Y: 320 Width: 49 (Height: 14)

・Character at In case of alarm
Copy the characters Run ⇒ After pasting, double click
String: Changed In case of alarm
[Placement/size]　X: 100 Y: 270 Width: 130 (Height: 18)

・STEP1 character
Copy the text In case of alarm ⇒ After pasting, double-click
Character string: STEP1, Character size: Changed to 14
[Placement/size]　X: 145 Y: 295 Width: 40 (Height: 14)

・The latest characters
Copy the characters in STEP1 ⇒ After pasting, double-click
String: change to latest
[Placement/size]　X: 105 Y: 320 Width: 34 (Height: 14)

・Vertical line
"Figure" tab ⇒ Select Line, click the screen, click the part
[Placement/size]　X: 142 Y: 290 Width: 1 Height: 50

Then, select the operation time log display of STEP1, the text of STEP1, and the vertical line, select the "Edit" tab ⇒ Consecutive copy, the total number after copying X direction: 9, Y direction: 1, figure / object Include: Check, X direction: 51, Increment setting: Batch, after setting to 1, press OK below.

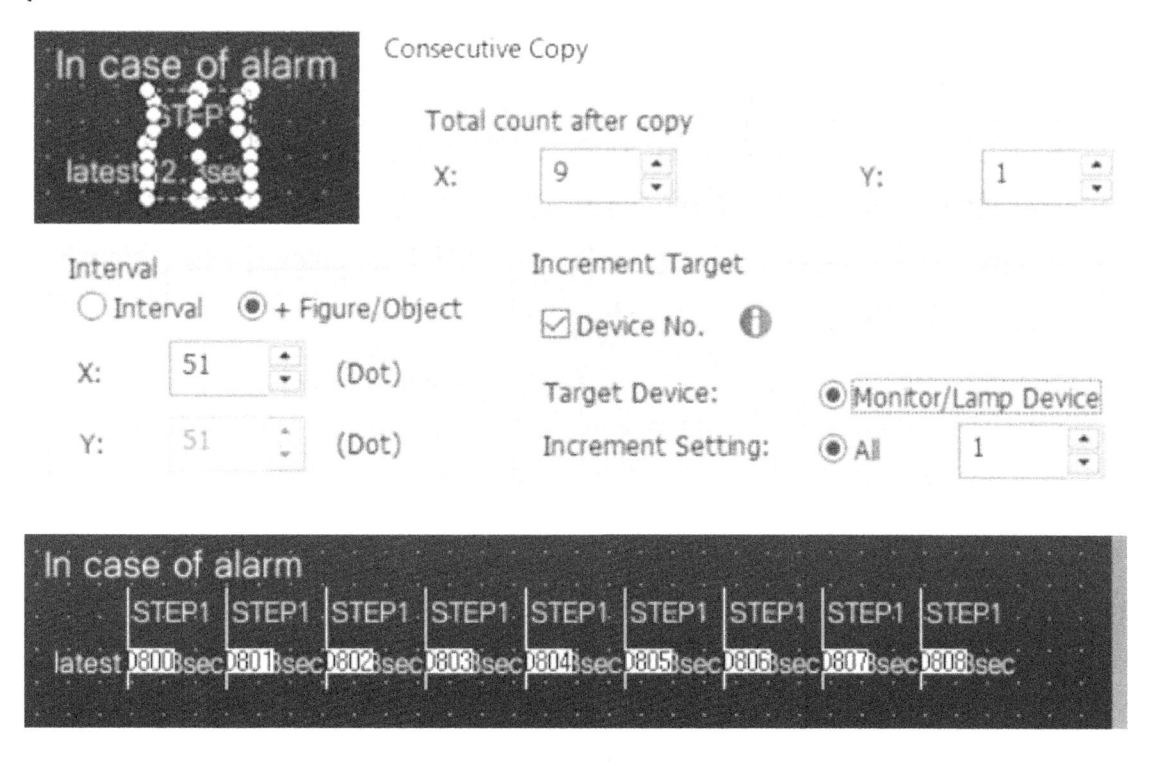

Next, create horizontal lines and borders.

·Horizontal line
Copy one of the vertical lines ⇒ Click after pasting
[Placement/size]　X: 100 Y: 313 Width: 493 Height: 1

·Frame border
Select the "Figure" tab ⇒ Rectangle, click the screen, click the part
[Placement/size]　X: 100 Y: 290 Width: 493 Height: 50

Finally, change the letters in STEP1 to STEP1 to STEP8, TOTAL.

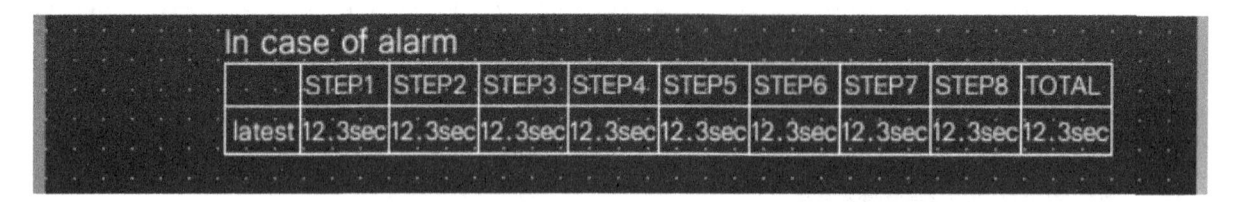

It is convenient to use the property sheet to change characters. Change the character in the style by clicking the character you want to change. If the property sheet is not visible, press Alt+1 to display it.

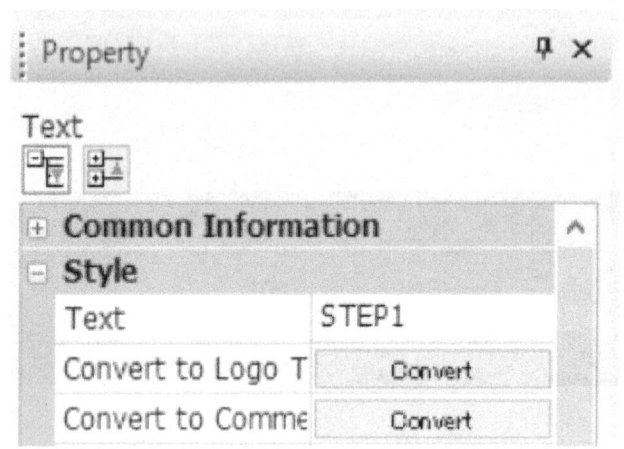

2. Next, create a log acquisition display during normal operation. After selecting all the parts that were created at the time of alarm occurrence, copy ⇒ paste, and paste by clicking so that the left end is in the position of the left frame as shown in the figure below.

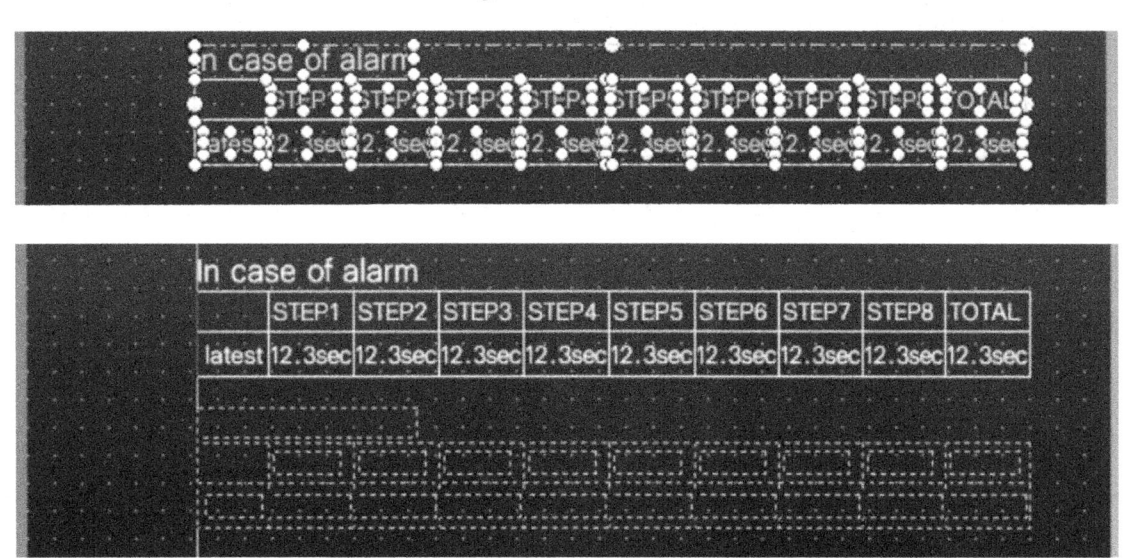

After pasting, if you select only the character at the time of alarm occurrence, the position will be displayed in the lower right. X: 100 is 100 because I made it to the left end at the position of the left frame earlier. I want Y to be 350, so in the case of Y: 362 in the figure below, it needs to be moved up by 12. After confirming that the movement amount at the top is 1, select all the pasted parts, press the cursor up button 13 times and set Y to 350.

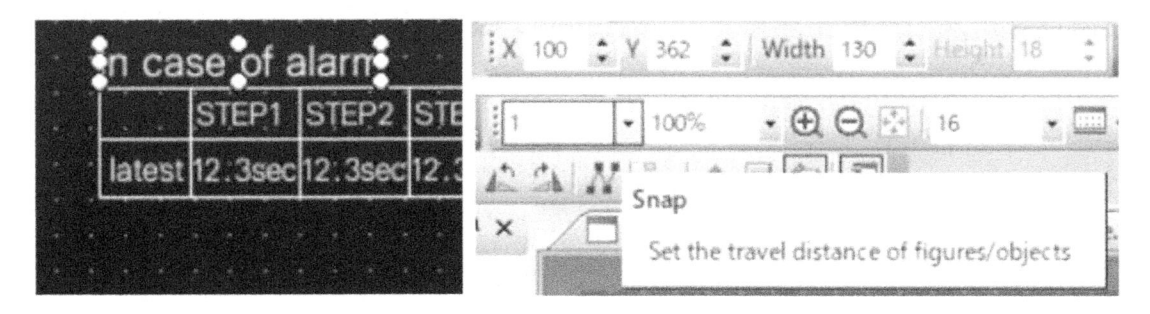

After moving, change the character at the time of alarm occurrence to normal, select only the character at normal time, and confirm that it is Y: 350.

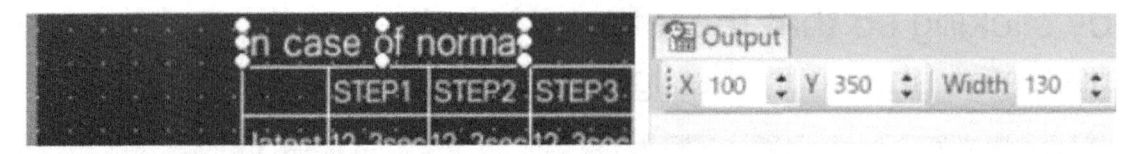

3. Select all the time displays in the latest normal time and press Ctrl + F3 to display the device batch change screen. Put the D850 in the device after changing the word and press the change button at the bottom right to replace all at once, then press the close button at the bottom right to close the device batch change screen.

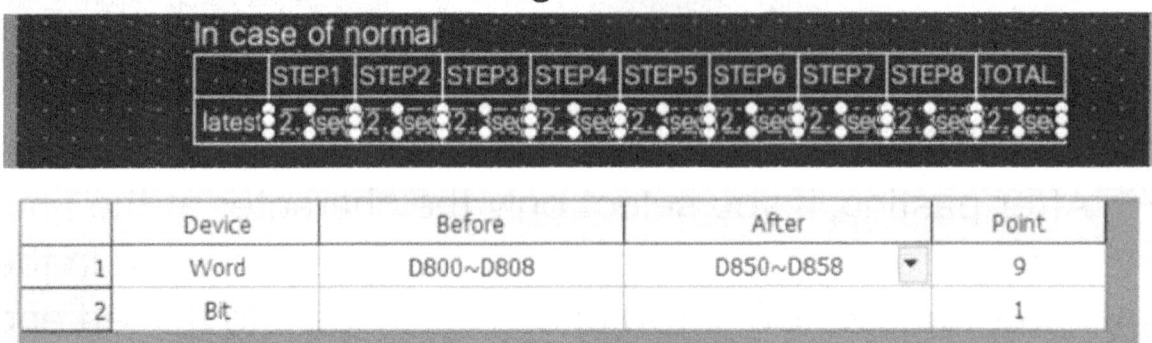

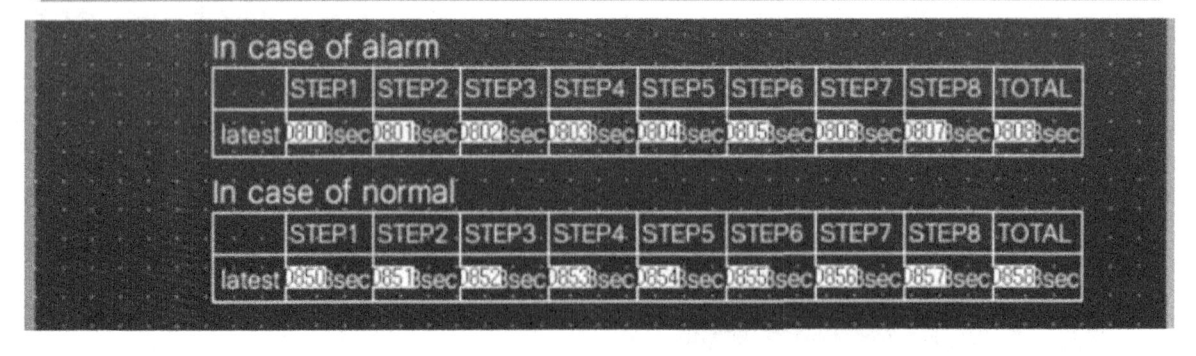

	Device	Before	After	Point
1	Word	D800~D808	D850~D858	9
2	Bit			1

4. Create the time display of the 1st and 2nd times before the normal time. After selecting each character from the latest to the total and the upper horizontal bar, select the "Edit" tab ⇒ Continuous copy, the total number after copying X direction: 1, Y direction: 3, Spacing Y direction: 26, Increment Check the target device number, batch number: After changing to 10, press OK below to perform continuous copying.

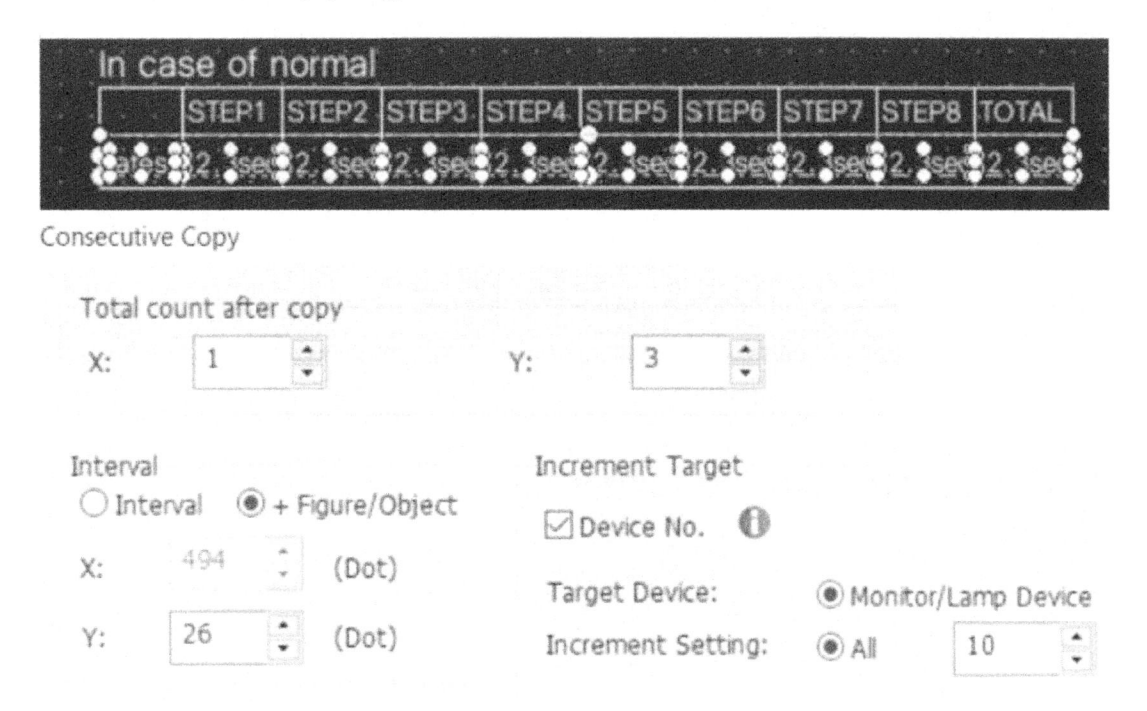

After pasting, change the latest character on the 2nd row to 1 time before, 3rd row to 2 times before, select the outer frame, and change the height at the bottom right of the screen to 100.

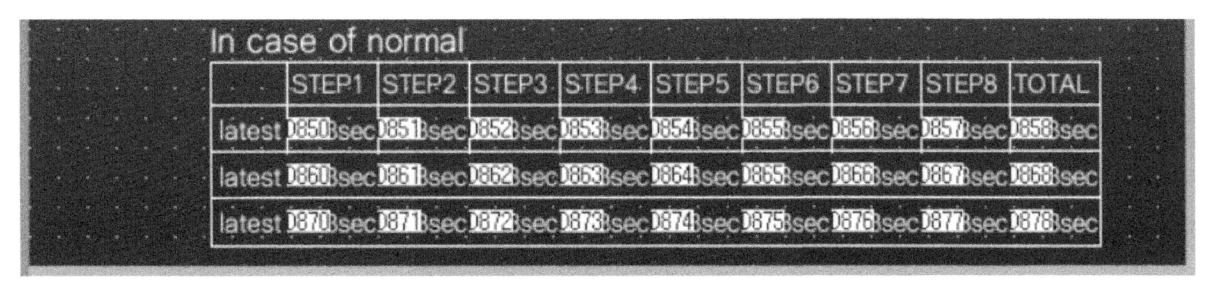

Click the vertical lines in STEP1 to STEP8 while holding down the Shift key and change the height at the bottom right of the screen to 100. If you accidentally select a different location by clicking on it, you can deselect it by clicking the same location again.

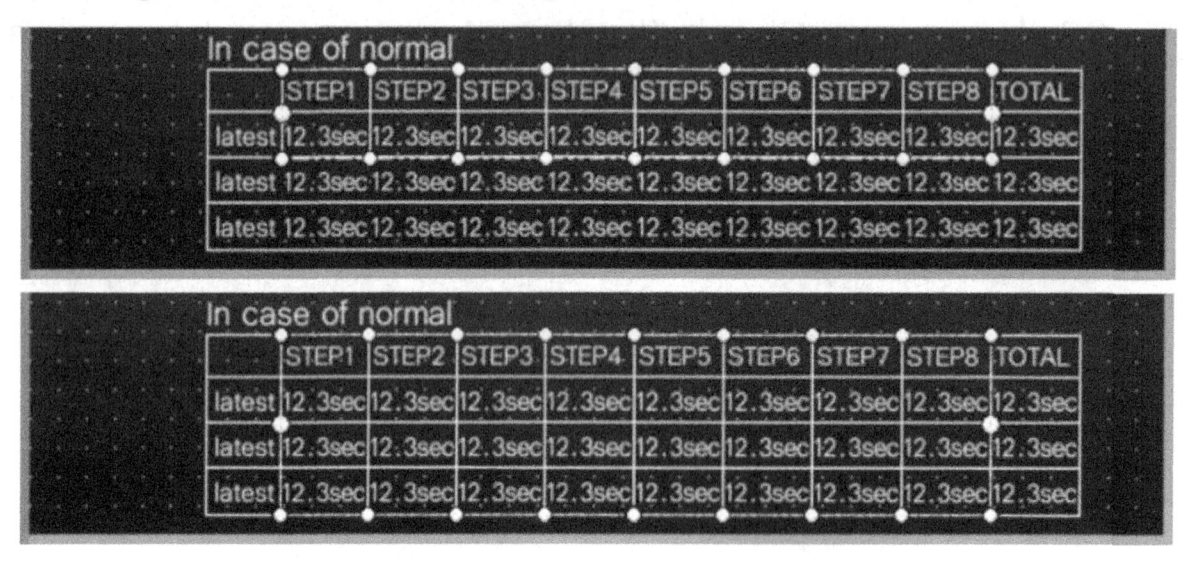

This completes screen creation.

5. Next, create a circuit for log acquisition at the bottom of the circuit. First, create a flag for operation delay (when an alarm occurs) and no operation delay (when normal). When bottle transfer flow completion M387 is turned ON, M390 with operation delay is turned ON if the flow operation time is longer than the alarm set time, and M391 without operation delay is turned ON if the flow operation time is less than the alarm set time. Now you have created a signal for logging when an alarm occurs and when it is normal.

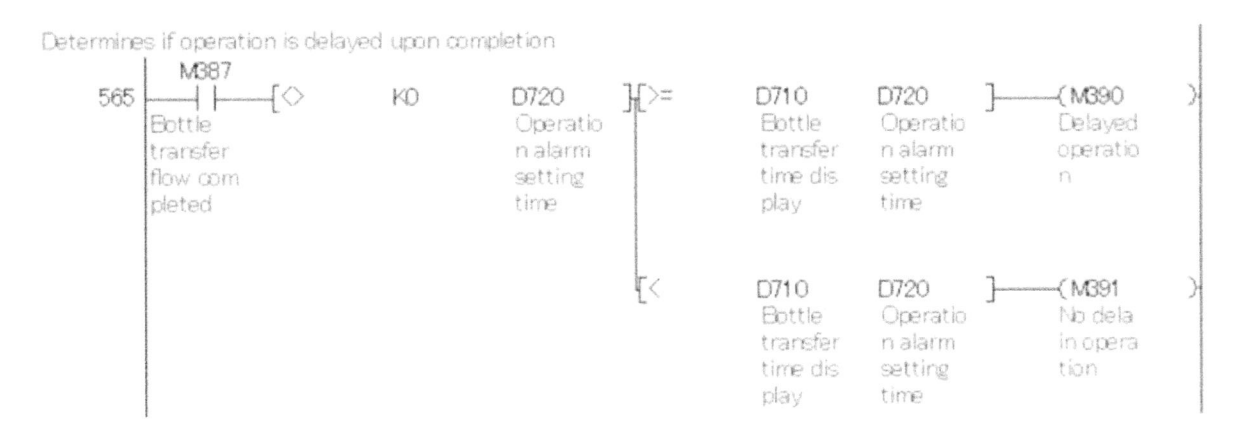

```
Determines if operation is delayed upon completion
        M387
565 ─┤├──[◇  K0  D720 ]─[>=  D710  D720 ]────(M390)
     Bottle         Operatio    Bottle    Operatio   Delayed
     transfer       n alarm     transfer  n alarm    operatio
     flow com       setting     time dis  setting    n
     pleted         time        play      time

                              ─[<  D710  D720 ]────(M391)
                                   Bottle    Operatio   No dela
                                   transfer  n alarm    in opera
                                   time dis  setting    tion
                                   play      time
```

6. Create a log acquisition circuit at the time of alarm occurrence at the bottom of the circuit. With operation delay When M390 is turned ON, the time display devices D700 to D707 from STEP1 to STEP8 are batch transferred to the alarm log acquisition devices D800 to D807. Batch transfer uses the BMOV instruction, press F8 and enter "BMOV D700 D800 K8". In addition, the time display device D710 for the entire bottle transfer flow is transferred to the log acquisition device D808 using MOV when an alarm occurs. You do not need to enter comments for D800 to D808 here, as I will explain how to easily enter them later.

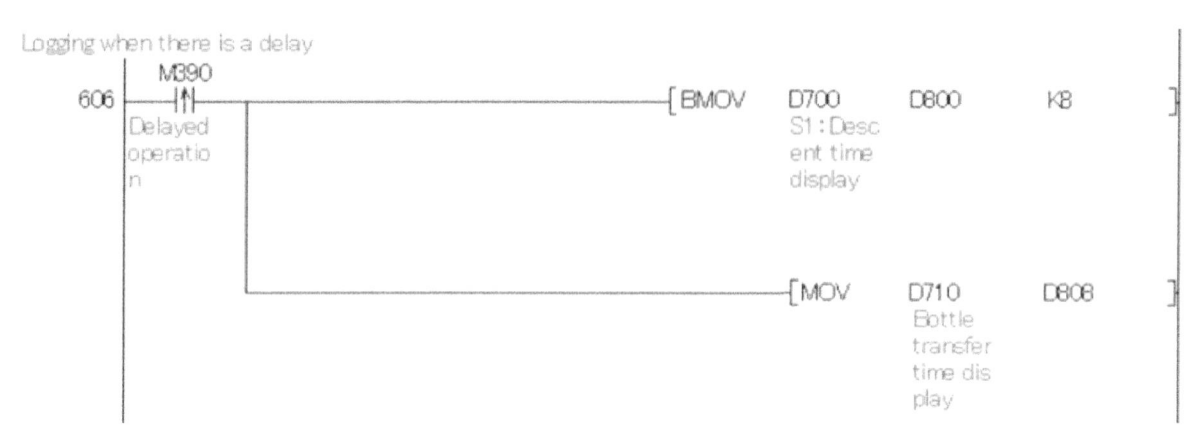

```
Logging when there is a delay
         M390
606     ─┤↑├─                          ─[BMOV   D700      D800    K8   ]
        Delayed                                 S1:Desc
        operatio                                ent time
        n                                       display

                                        ─[MOV   D710              D808 ]
                                                Bottle
                                                transfer
                                                time dis
                                                play
```

Comments for D800 to D808 are entered using the global device comment in the navigation on the left side of the screen.

Double-click the global device comment, enter D800 in the device name, and press Enter to display the comment column from D800. A common method is to enter the D800 comment, paste the D800 comment to D801 to D808, and then correct the characters for each device, but it is not very efficient.

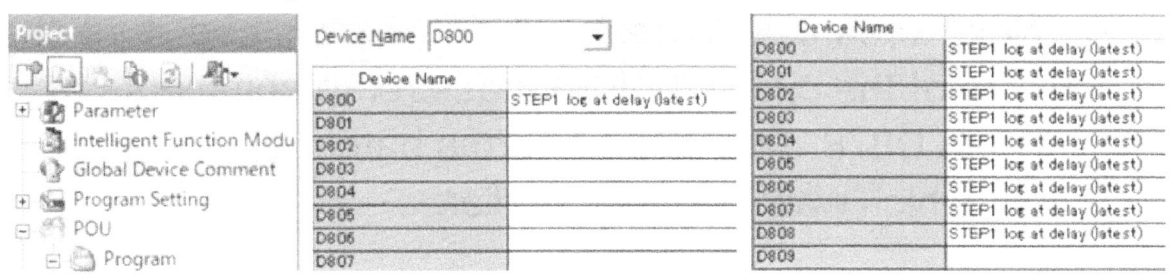

It is convenient to use Excel when the number increases like in STEP1 to STEP8 this time, or when you want to replace a certain number of characters.

In this case, after writing the D800 character in Excel, create up to STEP9 while holding down the left click on the lower right of the cell. Then, after changing the characters in STEP9 to total, copy all the characters in Excel and paste them into the global device comment. This allows you to enter comments more efficiently than working on global device comments.

When creating a PLC program, there are many occasions where similar comments are made. At that time, it is troublesome to change the comments one by one on the global device comment, so it is recommended to work on Excel as described above.

7. Next, create a normal log acquisition circuit at the bottom of the circuit. Before that, create comments from D850 to D878. This also performs batch replacement on Excel, which was explained earlier.

After selecting all the previous comments, press CTRL to bring up Find and Replace and select the Replace tab. Then, put "operation delay" in the string to be searched and "normal" in the string after replacement and press the replace all button at the bottom left to make comments for D850 to D858, so copy it on Excel and make a global device comment Paste to

STEP1 log at delay (latest)		STEP1 log at normal (latest)			
STEP2 log at delay (latest)		STEP2 log at normal (latest)	D850		STEP1 log at normal (latest)
STEP3 log at delay (latest)		STEP3 log at normal (latest)	D851		STEP2 log at normal (latest)
STEP4 log at delay (latest)	→	STEP4 log at normal (latest)	D852		STEP3 log at normal (latest)
STEP5 log at delay (latest)		STEP5 log at normal (latest)	D853		STEP4 log at normal (latest)
STEP6 log at delay (latest)		STEP6 log at normal (latest)	D854		STEP5 log at normal (latest)
STEP7 log at delay (latest)		STEP7 log at normal (latest)	D855		STEP6 log at normal (latest)
STEP8 log at delay (latest)		STEP8 log at normal (latest)	D856		STEP7 log at normal (latest)
TOTAL log at delay (latest)		TOTAL log at normal (latest)	D857		STEP8 log at normal (latest)
			D858		TOTAL log at normal (latest)
			D859		

Create comments for D860 to D868 and D870 to D878 in the same way.

D860	STEP1 log at normal (1 Prev.)
D861	STEP2 log at normal (1 Prev.)
D862	STEP3 log at normal (1 Prev.)
D863	STEP4 log at normal (1 Prev.)
D864	STEP5 log at normal (1 Prev.)
D865	STEP6 log at normal (1 Prev.)
D866	STEP7 log at normal (1 Prev.)
D867	STEP8 log at normal (1 Prev.)
D868	TOTAL log at normal (1 Prev.)
D869	

D870	STEP1 log at normal (2 Prev.)
D871	STEP2 log at normal (2 Prev.)
D872	STEP3 log at normal (2 Prev.)
D873	STEP4 log at normal (2 Prev.)
D874	STEP5 log at normal (2 Prev.)
D875	STEP6 log at normal (2 Prev.)
D876	STEP7 log at normal (2 Prev.)
D877	STEP8 log at normal (2 Prev.)
D878	TOTAL log at normal (2 Prev.)
D879	

Different from when an alarm occurs, the normal log remains three times. The latest log is entered in D850 to D858 each time, but if the previous data remains in D850 to D858, that data will disappear.

To prevent this from happening, it is necessary to transfer the previously entered data from D850 to D858 to D860 to D868 before inserting the data. Similarly, the data of D860 to D868 must be transferred to D870 to D878.

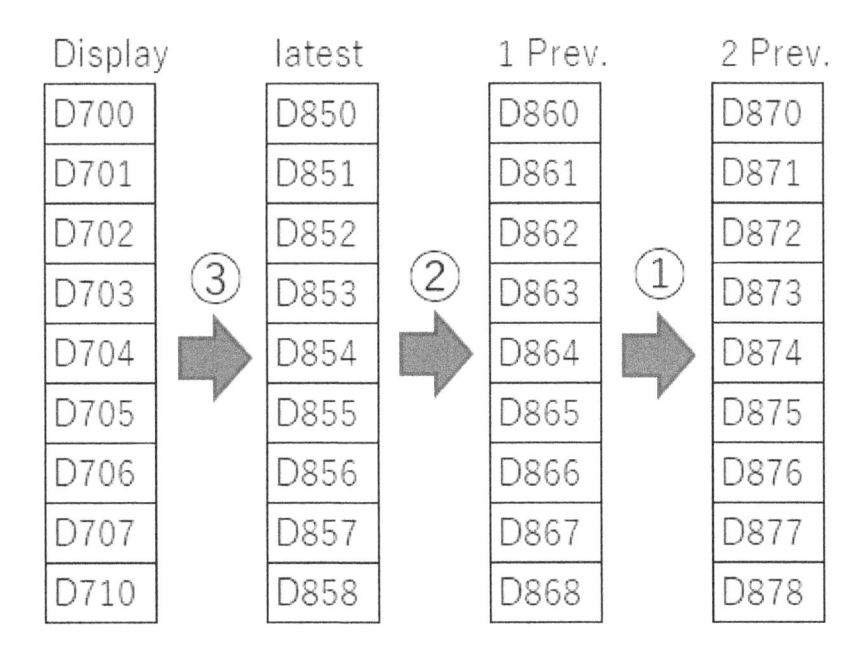

Display	latest	1 Prev.	2 Prev.
D700	D850	D860	D870
D701	D851	D861	D871
D702	D852	D862	D872
D703	D853	D863	D873
D704	D854	D864	D874
D705	D855	D865	D875
D706	D856	D866	D876
D707	D857	D867	D877
D710	D858	D868	D878

③ ← ② ← ①

Therefore, first create a circuit that transfers data from D860 to D868 to D870 to D878, and then transfers data from D850 to D858 to D860 to D868. Here, ① and ② above are executed by collectively transferring data from D850 to D869 to D860 to D879.

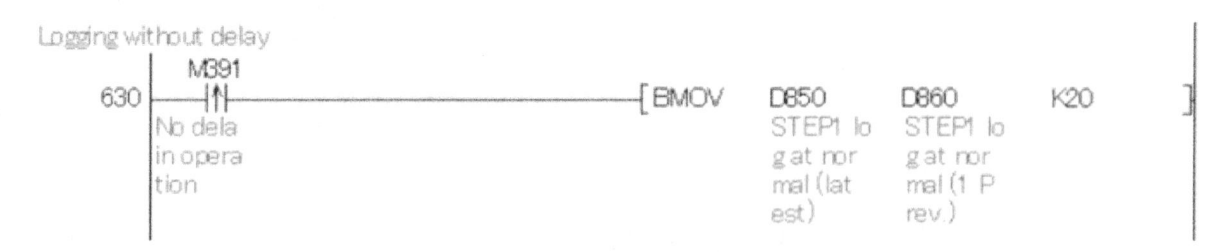

```
Logging without delay
         M391
630 ─────┤↑├──────────────────────[BMOV  D850      D860      K20 ]
         No dela                         STEP1 lo  STEP1 lo
         in opera                        g at nor  g at nor
         tion                            mal (lat  mal (1 P
                                         est)      rev.)
```

Then create the circuit of ③ under the instruction of ①②. The order of transfer is important here, so be careful not to place the circuit of ③ on top of the circuit of ① and ②.

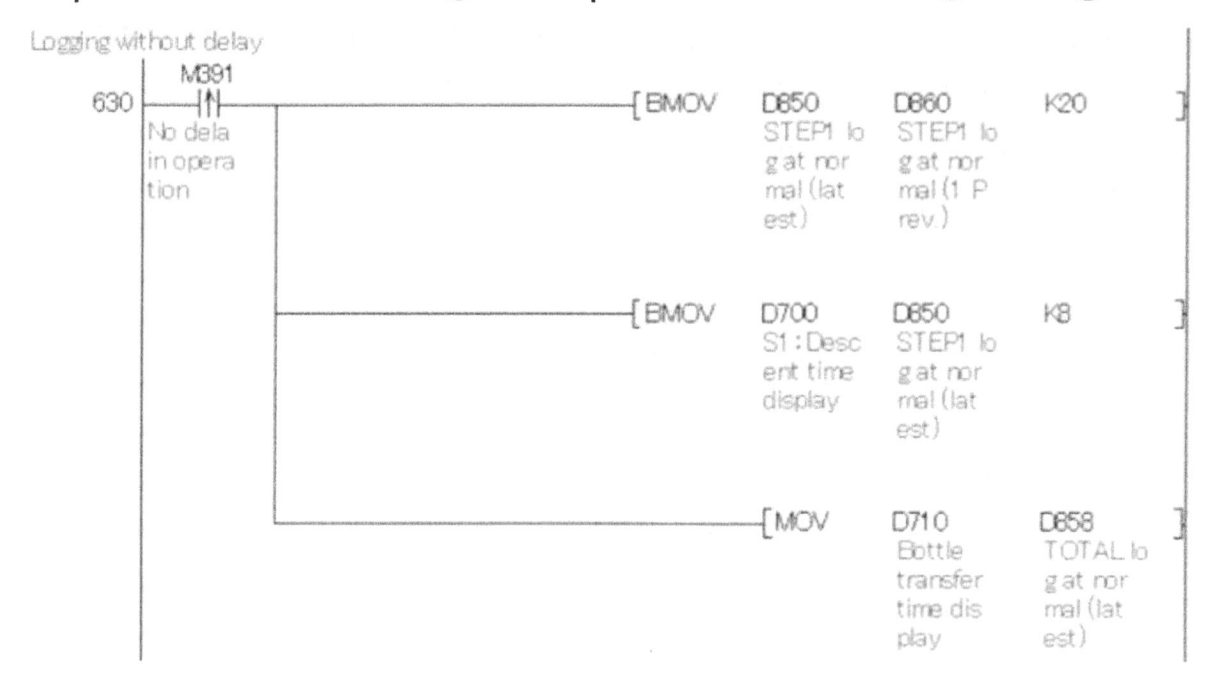

```
Logging without delay
         M391
630 ─────┤↑├──────────────────────[BMOV  D850      D860      K20 ]
         No dela                         STEP1 lo  STEP1 lo
         in opera                        g at nor  g at nor
         tion                            mal (lat  mal (1 P
                                         est)      rev.)

                                  [BMOV  D700      D850      K8  ]
                                         S1:Desc   STEP1 lo
                                         ent time  g at nor
                                         display   mal (lat
                                                   est)

                                  [MOV   D710      D858      ]
                                         Bottle    TOTAL lo
                                         transfer  g at nor
                                         time dis  mal (lat
                                         play      est)
```

Finally, if an alarm occurs during operation confirmation and it switches to screen 5, it is difficult to confirm operation, so insert SM401 that is always OFF and disable it.

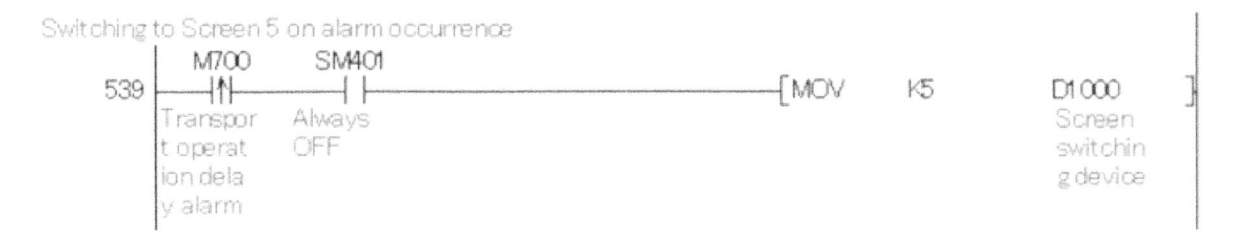

```
Switching to Screen 5 on alarm occurrence
         M700      SM401
  539 ───┤↑├───────┤ ├────────────────────[MOV   K5    D1000 ]
         Transpor  Always                              Screen
         t operat  OFF                                 switchin
         ion dela                                      g device
         y alarm
```

This completes the creation of the PLC program.

If you want to display the log multiple times on the screen, remember the shape of the circuit explained above and you will be able to apply it to other things, so please remember it.

8. Please perform a simulation that links the PLC program and the screen and check the operation.

・Set the set time to 99.9 seconds on the bottle transfer flow screen, start automatic operation with the transfer start conditions OK (right bottle, rise, right position, chuck open are all ON), and complete all steps in 99.9 seconds After proceeding with the operation confirmation button within seconds, when you move to the alarm screen, each time is acquired in the latest log at normal time.

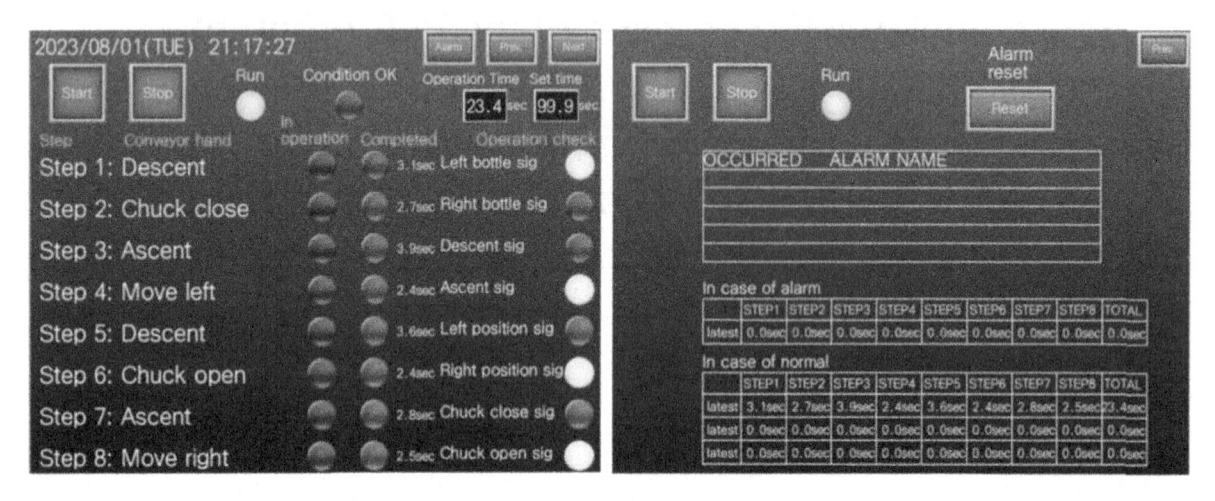

In case of normal

	STEP1	STEP2	STEP3	STEP4	STEP5	STEP6	STEP7	STEP8	TOTAL
latest	3.1sec	2.7sec	3.9sec	2.4sec	3.6sec	2.4sec	2.8sec	2.5sec	23.4sec
latest	0.0sec	0.0sec	0.0sec	0.0sec	0.0sec	0.0sec	0.0sec	0.0sec	0.0sec
latest	0.0sec	0.0sec	0.0sec	0.0sec	0.0sec	0.0sec	0.0sec	0.0sec	0.0sec

・Returns to the bottle transfer flow screen, the left side bottle detection is turned off and the right side bottle detection is turned on, and automatic operation resumes. The previous data is included in the previous data, and the latest normal log contains each time of this time.

In case of normal

	STEP1	STEP2	STEP3	STEP4	STEP5	STEP6	STEP7	STEP8	TOTAL
latest	5.4sec	3.9sec	5.0sec	3.4sec	5.1sec	3.1sec	5.0sec	6.1sec	37.0sec
latest	3.1sec	2.7sec	3.9sec	2.4sec	3.6sec	2.4sec	2.8sec	2.5sec	23.4sec
latest	0.0sec	0.0sec	0.0sec	0.0sec	0.0sec	0.0sec	0.0sec	0.0sec	0.0sec

・Returns to the bottle transfer flow screen, the left side bottle detection is turned off and the right side bottle detection is turned on, and automatic operation resumes. Press the operation confirmation button within 99.9 seconds until all steps are completed, and then move to the alarm screen to display the latest, the previous data moves to the previous 1st and 2nd previous data, and each time of this time is acquired in the latest log at normal time.

In case of normal

	STEP1	STEP2	STEP3	STEP4	STEP5	STEP6	STEP7	STEP8	TOTAL
latest	1.1sec	1.7sec	4.2sec	2.1sec	3.2sec	1.7sec	1.7sec	2.8sec	18.5sec
latest	5.4sec	3.9sec	5.0sec	3.4sec	5.1sec	3.1sec	5.0sec	6.1sec	37.0sec
latest	3.1sec	2.7sec	3.9sec	2.4sec	3.6sec	2.4sec	2.8sec	2.5sec	23.4sec

- Return to the bottle transfer flow screen, stop automatic operation, set the set time to 40 seconds, and start automatic operation with the transfer start conditions OK (right bottle, rise, right position, chuck open are all ON). Then, after proceeding with the operation confirmation button so that all steps are completed in 40 seconds or more, when you move to the alarm screen, "bottle transfer flow operation delay alarm" is displayed on the alarm display, and the latest log at the time of the alarm is displayed. is obtained each time.

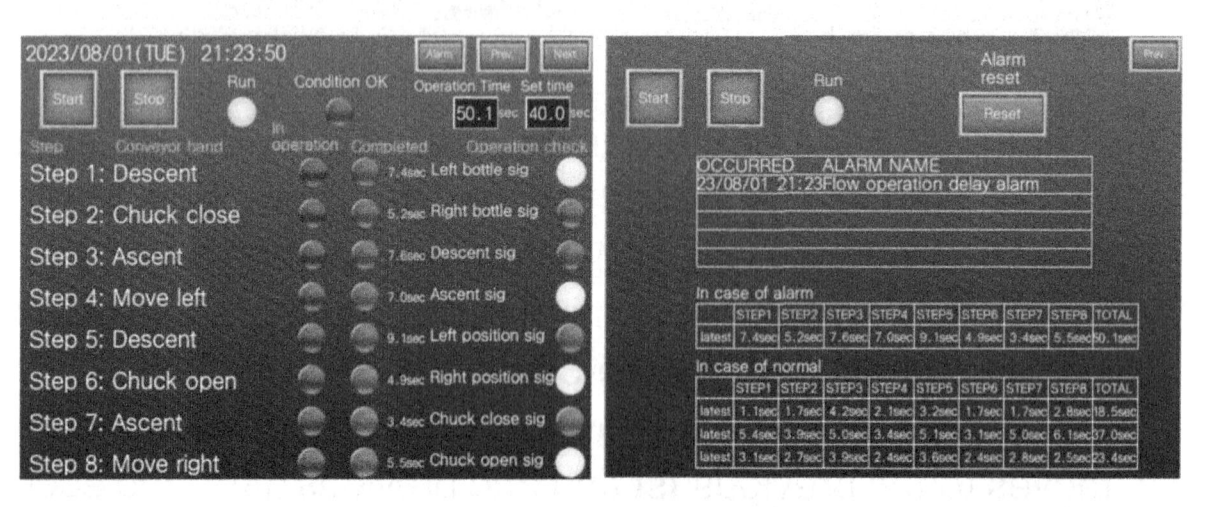

In case of alarm

	STEP1	STEP2	STEP3	STEP4	STEP5	STEP6	STEP7	STEP8	TOTAL
latest	7.4sec	5.2sec	7.6sec	7.0sec	9.1sec	4.9sec	3.4sec	5.5sec	50.1sec

This concludes the explanation of how to create a circuit and screen that acquires and records each operation time as a log during normal operation and when an alarm occurs. In addition to time, it is also possible to log the number of production and the number of defects every 10 minutes, for example. Please make use of it on site.

3-1 to 3-4 Summary

this time,

・[Energy saving] Creation of energy saving operation circuits for equipment/machinery
・[Equipment failure prevention] Maintenance alarm circuit and screen creation based on the number of operations
・[Prevention of decrease in production volume] Creation of alarm circuit and screen due to decrease in production operation time
・[Abnormality detection] Creating a circuit and screen that acquires each operation time as a log

We have introduced four improvement cases.

There are many facilities that require energy-saving measures due to the recent trend of SDGs, carbon neutrality, and soaring electricity rates. I think. In that case, it is possible to improve the equipment by adding a circuit that "stops when it is not needed".

again, **Delay in noticing equipment failures and production volume declines can lead to major losses.** Please use the above prevention circuits and screens to prevent them from happening.

again, **Acquisition of logs can be used not only for each operation time and equipment status when an error occurs, but also for acquisition of production numbers and defect numbers for each hour, and acquisition of each parameter when parameters change.** If you have a need to "get a log" in your equipment, please remember this circuit and screen and make use of it.

We hope that this improvement case study will be of some help to you in improving your facilities.

Chapter 4 3 Selections of Program Investigation Methods Useful in Trouble

In this chapter, I would like to introduce how to proceed with the investigation when a problem occurs in equipment or machinery.

4-1 Contact coil search "Ctrl + Alt + F7"

First, when some kind of problem occurs on the PLC program side, it is useful when investigating the cause. **Contact coil search**" will be explained.

As an example, let's say you want to investigate the reason why automatic operation does not start even if you press the start button when you turn on the power of the created washing machine operation screen and select the manual course.

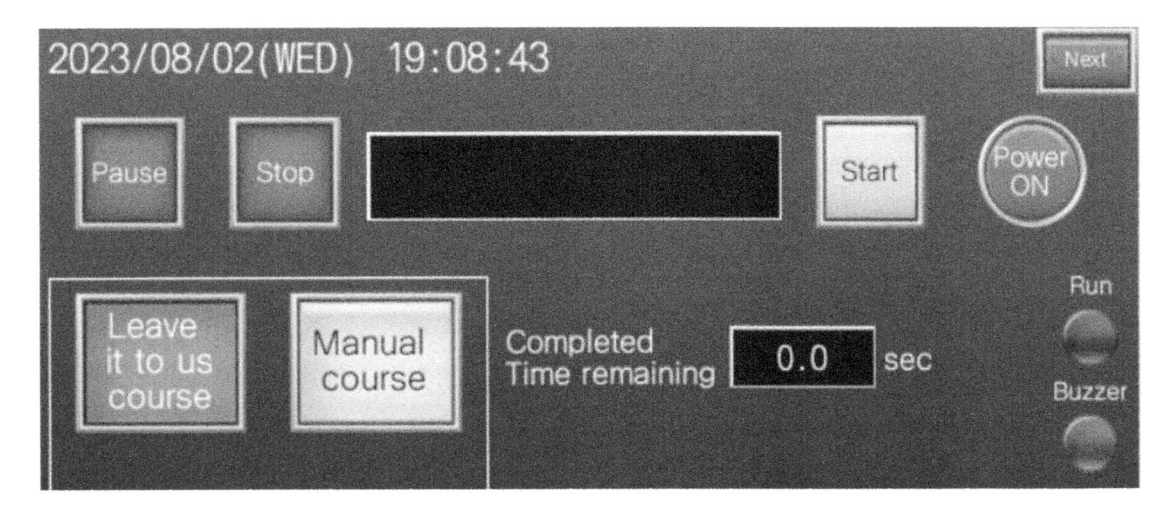

First, press Ctrl + F on the start button X330 and search by device search. Then you can see that the conditions for M354 are not met.

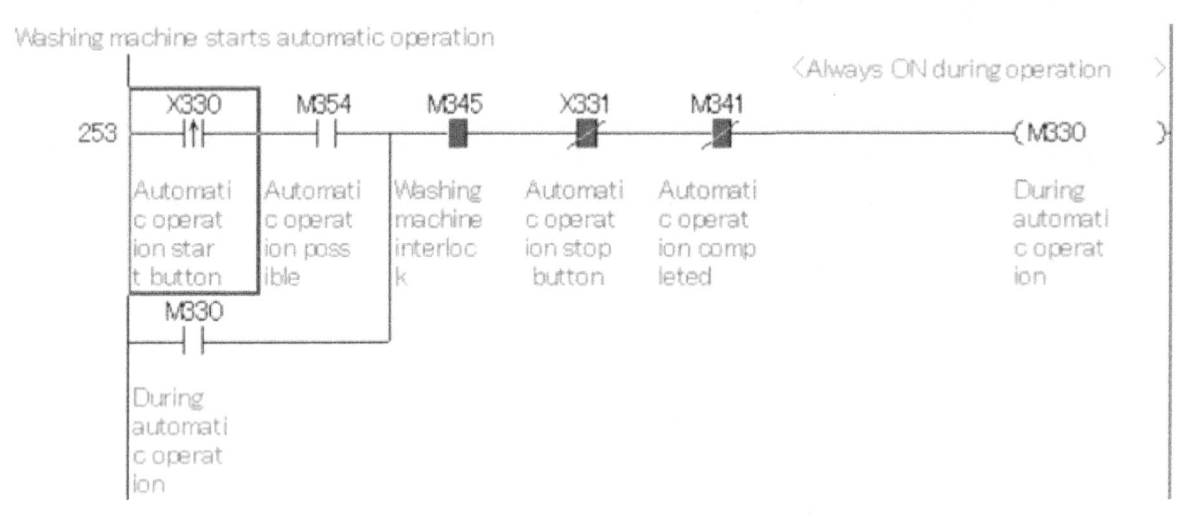

In the normal device search, all M354 contacts and coils are searched, so if there are many contacts, press the "Find Next" button or the Enter key (option: If you check the consecutive search with enter key) many times. is needed.

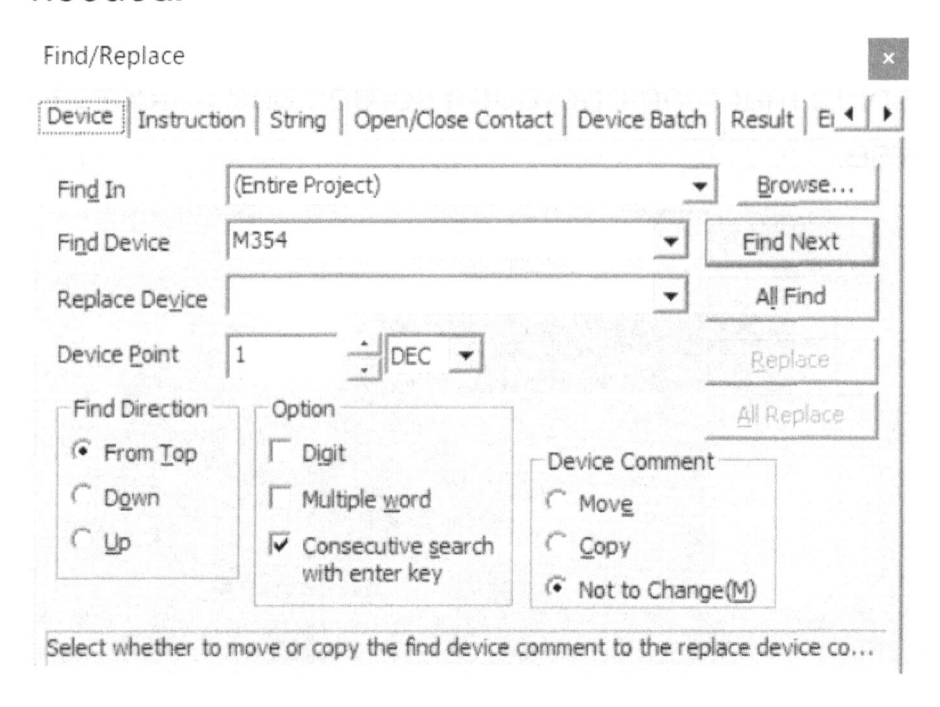

This is inefficient, so when searching for M354 coils, "**Contact coil search**" Use the. To use it, move the cursor to M354 and go to the "Find/Replace" tab ⇒ "Find contact or coil" or Ctrl + Alt + F7 to move to the M354 coil. Especially this Ctrl + Alt + F7 is convenient, so please remember it.

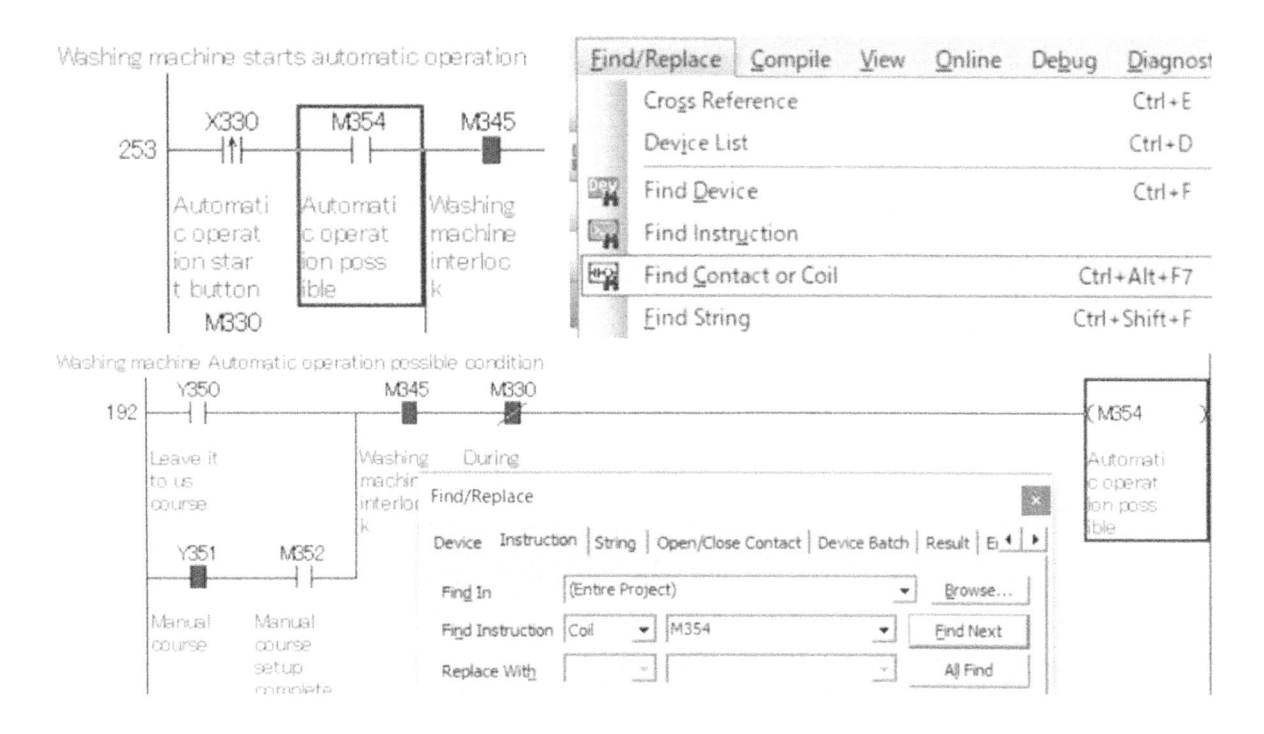

Looking at the coil conditions for M354, the conditions for M352 are not met, so move the cursor to M352 and press Ctrl + Alt + F7. Looking at the conditions of M352, you can see that automatic operation cannot be started because the washing machine rinse time setting D352 is not set.

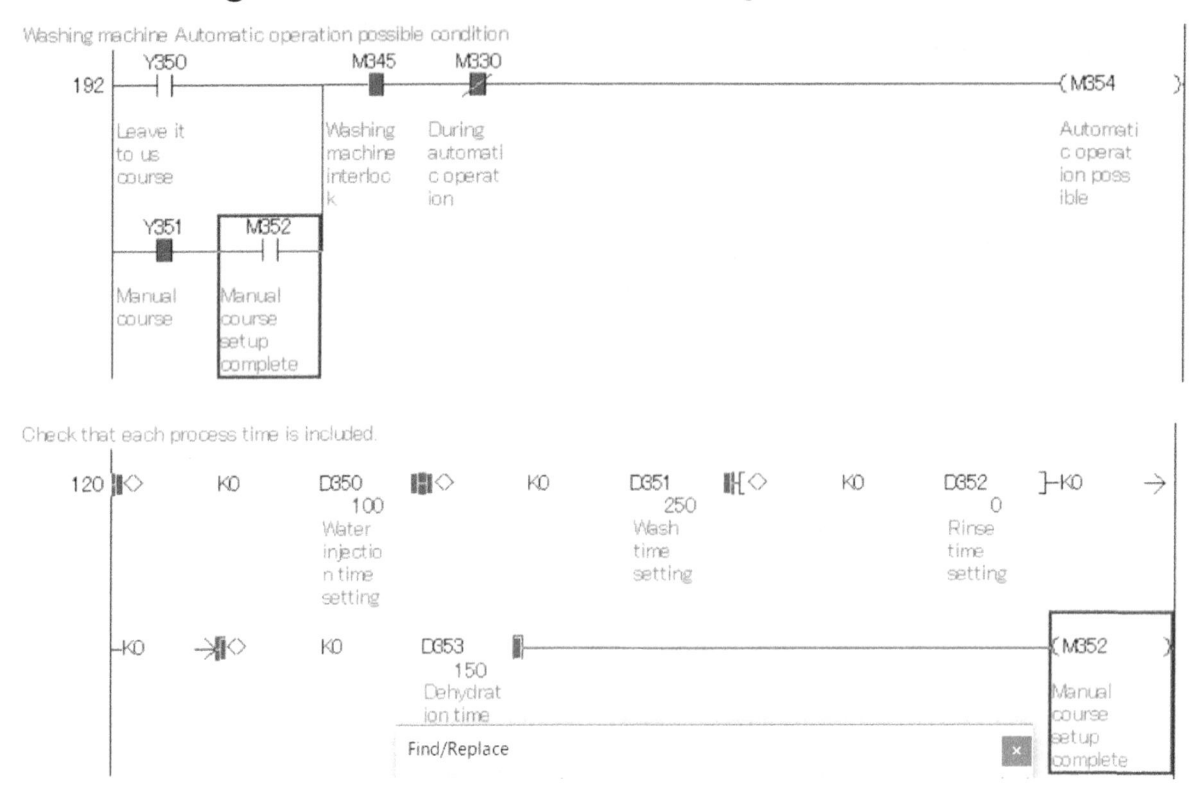

```
Washing machine Automatic operation possible condition
        Y350              M345      M330
192 ────┤ ├───────┬───────┤/├───────┤/├──────────────────────────( M354 )
        Leave it  │       Washing   During                        Automati
        to us     │       machine   automati                      c operat
        course    │       interloc  c operat                      ion poss
                  │       k         ion                           ible
        Y351      M352
        ────┤ ├───┤ ├
        Manual    Manual
        course    course
                  setup
                  complete

Check that each process time is included.
120 ├◇──── K0 ────D350 ├◇──── K0 ────D351 ├◇──── K0 ────D352 ├─K0 →
         100                    250                    0
         Water                  Wash                   Rinse
         injectio               time                   time
         n time                 setting                setting
         setting
    ├─K0 →├◇──── K0 ────D353
                         150                                    ( M352 )
                         Dehydrat                               Manual
                         ion time                               course
                                        Find/Replace    [x]     setup
                                                                complete
```

The program example this time was simple, but if the program is complicated, it is necessary to repeat the contact coil search many times to find the points where the conditions are not met.

This is the most basic investigation procedure when a problem occurs, so please be sure to memorize it.

4-2 Investigation of defect cause using increment (INC) instruction

Next, we will use an example to explain how to investigate the cause of a problem using the increment (INC) instruction.

For example, if the robot is carrying an item, sensors 1 to 4 will turn ON, and if any sensor turns OFF while the item is being transported, an alarm "Robot transporting sensor error" will occur and the robot will stop.

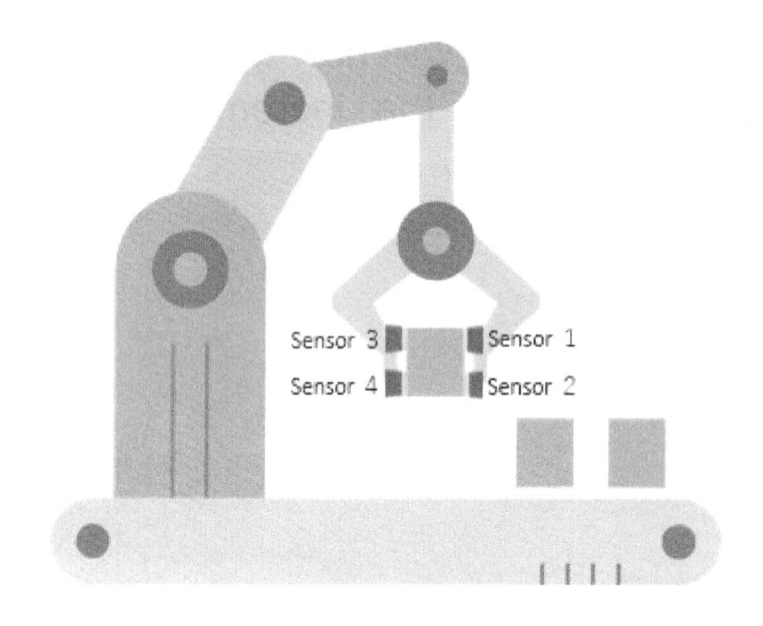

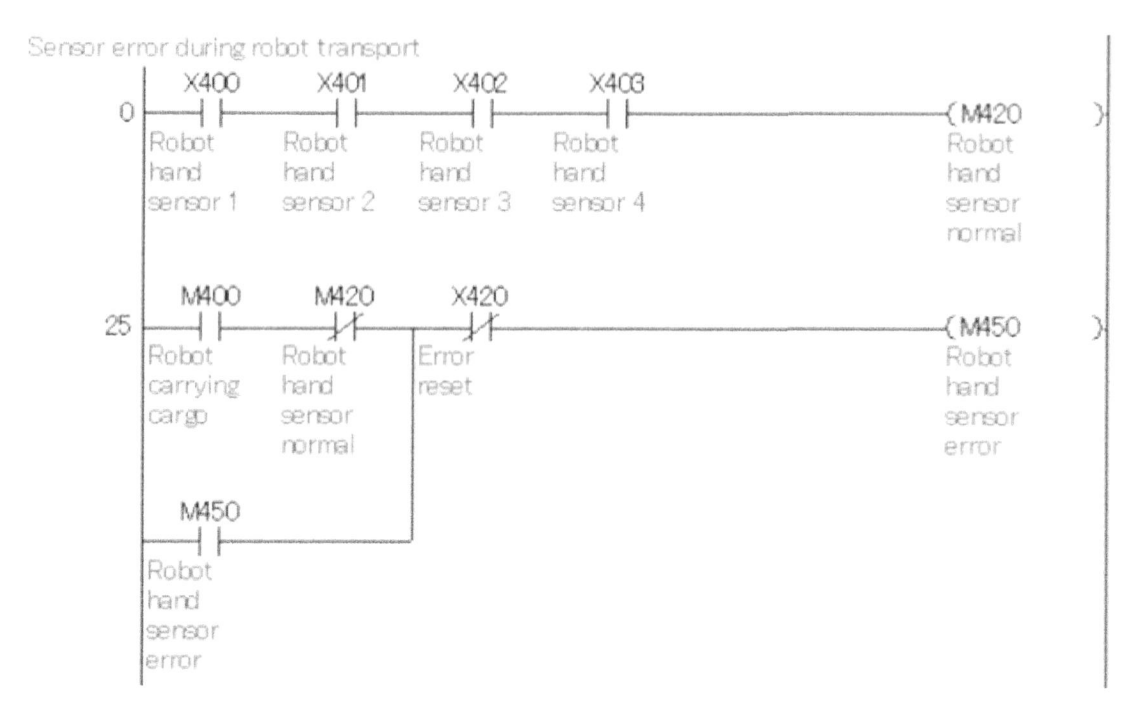

Sensor error during robot transport

```
        X400        X401        X402        X403
  0 ────┤├──────────┤├──────────┤├──────────┤├────────────────────────( M420 )
        Robot       Robot       Robot       Robot                       Robot
        hand        hand        hand        hand                        hand
        sensor 1    sensor 2    sensor 3    sensor 4                    sensor
                                                                        normal

        M400        M420        X420
 25 ────┤├──────────┤/├─────────┤/├──────────────────────────────────( M450 )
        Robot       Robot       Error                                   Robot
        carrying    hand        reset                                   hand
        cargo       sensor                                              sensor
                    normal                                              error

        M450
     ───┤├───
        Robot
        hand
        sensor
        error
```

If sensor 3 is turned off during transport and an abnormality occurs, if the package does not fall from the robot, you can tell by looking at the screen if the PLC program or touch panel displays that sensor 3 is disconnected.

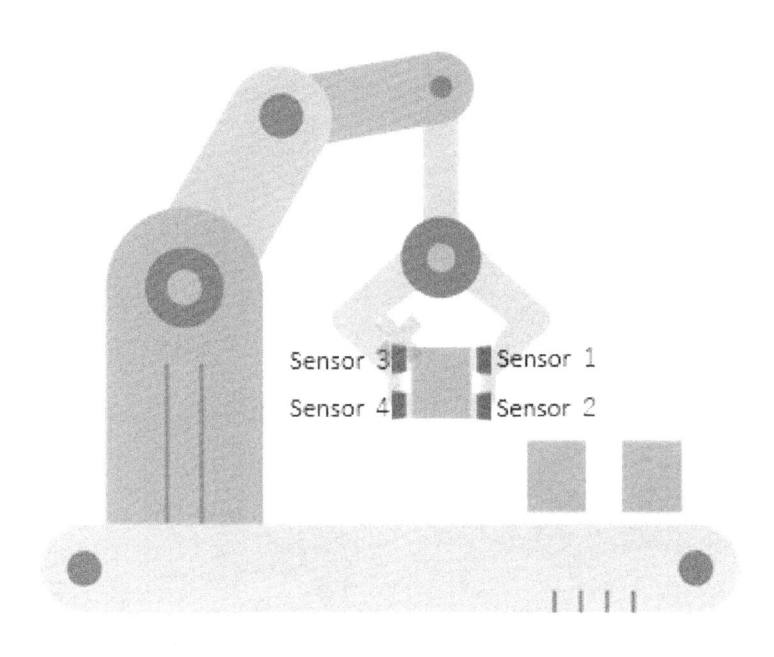

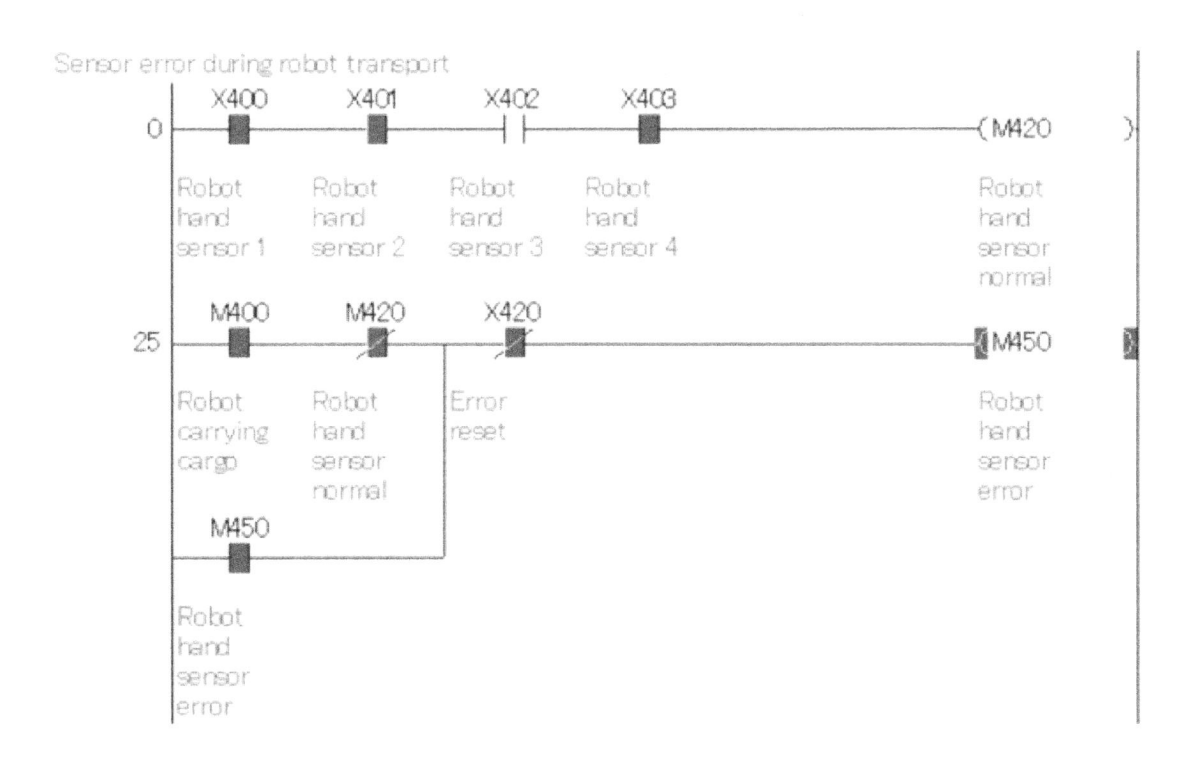

Sensor error during robot transport

```
     X400      X401      X402      X403
0 ----| |------| |------|/|------| |----------------( M420 )
     Robot     Robot     Robot     Robot                    Robot
     hand      hand      hand      hand                     hand
     sensor 1  sensor 2  sensor 3  sensor 4                 sensor
                                                            normal

      M400      M420      X420
25 ---| |------|/|-------|/|-----------------------( M450 )
     Robot     Robot     Error                              Robot
     carrying  hand      reset                              hand
     cargo     sensor                                       sensor
               normal                                       error

      M450
    ---| |---
     Robot
     hand
     sensor
     error
```

However, if sensor 3 turns off during transportation and an abnormality occurs, and if the package falls from the robot, it is not possible to tell from the PLC program or the touch panel display that sensor 3 is disconnected.

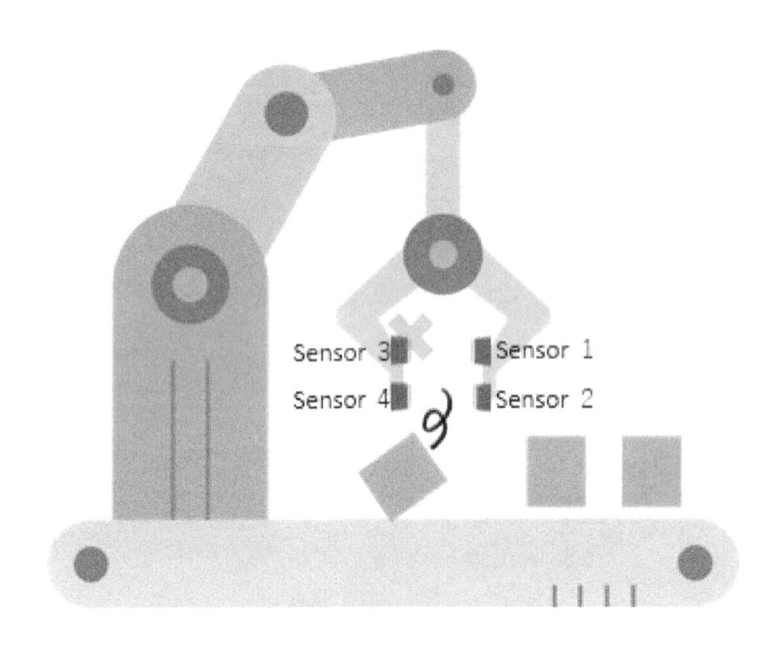

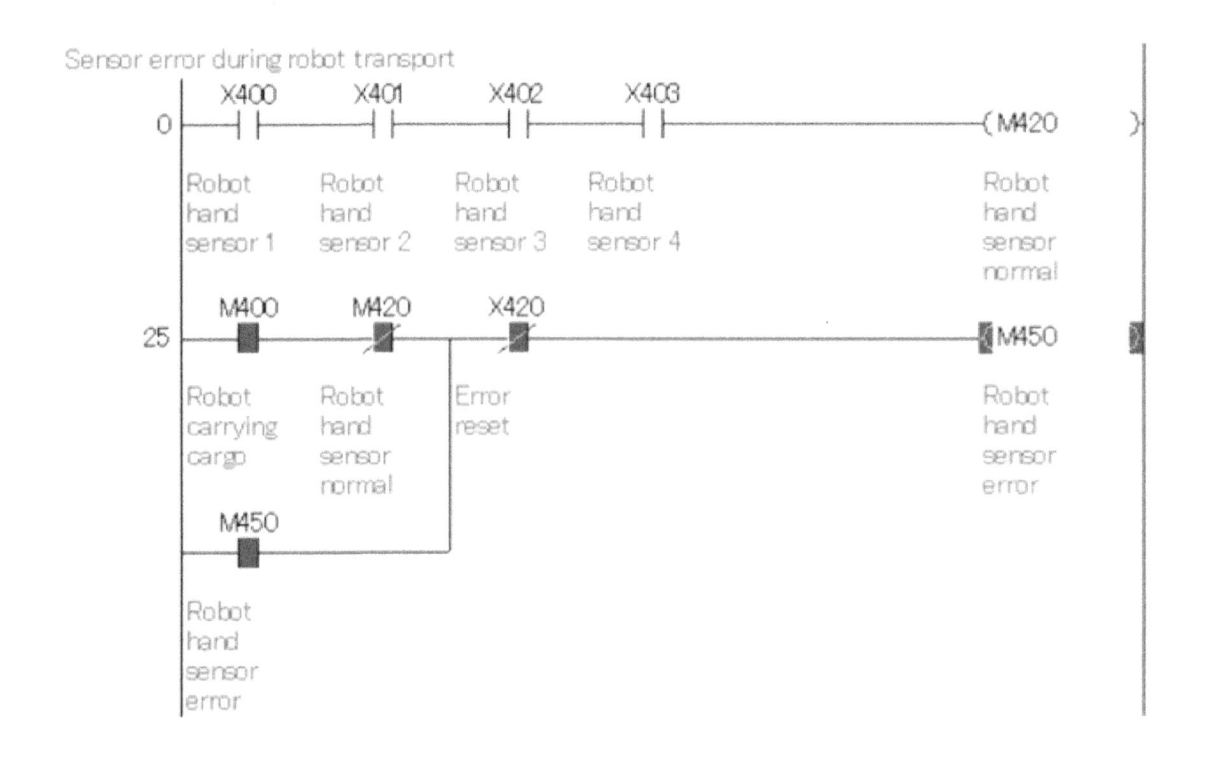

Sensor error during robot transport

```
      X400      X401      X402      X403
0 ────┤├────────┤├────────┤├────────┤├──────────────────(M420)
      Robot     Robot     Robot     Robot                Robot
      hand      hand      hand      hand                 hand
      sensor 1  sensor 2  sensor 3  sensor 4             sensor
                                                         normal

       M400     M420      X420
25 ────┤├──────┤/├───────┤/├─────────────────────────────(M450)
      Robot     Robot     Error                          Robot
      carrying  hand      reset                          hand
      cargo     sensor                                   sensor
                normal                                   error
       M450
      ─┤├─
      Robot
      hand
      sensor
      error
```

Such an anomaly may not be reproduced even if you try to reproduce the same operation again, and it is not possible to visually observe it all the time. Also, it may not be possible to know which sensor is bad at the timing of occurrence. Therefore **Increment (INC) instruction** Use the.

In this case, we want to identify which sensor is bad, so we create the following circuit using the increment (INC) command. For the increment (INC) command, press F8 and enter "INCP D1500". The P after INC is a rising pulse, so it turns ON only for one scan. Also, since the robot will stop at the timing of the next scan and M400 will turn off, create this circuit right below the abnormal circuit.

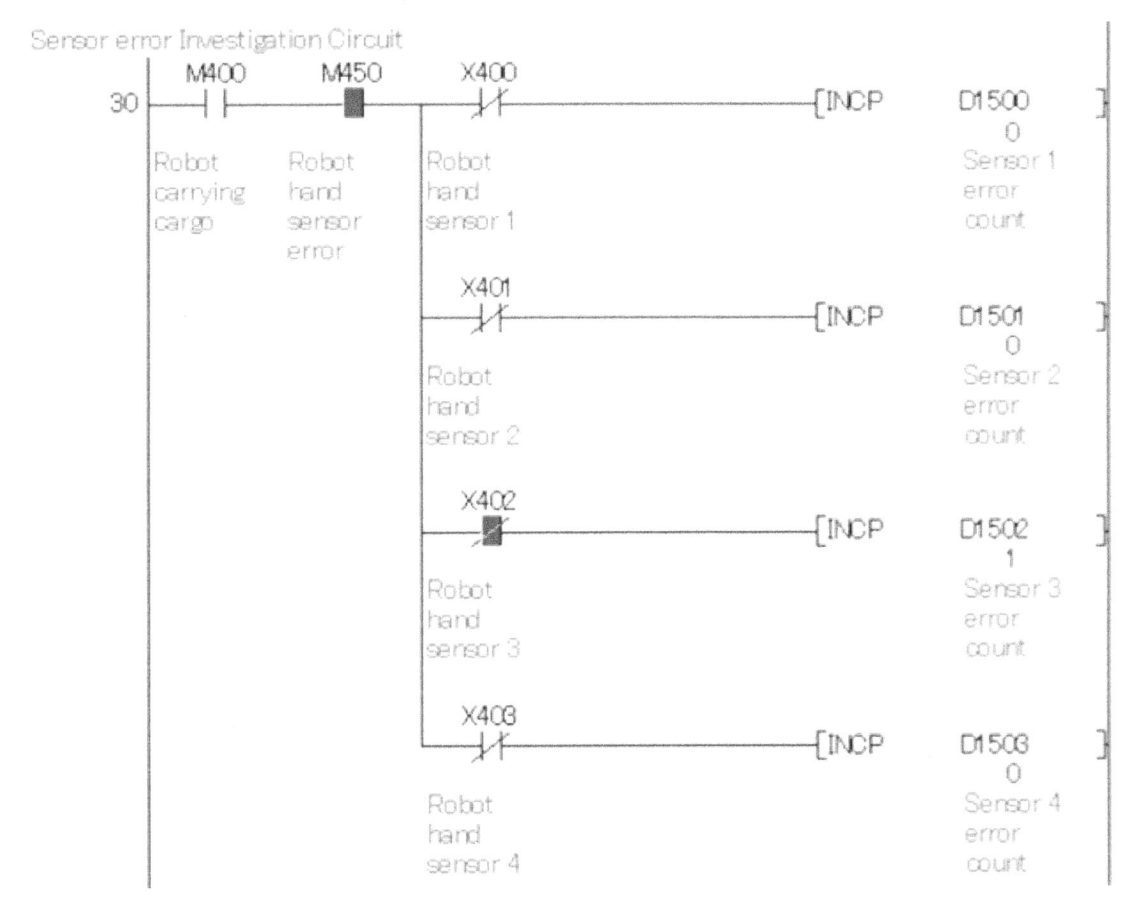

Sensor error Investigation Circuit

```
     M400      M450       X400
30 ───┤ ├──────┤ ├────────┤/├──────────────[INCP   D1500 ]
    Robot     Robot      Robot                      0
    carrying  hand       hand                     Sensor 1
    cargo     sensor     sensor 1                 error
              error                               count

                          X401
                         ─┤/├───────────────────[INCP   D1501 ]
                                                         0
                          Robot                         Sensor 2
                          hand                          error
                          sensor 2                      count

                          X402
                         ─┤ ├───────────────────[INCP   D1502 ]
                                                         1
                          Robot                         Sensor 3
                          hand                          error
                          sensor 3                      count

                          X403
                         ─┤/├───────────────────[INCP   D1503 ]
                                                         0
                          Robot                         Sensor 4
                          hand                          error
                          sensor 4                      count
```

By adding such an investigation circuit, it will be possible to keep a count of which sensors were OFF at the timing when a sensor abnormality occurred while the robot was being transported. This is particularly effective when investigating the cause of anomalies that rarely occur, or when the cause of an anomaly with multiple conditions is unknown.

And after the investigation is completed successfully and the adjustment and replacement of the sensor are completed, the circuit created this time will be unnecessary in many cases, so I will delete it. When deleting, don't forget to delete the comment as well.

4-3 Investigation of defect occurrence step using increment (INC) instruction

Next, we will explain how to investigate the step where the problem occurred using the increment (INC) instruction, also using an example.

As an example, the washing machine automatic operation flow created in Chapter 2 will be explained. For example, suppose that the washing machine lid opening X325 is turned ON during automatic operation of the washing machine, and the automatic operation of the washing machine stops due to an interlock. This time, we will identify at which step the washing machine lid open X325 is ON.

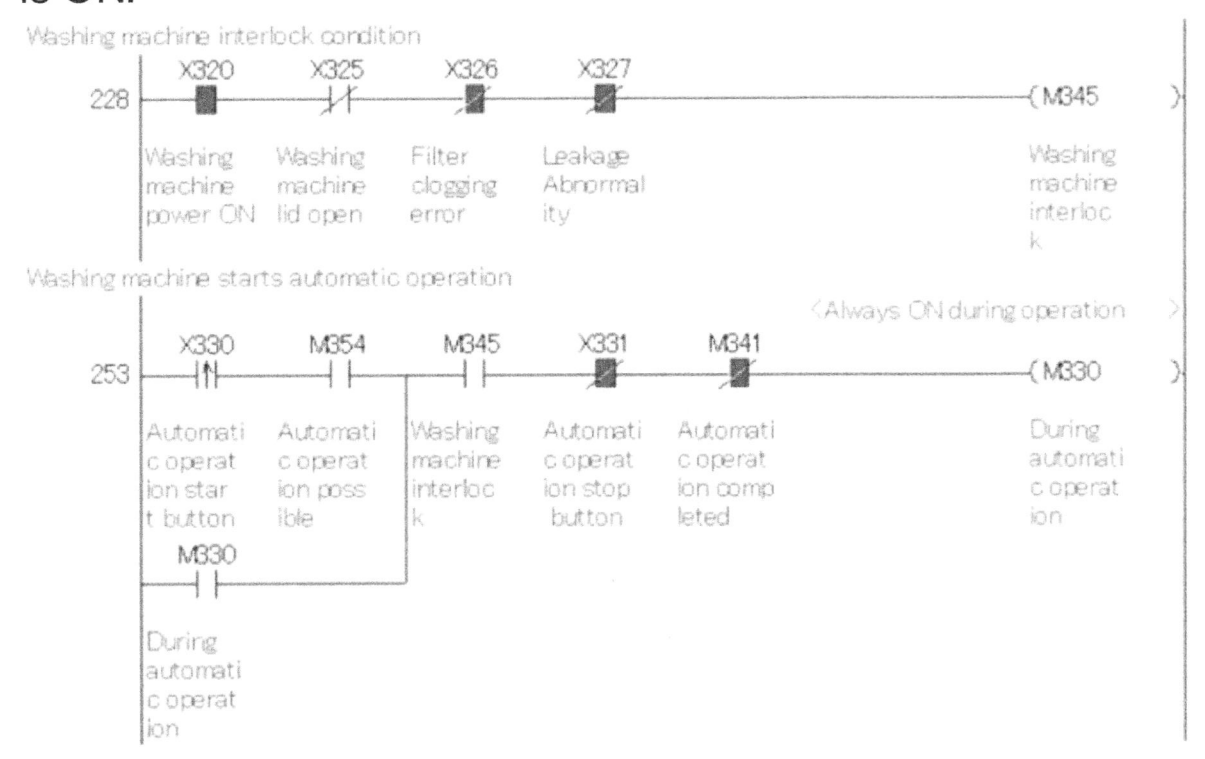

```
Washing machine interlock condition
        X320      X325      X326      X327
228 ─────┤├───────┤/├───────┤├────────┤├──────────────────( M345 )
      Washing   Washing    Filter    Leakage              Washing
      machine   machine    clogging  Abnormal             machine
      power ON  lid open   error     ity                  interlock

Washing machine starts automatic operation
                                                <Always ON during operation>
        X330      M354      M345      X331      M341
253 ─────┤↑├──────┤├────────┤├────────┤├────────┤├────────( M330 )
        │    M330                                         During
        ├─────┤├──                                        automati
      Automati Automati  Washing   Automati  Automati     c operat
      c operat c operat  machine   c operat  c operat    ion
      ion star ion poss  interloc  ion stop  ion comp
      t button ible      k         button    leted
        M330
        ┤├
        During
        automati
        c operat
        ion
```

This assumes that in the case of equipment or machinery operating at high speed with complex sequence control, it is not known at which step the equipment has stopped.

Of course, it is positive that detailed alarms are set for each step and there is a monitor display so that you can see at which step it stopped, but if that is not the case, you can quickly find the step that caused the problem. To identify, also **Increment (INC) instruction** use to investigate.

In this case, we want to identify at which step the lid is opened, so we create the following circuit using the increment (INC) instruction. In addition, since M330 is turned off during automatic operation of the washing machine by scanning when the washing machine lid is open X325 is ON, create this circuit above the output of M330.

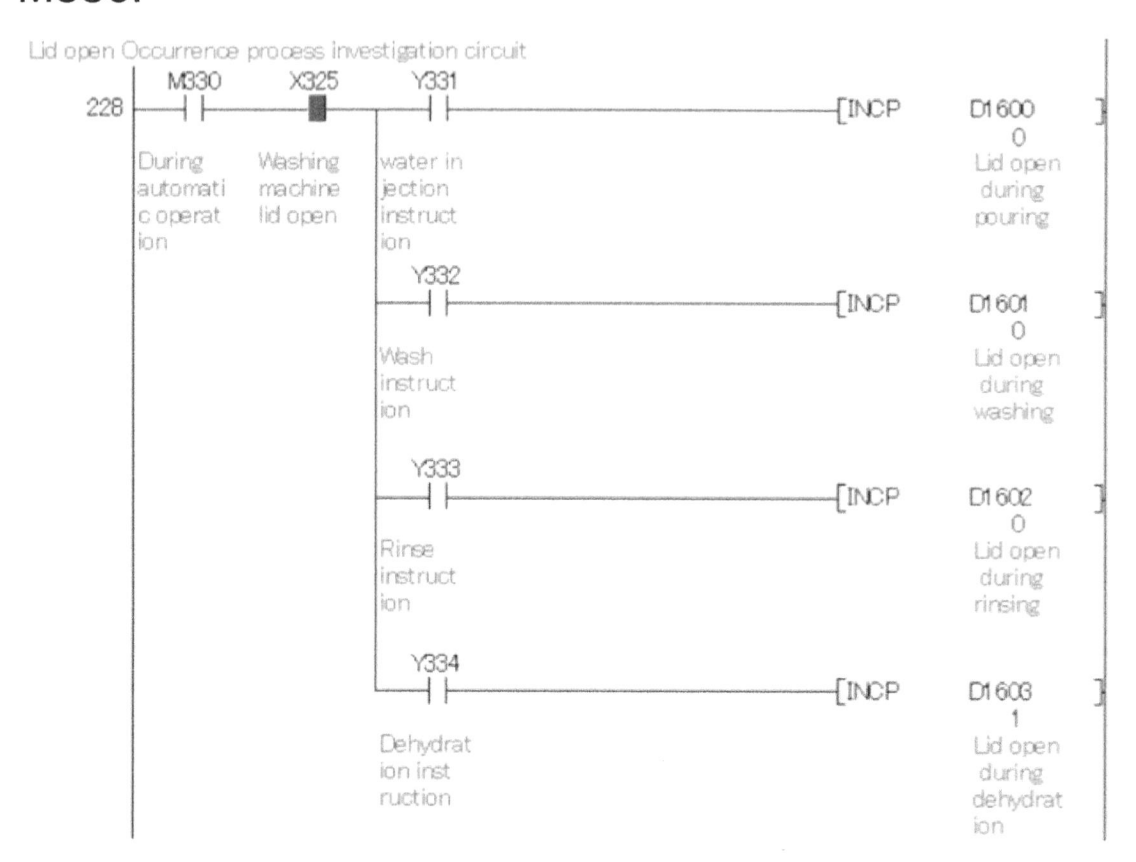

Lid open Occurrence process investigation circuit

```
           M330      X325      Y331
228       ──┤├───────┤▐───────┤├──────────────────[INCP   D1600  ]
                                                             0
          During    Washing   water in                    Lid open
          automati  machine   jection                     during
          c operat  lid open  instruct                    pouring
          ion                 ion
                              Y332
                            ──┤├──────────────────[INCP   D1601  ]
                                                             0
                              Wash                        Lid open
                              instruct                    during
                              ion                         washing

                              Y333
                            ──┤├──────────────────[INCP   D1602  ]
                                                             0
                              Rinse                       Lid open
                              instruct                    during
                              ion                         rinsing

                              Y334
                            ──┤├──────────────────[INCP   D1603  ]
                                                             1
                              Dehydrat                    Lid open
                              ion inst                    during
                              ruction                     dehydrat
                                                          ion
```

In this case, it turned out that the lid had been opened during the spin-drying process. It is possible to guess the cause.

By narrowing down the steps with the cause in this way, it may be possible to quickly take measures to address the cause.

Also, as before, after the investigation is successfully completed and the sensor is adjusted or replaced, there are many cases where the circuit created this time will not be needed, so I will delete it. When deleting, don't forget to delete the comment as well.

The above is a useful program investigation method when trouble occurs.

Failure investigation is based on contact coil search method and cause identification using increment (INC) command. Please try these methods on site.

4-1 to 4-3 Summary

· When some kind of trouble occurs on the PLC program side, it is useful when investigating the cause **Contact coil search'** shortcut is **Ctrl+Alt+F7**is.

· **When there are multiple conditions for an error occurrence and you do not know which condition has occurred**, with each condition Ac**count with increment (INC) instruction** This makes it possible to determine under what conditions an error occurred.

· **If you do not know at which step the error occurred** Also, each step operation signal + abnormal signal is a condition **Count with increment (INC) instruction** By doing so, it is possible to determine at which step an error occurred.

At the end

Thank you for reading to the end.

As with any programming, you can experience an indescribable excitement when you create, try to run, repeat trial, and error, and finally complete it.

Repetition is the fastest way to improve your skills.

This time in this book

· Shortcuts to improve the efficiency of PLC program creation
 · How to write a basic sequence control program
 · Specific PLC/GOT improvement cases: 4 cases
 · Three selections of program investigation methods that are useful when problems occur

I was introduced and explained about.

Based on the contents explained this time, I hope that you will work on the actual creation of PLC / GOT and improvement of the site. I hope that this book will be of some help to you in your work.

Finally, I look forward to working with everyone who reads this book in the FA and PLC industries.

Made in the USA
Coppell, TX
07 June 2024